BENCHMARK SERIES

MICROSOFT® EXCEL® 2013
LEVEL 1

NITA RUTKOSKY
Pierce College Puyallup
Puyallup, Washington

AUDREY ROGGENKAMP
Pierce College Puyallup
Puyallup, Washington

IAN RUTKOSKY
Pierce College Puyallup
Puyallup, Washington

PARADIGM
EDUCATION SOLUTIONS

St. Paul

Managing Editor	Christine Hurney
Director of Production	Timothy W. Larson
Production Editor	Sarah Kearin
Cover and Text Designers	Leslie Anderson and Jaana Bykonich
Copy Editors	Communicáto, Ltd.; Nan Brooks, Abshier House
Desktop Production	Jaana Bykonich, Julie Johnston, Valerie King, Timothy W. Larson, Jack Ross, and Sara Schmidt Boldon
Indexer	Terry Casey
VP & Director of Digital Projects	Chuck Bratton
Digital Projects Manager	Tom Modl

Acknowledgements: The authors, editors, and publisher thank the following instructors for their helpful suggestions during the planning and development of the books in the Benchmark Office 2013 Series: Olugbemiga Adekunle, Blue Ridge Community College, Harrisonburg, VA; Letty Barnes, Lake WA Institute of Technology, Kirkland, WA; Erika Nadas, Wilbur Wright College, Chicago, IL; Carolyn Walker, Greenville Technical College, Greenville, SC; Carla Anderson, National College, Lynchburg, VA; Judy A. McLaney, Lurleen B. Wallace Community College, Opp, AL; Sue Canter, Guilford Technical Community College, Jamestown, NC; Reuel Sample, National College, Knoxville, TN; Regina Young, Wiregrass Georgia Technical College, Valdosta, GA; William Roxbury, National College, Stow, OH; Charles Adams, II, Danville Community College, Danville, VA; Karen Spray, Northeast Community College, Norfolk, NE; Deborah Miller, Augusta Technical College, Augusta, GA; Wanda Stuparits, Lanier Technical College, Cumming, GA; Gale Wilson, Brookhaven College, Farmers Branch, TX; Jocelyn S. Pinkard, Arlington Career Institute, Grand Prairie, TX; Ann Blackman, Parkland College, Champaign, IL; Fathia Williams, Fletcher Technical Community College, Houma, LA; Leslie Martin, Gaston College, Dallas, NC; Tom Rose, Kellogg Community College, Battle Creek, MI; Casey Thompson, Wiregrass Georgia Technical College, Douglas, GA; Larry Bush, University of Cincinnati, Clermont College, Amelia, OH; Tim Ellis, Schoolcraft College, Liconia, MI; Miles Cannon, Lanier Technical College, Oakwood, GA; Irvin LaFleur, Lanier Technical College, Cumming, GA; Patricia Partyka, Schoolcraft College, Prudenville, MI.

The authors and publishing team also thanks the following individuals for their contributions to this project: checking the accuracy of the instruction and exercises—Brienna McWade, Traci Post, and Janet Blum, Fanshawe College, London, Ontario; creating annotated model answers and developing lesson plans—Ann Mills, Ivy Tech Community College, Evansville, Indiana; developing rubrics—Marjory Wooten, Laneir Techncial College, Cumming, Georgia.

Trademarks: Access, Excel, Internet Explorer, Microsoft, PowerPoint, and Windows are trademarks or registered trademarks of Microsoft Corporation in the United States and/or other countries. Some of the product names and company names included in this book have been used for identification purposes only and may be trademarks or registered trade names of their respective manufacturers and sellers. The authors, editors, and publisher disclaim any affiliation, association, or connection with, or sponsorship or endorsement by, such owners.

We have made every effort to trace the ownership of all copyrighted material and to secure permission from copyright holders. In the event of any question arising as to the use of any material, we will be pleased to make the necessary corrections in future printings. Thanks are due to the aforementioned authors, publishers, and agents for permission to use the materials indicated.

Paradigm Publishing is independent from Microsoft Corporation, and not affiliated with Microsoft in any manner. While this publication may be used in assisting individuals to prepare for a Microsoft Office Specialist certification exam, Microsoft, its designated program administrator, and Paradigm Publishing do not warrant that use of this publication will ensure passing a Microsoft Office Specialist certification exam.

ISBN 978-0-76385-347-1 (Text)
ISBN 978-0-76385-390-7 (Text + CD)
ISBN 978-0-76385-369-3 (ebook via email)
ISBN 978-0-76385-412-6 (ebook via mail)

Printed in the United States of America

23 22 21 20 19 18 17 16 15   4 5 6 7 8 9 10 11 12

Contents

Microsoft Excel 2013 Level 1

Benchmark Series Microsoft Excel 2013 is designed for students who want to learn how to use this powerful spreadsheet program to manipulate numerical data in resolving issues related to finances or other numbers-based information. No prior knowledge of spreadsheets is required. After successfully completing a course using this textbook, students will be able to

- Create and edit spreadsheets of varying complexity
- Format cells, columns, and rows as well as entire workbooks in a uniform, attractive style
- Analyze numerical data and project outcomes to make informed decisions
- Plan, research, create, revise, and publish worksheets and workbooks to meet specific communication needs
- Given a workplace scenario requiring a numbers-based solution, assess the information requirements and then prepare the materials that achieve the goal efficiently and effectively

In addition to mastering Excel skills, students will learn the essential features and functions of computer hardware, the Windows 8 operating system, and Internet Explorer 10. Upon completing the text, they can expect to be proficient in using Excel to organize, analyze, and present information.

Well-designed textbook pedagogy is important, but students learn technology skills from practice and problem solving. Technology provides opportunities for interactive learning as well as excellent ways to quickly and accurately assess student performance. To this end, this textbook is supported with SNAP, Paradigm Publishing's web-based training and assessment learning management system. Details about SNAP as well as additional student courseware and instructor resources can be found on page xiv.

Achieving Proficiency in Excel 2013 ■■■■■■■■

Since its inception several Office versions ago, the Benchmark Series has served as a standard of excellence in software instruction. Elements of the book function individually and collectively to create an inviting, comprehensive learning environment that produces successful computer users. The following visual tour highlights the text's features.

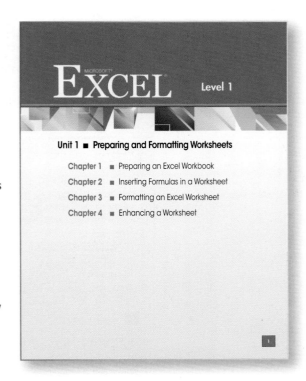

UNIT OPENERS display the unit's four chapter titles. Each level has two units, which conclude with a comprehensive unit performance assessment.

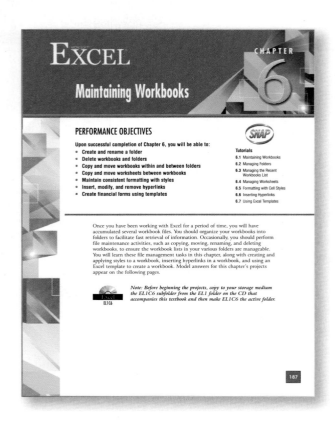

CHAPTER OPENERS present the performance objectives and an overview of the skills taught.

SNAP interactive tutorials are available to support chapter-specific skills at snap2013.emcp.com.

DATA FILES are provided for each chapter. A prominent note reminds students to copy the appropriate chapter data folder and make it active.

PROJECT APPROACH: Builds Skill Mastery within Realistic Context

MODEL ANSWERS provide a preview of the finished chapter projects and allow students to confirm they have created the materials accurately.

MULTIPART PROJECTS provide a framework for the instruction and practice on software features. A project overview identifies tasks to accomplish and key features to use in completing the work.

Project 1 Format a Product Pricing Worksheet   **7 Parts**

You will open a workbook containing a worksheet with product pricing data and then format the worksheet by changing column widths and row heights, inserting and deleting rows and columns, and clearing data in cells. You will also apply font and alignment formatting to data in cells.

Changing Column Width ■■■■■■■■■■■■■■■■■■■■

Columns in a worksheet are the same width by default. In some worksheets, you may want to change column widths to accommodate more or less data. Change column width using the mouse on column boundaries or at a dialog box.

Changing Column Width Using Column Boundaries

As you learned in Chapter 1, you can adjust the width of a column by dragging the column boundary line or adjust a column width to the longest entry by double-clicking the boundary line. When you drag a column boundary, the column width displays in a box above the mouse pointer. The column width number that displays represents the average number of characters in the standard font that can fit in a cell.

You can change the width of selected adjacent columns at the same time. To do this, select the columns and then drag one of the column boundaries within the selected columns. As you drag the boundary, the column width changes for all selected columns. To select adjacent columns, position the cell pointer on the first desired column header (the mouse pointer turns into a black, down-pointing arrow), hold down the left mouse button, drag the cell pointer to the last desired column header, and then release the mouse button.

H|I|N|T

To change the width of all columns in a worksheet, click the Select All button and then drag a column boundary to the desired position.

Project 1a Changing Column Width Using a Column Boundary   Part 1 of 7

1. Open **CMProducts.xlsx**.
2. Save the workbook with Save As and name it **EL1-C3-P1-CMProducts**.
3. Insert a formula in cell D2 that multiplies the price in cell B2 with the number in cell C2. Copy the formula in cell D2 down to cells D3 through D14.
4. Change the width of column D by completing the following steps:
   a. Position the mouse pointer on the column boundary in the column header between columns D and E until it turns into a double-headed arrow pointing left and right.
   b. Hold down the left mouse button, drag the column boundary to the right until *Width: 11.00 (106 pixels)* displays in the box, and then release the mouse button.

   Step 4b

5. Make cell D15 active and then insert the sum of cells D2 through D14.
6. Change the width of columns A and B by completing the following steps:
   a. Select columns A and B. To do this, position the cell pointer on the column A header, hold down the left mouse button, drag the cell pointer to the column B header, and then release the mouse button.

Chapter 3 ■ Formatting an E...

STEP-BY-STEP INSTRUCTIONS guide students to the desired outcome for each project part. Screen captures illustrate what the student's screen should look like at key points.

Between project parts, the text presents instruction on the features and skills necessary to accomplish the next section of the project.

Typically, a file remains open throughout all parts of the project. Students save their work incrementally.

   b. Position the cell pointer on the column boundary between columns A and B until it turns into a double-headed arrow pointing left and right.
   c. Hold down the left mouse button, drag the column boundary to the right until *Width: 10.33 (100 pixels)* displays in the box, and then release the mouse button.
7. Adjust the width of column C to accommodate the longest entry by double-clicking on the column boundary between columns C and D.
8. Save **EL1-C3-P1-CMProducts.xlsx**.

   Step 6c

Changing Column Width at the Column Width Dialog Box

At the Column Width dialog box, shown in Figure 3.1, you can specify a column width number. Increase the column width number to make the column wider or decrease the column width number to make the column narrower.

To display the Column Width dialog box, click the Format button in the Cells group on the HOME tab and then click *Column Width* at the drop-down list. At the Column Width dialog box, type the number representing the average number of characters in the standard font that you want to fit in the column and then press Enter or click OK.

♥ Quick Steps

Change Column Width

Drag column boundary line.
OR
Double-click column boundary.
OR
1. Click Format button.
2. Click *Column Width* at drop-down list.
3. Type desired width.
4. Click OK.

Format

Figure 3.1 Column Width Dialog Box

Type the column width in this text box.

Project 1b Changing Column Width at the Column Width Dialog Box   Part 2 of 7

1. With **EL1-C3-P1-CMProducts.xlsx** open, change the width of column A by completing the following steps:
   a. Make any cell in column A active.
   b. Click the Format button in the Cells group on the HOME tab and then click *Column Width* at the drop-down list.
   c. At the Column Width dialog box, type 12.7 in the *Column width* text box.
   d. Click OK to close the dialog box.
2. Make any cell in column B active and then change the width of column B to *12.5* by completing steps similar to those in Step 1.
3. Make any cell in column C active and then change the width of column C to *8* by completing steps similar to those in Step 1.
4. Save **EL1-C3-P1-CMProducts.xlsx**.

   Step 1c

   Step 1d

Working with Ranges

A selected group of cells is referred to as a *range*. A range of cells can be formatted, moved, copied, or deleted. You can also name a range of cells and then move the insertion point to the range or use a named range as part of a formula.

To name a range, select the cells and then click in the Name box located at the left of the Formula bar. Type a name for the range (do not use a space) and then press Enter. To move the insertion point to a specific range and select the range, click the down-pointing arrow at the right side of the Name box and then click the range name.

You can also name a range using the Define Name button in the FORMULAS tab. To do this, click the FORMULAS tab and then click the Define Name button in the Defined Names group. At the New Name dialog box, type a name for the range and then click OK.

A range name can be used in a formula. For example, if a range is named *Profit* and you want to insert the average of all cells in the Profit range, make the desired cell active and then type *=AVERAGE(Profit)*. Use a named range in the current worksheet or in another worksheet within the workbook.

♦ Quick Steps

Name a Range
1. Select cells.
2. Click in Name box.
3. Type range name.
4. Press Enter.

Define Name

H I N T
Another method for moving to a range is to click the Find & Select button in the Editing group on the HOME tab and then click Go To. At the Go To dialog box, double-click the range name.

Project 2b Naming a Range and Using a Range in a Formula   Part 2 of 2

1. With **EL1-C5-P2-HCEqpRpt.xlsx** open, click the Sheet2 tab and then type the following text in the specified cells:
   A1: EQUIPMENT USAGE REPORT
   A2: Yearly hours
   A3: Avoidable delays
   A4: Unavoidable delays
   A5: Total delay hours
   A6: (leave blank)
   A7: Repairs
   A8: Servicing
   A9: Total repair/servicing hours
2. Make the following formatting changes to the worksheet:
   a. Automatically adjust the width of column A.
   b. Center and bold the text in cells A1 and A2.
3. Select a range of cells in Sheet1, name the range, and use it in a formula in Sheet2 by completing the following steps:
   a. Click the Sheet1 tab.
   b. Select cells B5 through M5.
   c. Click in the Name box located to the left of the Formula bar.
   d. Type adhours (for Avoidable Delays Hours) and then press Enter.
   e. Click the Sheet2 tab.
   f. Make cell B3 active.
   g. Type the equation =SUM(a... then press Enter.

---

4. Click the Sheet1 tab and then complete the following steps:
   a. Select cells B6 through M6.
   b. Click the FORMULAS tab.
   c. Click the Define Name button in the Defined Names group.
   d. At the New Name dialog box, type udhours and then click OK.
   e. Click the Sheet2 tab, make sure cell B4 is active, type the equation =SUM(udhours), and then press Enter.
5. Click the Sheet1 tab and then complete the following steps:
   a. Select cells B7 through M7 and then name the range *rhours*.
   b. Click the Sheet2 tab, make cell B7 active, type the equation =SUM(rhours), and then press Enter.
   c. Click the Sheet1 tab.
   d. Select cells B8 through M8 and then name the range *shours*.
   e. Click the Sheet2 tab, make sure cell B8 is active, type the equation =SUM(shours), and then press Enter.
6. With Sheet2 still active, make the following changes:
   a. Make cell B5 active.
   b. Double-click the AutoSum button in the Editing group on the HOME tab.
   c. Make cell B9 active.
   d. Double-click the AutoSum button in the Editing group.
7. Click the Sheet1 tab and then move to the adhours range by clicking the down-pointing arrow at the right side of the Name box and then clicking *adhours* at the drop-down list.
8. Select both sheet tabs, change the orientation to landscape, scale the contents to fit on one page (by changing the width to *1 page* on the PAGE LAYOUT tab), and then insert a custom footer with your name, the page number, and the date.
9. With both worksheet tabs selected, print both worksheets in the workbook.
10. Save and then close **EL1-C5-P2-HCEqpRpt.xlsx**.

Project 3 Arrange, Size, and Copy Data between Workbooks   3 Parts

You will open, arrange, hide, unhide, size, and move multiple workbooks. You will also copy cells from one workbook and paste them in another workbook.

Working with Windows

You can open multiple workbooks in Excel, open a new window with the current workbook, and arrange the open workbooks in the Excel window. With multiple workbooks open, you can cut and paste or copy and paste cell entries from one workbook to another using the same techniques discussed earlier in this chapter with the exception that you make the destination workbook active before using the Paste command.

QUICK STEPS provide feature summaries for reference and review.

HINTS provide useful tips on how to use features efficiently and effectively.

MAGENTA TEXT identifies material to type.

At the end of the project, students save, print, and then close the file.

CHAPTER REVIEW ACTIVITIES: A Hierarchy of Learning Assessments

Chapter Summary

- The Page Setup group on the PAGE LAYOUT tab contains buttons for changing the margins and page orientation and size, as well as buttons for establishing the print area, inserting a page break, applying a picture background, and printing titles.
- The default left and right margins are 0.7 inch and the default top and bottom margins are 0.75 inch. Change these default margins with the Margins button in the Page Setup group on the PAGE LAYOUT tab.
- Display the Page Setup dialog box with the Margins tab selected by clicking the Margins button in the Page Setup group on the PAGE LAYOUT tab and then clicking *Custom Margins* at the drop-down list.
- Center a worksheet on the page with the *Horizontally* and *Vertically* options at the Page Setup dialog box with the Margins tab selected.
- Click the Orientation button in the Page Setup group on the PAGE LAYOUT tab to display the two orientation choices: *Portrait* and *Landscape*.
- Insert a page break by selecting the column or row, clicking the Breaks button in the Page Setup group on the PAGE LAYOUT tab, and then clicking *Insert Page Break* at the drop-down list.
- To insert both horizontal and vertical page breaks at the same time, make a cell active, click the Br...
  down list.
- Preview the page break...
  button in the view area...
  clicking the Page Break...
- Use options at the Page...
  printing column and/or...
  the Print Titles button i...
- Use options in the Scal...
  to fit on a specific num...
- Use the Background bu...
  to insert a worksheet b...
  screen but does not pri...
- Use options in the She...
  whether to view and/or...
- Specify the print area b...
  button in the Page Setu...
  Set Print Area at the dr...
  desired cells, clicking t...
  at the drop-down list.
- Create a header and/or...
  group on the INSERT...
  Setup dialog box with...
- Customize a print job...
- To check spelling in a...
  Spelling button.

130 Excel Level 1 ■ Unit 1

CHAPTER SUMMARY captures the purpose and execution of key features.

- Click the Undo button on the Quick Access toolbar to reverse the most recent action and click the Redo button to redo a previously reversed action.
- Use options at the Find and Replace dialog box with the Find tab selected to find specific data and/or formatting in a worksheet.
- Use options at the Find and Replace dialog box with the Replace tab selected to find specific data and/or formatting and replace it with other data and/or formatting.
- Sort data in a worksheet with options from the Sort & Filter button in the Editing group on the HOME tab.
- Create a custom sort with options at the Sort dialog box. Display this dialog box by clicking the Sort & Filter button and then clicking *Custom Sort* at the drop-down list.
- Use filtering to temporarily isolate specific data. Turn on the filter feature by clicking the Sort & Filter button in the Editing group on the HOME tab and then clicking *Filter* at the drop-down list. This inserts filter arrows with each column label. Click a filter arrow and then use options at the drop-down list that displays to specify the filter data.

COMMANDS REVIEW summarizes visually the major features and alternative methods of access.

Commands Review

FEATURE	RIBBON TAB, GROUP	BUTTON, OPTION	KEYBOARD SHORTCUT
background picture	PAGE LAYOUT, Page Setup		
filter data	HOME, Editin		
Find and Replace dialog box with Find tab selected	HOME, Editin		
Find and Replace dialog box with Replace tab selected	HOME, Editin		
header and footer	INSERT, Text		
insert page break	PAGE LAYOU		
margins	PAGE LAYOU		
orientation	PAGE LAYOU		
Page Layout view	VIEW, Work		
Page Setup dialog box with Margins tab selected	PAGE LAYOU		
Page Setup dialog box with Sheet tab selected	PAGE LAYOU		
preview page break	VIEW, Work		

FEATURE	RIBBON TAB, GROUP	BUTTON, OPTION	KEYBOARD SHORTCUT
print area	PAGE LAYOUT, Page Setup		
remove page break	PAGE LAYOUT, Page Setup	*Remove Page Break*	
scale height	PAGE LAYOUT, Scale to Fit		
scale to fit	PAGE LAYOUT, Scale to Fit		
scale width	PAGE LAYOUT, Scale to Fit		
size	PAGE LAYOUT, Page Setup		
sort data	HOME, Editing		
spelling checker	REVIEW, Proofing		F7

Concepts Check   Test Your Knowledge   SNAP

Completion: In the space provided at the right, indicate the correct term, symbol, or command.

1. This is the default left and right margin measurement.

2. This is the default top and bottom margin measurement.

3. The Margins button is located on this tab.

4. By default, a worksheet prints in this orientation on a page.

5. Click the Print Titles button in the Page Setup group on the PAGE LAYOUT tab and the Page Setup dialog box displays with this tab selected.

6. Use options in this group on the PAGE LAYOUT tab to adjust the printed output by a percentage to fit the number of pages specified.

7. Use this button in the Page Setup group on the PAGE LAYOUT tab to select and print specific areas in a worksheet.

8. Click the Header & Footer button in the Text group on the INSERT tab and the worksheet displays in this view.

9. This tab contains options for formatting and customizing a header and/or footer.

CONCEPTS CHECK questions assess knowledge recall. Students enrolled in SNAP can complete the Concepts Check online. SNAP automatically scores student work.

132 Excel Level 1 ■ Unit 1

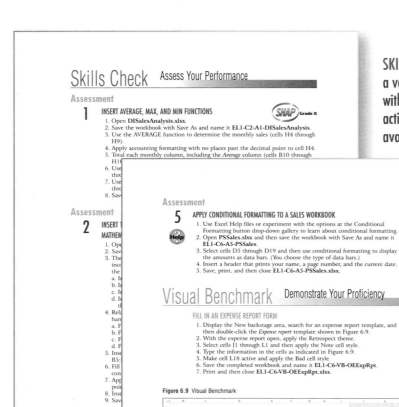

Skills Check — Assess Your Performance

Assessment 1
INSERT AVERAGE, MAX, AND MIN FUNCTIONS

SNAP Grade It

1. Open **DISalesAnalysis.xlsx**.
2. Save the workbook with Save As and name it **EL1-C2-A1-DISalesAnalysis**.
3. Use the AVERAGE function to determine the monthly sales (cells H4 through H9).
4. Apply accounting formatting with no places past the decimal point to cell H4.
5. Total each monthly column, including the *Average* column (cells B10 through H10...
6. Use...
7. Use...
8. Sav...

Assessment 2
**INSERT ...
MATHEM...**

1. Ope...
2. Sav...
3. The...
   inco...
   the...
   a. I...
   b. I...
   c. I...
   d. I...
   t...
4. Rela...
   han...
   a. F...
   b. F...
   c. F...
   d. F...
5. Inse...
   B5:...
6. Fill...
   con...
7. App...
   poi...
8. Inse...
9. Sav...

56   Excel Level 1 ■ Unit 1

SKILLS CHECK exercises ask students to create a variety of documents using multiple features without how-to directions. Versions of the activities marked with a SNAP Grade It icon are available for automatic scoring in SNAP.

Assessment 5
APPLY CONDITIONAL FORMATTING TO A SALES WORKBOOK

Help

1. Use Excel Help files or experiment with the options at the Conditional Formatting button drop-down gallery to learn about conditional formatting.
2. Open **PSSales.xlsx** and then save the workbook with Save As and name it **EL1-C6-A5-PSSales**.
3. Select cells D5 through D19 and then use conditional formatting to display the amounts as data bars. (You choose the type of data bars.)
4. Insert a header that prints your name, a page number, and the current date.
5. Save, print, and then close **EL1-C6-A5-PSSales.xlsx**.

Visual Benchmark — Demonstrate Your Proficiency

FILL IN AN EXPENSE REPORT FORM

1. Display the New backstage area, search for an expense report template, and then double-click the *Expense report* template shown in Figure 6.9.
2. With the expense report open, apply the Retrospect theme.
3. Select cells J1 through L1 and then apply the Note cell style.
4. Type the information in the cells as indicated in Figure 6.9.
5. Make cell L18 active and apply the Bad cell style.
6. Save the completed workbook and name it **EL1-C6-VB-OEExpRpt**.
7. Print and then close **EL1-C6-VB-OEExpRpt.xlsx**.

Figure 6.9 Visual Benchmark

VISUAL BENCHMARK assessments test students' problem-solving skills and mastery of program features.

Case Study — Apply Your Skills

Part 1

You are the office manager for Allenmore Auto Sales and are responsible for preparing the monthly sales worksheet. Open **AASFebSales.xlsx** and then save the workbook with Save As and name it **EL1-C2-CS-AASFebSales**. Complete the workbook by inserting the following formulas:

- In column F, insert a formula that displays the gross profit, which is the price minus the dealer cost.
- In column H, insert a formula that multiplies the gross profit by the commission percentage.
- In column I, insert a formula that displays the net profit, which is the gross profit minus the total commission.
- Apply accounting formatting with a dollar sign to the amounts in cells D4, E4, F4, H4, and I4.

Save the workbook, print the workbook (it will print on two pages), and then close the workbook.

Part 2

The sales manager at Allenmore Auto Sales has asked you to determine the percentage of total commissions each salesperson has earned for the month of February. Open **AASFebCommissions.xlsx** and then save the workbook with Save As and name it **EL1-C2-CS-AASFebCommissions**. Insert a formula in cell C5 that divides B5 by the amount in cell C3. Use an absolute cell reference for cell C3 when writing the formula. Copy the formula down to cells C6 through C12. Save, print, and then close the workbook.

Part 3

You have created a workbook for automobile trade-ins for the month of February. The sales manager wants used automobiles to be wholesaled if they are not sold within a specific period of time. She wants you to determine the date each February trade-in is to be wholesaled. She wants any used automobile older than 2010 to be wholesaled after 45 days and any automobile newer than 2009 to be wholesaled after 60 days. Open **AASFebTradeIns.xlsx** and then save the workbook with Save As and name it **EL1-C2-CS-AASFebTradeIns**. Insert a formula in column G that adds 45 days to the date in column B for trade-ins 2009 and older and adds 60 days to trade-ins 2010 and newer. Save, print, and then close the workbook.

Part 4

Help *WWW*

The sales manager has asked you to locate at least two websites that provide estimates on the value of used automobiles (such as Kelley Blue Book (kbb.com) and Edmunds.com). She wants you to add at least two hyperlinks to the February trade-ins workbook. Sales people can use the hyperlinks in the worksheet to quickly determine the value of a used automobile. Use the Help feature to learn how to create hyperlinks in Excel. Open **EL1-C2-CS-AASFebTradeIns.xlsx** workbook and save it with Save As and name it **EL1-C2-CS-AASFebTradeIns-2**. Add at least two hyperlinks to the workbook that link to websites that provide estimates on the value of used automobiles. Save, print, and then close the workbook.

60   Excel Level 1 ■ Unit 1

CASE STUDY requires analyzing a workplace scenario and then planning and executing multipart projects.

Students search the Web and/or use the program's Help feature to locate additional information required to complete the Case Study.

UNIT PERFORMANCE ASSESSMENT: Cross-Disciplinary, Comprehensive Evaluation

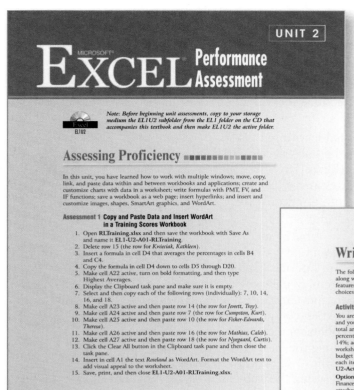

UNIT 2

MICROSOFT EXCEL Performance Assessment

Note: Before beginning unit assessments, copy to your storage medium the EL1U2 subfolder from the EL1 folder on the CD that accompanies this textbook and then make EL1U2 the active folder.

EL1U2

Assessing Proficiency

In this unit, you have learned how to work with multiple windows; move, copy, link, and paste data within and between workbooks and applications; create and customize charts with data in a worksheet; write formulas with PMT, FV, and IF functions; save a workbook as a web page; insert hyperlinks; and insert and customize images, shapes, SmartArt graphics, and WordArt.

Assessment 1 Copy and Paste Data and Insert WordArt in a Training Scores Workbook

1. Open **RLTraining.xlsx** and then save the workbook with Save As and name it **EL1-U2-A01-RLTraining**.
2. Delete row 15 (the row for *Kwieciak, Kathleen*).
3. Insert a formula in cell D4 that averages the percentages in cells B4 and C4.
4. Copy the formula in cell D4 down to cells D5 through D20.
5. Make cell A22 active, turn on bold formatting, and then type Highest Averages.
6. Display the Clipboard task pane and make sure it is empty.
7. Select and then copy each of the following rows (individually): 7, 10, 14, 16, and 18.
8. Make cell A23 active and then paste row 14 (the row for *Jewett, Troy*).
9. Make cell A24 active and then paste row 7 (the row for *Cumpston, Kurt*).
10. Make cell A25 active and then paste row 10 (the row for *Fisher-Edwards, Theresa*).
11. Make cell A26 active and then paste row 16 (the row for *Mathias, Caleb*).
12. Make cell A27 active and then paste row 18 (the row for *Nyegaard, Curtis*).
13. Click the Clear All button in the Clipboard task pane and then close the task pane.
14. Insert in cell A1 the text *Roseland* as WordArt. Format the WordArt text to add visual appeal to the worksheet.
15. Save, print, and then close **EL1-U2-A01-RLTraining.xlsx**.

ASSESSING PROFICIENCY checks mastery of features.

WRITING ACTIVITIES involve applying program skills in a communication context.

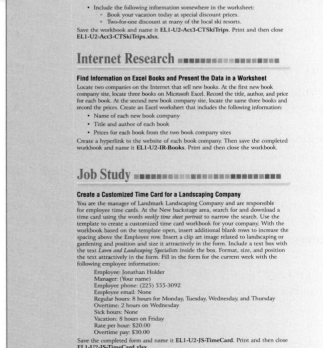

Writing Activities

The following activities give you the opportunity to practice your writing skills along with demonstrating an understanding of some of the important Excel features you have mastered in this unit. Use correct grammar, appropriate word choices, and clear sentence constructions.

Activity 1 Prepare a Projected Budget

You are the accounting assistant in the financial department of McCormack Funds and you have been asked to prepare a proposed annual department budget. The total amount available to the department is $1,450,000. You are given these percentages for the proposed budget items: salaries, 45%; benefits, 12%; training, 14%; administrative costs, 10%; equipment, 11%; and supplies, 8%. Create a worksheet with this information that shows the projected yearly budget, the budget items in the department, the percentage for each item, and the amount for each item. After the worksheet is completed, save the workbook and name it **EL1-U2-Act1-MFBudget**. Print and then close the workbook.

Optional: Using Word 2013, write a memo to members of the McCormack Funds Finance Department explaining that the proposed annual department budget is attached for their review. Comments and suggestions are to be sent to you within one week. Save the file and name it **EL1-U2-Act1-MFMemo**. Print and then close the file.

Activity 2 Create a Travel Tours Bar Chart

- Include the following information somewhere in the worksheet:
  - Book your vacation today at special discount prices.
  - Two-for-one discount at many of the local ski resorts.
Save the workbook and name it **EL1-U2-Act3-CTSkiTrips**. Print and then close **EL1-U2-Act3-CTSkiTrips.xlsx**.

Internet Research

Find Information on Excel Books and Present the Data in a Worksheet

Locate two companies on the Internet that sell new books. At the first new book company site, locate three books on Microsoft Excel. Record the title, author, and price for each book. At the second new book company site, locate the same three books and record the prices. Create an Excel worksheet that includes the following information:

- Name of each new book company
- Title and author of each book
- Prices for each book from the two book company sites

Create a hyperlink to the website of each book company. Then save the completed workbook and name it **EL1-U2-IR-Books**. Print and then close the workbook.

Job Study

Create a Customized Time Card for a Landscaping Company

You are the manager of Landmark Landscaping Company and are responsible for employee time cards. At the New backstage area, search for and download a time card using the words *weekly time sheet portrait* to narrow the search. Use the template to create a customized time card workbook for your company. With the workbook based on the template open, insert additional blank rows to increase the spacing above the Employee row. Insert a clip art image related to landscaping or gardening and position and size it attractively in the form. Include a text box with the text *Lawn and Landscaping Specialists* inside the box. Format, size, and position the text attractively in the form. Fill in the form for the current week with the following employee information:

    Employee: Jonathan Holder
    Manager: (Your name)
    Employee phone: (225) 555-3092
    Employee email: None
    Regular hours: 8 hours for Monday, Tuesday, Wednesday, and Thursday
    Overtime: 2 hours on Wednesday
    Sick hours: None
    Vacation: 8 hours on Friday
    Rate per hour: $20.00
    Overtime pay: $30.00

Save the completed form and name it **EL1-U2-JS-TimeCard**. Print and then close **EL1-U2-JS-TimeCard.xlsx**.

INTERNET RESEARCH project reinforces research and word processing skills.

JOB STUDY at the end of Unit 2 presents a capstone assessment requiring critical thinking and problem solving.

Student Courseware ■■■■■■■■■■■■■■■■■■■■■■■■■■■■■■■■■■

Student Resources CD Each Benchmark Series textbook is packaged with a Student Resources CD containing the data files required for completing the projects and assessments. A CD icon and folder name displayed on the opening page of chapters reminds students to copy a folder of files from the CD to the desired storage medium before beginning the project exercises. Directions for copying folders are printed on the inside back cover.

Internet Resource Center Additional learning tools and reference materials are available at the book-specific website at www.paradigmcollege.net/BenchmarkExcel13. Students can access the same files that are on the Student Resources CD along with study aids, web links, and tips for using computers effectively in academic and workplace settings.

SNAP Training and Assessment Available at snap2013.emcp.com, SNAP is a web-based program offering an interactive venue for learning Microsoft Office 2013, Windows 8, and Internet Explorer 10. Along with a web-based learning management system, SNAP provides multimedia tutorials, performance skill items, Concepts Check matching activities, Grade It Skills Check Assessment activities, comprehensive performance evaluations, a concepts test bank, an online grade book, and a set of course planning tools. A CD of tutorials teaching the basics of Office, Windows, and Internet Explorer is also available if instructors wish to assign additional SNAP tutorial work without using the web-based SNAP program.

eBook For students who prefer studying with an eBook, the texts in the Benchmark Series are available in an electronic form. The web-based, password-protected eBooks feature dynamic navigation tools, including bookmarking, a linked table of contents, and the ability to jump to a specific page. The eBook format also supports helpful study tools, such as highlighting and note taking.

Instructor Resources ■■■■■■■■■■■■■■■■■■■■■■■■■■■■■■■

Instructor's Guide and Disc Instructor support for the Benchmark Series includes an *Instructor's Guide and Instructor Resources Disc* package. This resource includes planning information, such as Lesson Blueprints, teaching hints, and sample course syllabi; presentation resources, such as PowerPoint slide shows with lecture notes and audio support; and assessment resources, including an overview of available assessment venues, live model answers for chapter activities, and live and PDF model answers for end-of-chapter exercises. Contents of the *Instructor's Guide and Instructor Resources Disc* package are also available on the password-protected section of the Internet Resource Center for this title at www.paradigmcollege.net/BenchmarkExcel13.

Computerized Test Generator Instructors can use the ExamView® Assessment Suite and test banks of multiple-choice items to create customized web-based or print tests.

Blackboard Cartridge This set of files allows instructors to create a personalized Blackboard website for their course and provides course content, tests, and the mechanisms for establishing communication via e-discussions and online group conferences. Available content includes a syllabus, test banks, PowerPoint presentations with audio support, and supplementary course materials. Upon request, the files can be available within 24–48 hours. Hosting the site is the responsibility of the educational institution.

System Requirements ■■■■■■■■■■■■■■■■■■■■■■■■■■■■■■■■■

This text is designed for the student to complete projects and assessments on a computer running a standard installation of Microsoft Office Professional Plus 2013 and the Microsoft Windows 8 operating system. To effectively run this suite and operating system, your computer should be outfitted with the following:

- 1 gigahertz (GHz) processor or higher; 1 gigabyte (GB) of RAM (32 bit) or 2 GB of RAM (64 bit)
- 3 GB of available hard-disk space
- .NET version 3.5, 4.0, or 4.5
- DirectX 10 graphics card
- Minimum 1024 × 576 resolution (or 1366 × 768 to use Windows Snap feature)
- Computer mouse, multi-touch device, or other compatible pointing device

Office 2013 will also operate on computers running the Windows 7 operating system.

Screen captures in this book were created using a screen resolution display setting of 1600 × 900. Refer to the *Customizing Settings* section of *Getting Started in Office 2013* following this preface for instructions on changing your monitor's resolution. Figure G.9 on page 10 shows the Microsoft Office Word ribbon at three resolutions for comparison purposes. Choose the resolution that best matches your computer; however, be aware that using a resolution other than 1600 × 900 means that your screens may not match the illustrations in this book.

About the Authors ■■■■■■■■■■■■■■■■■■■■■■■■■■■■■■■■■

Nita Rutkosky began teaching business education courses at Pierce College Puyallup, Washington, in 1978. Since then she has taught a variety of software applications to students in postsecondary Information Technology certificate and degree programs. In addition to *Benchmark Office 2013,* she has co-authored *Marquee Series: Microsoft Office 2013, 2010, 2007,* and *2003; Signature Series: Microsoft Word 2013, 2010, 2007,* and *2003; Using Computers in the Medical Office: Microsoft Word, Excel, and PowerPoint 2010, 2007* and *2003;* and *Computer and Internet Essentials: Preparing for IC³.* She has also authored textbooks on keyboarding, WordPerfect, desktop publishing, and voice recognition for Paradigm Publishing, Inc.

Audrey Roggenkamp has been teaching courses in the Business Information Technology department at Pierce College Puyallup since 2005. Her courses have included keyboarding, skill building, and Microsoft Office programs. In addition to this title, she has co-authored *Marquee Series: Microsoft Office 2013, 2010,* and *2007; Signature Series: Microsoft Word 2013, 2010,* and *2007; Using Computers in the Medical Office: Microsoft Word, Excel, and PowerPoint 2010, 2007,* and *2003;* and *Computer and Internet Essentials: Preparing for IC³* for Paradigm Publishing, Inc.

Ian Rutkosky teaches Business Technology courses at Pierce College Puyallup, Washington. In addition to this title, he has coauthored *Computer and Internet Essentials: Preparing for IC³, Marquee Series: Microsoft Office 2013,* and *Using Computers in the Medical Office: Microsoft Word, Excel, and PowerPoint 2010.* He is also a co-author and consultant for Paradigm's SNAP training and assessment software.

Getting Started in Office 2013

In this textbook, you will learn to operate several computer programs that combine to make the Microsoft Office 2013 application suite. The programs you will learn are known as *software*, and they contain instructions that tell the computer what to do. Some of the application programs in the suite include Word, a word processing program; Excel, a spreadsheet program; Access, a database program; and PowerPoint, a presentation program.

Identifying Computer Hardware

The computer equipment you will use to operate the Microsoft Office suite is referred to as *hardware*. You will need access to a computer system that includes a CPU, monitor, keyboard, printer, drives, and mouse. If you are not sure what equipment you will be operating, check with your instructor. The computer system shown in Figure G.1 consists of six components. Each component is discussed separately in the material that follows.

Figure G.1 Computer System

CPU

CD-ROM

DVD±RW

USB drive

monitor

printer

keyboard

mouse

CPU

The *central processing unit (CPU)* is the brain of the computer and is where all processing occurs. Silicon chips, which contain miniaturized circuitry, are placed on boards that are plugged into slots within the CPU. Whenever an instruction is given to the computer, it is processed through the circuitry in the CPU.

Monitor

A computer *monitor* looks like a television screen. It displays the information in a program and the text you input using the keyboard. The quality of display for monitors varies depending on the type of monitor and the level of resolution. Monitors can also vary in size—generally from 13 inches to 26 inches or larger.

Keyboard

The *keyboard* is used to input information into the computer. The number and location of the keys on a keyboard can vary. In addition to letters, numbers, and symbols, most computer keyboards contain function keys, arrow keys, and a numeric keypad. Figure G.2 shows an enhanced keyboard.

The 12 keys at the top of the keyboard, labeled with the letter F followed by a number, are called *function keys*. Use these keys to perform functions within each of the Office programs. To the right of the regular keys is a group of *special* or *dedicated keys*. These keys are labeled with specific functions that will be performed when you press the key. Below the special keys are arrow keys. Use these keys to move the insertion point in the document screen.

Some keyboards include mode indicator lights. When you select certain modes, a light appears on the keyboard. For example, if you press the Caps Lock key, which disables the lowercase alphabet, a light appears next to Caps Lock. Similarly, pressing the Num Lock key will disable the special functions on the numeric keypad, which is located at the right side of the keyboard.

Figure G.2 Keyboard

function keys

Media Center

function keys

mode indicator lights

special or dedicated keys

special or dedicated keys

alphanumeric keys

insertion point control keys

numeric, insertion point control, and special keys

Drives and Ports

Depending on the computer system you are using, Microsoft Office 2013 is installed on a hard drive or as part of a network system. Either way, you will need to have a CD or DVD drive to complete the projects and assessments in this book. If you plan to use a USB drive as your storage medium, you will also need a USB port. You will insert the CD that accompanies this textbook into the CD or DVD drive and then copy folders from the disc to your storage medium. You will also save documents you create to folders on your storage medium.

Printer

An electronic version of a file is known as a **soft copy**. If you want to create a **hard copy** of a file, you need to print it. To print documents you will need to access a printer, which will probably be either a laser printer or an ink-jet printer. A **laser printer** uses a laser beam combined with heat and pressure to print documents, while an **ink-jet printer** prints a document by spraying a fine mist of ink on the page.

Mouse or Touchpad

Most functions and commands in the Microsoft Office suite are designed to be performed using a mouse or a similar pointing device. A **mouse** is an input device that sits on a flat surface next to the computer. You can operate a mouse with your left or right hand. Moving the mouse on the flat surface causes a corresponding pointer to move on the screen, and clicking the left or right mouse buttons allows you to select various objects and commands. Figure G.1 contains an image of a mouse.

If you are working on a laptop computer, you may use a touchpad instead of a mouse. A **touchpad** allows you to move the mouse pointer by moving your finger across a surface at the base of the keyboard. You click by using your thumb to press the button located at the bottom of the touchpad.

Using the Mouse

The programs in the Microsoft Office suite can be operated with the keyboard and a mouse. The mouse generally has two buttons on top, which you press to execute specific functions and commands. A mouse may also contain a wheel, which can be used to scroll in a window or as a third button. To use the mouse, rest it on a flat surface or a mouse pad. Put your hand over it with your palm resting on top of the mouse, your wrist resting on the table surface, and your index finger resting on the left mouse button. As you move your hand, and thus the mouse, a corresponding pointer moves on the screen.

When using the mouse, you should understand four terms — point, click, double-click, and drag. When operating the mouse, you may need to point to a specific command, button, or icon. To **point** means to position the mouse pointer on the desired item. With the mouse pointer positioned on the desired item, you may need to click a button on the mouse to select the item. To **click** means to quickly tap a button on the mouse once. To complete two steps at one time, such as choosing and then executing a function, double-click the mouse button. To **double-click** means to tap the left mouse button twice in quick succession. The term **drag** means to press and hold the left mouse button, move the mouse pointer to a specific location, and then release the button.

Using the Mouse Pointer

The mouse pointer will look different depending on where you have positioned it and what function you are performing. The following are some of the ways the mouse pointer can appear when you are working in the Office suite:

- The mouse pointer appears as an I-beam (called the *I-beam pointer*) when you are inserting text in a file. The I-beam pointer can be used to move the insertion point or to select text.
- The mouse pointer appears as an arrow pointing up and to the left (called the *arrow pointer*) when it is moved to the Title bar, Quick Access toolbar, ribbon, or an option in a dialog box, among other locations.
- The mouse pointer becomes a double-headed arrow (either pointing left and right, pointing up and down, or pointing diagonally) when you perform certain functions such as changing the size of an object.
- In certain situations, such as when you move an object or image, the mouse pointer displays with a four-headed arrow attached. The four-headed arrow means that you can move the object left, right, up, or down.
- When a request is being processed or when a program is being loaded, the mouse pointer may appear as a moving circle. The moving circle means "please wait." When the process is completed, the circle is replaced with a normal arrow pointer.
- When the mouse pointer displays as a hand with a pointing index finger, it indicates that more information is available about an item. The mouse pointer also displays as a hand with a pointing index finger when you hover the mouse over a hyperlink.

Choosing Commands

Once a program is open, you can use several methods in the program to choose commands. A *command* is an instruction that tells the program to do something. You can choose a command using the mouse or the keyboard. When a program such as Word or PowerPoint is open, the ribbon contains buttons and options for completing tasks, as well as tabs you can click to display additional buttons and options. To choose a button on the Quick Access toolbar or on the ribbon, position the tip of the mouse arrow pointer on the button and then click the left mouse button.

The Office suite provides *accelerator keys* you can press to use a command in a program. Press the Alt key on the keyboard to display KeyTips that identify the accelerator key you can press to execute a command. For example, if you press the Alt key in a Word document with the HOME tab active, KeyTips display as shown in Figure G.3. Continue pressing accelerator keys until you execute the desired command. For example, to begin spell checking a document, press the Alt key, press the R key on the keyboard to display the REVIEW tab, and then press the letter S on the keyboard.

Figure G.3 Word HOME Tab KeyTips

Choosing Commands from Drop-Down Lists

To choose a command from a drop-down list with the mouse, position the mouse pointer on the desired option and then click the left mouse button. To make a selection from a drop-down list with the keyboard, type the underlined letter in the desired option.

Some options at a drop-down list may appear in gray (dimmed), indicating that the option is currently unavailable. If an option at a drop-down list displays preceded by a check mark, it means the option is currently active. If an option at a drop-down list displays followed by an ellipsis (…), clicking that option will display a dialog box.

Choosing Options from a Dialog Box

A *dialog box* contains options for applying formatting or otherwise modifying a file or data within a file. Some dialog boxes display with tabs along the top that provide additional options. For example, the Font dialog box shown in Figure G.4 contains two tabs — the Font tab and the Advanced tab. The tab that displays in the front is the active tab. To make a tab active using the mouse, position the arrow pointer on the desired tab and then click the left mouse button. If you are using the keyboard, press Ctrl + Tab or press Alt + the underlined letter on the desired tab.

Figure G.4 Word Font Dialog Box

To choose options from a dialog box with the mouse, position the arrow pointer on the desired option and then click the left mouse button. If you are using the keyboard, press the Tab key to move the insertion point forward from option to option. Press Shift + Tab to move the insertion point backward from option to option. You can also hold down the Alt key and then press the underlined letter of the desired option. When an option is selected, it displays with a blue background or surrounded by a dashed box called a *marquee*. A dialog box contains one or more of the following elements: list boxes, option boxes, check boxes, text boxes, option buttons, measurement boxes, and command buttons.

List Boxes and Option Boxes

The fonts below the *Font* option in the Font dialog box in Figure G.4 are contained in a **list box**. To make a selection from a list box with the mouse, move the arrow pointer to the desired option and then click the left mouse button.

Some list boxes may contain a scroll bar. This scroll bar will display at the right side of the list box (a vertical scroll bar) or at the bottom of the list box (a horizontal scroll bar). Use a vertical scroll bar or a horizontal scroll bar to move through the list if the list is longer (or wider) than the box. To move down a list using a vertical scroll bar, position the arrow pointer on the down-pointing arrow and hold down the left mouse button. To scroll up through the list, position the arrow pointer on the up-pointing arrow and hold down the left mouse button. You can also move the arrow pointer above the scroll box and click the left mouse button to scroll up the list or move the arrow pointer below the scroll box and click the left mouse button to move down the list. To navigate a list with a horizontal scroll bar, click the left-pointing arrow to scroll to the left of the list or click the right-pointing arrow to scroll to the right of the list.

To use the keyboard to make a selection from a list box, move the insertion point into the box by holding down the Alt key and pressing the underlined letter of the desired option. Press the Up and/or Down Arrow keys on the keyboard to move through the list, and press Enter once the desired option is selected.

In some dialog boxes where there is not enough room for a list box, lists of options are contained in a drop-down list box called an **option box**. Option boxes display with a down-pointing arrow. For example, in Figure G.4, the font color options are contained in an option box. To display the different color options, click the down-pointing arrow at the right of the *Font color* option box. If you are using the keyboard, press Alt + C.

Check Boxes

Some dialog boxes contain options preceded by a box. A check mark may or may not appear in the box. The Word Font dialog box shown in Figure G.4 displays a variety of check boxes within the *Effects* section. If a check mark appears in the box, the option is active (turned on). If the check box does not contain a check mark, the option is inactive (turned off). Any number of check boxes can be active. For example, in the Word Font dialog box, you can insert a check mark in several of the boxes in the *Effects* section to activate the options.

To make a check box active or inactive with the mouse, position the tip of the arrow pointer in the check box and then click the left mouse button. If you are using the keyboard, press Alt + the underlined letter of the desired option.

Text Boxes

Some options in a dialog box require you to enter text. For example, the boxes below the *Find what* and *Replace with* options at the Excel Find and Replace dialog box shown in Figure G.5 are text boxes. In a text box, you type text or edit existing text. Edit text in a text box in the same manner as normal text. Use the Left and Right Arrow keys on the keyboard to move the insertion point without deleting text and use the Delete key or Backspace key to delete text.

Option Buttons

The Word Insert Table dialog box shown in Figure G.6 contains options in the *AutoFit behavior* section preceded by **option button**s. Only one option button can be selected at any time. When an option button is selected, a blue or black circle displays in the button. To select an option button with the mouse, position the tip of the arrow pointer inside the option button or on the option and then click the left mouse button. To make a selection with the keyboard, hold down the Alt key and then press the underlined letter of the desired option.

Measurement Boxes

Some options in a dialog box contain measurements or amounts you can increase or decrease. These options are generally located in a **measurement box**. For example, the Word Insert Table dialog box shown in Figure G.6 contains the *Number of columns* and *Number of rows* measurement boxes. To increase a number in a measurement box, position the tip of the arrow pointer on the up-pointing arrow at the right of the desired option and then click the left mouse button. To decrease the number, click the down-pointing arrow. If you are using the keyboard, press and hold down Alt + the underlined letter of the desired option and then press the Up Arrow key to increase the number or the Down Arrow key to decrease the number.

Command Buttons

The buttons at the bottom of the Excel Find and Replace dialog box shown in Figure G.5 are called **command buttons**. Use a command button to execute or cancel a command. Some command buttons display with an ellipsis (...), which means another dialog box will open if you click that button. To choose a command button with the mouse, position the arrow pointer on the desired button and then click the left mouse button. To choose a command button with the keyboard, press the Tab key until the desired command button is surrounded by a marquee and then press the Enter key.

Figure G.5 Excel Find and Replace Dialog Box

Choosing Commands with Keyboard Shortcuts

Applications in the Office suite offer a variety of keyboard shortcuts you can use to execute specific commands. Keyboard shortcuts generally require two or more keys. For example, the keyboard shortcut to display the Open dialog box in an application is Ctrl + F12. To use this keyboard shortcut, hold down the Ctrl key, press the F12 function on the keyboard, and then release the Ctrl key. For a list of keyboard shortcuts, refer to the Help files.

Choosing Commands with Shortcut Menus

The software programs in the Office suite include shortcut menus that contain commands related to different items. To display a shortcut menu, position the mouse pointer over the item for which you want to view more options, and then click the right mouse button or press Shift + F10. The shortcut menu will appear wherever the insertion point is positioned. For example, if the insertion point is positioned in a paragraph of text in a Word document, clicking the right mouse button or pressing Shift + F10 will cause the shortcut menu shown in Figure G.7 to display in the document screen (along with the Mini toolbar).

To select an option from a shortcut menu with the mouse, click the desired option. If you are using the keyboard, press the Up or Down Arrow key until the desired option is selected and then press the Enter key. To close a shortcut menu without choosing an option, click anywhere outside the shortcut menu or press the Esc key.

Figure G.6 Word Insert Table Dialog Box

option buttons

Figure G.7 Word Shortcut Menu

Working with Multiple Programs ■■■■■■■■■■■■■■■■■■

As you learn the various programs in the Microsoft Office suite, you will notice many similarities between them. For example, the steps to save, close, and print are virtually the same whether you are working in Word, Excel, or PowerPoint. This consistency between programs greatly enhances a user's ability to transfer knowledge learned in one program to another within the suite. Another benefit to using Microsoft Office is the ability to have more than one program open at the same time and to integrate content from one program with another. For example, you can open Word and create a document, open Excel and create a spreadsheet, and then copy the Excel spreadsheet into Word.

When you open a program, a button containing an icon representing the program displays on the Taskbar. If you open another program, a button containing an icon representing that program displays to the right of the first program button on the Taskbar. Figure G.8 on the next page, shows the Taskbar with Word, Excel, Access, and PowerPoint open. To move from one program to another, click the Taskbar button representing the desired program.

Figure G.8 Taskbar with Word, Excel, Access, and PowerPoint Open

Customizing Settings ■■■■■■■■■■■■■■■■■■■■■■■■■■

Before beginning computer projects in this textbook, you may need to customize your monitor's settings and turn on the display of file extensions. Projects in the chapters in this textbook assume that the monitor display is set at 1600 x 900 pixels and that the display of file extensions is turned on.

Before you begin learning the applications in the Microsoft Office 2013 suite, take a moment to check the display settings on the computer you are using. Your monitor's display settings are important because the ribbon in the Microsoft Office suite adjusts to the screen resolution setting of your computer monitor. A computer monitor set at a high resolution will have the ability to show more buttons in the ribbon than will a monitor set to a low resolution. The illustrations in this textbook were created with a screen resolution display set at 1600 × 900 pixels. In Figure G.9 on the next page, the Word ribbon is shown three ways: at a lower screen resolution (1366 × 768 pixels), at the screen resolution featured throughout this textbook, and at a higher screen resolution (1920 × 1080 pixels). Note the variances in the ribbon in all three examples. If possible, set your display to 1600 × 900 pixels to match the illustrations you will see in this textbook.

Figure G.9 Monitor Resolution

1366 × 768 screen resolution

1600 × 900 screen resolution

1920 × 1080 screen resolution

Project 1 Setting Monitor Display to 1600 by 900

1. At the Windows desktop, right-click a blank area of the screen.
2. At the shortcut menu, click the *Screen resolution* option.
3. At the Screen Resolution window, click the *Resolution* option box. (This displays a slider bar. Your slider bar may display differently than what you see in the image at the right.)
4. Drag the button on the slider bar until *1600 × 900* displays to the right of the slider bar.
5. Click in the Screen Resolution window to remove the slider bar.
6. Click the Apply button.
7. Click the Keep Changes button.
8. Click the OK button.

Project 2   Displaying File Extensions

1. At the Windows desktop, position the mouse pointer in the lower left corner of the Taskbar until the Start screen thumbnail displays and then click the right mouse button.
2. At the pop-up list, click the *File Explorer* option.
3. At the Computer window, click the View tab on the ribbon and then click the *File name extensions* check box in the Show/hide group to insert a check mark.
4. Close the Computer window.

Completing Computer Projects ■■■■■■■■■■■■■■■■■■

Some projects in this textbook require that you open an existing file. Project files are saved on the Student Resources CD in individual chapter folders. Before beginning a chapter, copy the necessary folder from the CD to your storage medium (such as a USB flash drive or your OneDrive) using the Computer window. To maximize storage capacity, delete previous chapter folders before copying a new chapter folder onto your storage medium.

Project 3   Copying a Folder from the Student Resources CD to a USB Flash Drive

1. Insert the CD that accompanies this textbook into your computer's CD/DVD drive.
2. Insert your USB flash drive into an available USB port.
3. At the Windows Start screen, click the Desktop tile.
4. Open File Explorer by clicking the File Explorer button on the Taskbar.
5. Click *Computer* in the Navigation pane at the left side of the File Explorer window.
6. Double-click the CD/DVD drive that displays with the name *BM13StudentResources* preceded by the drive letter.
7. Double-click **StudentDataFiles** in the Content pane.
8. Double-click the desired program folder name (and level number, if appropriate) in the Content pane.
9. Click once on the desired chapter (or unit performance assessment) folder name to select it.
10. Click the Home tab and then click the Copy button in the Clipboard group.
11. Click your USB flash drive that displays in the Navigation pane at the left side of the window.
12. Click the Home tab and then click the Paste button in the Clipboard group.
13. Close the File Explorer window by clicking the Close button located in the upper right corner of the window.

Project 4 Copying a Folder from the Student Resources CD to your OneDrive Account

Note: OneDrive is updated periodically, so the steps to create folders and upload files may vary from the steps below.
1. Insert the CD that accompanies this textbook into your computer's CD/DVD drive.
2. At the Windows Start screen, click the Desktop tile.
3. Open Internet Explorer by clicking the Internet Explorer button on the Taskbar.
4. At the Internet Explorer home page, click in the Address bar, type **www.onedrive.com**, and then press Enter.
5. At the Microsoft OneDrive login page, type your Windows Live ID (such as your email address).
6. Press the Tab key, type your password, and then press Enter.
7. Click the Documents tile in your OneDrive.
8. Click the Create option on the OneDrive menu bar and then click *Folder* at the drop-down list.
9. Type the name of the folder that you want to copy from the Student Resources CD and then press the Enter key.
10. Click the folder tile you created in the previous step.
11. Click the Upload option on the menu bar.
12. Click the CD/DVD drive that displays in the Navigation pane at the left side of the Choose File to Upload dialog box.
13. Open the chapter folder on the CD that contains the required student data files.
14. Select all of the files in the folder by pressing Ctrl + A and then click the Open button.

Project 5 Deleting a Folder

Note: Check with your instructor before deleting a folder.
1. Insert your storage medium (such as a USB flash drive) into your computer's USB port.
2. At the Windows desktop, open File Explorer by right-clicking the Start screen thumbnail and then clicking *File Explorer* at the shortcut menu.
3. Double-click the drive letter for your storage medium (the drive containing your USB flash drive, such as *Removable Disk (F:)*).
4. Click the chapter folder in the Content pane.
5. Click the Home tab and then click the Delete button in the Organize group.
6. At the message asking if you want to delete the folder, click the Yes button.
7. Close the Computer window by clicking the Close button located in the upper right corner of the window.

Using Windows 8

A computer requires an operating system to provide necessary instructions on a multitude of processes including loading programs, managing data, directing the flow of information to peripheral equipment, and displaying information. Windows 8 is an operating system that provides functions of this type (along with much more) in a graphical environment. Windows is referred to as a *graphical user interface* (GUI—pronounced *gooey*) that provides a visual display of information with features such as icons (pictures) and buttons. In this introduction, you will learn these basic features of Windows 8:

- Use the Start screen to launch programs
- Use desktop icons and the Taskbar to launch programs and open files or folders
- Organize and manage data, including copying, moving, creating, and deleting files and folders; and create a shortcut
- Explore the Control Panel and personalize the desktop
- Use the Windows Help and Support features
- Use search tools
- Customize monitor settings

Before using the software programs in the Microsoft Office suite, you will need to start the Windows 8 operating system. To do this, turn on the computer. Depending on your computer equipment configuration, you may also need to turn on the monitor and printer. If you are using a computer that is part of a network system or if your computer is set up for multiple users, a screen will display showing the user accounts defined for your computer system. At this screen, click your user account name; if necessary, type your password; and then press the Enter key. The Windows 8 operating system will start and, after a few moments, the Windows 8 Start screen will display as shown in Figure W.1. (Your Windows 8 Start screen may vary from what you see in Figure W.1.)

Exploring the Start Screen and Desktop ■■■■■■■■■■■

When Windows is loaded, the Windows 8 Start screen displays. This screen contains tiles that open various applications. Open an application by clicking an application's tile or display the Windows 8 desktop by clicking the Desktop tile. Click the Desktop tile and the screen displays as shown in Figure W.2. Think of the desktop in Windows as the top of a desk in an office. A businessperson places necessary tools—such as pencils, pens, paper, files, calculator—on the desktop to perform functions. Like the tools that are located on a desk, the Windows 8 desktop contains tools for operating the computer. These tools are logically grouped and placed in dialog boxes or panels that you can display using icons on the desktop. The desktop contains a variety of features for using your computer and applications installed on the computer.

Figure W.1 Windows 8 Start Screen

current user

tiles

Start

Student
Name

Click this tile
to display the
Windows 8
desktop.

scroll bar

zoom out

Figure W.2 Windows 8 Desktop

Recycle Bin icon

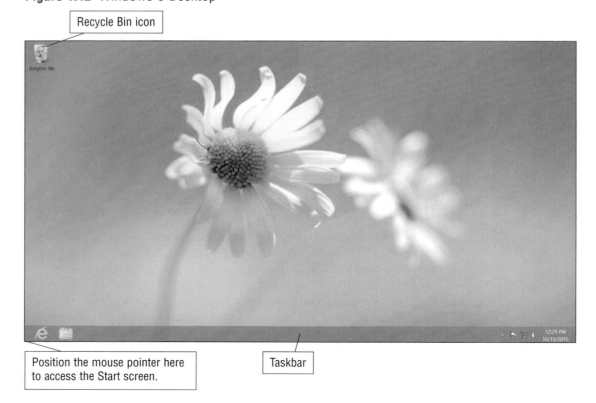

Position the mouse pointer here
to access the Start screen.

Taskbar

Using Icons

Icons are visual symbols that represent programs, files, or folders. Figure W.2 identifies the Recycle Bin icon on the Windows desktop. The Windows desktop on your computer may contain additional icons. Applications that have been installed on your computer may be represented by an icon on the desktop. Icons that represent files or folders may also display on your desktop. Double-click an icon and the application, file, or folder it represents opens on the desktop.

Using the Taskbar

The bar that displays at the bottom of the desktop (see Figure W.2) is called the *Taskbar*. The Taskbar, shown in Figure W.3, contains the Start screen area (a spot where you point to access the Start screen), pinned items, a section that displays task buttons representing active tasks, the notification area, and the Show desktop button.

Position the mouse pointer in the lower left corner of the Taskbar to display the Start screen thumbnail. When the Start screen thumbnail displays, click the left mouse button to access the Windows 8 Start screen, shown in Figure W.1. (Your Start screen may look different.) You can also display the Start screen by pressing the Windows key on your keyboard or by pressing Ctrl + Esc. The left side of the Start menu contains tiles you can click to access the most frequently used applications. The name of the active user (the person who is currently logged on) displays in the upper right corner of the Start screen.

To open an application from the Start screen, drag the arrow pointer to the desired tile (referred to as *pointing*) and then click the left mouse button. When a program is open, a task button representing the program appears on the Taskbar. If multiple programs are open, each program will appear as a task button on the Taskbar (a few specialized tools may not).

Figure W.3 Windows 8 Taskbar

Show desktop button

pinned items

buttons for active programs

notification area

Manipulating Windows

When you open a program, a defined work area known as a *window* displays on the screen. A Title bar displays at the top of the window and contains buttons at the right side for minimizing, maximizing, and restoring the size of the window, as well as for closing it. You can open more than one window at a time and the open windows can be cascaded or stacked. Windows 8 contains a Snap feature that causes a window to "stick" to the edge of the screen when the window is moved to the left or right side of the screen. Move a window to the top of the screen and the window is automatically maximized. If you drag down a maximized window, the window is automatically restored down (returned to its previous smaller size).

In addition to moving and sizing a window, you can change the display of all open windows. To do this, position the mouse pointer on the Taskbar and then click the right mouse button. At the pop-up menu that displays, you can choose to cascade all open windows, stack all open windows, or display all open windows side by side.

Project 1   Opening Programs, Switching between Programs, and Manipulating Windows

1. Open Windows 8. (To do this, turn on the computer and, if necessary, turn on the monitor and/or printer. If you are using a computer that is part of a network system or if your computer is set up for multiple users, you may need to click your user account name, type your password, and then press the Enter key. Check with your instructor to determine if you need to complete any additional steps.)
2. When the Windows 8 Start screen displays, open Microsoft Word by positioning the mouse pointer on the *Word 2013* tile and then clicking the left mouse button. (You may need to scroll to the right to display the Word 2013 tile.)

3. When the Microsoft Word program is open, notice that a task button representing Word displays on the Taskbar.

Step 3

4. Open Microsoft Excel by completing the following steps:
   a. Position the arrow pointer in the lower left corner of the Taskbar until the Start screen thumbnail displays and then click the left mouse button.
   b. At the Start screen, position the mouse pointer on the *Excel 2013* tile and then click the left mouse button.
5. When the Microsoft Excel program is open, notice that a task button representing Excel displays on the Taskbar to the right of the task button representing Word.

6. Switch to the Word program by clicking the Word task button on the Taskbar.
7. Switch to the Excel program by clicking the Excel task button on the Taskbar.

Step 6

8. Restore down the Excel window by clicking the Restore Down button that displays immediately left of the Close button in the upper right corner of the screen. (This reduces the Excel window so it displays along the bottom half of the screen.)
9. Restore down the Word window by clicking the Restore Down button located immediately left of the Close button in the upper right corner of the screen.

Step 8

10. Position the mouse pointer at the top of the Word window screen, hold down the left mouse button, drag to the left side of the screen until an outline of the window displays in the left half of the screen, and then release the mouse button. (This "sticks" the window to the left side of the screen.)

11. Position the mouse pointer at the top of the Excel window screen, hold down the left mouse button, drag to the right until an outline of the window displays in the right half of the screen, and then release the mouse button.

12. Minimize the Excel window by clicking the Minimize button that displays in the upper right corner of the Excel window screen.

13. Hover your mouse over the Excel button on the Taskbar and then click the Excel window thumbnail that displays. (This displays the Excel window at the right side of the screen.)

14. Cascade the Word and Excel windows by positioning the arrow pointer in an empty area of the Taskbar, clicking the right mouse button, and then clicking *Cascade windows* at the shortcut menu.

15. After viewing the windows cascaded, display them stacked by right-clicking an empty area of the Taskbar and then clicking *Show windows stacked* at the shortcut menu.

16. Display the desktop by right-clicking an empty area of the Taskbar and then clicking *Show the desktop* at the shortcut menu.

17. Display the windows stacked by right-clicking an empty area of the Taskbar and then clicking *Show open windows* at the shortcut menu.

18. Position the mouse pointer at the top of the Word window screen, hold down the left mouse button, drag the window to the top of the screen, and then release the mouse button. This maximizes the Word window so it fills the screen.

19. Close the Word window by clicking the Close button located in the upper right corner of the window.

20. At the Excel window, click the Maximize button located immediately left of the Close button in the upper right corner of the Excel window.

21. Close the Excel window by clicking the Close button located in the upper right corner of the window.

Using the Pinned Area

The icons that display immediately right of the Start screen area represent *pinned applications*. Clicking an icon opens the application associated with the icon. Click the first icon to open the Internet Explorer web browser and click the second icon to open a File Explorer window containing Libraries.

Exploring the Notification Area

The notification area is located at the right side of the Taskbar and contains icons that show the status of certain system functions such as a network connection or battery power. The notification area contains icons for managing certain programs and Windows 8 features, as well as the system clock and date. Click the time or date in the notification area and a window displays with a clock and a calendar of the current month. Click the <u>Change date and time settings</u> hyperlink that displays at the bottom of the window and the Date and Time dialog box displays. To change the date and/or time, click the Change date and time button and the Date and Time Settings dialog box displays, similar to the dialog box shown in Figure W.4. (If a dialog box displays telling you that Windows needs your permission to continue, click the Continue button.)

Change the month and year by clicking the left-pointing or right-pointing arrow at the top of the calendar. Click the left-pointing arrow to display the previous month(s) and click the right-pointing arrow to display the next month(s).

To change the day, click the desired day in the monthly calendar that displays in the dialog box. To change the time, double-click either the hour, minute, or seconds number and then type the appropriate time or use the up- and down-pointing arrows in the measurement boxes to adjust the time.

Figure W.4 Date and Time Settings Dialog Box

Some applications, when installed, will add an icon to the notification area of the Taskbar. To determine the name of an icon, position the mouse pointer on the icon and, after approximately one second, its label will display. If more icons have been inserted in the notification area than can be viewed at one time, an up-pointing arrow button displays at the left side of the notification area. Click this up-pointing arrow to display the remaining icons.

Setting Taskbar Properties

Customize the Taskbar with options at the Taskbar shortcut menu. Display this menu by right-clicking in an empty portion of the Taskbar. The Taskbar shortcut menu contains options for turning on or off the display of specific toolbars, specifying the display of multiple windows, displaying the Start Task Manager dialog box, locking or unlocking the Taskbar, and displaying the Taskbar Properties dialog box.

With options in the Taskbar Properties dialog box, shown in Figure W.5, you can change settings for the Taskbar. Display this dialog box by right-clicking an empty area on the Taskbar and then clicking *Properties* at the shortcut menu.

Each Taskbar property is controlled by a check box or an option box. If a property's check box contains a check mark, that property is active. Click the check box to remove the check mark and make the option inactive. If an option is inactive, clicking the check box will insert a check mark and turn on the option (make it active). A property option box displays the name of the currently active option. Click the option box to select a different option from the drop-down list.

Figure W.5 Taskbar Properties Dialog Box

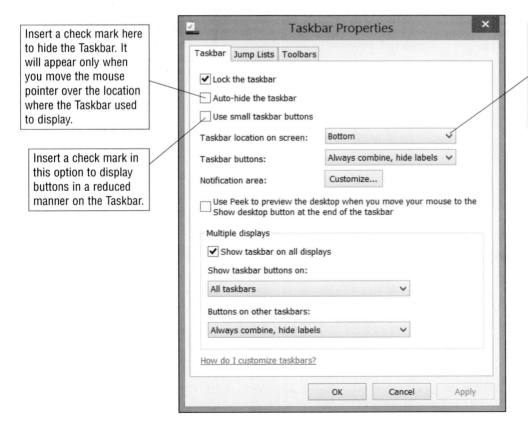

Insert a check mark here to hide the Taskbar. It will appear only when you move the mouse pointer over the location where the Taskbar used to display.

Insert a check mark in this option to display buttons in a reduced manner on the Taskbar.

Use this option box to change the location of the Taskbar from the bottom of the desktop to the left side, right side, or top of the desktop.

1. Make sure the Windows 8 desktop displays.
2. Change the Taskbar properties by completing the following steps:
   a. Position the arrow pointer in an empty area of the Taskbar and then click the right mouse button.
   b. At the shortcut menu that displays, click *Properties*.
   c. At the Taskbar Properties dialog box, click the *Auto-hide the taskbar* check box to insert a check mark.
   d. Click the *Use small taskbar buttons* check box to insert a check mark.
   e. Click the option box (contains the word *Bottom*) that displays at the right side of the *Taskbar location on screen:* option and then click *Right* at the drop-down list.
   f. Click OK to close the dialog box.

3. Since the *Auto-hide the taskbar* check box contains a check mark, the Taskbar does not display. Display the Taskbar by moving the mouse pointer to the right side of the screen. Notice that the buttons on the Taskbar are smaller than they were before.
4. Return to the default Taskbar properties by completing the following steps:
   a. Move the mouse pointer to the right side of the screen to display the Taskbar.
   b. Right-click an empty area of the Taskbar and then click *Properties* at the shortcut menu.
   c. Click the *Auto-hide the taskbar* check box to remove the check mark.
   d. Click the *Use small taskbar buttons* check box to remove the check mark.
   e. Click the *Taskbar location on screen* option box (displays with the word *Right*) and then click *Bottom* at the drop-down list.
   f. Click OK to close the dialog box.

Using the Charm Bar ▪▪▪▪▪▪▪▪▪▪▪▪▪▪▪▪▪▪▪▪▪▪▪▪▪▪

Windows 8 contains a new feature called the ***Charm bar***. The Charm bar is a bar that displays when you position the mouse pointer in the upper or lower right corner of the screen. Use the buttons on the Charm bar, shown in Figure W.6, to access certain features or tools. Use the Search button to search the computer for applications, files, folders and settings. With the Share button, you can share information with others via email or social networks. Clicking the Start button displays the Windows 8 Start screen. Access settings for various devices such as printers, monitors, and so on with the Devices button. The Settings button gives you access to common computer settings and is also used to power down the computer.

Figure W.6 Charm Bar

Click this button to search for applications, files, and settings.

Click this button to share information with others.

Click this button to display the Windows 8 Start screen.

Click this button to change device settings.

Click this button to change computer settings and power down the computer.

Search

Share

Start

Devices

Settings

Powering Down the Computer ■■■■■■■■■■■■■■■■■■■■

If you want to shut down Windows, first close any open programs and then display the Charm bar. Click the Settings button on the Charm bar, click the Power tile, and then click the *Shut down* option. The Power tile also contains options for restarting the computer or putting the computer to sleep. Restarting the computer may be useful when installing new applications or if Windows 8 stops working properly. In sleep mode, Windows saves files and information about applications and then powers down the computer to a low-power state. To "wake up" the computer, press the computer's power button.

In a multi-user environment, you can sign out of or lock your account so that no one can tamper with your work. To access these features, display the Windows 8 Start screen and then click your user account tile in the upper right corner. This displays a shortcut menu with three options. The *Lock* option locks the computer, which means that it is still powered on but requires a user password in order to access any applications or files that were previously opened. (To unlock the computer, click the icon on the login screen representing your account, type your password, and then press Enter.) Use the *Sign out* option to sign out of your user account while still keeping the computer turned on so that others may log on to it. Click the *Change account picture* option if you want to change the picture associated with your user account.

Managing Files and Folders ■■■■■■■■■■■■■■■■■■■■■■

As you begin working with programs in Windows 8, you will create files in which data (information) is saved. A file might be a Word document, an Excel workbook, an Access database, or a PowerPoint presentation. As you begin creating files, consider creating folders in which to store these files. Complete file management tasks such as creating a folder or moving a file at the Computer window. To display the Computer window, shown in Figure W.7, position your mouse pointer in the lower left corner of the screen to display the Start screen thumbnail, click the right mouse button, and then click *File Explorer* at the shortcut menu. The various components of the Computer window are identified in Figure W.7.

In the Content pane of the Computer window, icons display representing each hard disk drive and removable storage medium (such as a CD, DVD, or USB device) connected to your computer. Next to each storage device icon, Windows displays the amount of storage space available as well as a bar with the amount of used space shaded with color. This visual cue allows you to see at a glance the amount of space available relative to the capacity of the device. Double-click a device icon in the Content pane to change the display to show the contents stored on the device. Display contents from another device or folder using the Navigation pane or the Address bar on the Computer window.

Figure W.7 Computer Window

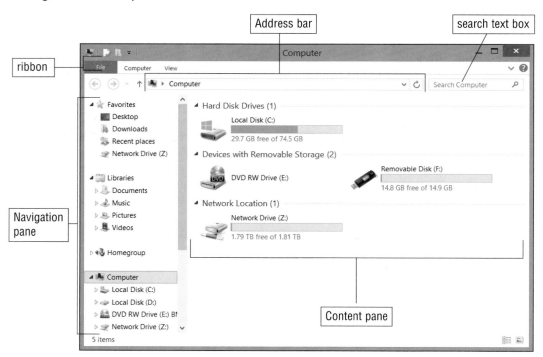

Copying, Moving, and Deleting Files and Folders

File and folder management activities include copying and moving files and folders from one folder or drive to another, as well as deleting files and folders. The Computer window offers a variety of methods for performing these actions. This section will provide you with steps for copying, moving, and deleting files and folders using options from the Home tab (shown in Figure W.8) and the shortcut menu (shown in Figure W.9).

To copy a file to another folder or drive, first display the file in the Content pane. If the file is located in the Documents folder, click the *Documents* folder in the *Libraries* section of the Navigation pane and then, in the Content pane, click the name of the file you want to copy. Click the Home tab on the ribbon and then click the Copy button in the Clipboard group. Use the Navigation pane to navigate to the location where you want to paste the file. Click the Home tab and then click the Paste button in the Clipboard group. Complete similar steps to copy and paste a folder to another location.

If the desired file is located on a storage medium such as a CD, DVD, or USB device, double-click the device in the section of the Content pane labeled *Devices with Removable Storage*. (Each removable device is assigned an alphabetic drive letter by Windows, usually starting at E or F and continuing through the alphabet depending on the number of removable devices that are currently in use.) After double-clicking the storage medium in the Content pane, navigate to the desired folder and then click the file to select it. Click the Home tab on the ribbon and then click the Copy button in the Clipboard group. Navigate to the desired folder, click the Home tab, and then click the Paste button in the Clipboard group.

To move a file, click the desired file in the Content pane, click the Home tab on the ribbon, and then click the Cut button in the Clipboard group. Navigate to the desired location, click the Home tab, and then click the Paste button in the Clipboard group.

To delete a file or folder, click the file or folder in the Content pane in the Computer window. Click the Home tab and then click the Delete button in the Organize group. At the message asking if you want to move the file or folder to the Recycle Bin, click the Yes button.

Figure W.8 File Explorer Home tab

Figure W.9 Shortcut Menu

Open
Edit
New
Print
SkyDrive Pro ▸
Open with ▸
Restore previous versions
Send to ▸
Cut
Copy
Create shortcut
Delete
Rename
Properties

Project 3 Copying a File and Folder and Deleting a File

1. Insert the CD that accompanies this textbook into the appropriate drive.
2. Insert your storage medium (such as a USB flash drive) into the appropriate drive.
3. At the Windows 8 desktop, position the mouse pointer in the lower left corner of the Taskbar to display the Start screen thumbnail, click the right mouse button, and then click *File Explorer* at the shortcut menu.
4. Copy a file from the CD that accompanies this textbook to the drive containing your storage medium by completing the following steps:
   a. In the Content pane, double-click the drive into which you inserted the CD that accompanies this textbook.
   b. Double-click the *StudentDataFiles* folder in the Content pane.
   c. Double-click the *Windows8* folder in the Content pane.
   d. Click *WordDocument01.docx* in the Content pane.
   e. Click the Home tab and then click *Copy* in the Clipboard group.

   f. In the Computer section in the Navigation pane, click the drive containing your storage medium. (You may need to scroll down the Navigation pane.)
   g. Click the Home tab and then click the Paste button in the Clipboard group.
5. Delete *WordDocument01.docx* from your storage medium by completing the following steps:
   a. Make sure the contents of your storage medium display in the Content pane in the Computer window.

b. Click *WordDocument01.docx* in the Content pane to select it.

c. Click the Home tab and then click the Delete button in the Organize group.

d. At the message asking if you want to permanently delete the file, click the Yes button.

6. Copy the Windows8 folder from the CD to your storage medium by completing the following steps:

a. With the Computer window open, click the drive in the *Computer* section in the Navigation pane that contains the CD that accompanies this book.

b. Double-click *StudentDataFiles* in the Content pane.

c. Click the *Windows8* folder in the Content pane.

d. Click the Home tab and then click the Copy button in the Clipboard group.

e. In the *Computer* section in the Navigation pane, click the drive containing your storage medium.

f. Click the Home tab and then click the Paste button in the Clipboard group.

7. Close the Computer window by clicking the Close button located in the upper right corner of the window.

In addition to options on the Home tab, you can use options in a shortcut menu to copy, move, and delete files or folders. To use a shortcut menu, select the desired file(s) or folder(s), position the mouse pointer on the selected item, and then click the right mouse button. At the shortcut menu that displays, click the desired option, such as *Copy*, *Cut*, or *Delete*.

Selecting Files and Folders

You can move, copy, or delete more than one file or folder at the same time. Before moving, copying, or deleting files or folders, select the desired files or folders. To make selecting easier, consider displaying the files in the Content pane in a list or detailed list format. To change the display, click the View tab on the ribbon and then click *List* or *Details* in the Layout group.

To select adjacent files or folders, click the first file or folder, hold down the Shift key, and then click the last file or folder. To select nonadjacent files or folders, click the first file or folder, hold down the Ctrl key, and then click the other files or folders you wish to select.

Project 4 **Copying and Deleting Files**

1. At the Windows 8 desktop, position the mouse pointer in the lower left corner of the Taskbar to display the Start screen thumbnail, click the right mouse button, and then click *File Explorer* at the shortcut menu.

2. Copy files from the CD that accompanies this textbook to the drive containing your storage medium by completing the following steps:

a. Make sure the CD that accompanies this textbook and your storage medium are inserted in the appropriate drives.

b. Double-click the CD drive in the Content pane in the Computer window.

c. Double-click the *StudentDataFiles* folder in the Content pane.
d. Double-click the *Windows8* folder in the Content pane.
e. Change the display to List by clicking the View tab and then clicking *List* in the Layout group list box.

f. Click ***WordDocument01.docx*** in the Content pane.
g. Hold down the Shift key, click ***WordDocument05.docx***, and then release the Shift key. (This selects five documents.)

h. Click the Home tab and then click the Copy button in the Clipboard group.
i. In the *Computer* section of the Navigation pane, click the drive containing your storage medium.
j. Click the Home tab and then click the Paste button in the Clipboard group.
3. Delete the files you just copied to your storage medium by completing the following steps:
   a. Change the display by clicking the View tab and then clicking *List* in the Layout group.
   b. Click ***WordDocument01.docx*** in the Content pane.
   c. Hold down the Shift key, click ***WordDocument05.docx***, and then release the Shift key.
   d. Position the mouse pointer on any selected file, click the right mouse button, and then click *Delete* at the shortcut menu.
   e. At the message asking if you are sure you want to permanently delete the files, click Yes.
4. Close the Computer window by clicking the Close button located in the upper right corner of the window.

Manipulating and Creating Folders

As you begin working with and creating multiple files, consider creating folders in which you can logically group and store the files. To create a folder, display the Computer window and then display the drive or folder where you want to create the folder in the Content pane. To create the new folder, click the New folder button in the New group on the Home tab; click the New folder button on the Quick Access toolbar; or click in a blank area in the Content pane, click the right mouse button, point to *New* in the shortcut menu, and then click *Folder* at the side menu. Any of the three methods inserts a folder icon in the Content pane and names the folder *New folder*. Type the desired name for the new folder and then press Enter.

Project 5   Creating a New Folder

1. At the Windows 8 desktop, open the Computer window.
2. Create a new folder by completing the following steps:
    a. In the Content pane, double-click the drive that contains your storage medium.
    b. Double-click the *Windows8* folder in the Content pane. (This opens the folder.)
    c. Click the View tab and then click *List* in the Layout group.
    d. Click the Home tab and then click the New folder button in the New group.
    e. Type **SpellCheckFiles** and then press Enter. (This changes the name from *New folder* to *SpellCheckFiles*.)

Step 2d

Step 2e

3. Copy **WordSpellCheck01.docx**, **WordSpellCheck02.docx**, and **WordSpellCheck03.docx** into the SpellCheckFiles folder you just created by completing the following steps:
    a. Click the View tab and then click *List* in the Layout group. (Skip this step if *List* is already selected.)
    b. Click *WordSpellCheck01.docx* in the Content pane.
    c. Hold down the Shift key, click *WordSpellCheck03.docx*, and then release the Shift key. (This selects three documents.)
    d. Click the Home tab and then click the Copy button in the Clipboard group.
    e. Double-click the *SpellCheckFiles* folder in the Content pane.
    f. Click the Home tab and then click the Paste button in the Clipboard group.

4. Delete the SpellCheckFiles folder and its contents by completing the following steps:
   a. Click the Back button (contains a left-pointing arrow) located at the left side of the Address bar.
   b. With the SpellCheckFiles folder selected in the Content pane, click the Home tab and then click the Delete button in the Organize group.
   c. At the message asking you to confirm the deletion, click Yes.
5. Close the window by clicking the Close button located in the upper right corner of the window.

Using the Recycle Bin

Deleting the wrong file can be a disaster, but Windows 8 helps protect your work with the *Recycle Bin*. The Recycle Bin acts just like an office wastepaper basket; you can "throw away" (delete) unwanted files, but you can also "reach in" to the Recycle Bin and take out (restore) a file if you threw it away by accident.

Deleting Files to the Recycle Bin

Files and folders you delete from the hard drive are sent automatically to the Recycle Bin. If you want to permanently delete files or folders from the hard drive without first sending them to the Recycle Bin, select the desired file(s) or folder(s), right-click one of the selected files or folders, hold down the Shift key, and then click *Delete* at the shortcut menu.

Files and folders deleted from a USB flash drive or disc are deleted permanently. (Recovery programs are available, however, that will help you recover deleted files or folders. If you accidentally delete a file or folder from a USB flash drive or disc, do not do anything more with the USB flash drive or disc until you can run a recovery program.)

You can delete files in the manner described earlier in this section and you can also delete a file by dragging the file icon to the Recycle Bin. To do this, click the desired file in the Content pane in the Computer window, drag the file icon to the Recycle Bin icon on the desktop until the text *Move to Recycle Bin* displays, and then release the mouse button.

Restoring Files from the Recycle Bin

To restore a file from the Recycle Bin, double-click the Recycle Bin icon on the desktop. This opens the Recycle Bin window, shown in Figure W.10. (The contents of the Recycle Bin will vary.) To restore a file, click the file you want restored, click the Recycle Bin Tools Manage tab and then click the Restore the selected items button in the Restore group. This removes the file from the Recycle Bin and returns it to its original location. You can also restore a file by positioning the mouse pointer on the file, clicking the right mouse button, and then clicking *Restore* at the shortcut menu.

Figure W.10 Recycle Bin Window

Project 6 Deleting Files to and Restoring Files from the Recycle Bin

Before beginning this project, check with your instructor to determine if you can copy files to the hard drive.

1. At the Windows 8 desktop, open the Computer window.
2. Copy files from your storage medium to the Documents folder on your hard drive by completing the following steps:
   a. In the Content pane, double-click the drive containing your storage medium.
   b. Double-click the *Windows8* folder in the Content pane.
   c. Click the View tab and then click *List* in the Layout group. (Skip this step if *List* is already selected.)
   d. Click *WordSpellCheck01.docx* in the Content pane.
   e. Hold down the Shift key, click *WordSpellCheck03.docx*, and then release the Shift key.
   f. Click the Home tab and then click the Copy button in the Clipboard group.
   g. Click the *Documents* folder in the *Libraries* section of the Navigation pane.
   h. Click the Home tab and then click the Paste button in the Clipboard group.

3. With **WordSpellCheck01.docx** through **WordSpellCheck03.docx** selected in the Content pane, click the Home tab and then click the Delete button in the Organize group to delete the files to the Recycle Bin.
4. Close the Computer window.
5. At the Windows 8 desktop, display the contents of the Recycle Bin by double-clicking the Recycle Bin icon.
6. Restore the files you just deleted by completing the following steps:
   a. Select **WordSpellCheck01.docx** through **WordSpellCheck03.docx** in the Recycle Bin Content pane. (If these files are not visible, you will need to scroll down the list of files in the Content pane.)
   b. Click the Recycle Bin Tools Manage tab and then click the Restore the selected items button in the Restore group.

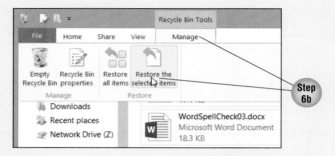

7. Close the Recycle Bin by clicking the Close button located in the upper right corner of the window.
8. Display the Computer window.
9. Click the *Documents* folder in the *Libraries* section of the Navigation pane.
10. Delete the files you restored.
11. Close the Computer window.

Emptying the Recycle Bin

Just like a wastepaper basket, the Recycle Bin can get full. To empty the Recycle Bin, position the arrow pointer on the Recycle Bin icon on the desktop and then click the right mouse button. At the shortcut menu that displays, click the *Empty Recycle Bin* option. At the message asking if you want to permanently delete the items, click Yes. You can also empty the Recycle Bin by displaying the Recycle Bin window and then clicking the Empty Recycle Bin button in the Manage group on the Recycle Bin Tools Manage tab. At the message asking if you want to permanently delete the items, click Yes. To delete a specific file from the Recycle Bin window, click the desired file in the Recycle Bin window, click the Home tab, and then click the Delete button in the Organize group. At the message asking if you want to permanently delete the file, click Yes. When you empty the Recycle Bin, the files cannot be recovered by the Recycle Bin or by Windows 8. If you have to recover a file, you will need to use a file recovery program.

Note: Before beginning this project, check with your instructor to determine if you can delete files/folders from the Recycle Bin.

1. At the Windows 8 desktop, double-click the Recycle Bin icon.
2. At the Recycle Bin window, empty the contents by clicking the Empty Recycle Bin button in the Manage group on the Recycle Bin Tools Manage tab.
3. At the message asking you if you want to permanently delete the items, click Yes.
4. Close the Recycle Bin by clicking the Close button located in the upper right corner of the window.

Creating a Shortcut ▪▪▪▪▪▪▪▪▪▪▪▪▪▪▪▪▪▪▪▪▪▪▪▪▪▪▪▪▪▪▪

If you use a file or application on a consistent basis, consider creating a shortcut to the file or application. A *shortcut* is a specialized icon that points the operating system to an actual file, folder, or application. If you create a shortcut to a Word document, the shortcut icon is not the actual document but a very small file that contains the path to the document. Double-click the shortcut icon and Windows 8 opens the document in Word.

One method for creating a shortcut is to display the Computer window and then make active the drive or folder where the file is located. Right-click the desired file, point to *Send to*, and then click *Desktop (create shortcut)*. You can easily delete a shortcut icon from the desktop by dragging the shortcut icon to the Recycle Bin icon. This deletes the shortcut icon but does not delete the file to which the shortcut pointed.

1. At the Windows 8 desktop, display the Computer window.
2. Double-click the drive containing your storage medium.
3. Double-click the *Windows8* folder in the Content pane.
4. Change the display of files to a list by clicking the View tab and then clicking *List* in the Layout group. (Skip this step if *List* is already selected.)
5. Create a shortcut to the file named **WordQuiz.docx** by right-clicking **WordQuiz.docx**, pointing to *Send to*, and then clicking *Desktop (create shortcut)*.
6. Close the Computer window.

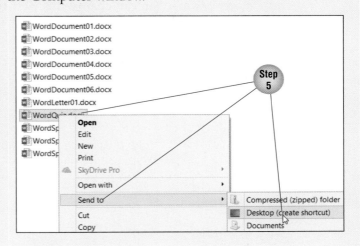

7. Open Word and **WordQuiz.docx** by double-clicking the *WordQuiz.docx* shortcut icon on the desktop.
8. After viewing the file in Word, close Word by clicking the Close button that displays in the upper right corner of the window.
9. Delete the *WordQuiz.docx* shortcut icon by completing the following steps:
   a. At the desktop, position the mouse pointer on the *WordQuiz.docx* shortcut icon.
   b. Hold down the left mouse button, drag the icon on top of the Recycle Bin icon, and then release the mouse button.

Exploring the Control Panel

The Control Panel, shown in Figure W.11, contains a variety of icons for customizing the appearance and functionality of your computer as well as accessing and changing system settings. Display the Control Panel by right-clicking the Start screen thumbnail and then clicking *Control Panel* at the shortcut menu. The Control Panel organizes settings into categories to make them easier to find. Click a category icon and the Control Panel displays lower-level categories and tasks within each of them.

Hover your mouse over a category icon in the Control Panel and a ScreenTip displays with an explanation of what options are available. For example, if you hover the mouse over the Appearance and Personalization icon, a ScreenTip displays with information about the tasks available in the category, such as changing the appearance of desktop items, applying a theme or screen saver to your computer, or customizing the Taskbar.

If you click a category icon in the Control Panel, the Control Panel displays all of the available subcategories and tasks in the category. Also, the categories display in text form at the left side of the Control Panel. For example, if you click the Appearance and Personalization icon, the Control Panel displays as shown in Figure W.12. Notice how the Control Panel categories display at the left side of the Control Panel and options for changing the appearance and personalizing your computer display in the middle of the Control Panel.

By default, the Control Panel displays categories of tasks in what is called *Category* view. You can change this view to display large or small icons. To change the view, click the down-pointing arrow that displays at the right side of the text *View by* that displays in the upper right corner of the Control Panel, and then click the desired view at the drop-down list (see Figure W.11).

Figure W.11 The Control Panel

Click a category icon or hyperlink to display all of the category's options.

Use this option to change views.

Figure W.12 Appearance and Personalization Window

Click this option to return to the main Control Panel.

lower-level categories

task hyperlinks

Click a category to display category options.

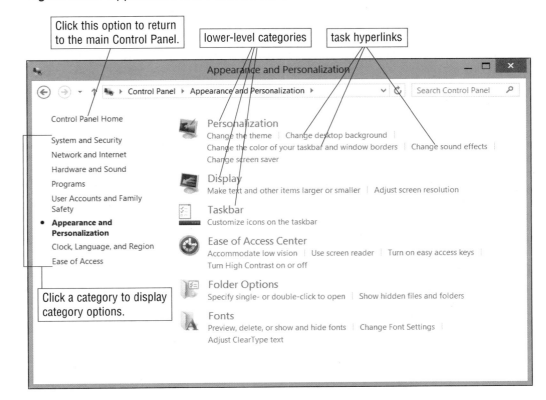

Project 9   **Changing the Desktop Theme**

1. At the Windows 8 desktop, right-click the Start screen thumbnail and then click *Control Panel* at the shortcut menu.
2. At the Control Panel, click the Appearance and Personalization icon.

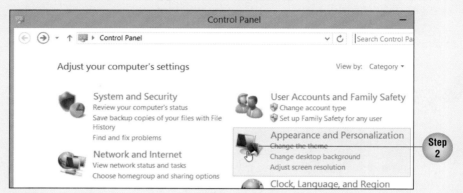

3. Click the <u>Change the theme</u> hyperlink that displays below *Personalization* in the panel at the right in the Control Panel.
4. At the window that displays with options for changing visuals and sounds on your computer, click *Earth* in the *Windows Default Themes* section.

5. Click the <u>Desktop Background</u> hyperlink that displays in the lower left corner of the panel.
6. Click the button that displays below the text *Change picture every* and then click *10 Seconds* at the drop-down list. (This tells Windows to change the picture on your desktop every 10 seconds.)
7. Click the Save changes button that displays in the lower right corner of the Control Panel.
8. Click the Close button located in the upper right corner to close the Control Panel.
9. Look at the picture that displays as the desktop background. Wait for 10 seconds and then look at the second picture that displays.
10. Right-click the Start screen thumbnail and then click *Control Panel* at the shortcut menu.
11. At the Control Panel, click the Appearance and Personalization icon.
12. Click the <u>Change the theme</u> hyperlink that displays below *Personalization* in the panel at the right.
13. At the window that displays with options for changing visuals and sounds on your computer, click *Windows* in the *Windows Default Themes* section. (This is the default theme.)
14. Click the Close button located in the upper right corner of the Control Panel.

Searching in the Control Panel

The Control Panel contains a large number of options for customizing the appearance and functionality of your computer. If you want to customize a feature and are not sure where the options for the feature are located, search for the feature. To do this, display the Control Panel and then type the name of the desired feature. By default, the insertion point is positioned in the *Search Control Panel* text box. When you type the feature name in the text box, options related to the feature display in the Control Panel.

Project 10 Customizing the Mouse

1. Right-click the Start screen thumbnail and then click *Control Panel*.
2. At the Control Panel, type **mouse**. (The insertion point is automatically located in the *Search Control Panel* text box when you open the Control Panel. When you type *mouse*, features for customizing the mouse display in the Control Panel.)
3. Click the Mouse icon that displays in the Control Panel.
4. At the Mouse Properties dialog box, notice the options that display. (The *Switch primary and secondary buttons* option might be useful, for example, if you are left-handed and want to switch the buttons on the mouse.)
5. Click the Cancel button to close the dialog box.
6. At the Control Panel, click the Change the mouse pointer display or speed hyperlink.

7. At the Mouse Properties dialog box with the Pointer Options tab selected, click the *Display pointer trails* check box in the *Visibility* section to insert a check mark.
8. Drag the button on the slider bar (located below the *Display pointer trails* check box) approximately to the middle of the bar.
9. Click OK to close the dialog box.
10. Close the Control Panel.
11. Move the mouse pointer around the screen to see the pointer trails.

Displaying Personalize Options with a Shortcut Command

In addition to the Control Panel, display customization options with a command from a shortcut menu. Display a shortcut menu by positioning the mouse pointer in the desired position and then clicking the right mouse button. For example, display a shortcut menu with options for customizing the desktop by positioning the mouse pointer in an empty area of the desktop and then clicking the right mouse button. At the shortcut menu that displays, click the desired shortcut command.

Project 11 **Customizing with a Shortcut Command**

1. At the Windows 8 desktop, position the mouse pointer in an empty area on the desktop, click the right mouse button, and then click *Personalize* at the shortcut menu.
2. At the Control Panel Appearance and Personalization window that displays, click the <u>Change mouse pointers</u> hyperlink that displays at the left side of the window.
3. At the Mouse Properties dialog box, click the Pointer Options tab.
4. Click in the *Display pointer trails* check box to remove the check mark.
5. Click OK to close the dialog box.
6. At the Control Panel Appearance and Personalization window, click the <u>Screen Saver</u> hyperlink that displays in the lower right corner of the window.
7. At the Screen Saver Settings dialog box, click the option button below the *Screen saver* option and then click *Ribbons* at the drop-down list.
8. Check the number in the *Wait* measurement box. If a number other than *1* displays, click the down-pointing arrow at the right side of the measurement box until *1* displays. (This tells Windows to display the screen saver after one minute of inactivity.)
9. Click OK to close the dialog box.
10. Close the Control Panel by clicking the Close button located in the upper right corner of the window.

Step 2

Step 7

Step 8

Step 9

11. Do not touch the mouse or keyboard and wait over one minute for the screen saver to display. After watching the screen saver, move the mouse. (This redisplays the desktop.)
12. Right-click in an empty area of the desktop and then click *Personalize* at the shortcut menu.
13. At the Control Panel Appearance and Personalization window, click the Screen Saver hyperlink.
14. At the Screen Saver Settings dialog box, click the option button below the *Screen saver* option and then click *(None)* at the drop-down list.
15. Click OK to close the dialog box.
16. Close the Control Panel Appearance and Personalization window.

Exploring Windows Help and Support

Windows 8 includes an on-screen reference guide providing information, explanations, and interactive help on learning Windows features. Get help at the Windows Help and Support window, shown in Figure W.13. Display this window by clicking the Start screen thumbnail to display the Windows 8 Start screen. Right-click a blank area of the Start screen, click the All apps button, and then click the *Help and Support* tile in the Windows System group. Use options in the Windows Help and Support window to search for help on a specific feature; display the opening Windows Help and Support window; print the current information; and display information on getting started with Windows 8, setting up a network, and protecting your computer.

Figure W.13 Windows Help and Support Window

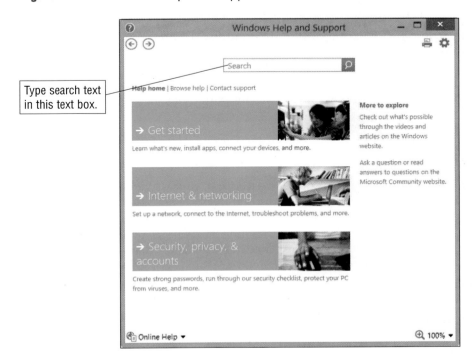

Type search text in this text box.

Project 12 Getting Help

1. Display the Windows 8 Help and Support window by following these steps:
   a. At the Windows 8 desktop, position the mouse pointer in the lower left corner of the screen and then click the Start screen thumbnail.
   b. Position the mouse in a blank area of the Windows 8 Start screen and then click the right mouse button.
   c. Click the All apps button that appears in the lower right corner of the Start screen and then scroll to the right of the Start screen.
   d. Click the *Help and Support* tile located in the *Windows System* category.
2. At the Windows Help and Support window, click the Get started hyperlink.
3. Click a hyperlink that interests you, read the information, and then click the Back button. (The Back button is located in the upper left corner of the window.)
4. Click another hyperlink that interests you and then read the information.
5. Click the Help home hyperlink that displays below the search text box. (This returns you to the opening Windows Help and Support window.)
6. Click in the search text box, type **delete files**, and then press Enter.
7. Click the How to work with files and folders hyperlink that displays in the window.
8. Read the information that displays about working with files or folders and then click the Print button located in the upper right corner of the Windows Help and Support window.
9. At the Print dialog box, click the Print button.
10. Click the Close button to close the Windows Help and Support window.

Using Search Tools ■■■■■■■■■■■■■■■■■■■■■■■■■■■■

The Charm bar contains a search tool you can use to quickly find an application or file on your computer. To use the search tool, display the Charm bar, click the Search button and then type in the search text box the first few characters of the application or file for which you are searching. As you type characters in the text box, a list displays with application names or file names that begin with the characters. As you continue typing characters, the search tool refines the list.

You can also search for programs or files with the search text box in the Computer window. The search text box displays in the upper right corner of the Computer window at the right side of the Address bar. If you want to search a specific folder, make that folder active in the Content pane and then type the search text in the text box.

When conducting a search, you can use the asterisk (*) as a wildcard character in place of any letters, numbers, or symbols within a file name. For example, in the following project you will search for file names containing *check* by typing ***check** in the search text box. The asterisk indicates that the file name can start with any letter but it must contain the letters *check* somewhere in the file name.

Project 13 | Searching for Programs and Files

1. At the Windows 8 desktop, display the Charm bar and then click the Search button.
2. With the insertion point positioned in the search text box, type **paint**. (Notice as you type the letters that Windows displays applications that begin with the same letters you are typing or that are associated with the same letters in a keyword. Notice that the Paint program displays below the heading *Apps* at the top of the list. Depending on the contents stored in the computer you are using, additional items may display below Paint.)

Step 2

3. Click *Paint* that displays below the *Apps* heading.
4. Close the Paint window.
5. Right-click the Start screen thumbnail and then click *File Explorer*.
6. At the Computer window, double-click the icon representing your storage medium.
7. Double-click the *Windows8* folder.
8. Click in the search text box located at the right of the Address bar and then type **document**. (As you begin typing the letters, Windows filters the list of files in the Content pane to those that contain the letters you type. Notice that the Address bar displays *Search Results in Windows8* to indicate that the files that display matching your criteria are limited to the current folder.)

Step 8

9. Select the text *document* that displays in the search text box and then type ***check**. (Notice that the Content pane displays file names containing the letters *check* no matter how the file name begins.)
10. Double-click ***WordSpellCheck02 .docx*** to open the document in Word.
11. Close the document and then close Word by clicking the Close button located in the upper right corner of the window.
12. Close the Computer window.

Browsing the Internet Using Internet Explorer 10

Microsoft Internet Explorer 10 is a web browser with options and features for displaying sites as well as navigating and searching for information on the Internet. The ***Internet*** is a network of computers connected around the world. Users access the Internet for several purposes: to communicate using instant messaging and/or email, to subscribe to newsgroups, to transfer files, to socialize with other users around the globe on social websites, and to access virtually any kind of information imaginable.

Using the Internet, people can find a phenomenal amount of information for private or public use. To use the Internet, three things are generally required: an ***Internet Service Provider (ISP)***, software to browse the Web (called a ***web browser***), and a ***search engine***. In this section, you will learn how to:

- Navigate the Internet using URLs and hyperlinks
- Use search engines to locate information
- Download web pages and images

You will use the Microsoft Internet Explorer web browser to locate information on the Internet. A ***Uniform Resource Locator***, referred to as a ***URL***, identifies a location on the Internet. The steps for browsing the Internet vary but generally include opening Internet Explorer, typing the URL for the desired site, navigating the various pages of the site, navigating to other sites using links, and then closing Internet Explorer.

To launch Internet Explorer 10, click the Internet Explorer icon on the Taskbar at the Windows desktop. Figure IE.1 identifies the elements of the Internet Explorer 10 window. The web page that displays in your Internet Explorer window may vary from what you see in Figure IE.1.

If you know the URL for a desired website, click in the Address bar, type the URL, and then press Enter. The website's home page displays in a tab within the Internet Explorer window. The format of a URL is *http://server-name.path*. The first part of the URL, *http*, stands for HyperText Transfer Protocol, which is the protocol or language used to transfer data within the World Wide Web. The colon and slashes separate the protocol from the server name. The server name is the second component of the URL. For example, in the URL http://www.microsoft.com, the server name is *microsoft*. The last part of the URL specifies the domain to which the server belongs. For example, *.com* refers to "commercial" and establishes that the URL is a commercial company. Examples of other domains include *.edu* for "educational," *.gov* for "government," and *.mil* for "military."

Internet Explorer 10 has been streamlined to provide users with more browsing space and reduced clutter. By default, Microsoft has turned off many features in Internet Explorer 10 such as the Menu bar, Command bar, and Status bar. You can turn these features on by right-clicking the empty space above the Address bar and to the right of the new tab button (see Figure IE.1) and then clicking the desired option at the drop-down list that displays. For example, if you want to turn on the Menu bar (the bar that contains File, Edit, and so on), right-click the empty space above the Address bar and then click *Menu bar* at the drop-down list. (This inserts a check mark next to *Menu bar*.)

Figure IE.1 Internet Explorer Window

Project 1 Browsing the Internet Using URLs

1. Make sure you are connected to the Internet through an Internet Service Provider and that the Windows 8 desktop displays. (Check with your instructor to determine if you need to complete steps for accessing the Internet such as typing a user name and password to log on.)
2. Launch Microsoft Internet Explorer by clicking the Internet Explorer icon located at the left side of the Windows Taskbar, which is located at the bottom of the Windows desktop.
3. Turn on the Command bar by right-clicking the empty space above the Address bar or to the right of the new tab button (see Figure IE.1) and then clicking *Command bar* at the drop-down list.
4. At the Internet Explorer window, explore the website for Yosemite National Park by completing the following steps:
   a. Click in the Address bar, type **www.nps.gov/yose**, and then press Enter.
   b. Scroll down the home page for Yosemite National Park by clicking the down-pointing arrow on the vertical scroll bar located at the right side of the Internet Explorer window.

c. Print the home page by clicking the Print button located on the Command bar. (Note that some websites have a printer-friendly button you can click to print the page.)

5. Explore the website for Glacier National Park by completing the following steps:
   a. Click in the Address bar, type **www.nps.gov/glac**, and then press Enter.
   b. Print the home page by clicking the Print button located on the Command bar.

6. Close Internet Explorer by clicking the Close button (contains an X) located in the upper right corner of the Internet Explorer window.

Navigating Using Hyperlinks ▩■▩■▩■▩■▩■▩■▩■▩■▩■▩■

Most web pages contain *hyperlinks* that you click to connect to another page within the website or to another site on the Internet. Hyperlinks may display in a web page as underlined text in a specific color or as images or icons. To use a hyperlink, position the mouse pointer on the desired hyperlink until the mouse pointer turns into a hand and then click the left mouse button. Use hyperlinks to navigate within and between sites on the Internet. The Internet Explorer window contains a Back button (see Figure IE.1) that, when clicked, takes you to the previous web page viewed. If you click the Back button and then want to return to the previous page, click the Forward button. You can continue clicking the Back button to back your way out of several linked pages in reverse order since Internet Explorer maintains a history of the websites you visit.

Project 2 | Navigating Using Hyperlinks

1. Make sure you are connected to the Internet and then click the Internet Explorer icon on the Windows Taskbar.
2. At the Internet Explorer window, display the White House web page and navigate in the page by completing the following steps:
   a. Click in the Address bar, type **whitehouse.gov**, and then press Enter.
   b. At the White House home page, position the mouse pointer on a hyperlink that interests you until the pointer turns into a hand and then click the left mouse button.
   c. At the linked web page, click the Back button. (This returns you to the White House home page.)
   d. At the White House home page, click the Forward button to return to the previous web page viewed.
   e. Print the web page by clicking the Print button on the Command bar.

3. Display the website for Amazon.com and navigate in the site by completing the following steps:
   a. Click in the Address bar, type www.amazon.com, and then press Enter.
   b. At the Amazon.com home page, click a hyperlink related to books.
   c. When a book web page displays, click the Print button on the Command bar.
4. Close Internet Explorer by clicking the Close button (contains an X) located in the upper right corner of the Internet Explorer window.

Step 3a

Searching for Specific Sites ■■■■■■■■■■■■■■■■■■■■■■■

If you do not know the URL for a specific site or you want to find information on the Internet but do not know what site to visit, complete a search with a search engine. A *search engine* is software created to search quickly and easily for desired information. A variety of search engines are available on the Internet, each offering the opportunity to search for specific information. One method for searching for information is to click in the Address bar, type a keyword or phrase related to your search, and then press Enter. Another method for completing a search is to visit the website for a search engine and use options at the site.

Bing is Microsoft's online search portal and is the default search engine used by Internet Explorer. Bing organizes search results by topic category and provides related search suggestions.

Project 3 Searching for Information by Topic

1. Start Internet Explorer.
2. At the Internet Explorer window, search for sites on bluegrass music by completing the following steps:
   a. Click in the Address bar.
   b. Type bluegrass music and then press Enter.
   c. When a list of sites displays in the Bing results window, click a site that interests you.
   d. When the page displays, click the Print button.
3. Use the Yahoo! search engine to find sites on bluegrass music by completing the following steps:
   a. Click in the Address bar, type www.yahoo.com, and then press Enter.
   b. At the Yahoo! website, with the insertion point positioned in the search text box, type bluegrass music and then press Enter. (Notice that the sites displayed vary from sites displayed in the earlier search.)

Step 2b

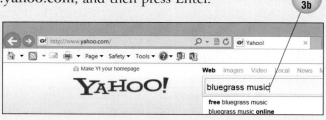

Step 3b

c. Click hyperlinks until a website displays that interests you.
d. Print the page.
4. Use the Google search engine to find sites on jazz music by completing the following steps:
   a. Click in the Address bar, type **www.google.com**, and then press Enter.
   b. At the Google website, with the insertion point positioned in the search text box, type **jazz music** and then press Enter.
   c. Click a site that interests you.
   d. Print the page.
5. Close Internet Explorer.

Step 4b

Using a Metasearch Engine

Bing, Yahoo!, and Google are search engines that search the Web for content and display search results. In addition to individual search engines, you can use a metasearch engine, such as Dogpile, that sends your search text to other search engines and then compiles the results in one list. With a metasearch engine, you type the search text once and then access results from a wider group of search engines. The Dogpile metasearch engine provides search results from Google, Yahoo!, and Yandex.

Project 4   Searching with a Metasearch Search Engine

1. Start Internet Explorer.
2. Click in the Address bar.
3. Type **www.dogpile.com** and then press Enter.
4. At the Dogpile website, type **jazz music** in the search text box and then press Enter.
5. Click a hyperlink that interests you.
6. Close the Internet Explorer window. If a message displays asking if you want to close all tabs, click the Close all tabs button.

Step 4

Completing Advanced Searches for Specific Sites

The Internet contains an enormous amount of information. Depending on what you are searching for on the Internet and the search engine you use, some searches can result in several thousand "hits" (sites). Wading through a large number of sites can be very time-consuming and counterproductive. Narrowing a search to very specific criteria can greatly reduce the number of hits for a search. To narrow a search, use the advanced search options offered by the search engine.

Project 5 Narrowing a Search

1. Start Internet Explorer.
2. Search for sites on skydiving in Oregon by completing the following steps:
   a. Click in the Address bar, type **www.yahoo.com**, and then press Enter.
   b. At the Yahoo! home page, click the Search button next to the search text box.
   c. Click the More hyperlink located above the search text box and then click *Advanced Search* at the drop-down list.

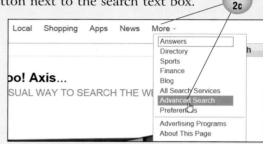

   d. At the Advanced Web Search page, click in the search text box next to *all of these words*.
   e. Type **skydiving Oregon tandem static line**. (This limits the search to web pages containing all of the words typed in the search text box.)
   f. Click the Yahoo! Search button.
   g. When the list of websites displays, click a hyperlink that interests you.
   h. Click the Back button until the Yahoo! Advanced Web Search page displays.

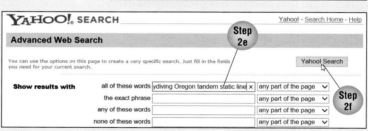

   i. Click in the *the exact phrase* text box and then type **skydiving in Oregon**.
   j. Click the *Only .com domains* option in the *Site/Domain* section.
   k. Click the Yahoo! Search button.
   l. When the list of websites displays, click a hyperlink that interests you.
   m. Print the page.
3. Close Internet Explorer.

Downloading Images, Text, and Web Pages from the Internet ■■■■■■■■■■■■■■■■■■■■■■■■■■■■■

The image(s) and/or text that display when you open a web page, as well as the web page itself, can be saved as a separate file. This separate file can be viewed, printed, or inserted in another file. The information you want to save in a separate file is downloaded from the Internet by Internet Explorer and saved in a folder of your choosing with the name you specify. Copyright laws protect much of the information on the Internet. Before using information downloaded from the Internet, check the site for restrictions. If you do use information, make sure you properly cite the source.

Project 6 **Downloading Images and Web Pages**

1. Start Internet Explorer.
2. Download a web page and image from Banff National Park by completing the following steps:
   a. Search for websites related to Banff National Park.
   b. From the list of sites that displays, choose a site that contains information about Banff National Park and at least one image of the park.
   c. Make sure the Command bar is turned on. (If the Command bar is turned off, turn it on by right-clicking the empty space above the Address bar or to the right of the new tab button and then clicking *Command bar* at the drop-down list.)

   d. Save the web page as a separate file by clicking the Page button on the Command bar and then clicking *Save as* at the drop-down list.
   e. At the Save Webpage dialog box, type **BanffWebPage**.
   f. Click the down-pointing arrow for the *Save as type* option and then click *Web Archive, single file (*.mht)*.
   g. Navigate to the drive containing your storage medium and then click the Save button.

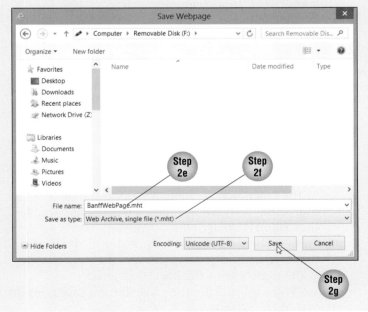

3. Save an image file by completing the following steps:
   a. Right-click an image that displays at the website.
   b. At the shortcut menu that displays, click *Save picture as*.

Step 3b

Step 3c

   c. At the Save Picture dialog box, type **BanffImage** in the *File name* text box.
   d. Navigate to the drive containing your storage medium and then click the Save button.
4. Close Internet Explorer.

Project 7   Opening the Saved Web Page and Image in a Word Document

1. Open Microsoft Word by positioning the mouse pointer in the lower left corner of the Taskbar, clicking the Start screen thumbnail, and then clicking the *Word 2013* tile in the Windows 8 Start screen. At the Word opening screen, click the *Blank document* template.
2. With Microsoft Word open, insert the image in a document by completing the following steps:
   a. Click the INSERT tab and then click the Pictures button in the Illustrations group.
   b. At the Insert Picture dialog box, navigate to the drive containing your storage medium and then double-click *BanffImage.jpg*.

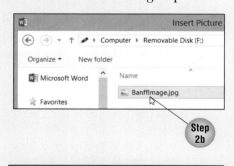

Step 2b

   c. When the image displays in the Word document, print the document by pressing Ctrl + P and then clicking the Print button.
   d. Close the document by clicking the FILE tab and then clicking the *Close* option. At the message asking if you want to save the changes, click the Don't Save button.
3. Open the **BanffWebPage.mht** file by completing the following steps:
   a. Click the FILE tab and then click the *Open* option.
   b. Double-click the *Computer* option.
   c. At the Open dialog box, navigate to the drive containing your storage medium and then double-click *BanffWebPage.mht*.

Step 3c

   d. Preview the web page(s) by pressing Ctrl + P. At the Print backstage area, preview the page shown at the right side of the backstage area.
4. Close Word by clicking the Close button (contains an X) that displays in the upper right corner of the screen.

MICROSOFT
EXCEL®

Level 1

Unit 1 ■ Preparing and Formatting Worksheets

MICROSOFT EXCEL

Preparing an Excel Workbook

CHAPTER 1

PERFORMANCE OBJECTIVES

Upon successful completion of Chapter 1, you will be able to:

- Identify the various elements of an Excel workbook
- Create, save, and print a workbook
- Enter data in a workbook
- Edit data in a workbook
- Insert a formula using the AutoSum button
- Apply basic formatting to cells in a workbook
- Use the Help feature

Tutorials

1.1 Opening, Saving, and Closing an Excel Workbook

1.2 Entering Data in Cells and Saving a Workbook with a New Name

1.3 Editing Cells and Using Proofing Tools

1.4 Printing a Worksheet

1.5 Performing Calculations Using the AutoSum Button

1.6 Navigating and Scrolling in a Worksheet

1.7 Applying Basic Formatting

1.8 Applying Number Formatting

1.9 Getting Help at the Excel Help Window

Many companies use spreadsheets to organize numerical and financial data and to analyze and evaluate information. An Excel spreadsheet can be used for such activities as creating financial statements, preparing budgets, managing inventory, and analyzing cash flow. In addition, numbers and values can be easily manipulated to create "What if?" situations. For example, using a spreadsheet, a person in a company can ask questions such as "What if the value in this category is decreased? How would that change affect the department budget?" Questions like these can be easily answered using the information in an Excel spreadsheet. Change the value in a category and Excel will recalculate formulas for the other values. In this way, a spreadsheet can be used not only for creating financial statements or budgets, but also as a planning tool. Model answers for this chapter's projects appear on the following page.

Note: Before beginning the projects, copy to your storage medium the EL1C1 subfolder from the EL1 folder on the CD that accompanies this textbook. Steps on how to copy a folder are presented on the inside of the back cover of this textbook. Do this every time you start a chapter's projects.

Team Net®

Employee	Location	Classification
Avery	West	Hourly
Bryant	North	Salaried
Estrada	West	Salaried
Juergens	West	Salaried
Mickulich	North	Hourly
Talbot	West	Hourly

Project 1 Prepare a Worksheet with Employee Information

EL1-C1-P1-EmpBene.xlsx

	January	February	March	April	May	June
Year 1	**100**	100	100	100	125	125
Year 3	**150**	150	150	150	175	175
Year 5	**200**	200	200	150	150	150
Year 7	**250**	250	250	250	250	250
Total	700	700	700	650	700	700

Qtr 1	$5,500	$6,250	$7,000	$8,500	$5,500	$4,500
Qtr 2	$6,000	$7,250	$6,500	$9,000	$4,000	$5,000
Qtr 3	$4,500	$8,000	$6,000	$7,500	$6,000	$5,000
Qtr 4	$6,500	$8,500	$7,000	$8,000	$5,500	$6,000
Average	$5,625	$7,500	$6,625	$8,250	$5,250	$5,125

Project 2 Open and Format a Workbook and Insert Formulas

EL1-C1-P2-FillCells.xlsx

Monthly Expenses
January, 2015

Expense	Budget	Actual
Accounting Services	$ 500	$ 423
Advertising	3,200	3,475
Utilities	2,700	3,045
Estimated Taxes	25,000	25,000
Health Insurance	9,420	9,595
Inventory Purchases	4,200	2,155
Equipment Repair	500	214
Loan Payment	5,586	5,586
Office Supplies	225	415
Total	$ 51,331	$ 49,908

Budget Percentages

Department	Percentage
Personnel	26%
Development	22%
Sales	18%
Production	13%
Maintenance	8%
Accounting	7%
Administration	6%

Project 3 Format a Worksheet

EL1-C1-P3-MoExps.xlsx

You will create a worksheet containing employee information, edit the contents, and then save and close the workbook.

Creating a Worksheet ▪▪▪▪▪▪▪▪▪▪▪▪▪▪▪▪▪▪▪▪▪▪▪▪▪▪▪▪

Open Excel by clicking the Excel 2013 tile at the Windows Start screen. (Depending on your operating system, these steps may vary.) At the Excel 2013 opening screen that displays, click the *Blank workbook* template. This displays a workbook with a blank worksheet, as shown in Figure 1.1. The elements of a blank Excel worksheet are described in Table 1.1.

A file created in Excel is referred to as a **workbook**. An Excel workbook consists of an individual worksheet (or *sheet*) by default, but it can contain multiple worksheets, like the sheets of paper in a notebook. Notice the tab named *Sheet1*, located toward the bottom of the Excel window. The area containing the gridlines in the Excel window is called the **worksheet area**. Figure 1.2 identifies the elements of the worksheet area. Create a worksheet in the worksheet area that will be saved as part of a workbook. Columns in a worksheet are labeled with letters of the alphabet and rows are numbered.

Figure 1.1 Blank Excel Worksheet

Table 1.1 Elements of an Excel Worksheet

Feature	Description
active cell	location in the worksheet that will display typed data or that will be affected by a command
cell pointer	when this icon appears, select cells by clicking or dragging the mouse
dialog box launcher	click to open a dialog box with more options for that group
FILE tab	displays the backstage area that contains options for working with and managing files
Formula bar	displays the contents stored in the active cell
horizontal and vertical scroll bars	used to view various parts of the worksheet beyond the current screen
Name box	displays the active cell address or name assigned to the active cell
New sheet button	click to insert a new worksheet in the workbook
Quick Access toolbar	contains buttons for commonly used commands that can be executed with a single mouse click
ribbon	area containing the tabs with commands and buttons
sheet tab	identifies the current worksheet in the workbook
Status bar	displays the current mode, action messages, view buttons, and Zoom slider bar
tab	contains commands and buttons organized into groups
Title bar	displays the workbook name followed by the application name
Collapse the Ribbon button	when clicked, removes the ribbon from the screen
worksheet area	contains the cells used to create a worksheet

Figure 1.2 Elements of a Worksheet Area

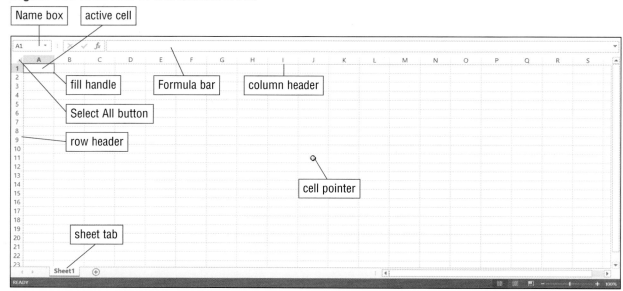

The horizontal and vertical lines that define the cells in the worksheet area are called *gridlines*. When a cell is active (displays with a green border), the *cell address*, also called the *cell reference*, displays in the *Name box*. The cell reference includes the column letter and row number. For example, if the first cell of the worksheet is active, the cell reference *A1* displays in the Name box. A green border surrounds the active cell.

Enter data such as text, a number, or a value in a cell. To enter data in a cell, make the desired cell active and then type the data. To make the next cell active, press the Tab key. Table 1.2 displays additional commands for making a specific cell active.

Another method for making a specific cell active is to use the Go To feature. To use this feature, click the Find & Select button in the Editing group on the HOME tab and then click *Go To*. At the Go To dialog box, type the cell reference in the *Reference* text box and then click OK.

When you are ready to type data into the active cell, check the Status bar. The word *READY* should display at the left side. As you type data, the word *Ready* changes to *ENTER*. Data you type in a cell displays in the cell as well as in the Formula bar. If the data you type is longer than the cell can accommodate, the data overlaps the next cell to the right. (It does not become a part of the next cell—it simply overlaps it.) You will learn how to change column widths to accommodate data later in this chapter.

HINT
To make a cell active, position the cell pointer in the cell and then click the left mouse button.

Find & Select

HINT
Ctrl + G is the keyboard shortcut to display the Go To dialog box.

Table 1.2 Commands for Making a Specific Cell Active

To make this cell active	Press
cell below current cell	Enter
cell above current cell	Shift + Enter
next cell	Tab
previous cell	Shift + Tab
cell at beginning of row	Home
next cell in direction of arrow	Up, Down, Left, or Right Arrow keys
last cell in worksheet	Ctrl + End
first cell in worksheet	Ctrl + Home
cell in next window	Page Down
cell in previous window	Page Up
cell in window to right	Alt + Page Down
cell in window to left	Alt + Page Up

If the data you enter in a cell consists of text and the text does not fit into the cell, it overlaps the next cell. If, however, you enter a number in a cell, specify it as a number (rather than text), and the number is too long to fit in the cell, Excel changes the display of the number to number symbols *(###)*. This change is made because Excel does not want you to be misled by a number when you see only a portion of it in the cell.

Along with the keyboard, the mouse can be used to make a specific cell active. To make a specific cell active with the mouse, position the mouse pointer, which displays as a white plus sign (called the ***cell pointer***), on the desired cell and then click the left mouse button. The cell pointer displays as a white plus sign when positioned in a cell in the worksheet and displays as an arrow pointer when positioned on other elements of the Excel window, such as options on tabs or scroll bars.

Scroll through a worksheet using the horizontal and/or vertical scroll bars. Scrolling shifts the display of cells in the worksheet area but does not change the active cell. Scroll through a worksheet until the desired cell is visible and then click the desired cell.

Saving a Workbook ■■■■■■■■■■■■■■■■■■■■■■■■■■■■■

▼ Quick Steps

Save a Workbook
1. Click Save button on Quick Access toolbar.
2. At Save As backstage area, click desired location.
3. Click Browse button.
4. At Save As dialog box, navigate to desired folder.
5. Type workbook name.
6. Press Enter.

Save

Ctrl + S is the keyboard shortcut to save a workbook.

Save an Excel workbook, which consists of one or more worksheets, by clicking the Save button on the Quick Access toolbar or by clicking the FILE tab and then clicking the *Save As* option at the backstage area. At the Save As backstage area, click the location where you want to save the workbook. For example, click the OneDrive option preceded by your name if you are saving to your OneDrive or click the *Computer* option if you are saving to a USB flash drive (or other location on your computer). After specifying the place, click the Browse button and the Save As dialog box displays. If you are saving the workbook to your computer or a flash drive, you can double-click the *Computer* option at the Save As backstage area to display the Save As dialog box. At the Save As dialog box, type a name for the workbook in the *File name* text box and then press Enter or click the Save button. You can bypass the Save As backstage area and go directly to the Save As dialog box by using the keyboard shortcut F12.

When you click your OneDrive or the *Computer* option at the Save As backstage area, the names of the most recently accessed folders display below the Recent Folders heading in the *Computer* section. Open a folder by clicking the folder name.

A workbook file name can contain up to 255 characters, including the drive letter and any folder names, and can include spaces. You cannot give a workbook the same name in first uppercase and then lowercase letters. Also, some symbols cannot be used in a file name, such as:

forward slash (/)	question mark (?)
backslash (\)	quotation mark (")
greater-than symbol (>)	colon (:)
less-than symbol (<)	semicolon (;)
asterisk (*)	pipe symbol (|)

To save an Excel workbook in the EL1C1 folder on your storage medium, display the Save As dialog box, click the drive representing your storage medium in the Navigation pane, and then double-click *EL1C1* in the Content pane.

1. Open Excel by clicking the Excel 2013 tile at the Windows Start screen. (Depending on your operating system, these steps may vary.)
2. At the Excel 2013 opening screen, click the *Blank workbook* template. (This opens a workbook with a blank worksheet.)
3. At the blank Excel worksheet that displays, create the worksheet shown in Figure 1.3 by completing the following steps:
   a. Press the Enter key once to make cell A2 the active cell.
   b. Type **Employee** in cell A2 .
   c. Press the Tab key. (This makes cell B2 active.)
   d. Type **Location** and then press the Tab key. (This makes cell C2 active.)
   e. Type **Benefits** and then press the Enter key to move the insertion point to cell A3.
   f. Type **Avery** (a name) in cell A3.
   g. Continue typing the data shown in Figure 1.3. (For commands that make specific cells active, refer to Table 1.2.)
4. After typing the data shown in the cells in Figure 1.3, save the workbook by completing the following steps:
   a. Click the Save button on the Quick Access toolbar.
   b. At the Save As backstage area, click the desired location, such as your OneDrive or *Computer,* and then click the Browse button.
   c. At the Save As dialog box, navigate to the EL1C1 folder in the Navigation pane and then double-click the *EL1C1* folder that displays in the Content pane.
   d. Select the text in the *File name* text box and then type **EL1-C1-P1-EmpBene** (for Excel Level 1, Chapter 1, Project 1, and the workbook that contains information about employee benefits).
   e. Press the Enter key or click the Save button.

Figure 1.3 Project 1a

	A	B	C	D
1				
2	Employee	Location	Benefits	
3	Avery			
4	Connors			
5	Estrada			
6	Juergens			
7	Mikulich			
8	Talbot			
9				

Editing Data in a Cell ■■■■■■■■■■■■■■■■■■■■■■■■■■■

Edit data being typed in a cell by pressing the Backspace key to delete the character to the left of the insertion point or pressing the Delete key to delete the character to the right of the insertion point. To change the data in a cell, click the cell once to make it active and then type the new data. When a cell containing data is active, anything typed will take the place of the existing data.

If you want to edit only a portion of the data in a cell, double-click in the cell. This makes the cell active, moves the insertion point inside the cell, and displays the word *Edit* at the left side of the Status bar. Move the insertion point using the arrow keys or the mouse and then make the needed corrections. If you are using the keyboard, press the Home key to move the insertion point to the first character in the cell or Formula bar or press the End key to move the insertion point to the last character.

When you are finished editing the data in the cell, be sure to change out of the Edit mode. To do this, make another cell active by pressing Enter, Tab, or Shift + Tab. You can also change out of the Edit mode and return to the Ready mode by clicking another cell or clicking the Enter button on the Formula bar.

Cancel

Enter

If the active cell does not contain data, the Formula bar displays only the cell reference (by column letter and row number). As you type data, two buttons display on the Formula bar to the right of the Name box, as shown in Figure 1.4. Click the Cancel button to delete the current cell entry. You can also delete the cell entry by pressing the Delete key. Click the Enter button to indicate that you are finished typing or editing the cell entry. When you click the Enter button on the Formula bar, the word *Enter* (or *Edit*) located at the left side of the Status bar changes to *Ready*.

Figure 1.4 Buttons on the Formula Bar

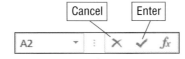

Project 1b   **Editing Data in a Cell**   **Part 2 of 3**

1. With **EL1-C1-P1-EmpBene.xlsx** open, double-click in cell A7 (contains *Mikulich*).
2. Move the insertion point immediately left of the *k* and then type c. (This changes the spelling to *Mickulich*.)
3. Click once in cell A4 (contains *Connors*), type **Bryant**, and then press the Tab key. (Clicking only once allows you to type over the existing data.)
4. Edit cell C2 by completing the following steps:
   a. Click the Find & Select button in the Editing group on the HOME tab and then click *Go To* at the drop-down list.

Step 4a

---

b. At the Go To dialog box, type C2 in the *Reference* text box and then click OK.

c. Type **Classification** (over *Benefits*).

5. Click once in any other cell.

6. Click the Save button on the Quick Access toolbar to save the workbook again.

Printing a Workbook ■■■■■■■■■■■■■■■■■■■■■■■■■■■

With a workbook open, click the FILE tab and the Info backstage area displays, as shown in Figure 1.5. Use buttons and options at the backstage area to perform functions such as opening, closing, saving, and printing a workbook. If you want to exit the backstage area without completing an action, click the Back button (located in the upper left corner of the backstage area) or press the Esc key on your keyboard.

Many of the computer projects you create will need to be printed. Print a workbook from the Print backstage area, as shown in Figure 1.6. To display this backstage area, click the FILE tab and then click the *Print* option. You can also display the Print backstage area with the keyboard shortcut Ctrl + P.

H I N T

Ctrl + P is the keyboard shortcut to display the Print backstage area.

Figure 1.5 Info Backstage Area

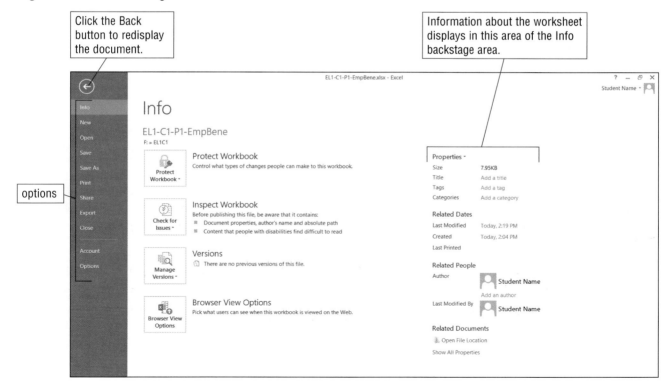

Click the Back button to redisplay the document.

Information about the worksheet displays in this area of the Info backstage area.

options

Figure 1.6 Print Backstage Area

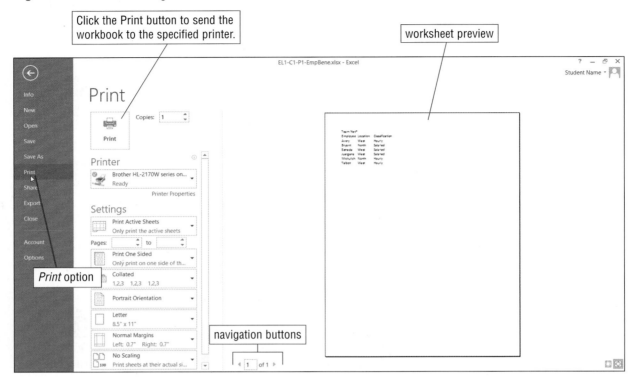

Click the Print button to send the workbook to the specified printer.

worksheet preview

Print

Print option

navigation buttons

▼ Quick Steps

Print a Workbook
1. Click FILE tab.
2. Click *Print* option.
3. Click Print button.
OR
Click Quick Print button on Quick Access toolbar.

The left side of the Print backstage area displays three categories: *Print, Printer,* and *Settings*. Click the Print button in the Print backstage area to send the workbook to the printer and use the *Copies* measurement box to specify the number of copies you want printed. Use the gallery in the *Printer* category to specify the desired printer. The *Settings* category contains a number of galleries, each with options for specifying how you want your workbook printed. Use the galleries to specify whether you want the pages collated when printed; what orientation, page size, and margins your workbook should have; and whether you want the worksheet scaled to print all rows and columns of data on one page.

Another method for printing a workbook is to insert the Quick Print button on the Quick Access toolbar and then click the button. This sends the workbook directly to the printer without displaying the Print backstage area. To insert this button on the Quick Access toolbar, click the Customize Quick Access Toolbar button that displays at the right side of the toolbar and then click *Quick Print* at the drop-down list. To remove the Quick Print button from the Quick Access toolbar, right-click the button and then click *Remove from Quick Access Toolbar* at the drop-down list.

▼ Quick Steps

Close a Workbook
1. Click FILE tab.
2. Click *Close* option.

Closing a Workbook ■■■■■■■■■■■■■■■■■■■■■■■■■■■

To close an Excel workbook without closing Excel, click the FILE tab and then click the *Close* option. You can also close a workbook with the keyboard shortcut Ctrl + F4.

Closing Excel ■■■■■■■■■■■■■■■■■■■■■■■■■■■■■■■■■■■■

To close Excel, click the Close button that displays in the upper right corner of the screen. The Close button contains an X, and if you position the mouse pointer on the button, a ScreenTip displays with the name *Close*. You can also close Excel with the keyboard shortcut Alt + F4.

▼ **Quick Steps**

Close Excel
Click Close button.

Close

Using Automatic Entering Features ■■■■■■■■■■■■■■■■

Excel contains several features that help you enter data into cells quickly and efficiently. These features include *AutoComplete*, which automatically inserts data in a cell that begins the same as a previous entry; *AutoCorrect*, which automatically corrects many common typographical errors; and *AutoFill*, which automatically inserts words, numbers, or formulas in a series.

Using AutoComplete

The AutoComplete feature automatically inserts data in a cell that begins the same as a previous entry. If the data inserted by AutoComplete is the data you want in the cell, press the Tab key or the Enter key. If it is not the desired data, simply continue typing the correct data. This feature can be very useful in a worksheet that contains repetitive data entries. For example, consider a worksheet that repeats the word *Payroll*. The second and subsequent times this word is to be inserted in a cell, simply typing the letter *P* will cause AutoComplete to insert the entire word.

Using AutoCorrect

The AutoCorrect feature automatically corrects many common typing errors. To see what symbols and words are in the AutoCorrect feature, click the FILE tab and then click *Options*. At the Excel Options dialog box, click *Proofing* in the left panel and then click the AutoCorrect Options button located in the right panel. This displays the AutoCorrect dialog box with the AutoCorrect tab selected, as shown in Figure 1.7, with a list box containing the replacement data.

Figure 1.7 AutoCorrect Dialog Box with AutoCorrect Tab Selected

When you type the text displayed in the first column of this list box in a worksheet and then press the spacebar, the text is replaced by the text in the second column of this list box.

At the AutoCorrect dialog box, type the text shown in the first column in the list box and the text in the second column is inserted in the cell. Along with symbols, the AutoCorrect dialog box contains commonly misspelled words and common typographical errors.

1. With **EL1-C1-P1-EmpBene.xlsx** open, make cell A1 active.
2. Type the text in cell A1, as shown in Figure 1.8. Insert the ® symbol by typing (r) and then pressing Enter. (AutoCorrect will change (r) to ®.)
3. Type the remaining text in the cells. When you type the W in *West* in cell B5, the AutoComplete feature will insert *West*. Accept this by pressing the Tab key. (Pressing the Tab key accepts *West* and also makes the cell to the right active.) Use the AutoComplete feature to enter *West* in cells B6 and B8 and *North* in cell B7. Use AutoComplete to enter the second and subsequent occurrences of *Salaried* and *Hourly*.
4. Click the Save button on the Quick Access toolbar.
5. Print **EL1-C1-P1-EmpBene.xlsx** by clicking the FILE tab, clicking the *Print* option, and then clicking the Print button at the Print backstage area. (The gridlines will not print.)

6. Close the workbook by clicking the FILE tab and then clicking the *Close* option at the backstage area.

Figure 1.8 Project 1c

	A	B	C	D
1	Team Net®			
2	Employee	Location	Classification	
3	Avery	West	Hourly	
4	Bryant	North	Salaried	
5	Estrada	West	Salaried	
6	Juergens	West	Salaried	
7	Mickulich	North	Hourly	
8	Talbot	West	Hourly	
9				

You will open an existing workbook and insert formulas to find the sums and averages of numbers.

Using AutoFill

When a cell is active, a thick, green border surrounds it and a small, green square displays in the bottom right corner of the border. This green square is called the AutoFill *fill handle* (see Figure 1.2 on page 6). With the fill handle, you can quickly fill a range of cells with the same data or with consecutive data. For example, suppose you need to insert the year 2015 in a row or column of cells. To do this quickly, type *2015* in the first cell, position the mouse pointer on the fill handle, hold down the left mouse button, drag across the cells in which you want the year inserted, and then release the mouse button.

You can also use the fill handle to insert a series in a row or column of cells. For example, suppose you are creating a worksheet with data for all of the months in the year. Type *January* in the first cell, position the mouse pointer on the fill handle, hold down the left mouse button, drag down or across to 11 more cells, and then release the mouse button. Excel automatically inserts the other 11 months in the year in the proper order. When using the fill handle, the cells must be adjacent. Table 1.3 identifies the sequences inserted in cells by Excel when specific types of data are entered.

Certain sequences, such as *2, 4* and *Jan 12, Jan 13,* require that both cells be selected before using the fill handle. If only the cell containing *2* is active, the fill handle will insert *2s* in the selected cells. The list in Table 1.3 is only a sampling of what the fill handle can do. You may find a variety of other sequences that can be inserted in a worksheet using the fill handle.

An Auto Fill Options button displays when you fill cells with the fill handle. Click this button and a list of options displays for filling the cells. By default, data and formatting are filled in each cell. You can choose to fill only the formatting in the cells or fill only the data without the formatting. You can also choose to copy data into the selected cells or fill the data as a series.

When filling cells with the fill handle, hold down the Ctrl key if you want to copy the same data instead of displaying the next instance in the series.

Auto Fill
Options

Table 1.3 AutoFill Fill Handle Series

Enter this data (commas represent data in separate cells)	And the fill handle will insert this sequence in adjacent cells
January	February, March, April, and so on
Jan	Feb, Mar, Apr, and so on
Jan 12, Jan 13	14-Jan, 15-Jan, 16-Jan, and so on
Monday	Tuesday, Wednesday, Thursday, and so on
Product 1	Product 2, Product 3, Product 4, and so on
Qtr 1	Qtr 2, Qtr 3, Qtr 4
2, 4	6, 8, 10, and so on

Opening a Workbook ■■■■■■■■■■■■■■■■■■■■■■■■■■■■

▼ Quick Steps

Open a Workbook
1. Click FILE tab.
2. Click *Open* option.
3. Click the desired location (your OneDrive or *Computer*).
4. Click the Browse button.
5. Display desired folder.
6. Double-click workbook name.

Open an Excel workbook at the Open dialog box. To display this dialog box, click the FILE tab and then click the *Open* option. This displays the Open backstage area. You can also display the Open backstage area with the keyboard shortcut Ctrl + O or by inserting an Open button on the Quick Access toolbar. At the Open backstage area, click the desired location, such as your OneDrive or *Computer*, and then click the Browse button. (If you are opening a workbook from your computer or USB flash drive, you can double-click the *Computer* option.) At the Open dialog box, navigate to the desired folder and then double-click the desired workbook name in the Content pane. You can bypass the Open backstage area and go directly to the Open dialog box by using the keyboard shortcut Ctrl + F12.

When you click your OneDrive or the *Computer* option at the Open backstage area, a list of the most recently accessed folders displays below the *Recent Folders* heading in the *Computer* section. Open a folder by clicking the folder name.

Opening a Workbook from the Recent Workbooks List

Click the *Recent Workbooks* option in the middle panel at the Open backstage area and a list of the most recently opened workbooks displays below the Recent Workbooks heading at the right side of the backstage area. Up to twenty-five workbook names display in the list by default. Open a workbook from this list by clicking the workbook name.

Pinning a Workbook to the Recent Workbooks List

If you want a workbook to remain in the Recent Workbooks list at the Open backstage area, "pin" the workbook to the list. To do this, position the mouse pointer over the desired workbook name and then click the small, left-pointing stick pin that displays at the right side of the workbook name. This changes it to a down-pointing stick pin. The next time you display the Open backstage area, the workbook you pinned displays at the top of the Recent Workbooks list. You can also pin a workbook to the Recent list at the Excel 2013 opening screen. When you pin a workbook here, it will display in the Recent Workbooks list at the Open backstage area as well. To "unpin" the workbook, click the stick pin to change it from a down-pointing pin to a left-pointing pin. You can pin more than one workbook to the list.

Project 2a | **Inserting Data in Cells with the Fill Handle** | **Part 1 of 3**

1. Open **FillCells.xlsx**. (This workbook is located in the EL1C1 folder on your storage medium.)
2. Save the workbook with Save As and name it **EL1-C1-P2-FillCells**.
3. Add data to cells as shown in Figure 1.9. Begin by making cell B1 active and then typing January.
4. Position the mouse pointer on the fill handle for cell B1, hold down the left mouse button, drag across to cell G1, and then release the mouse button.

◢	A	B	C	D	E	F	G
1		January	February	March	April	May	June
2		100					125	125
3		150	150	150	150	175	175

Step 4

5. Type a sequence and then use the fill handle to fill the remaining cells by completing the following steps:
   a. Make cell A2 active and then type **Year 1**.
   b. Make cell A3 active and then type **Year 3**.
   c. Select cells A2 and A3 by positioning the mouse pointer in cell A2, holding down the left mouse button, dragging down to cell A3, and then releasing the mouse button.
   d. Drag the fill handle for cell A3 to cell A5. (This inserts *Year 5* in cell A4 and *Year 7* in cell A5.)
6. Use the fill handle to fill adjacent cells with a number but not the formatting by completing the following steps:
   a. Make cell B2 active. (This cell contains *100* with bold formatting.)
   b. Drag the fill handle for cell B2 to cell E2. (This inserts *100* in cells C2, D2, and E2.)
   c. Click the Auto Fill Options button that displays at the bottom right of the selected cells.
   d. Click the *Fill Without Formatting* option at the drop-down list.
7. Use the fill handle to apply formatting only by completing the following steps:
   a. Make cell B2 active.
   b. Drag the fill handle to cell B5.
   c. Click the Auto Fill Options button and then click *Fill Formatting Only* at the drop-down list.
8. Make cell A10 active and then type **Qtr 1**.
9. Drag the fill handle for cell A10 to cell A13.
10. Save **EL1-C1-P2-FillCells.xlsx**.

Figure 1.9 Project 2a

	A	B	C	D	E	F	G	H
1		January	February	March	April	May	June	
2	Year 1	**100**	100	100	100	125	125	
3	Year 3	**150**	150	150	150	175	175	
4	Year 5	**200**	200	200	150	150	150	
5	Year 7	**250**	250	250	250	250	250	
6								
7								
8								
9								
10	Qtr 1	$5,500	$6,250	$7,000	$8,500	$5,500	$4,500	
11	Qtr 2	$6,000	$7,250	$6,500	$9,000	$4,000	$5,000	
12	Qtr 3	$4,500	$8,000	$6,000	$7,500	$6,000	$5,000	
13	Qtr 4	$6,500	$8,500	$7,000	$8,000	$5,500	$6,000	
14								

Inserting Formulas ■■■■■■■■■■■■■■■■■■■■■■■■■

▼ **Quick Steps**

Insert a Formula Using the AutoSum button
1. Click in desired cell.
2. Click AutoSum button.
3. Check range identified and make changes if necessary.
4. Press Enter.

AutoSum

H I N T

You can use the keyboard shortcut Alt + = to insert the SUM function in a cell.

Excel is a powerful decision-making tool you can use to manipulate data to answer questions in "What if?" situations. Insert a formula in a worksheet and then manipulate the data to make projections, answer specific questions, and plan for the future. For example, the manager of a department might use an Excel worksheet to prepare a department budget and then determine the impact on the budget of hiring a new employee or increasing the volume of production.

Insert a *formula* in a worksheet to perform calculations on values. A formula contains a mathematical operator, value, cell reference, cell range, and function. Formulas can be written that add, subtract, multiply, and/or divide values. Formulas can also be written that calculate averages, percentages, minimum and maximum values, and much more. Excel includes an AutoSum button in the Editing group on the HOME tab that inserts a formula to calculate the total of a range of cells.

Using the AutoSum Button to Add Numbers

You can use the AutoSum button in the Editing group on the HOME tab to insert a formula. The AutoSum button adds numbers automatically with the SUM function. Make active the cell in which you want to insert the formula (this cell should be empty) and then click the AutoSum button. Excel looks for a range of cells containing numbers that are above the active cell. If no cell above contains numbers, then Excel looks to the left of the active cell. Excel suggests the range of cells to be added. If the suggested range is not correct, drag through the desired range of cells with the mouse and then press Enter. You can also double-click the AutoSum button to insert the SUM function with the range Excel chooses.

Project 2b **Adding Values with the AutoSum Button**   Part 2 of 3

1. With **EL1-C1-P2-FillCells.xlsx** open, make cell A6 active and then type **Total**.
2. Make cell B6 active and then calculate the sum of the cells by clicking the AutoSum button in the Editing group on the HOME tab.
3. Excel inserts the formula *=SUM(B2:B5)* in cell B6. This is the correct range of cells, so press Enter.

4. Make cell C6 active and then click the AutoSum button in the Editing group.
5. Excel inserts the formula *=SUM(C2:C5)* in cell C6. This is the correct range of cells, so press Enter.

6. Make cell D6 active.
7. Double-click the AutoSum button. This inserts the formula *=SUM(D2:D5)* in cell D6 and inserts the sum *700*.
8. Insert the sum in cells E6, F6, and G6.
9. Save **EL1-C1-P2-FillCells.xlsx**.

Using the AutoSum Button to Average Numbers

A common function in a formula is the AVERAGE function. With this function, a range of cells is added together and then divided by the number of cell entries. The AVERAGE function is available on the AutoSum button. Click the AutoSum button arrow and a drop-down list displays with a number of common functions.

Using the Fill Handle to Copy a Formula

In a worksheet, you may want to insert the same basic formula in other cells. In a situation where a formula is copied to other locations in a worksheet, use a *relative cell reference*. Copy a formula containing relative cell references and the cell references change. For example, if you enter the formula *=SUM(A2:C2)* in cell D2 and then copy it relatively to cell D3, the formula in cell D3 displays as *=SUM(A3:C3)*. You can use the fill handle to copy a formula relatively in a worksheet. To do this, position the mouse pointer on the fill handle until the mouse pointer turns into a thin, black cross; hold down the left mouse button; drag and select the desired cells; and then release the mouse button.

▼ **Quick Steps**

Insert an Average Formula Using the AutoSum Button
1. Click in desired cell.
2. Click AutoSum button arrow.
3. Click *Average*.
4. Specify range.
5. Press Enter.

Copy a Formula Using the Fill Handle
1. Insert formula in cell.
2. Make active cell containing formula.
3. Using fill handle, drag through cells you want to contain formula.

Project 2c **Inserting the AVERAGE Function and Copying a Formula Relatively**   **Part 3 of 3**

1. With **EL1-C1-P2-FillCells.xlsx** open, make cell A14 active and then type **Average**.
2. Insert the average of cells B10 through B13 by completing the following steps:
   a. Make cell B14 active.
   b. Click the AutoSum button arrow in the Editing group and then click *Average* at the drop-down list.
   c. Excel inserts the formula *=AVERAGE(B10:B13)* in cell B14. This is the correct range of cells, so press Enter.
3. Copy the formula relatively to cells C14 through G14 by completing the following steps:
   a. Make cell B14 active.
   b. Position the mouse pointer on the fill handle, hold down the left mouse button, drag across to cell G14, and then release the mouse button.
4. Save, print, and then close **EL1-C1-P2-FillCells.xlsx**.

Step 2b

	Σ AutoSum	A
	Σ Sum	
Format	Average	nd & lect ▾
	Count Numbers	
	Max	
P	Min	S
	More Functions...	

9							
10	Qtr 1	$5,500	$6,250	$7,000	$8,500	$5,500	$4,500
11	Qtr 2	$6,000	$7,250	$6,500	$9,000	$4,000	$5,000
12	Qtr 3	$4,500	$8,000	$6,000	$7,500	$6,000	$5,000
13	Qtr 4	$6,500	$8,500	$7,000	$8,000	$5,500	$6,000
14	Average	$5,625	$7,500	$6,625	$8,250	$5,250	$5,125
15							
16							

Step 3b

<table>
<tr><td colspan="2">Project 3   Format a Worksheet   2 Parts</td></tr>
<tr><td colspan="2">You will open a monthly expenses workbook and then change column width, merge and center cells, and apply number formatting to numbers in cells.</td></tr>
</table>

Selecting Cells ▪■▪■▪■▪■▪■▪■▪■▪■▪■▪■▪■▪■▪■

You can use a variety of methods for formatting cells in a worksheet. For example, you can change the alignment of data in cells or rows or add character formatting. To identify the cells that are to be affected by the formatting, select the specific cells.

Selecting Cells Using the Mouse

Select specific cells in a worksheet using the mouse or select columns or rows. Table 1.4 displays the methods for selecting cells using the mouse.

The first cell in a range displays with a white background and is the active cell.

Selected cells, except the active cell, display with a gray background (this may vary) rather than a white background. The active cell is the first cell in the selection block and displays in the normal manner (white background with black data). Selected cells remain selected until you click a cell with the mouse or press an arrow key on the keyboard.

Selecting Cells Using the Keyboard

You can use the keyboard to select specific cells within a worksheet. Table 1.5 displays the commands for selecting specific cells. If a worksheet contains data, Ctrl + A selects the cells containing data. If the worksheet contains groups of data separated by empty cells, Ctrl + A or Ctrl + Shift + spacebar will select a group of cells rather than all of the cells.

Selecting Data within Cells

The selection commands presented select the entire cell. You can also select specific characters within a cell. To do this with the mouse, position the cell pointer in the desired cell and then double-click the left mouse button. Drag with the I-beam pointer through the data you want selected. Data selected within a cell displays in

Table 1.4 Selecting with the Mouse

To select this	Do this
column	Position the cell pointer on the column header (a letter) and then click the left mouse button.
row	Position the cell pointer on the row header (a number) and then click the left mouse button.
adjacent cells	Drag with the mouse to select specific cells.
nonadjacent cells	Hold down the Ctrl key while clicking the column header, row header, or specific cells.
all cells in worksheet	Click Select All button. (Refer to Figure 1.2 on page 6.)

Table 1.5 Selecting Cells Using the Keyboard

To select	Press
cells in direction of arrow key	Shift + arrow key
from active cell to beginning of row	Shift + Home
from active cell to beginning of worksheet	Shift + Ctrl + Home
from active cell to last cell in worksheet containing data	Shift + Ctrl + End
entire column	Ctrl + spacebar
entire row	Shift + spacebar
cells containing data	Ctrl + A
groups of data separated by empty cells	Ctrl + Shift + spacebar

black with a gray background. If you are using the keyboard to select data in a cell, hold down the Shift key and then press the arrow key that moves the insertion point in the desired direction. All data the insertion point passes through will be selected. You can also press F8 to turn on the Extend Selection mode, move the insertion point in the desired direction to select the data, and then press F8 to turn off the Extend Selection mode. When the Extend Selection mode is on, the words *EXTEND SELECTION* display toward the left side of the Status bar.

H I N T

Select nonadjacent columns or rows by holding down the Ctrl key while selecting cells.

Applying Basic Formatting

Excel provides a wide range of formatting options you can apply to cells in a worksheet. Some basic formatting options that are helpful when creating a worksheet include changing column width, merging and centering cells, and formatting numbers.

Changing Column Width

If data such as text or numbers overlaps in a cell, you can increase the width of the column to accommodate the data. To do this, position the mouse pointer on the gray boundary line between columns in the column header (Figure 1.2 identifies the column header) until the pointer turns into a left-and-right-pointing arrow and then drag the boundary to the desired location. If the column contains data, double-click the column boundary at the right side of the column to automatically adjust the width of the column to accommodate the longest entry.

Merging and Centering Cells

As you learned earlier in this chapter, if the text you type is longer than the cell can accommodate, the text overlaps the next cell to the right (unless you are typing numbers). You can merge cells to accommodate the text and also center the text within the merged cells. To merge cells and center the text, select the desired cells and then click the Merge & Center button located in the Alignment group on the HOME tab.

▼ Quick Steps

Change the Column Width
Drag column boundary line.
OR
Double-click column boundary.

Merge and Center Cells
1. Select cells.
2. Click Merge & Center button on HOME tab.

Merge & Center

1. Open **MoExps.xlsx** from the EL1C1 folder on your storage medium.
2. Save the workbook with Save As and name it **EL1-C1-P3-MoExps**.
3. Change the column width by completing the following steps:
   a. Position the mouse pointer in the column header on the boundary line between columns A and B until the pointer turns into a double-headed arrow pointing left and right.

Step 3a

   b. Double-click the left mouse button.
   c. Position the mouse pointer in the column header on the boundary line between columns E and F and then double-click the left mouse button.
   d. Position the mouse pointer in the column header on the boundary line between columns F and G and then double-click the left mouse button.
4. Merge and center cells by completing the following steps:
   a. Select cells A1 through C1.
   b. Click the Merge & Center button in the Alignment group on the HOME tab.

Step 4b

Step 4a

   c. Select cells A2 through C2.
   d. Click the Merge & Center button.
   e. Select cells E1 and F1 and then click the Merge & Center button.
5. Save **EL1-C1-P3-MoExps.xlsx**.

Formatting Numbers

Numbers in a cell, by default, are aligned at the right and decimals and commas do not display unless they are typed in the cell. Change the format of numbers with buttons in the Number group on the HOME tab. Symbols you can use to format numbers include a percent sign (%), a comma (,), and a dollar sign ($). For example, if you type the number *$45.50* in a cell, Excel automatically applies the Currency format to the number. If you type *45%*, Excel automatically applies the Percent format to the number. The Number group on the HOME tab contains five buttons you can use to format numbers in cells. The five buttons are shown and described in Table 1.6.

Specify the formatting for numbers in cells in a worksheet before typing the numbers or format existing numbers in a worksheet. The Increase Decimal and Decrease Decimal buttons in the Number group on the HOME tab will change decimal places for existing numbers only. The Number group on the HOME tab also contains the Number Format button. Click the Number Format button arrow and a drop-down list displays of common number formats. Click the desired format at the drop-down list to apply the number formatting to the cell or selected cells.

A general guideline in accounting is to insert a dollar sign before the first number amount in a column and before the total number amount but not before the number amounts in between. You can format a worksheet following this guideline by applying accounting formatting to the first amount and total amount (using the Accounting Number Format button) and applying comma formatting to the number amounts in between (using the Comma Style button).

Table 1.6 Number Formatting Buttons

Click this button		To do this
$ ▾	Accounting Number Format	Add a dollar sign, any necessary commas, and a decimal point followed by two decimal digits, if none are typed; right-align the number in the cell.
%	Percent Style	Multiply the cell value by 100 and display the result with a percent symbol; right-align the number in the cell.
,	Comma Style	Add any necessary commas and a decimal point followed by two decimal digits, if none are typed; right-align the number in the cell.
←.0 .00	Increase Decimal	Increase the number of decimal places displayed after the decimal point in the selected cell.
.00 →.0	Decrease Decimal	Decrease the number of decimal places displayed after the decimal point in the selected cell.

1. With **EL1-C1-P3-MoExps.xlsx** open, make cell B13 active and then double-click the AutoSum button. (This inserts the total of the numbers in cells B4 through B12.)
2. Make cell C13 active and then double-click the AutoSum button.
3. Apply accounting formatting to cells by completing the following steps:
   a. Select cells B4 and C4.
   b. Click the Accounting Number Format button in the Number group on the HOME tab.
   c. Decrease the decimals by clicking twice on the Decrease Decimal button in the Number group.

   d. Select cells B13 and C13.
   e. Click the Accounting Number Format button.
   f. Click twice on the Decrease Decimal button.
4. Apply comma formatting to numbers by completing the following steps:
   a. Select cells B5 through C12.
   b. Click the Comma Style button in the Number group.
   c. Click twice on the Decrease Decimal button.

5. Apply percent formatting to numbers by completing the following steps:
   a. Select cells F3 through F9.
   b. Click the Percent Style button in the Number group on the HOME tab.
6. Click in cell A1.
7. Save, print, and then close **EL1-C1-P3-MoExps.xlsx**.

Project 4 Use the Help Feature

2 Parts

You will use the Help feature to learn more about entering data in cells, printing a workbook, and number formats, as well as use the ScreenTip to display information about a specific button.

Using Help

Microsoft Excel includes a Help feature that contains information about Excel features and commands. This on-screen reference manual is similar to Windows Help and the Help features in Word, PowerPoint, and Access. Click the Microsoft Excel Help button (the question mark) located in the upper right corner of the screen or press the keyboard shortcut F1 to display the Excel Help window, as shown in Figure 1.10. In this window, type a topic, feature, or question in the search text box and then press the Enter key or click the Search help button. Topics related to the search text display in the Excel Help window. Click a topic that interests you. If the topic window contains a <u>Show All</u> hyperlink in the upper right corner, click this hyperlink and the topic options expand to show additional information related to the topic. When you click the <u>Show All</u> hyperlink, it becomes the <u>Hide All</u> hyperlink.

The Excel Help window contains five buttons that display to the left of the search text box as identified in Figure 1.10. Use the Back and Forward buttons to navigate in the window. Click the Home button to return to the Excel Help window opening screen. If you want to print information on a topic or feature,

▼ Quick Steps

Use the Help Feature
1. Click Microsoft Excel Help button.
2. Type topic or feature.
3. Press Enter.
4. Click desired topic.

Help

Figure 1.10 Excel Help Window

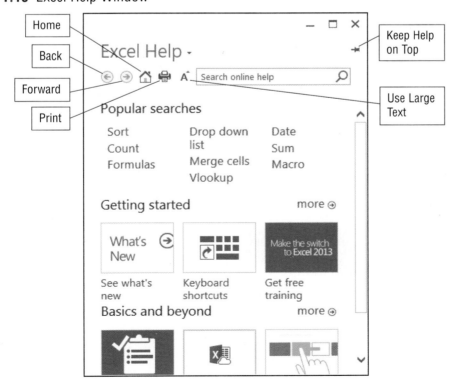

click the Print button and then click the Print button at the Print dialog box. Make the text in the Excel Help window larger by clicking the Use Large Text button. In addition to these five buttons, the Excel Help window contains a Keep Help on Top button located near the upper right corner of the window. Click this button and the Excel Help window remains on the screen (pinned to the screen) even when you work in a worksheet. Click the button again to remove the window from the screen.

Getting Help on a Button

When you position the mouse pointer on a button, a ScreenTip displays with information about the button. Some button ScreenTips display with a Help icon and the hyperlinked text <u>Tell me more</u>. Click this hyperlinked text or press F1 and the Excel Help window opens with information about the button feature.

Project 4a   **Using the Help Feature**   **Part 1 of 2**

1. At the blank screen, press Ctrl + N to display a blank workbook. (Ctrl + N is the keyboard shortcut to open a blank workbook.)
2. Click the Microsoft Excel Help button located in the upper right corner of the screen.
3. At the Excel Help window, type **enter data** in the search text box and then press the Enter key.
4. When the list of topics displays, click the <u>Enter data manually in worksheet cells</u> hyperlink.
5. Read the information about entering data in cells.
6. Click the Print button in the Excel Help window. This displays the Print dialog box. If you want to print the topic, click the Print button; otherwise, click the Cancel button to remove the dialog box.
7. Click the Use Large Text button in the Excel Help window to increase the size of the text.
8. Click the Use Large Text button again to return the text to the normal size.
9. Click the Back button to return to the previous window.
10. Click the Forward button to return to the article on entering data manually in worksheet cells.
11. Click the Home button to return to the original Excel Help window screen.
12. Click the Close button to close the Excel Help window.

13. Hover the mouse pointer over the Wrap Text button in the Alignment group on the HOME tab until the ScreenTip displays and then click the hyperlinked text <u>Tell me more</u> that displays at the bottom of the ScreenTip.

14. At the Excel Help window, read the information that displays and then close the window.

Step 13

Getting Help in a Dialog Box or Backstage Area

Some dialog boxes and backstage areas contain a help button you can click to display the Excel Help window with specific information about the dialog box or backstage area. After reading and/or printing the information, close the dialog box by clicking the Close button located in the upper right corner of the dialog box or close the backstage area by clicking the Back button or pressing the Esc key.

| **Project 4b** | **Getting Help in a Dialog Box or Backstage Area** | **Part 2 of 2** |

1. At the blank workbook, click the FILE tab and then click the *Print* option.
2. At the Print backstage area, click the Microsoft Excel Help button that displays in the upper right corner.
3. At the Excel Help window that displays, click the hyperlink to an article on printing that interests you. Read the article and then close the Excel Help window.
4. Click the Back button to return to the blank workbook.
5. At the blank workbook, click the Number group dialog box launcher.
6. At the Format Cells dialog box with the Number tab selected, click the Help button that displays in the upper right corner of the dialog box.

Step 5

Step 6

7. Click the hyperlink to the article on available number formats.
8. Read the article, close the Excel Help window and then close the Format Cells dialog box.

Chapter Summary

- A file created in Excel is called a workbook and it consists of individual worksheets.
- The intersection of columns and rows in a worksheet is referred to as a cell. Gridlines are the horizontal and vertical lines that define cells.
- When the insertion point is positioned in a cell, the cell name (also called the cell reference) displays in the Name box located at the left side of the Formula bar. The cell name includes the column letter and row number.
- If data entered in a cell consists of text (letters) and does not fit into the cell, it overlaps the cell to the right. If the data consists of numbers and does not fit into the cell, the numbers are changed to number symbols (###).
- Save a workbook by clicking the Save button on the Quick Access toolbar or by clicking the FILE tab and then clicking the *Save As* option. At the Save As backstage area, click the desired location and then click the Browse button. At the Save As dialog box, navigate to the desired folder, type the workbook name in the *File name* text box, and then press Enter.
- To replace data in a cell, click the cell once and then type the new data. To edit data within a cell, double-click the cell and then make necessary changes.
- Print a workbook by clicking the FILE tab, clicking the *Print* option, and then clicking the Print button.
- Close a workbook by clicking the FILE tab and then clicking the *Close* option or by using the keyboard shortcut Ctrl + F4.
- Close Excel by clicking the Close button located in the upper right corner of the screen or with the keyboard shortcut Alt + F4.
- The AutoComplete feature automatically inserts a previous entry if the character or characters being typed in a cell match a previous entry. The AutoCorrect feature corrects many common typographical errors. The AutoFill fill handle fills a range of cells with the same or consecutive data.
- Open a workbook by clicking the FILE tab and then clicking the *Open* option. At the Open backstage area, click the desired location and then click the Browse button. At the Open dialog box, double-click the desired workbook.
- Use the AutoSum button in the Editing group on the HOME tab to find the total or average of data in columns or rows.
- Select all cells in a column by clicking the column header. Select all cells in a row by clicking the row header. Select all cells in a worksheet by clicking the Select All button located immediately to the left of the column headers.
- Change column width by dragging or double-clicking the column boundary.
- Merge and center cells by selecting the desired cells and then clicking the Merge & Center button in the Alignment group on the HOME tab.
- Format numbers in cells with buttons in the Number group on the HOME tab.
- Click the Microsoft Excel Help button or press F1 to display the Excel Help window. At this window, type a topic in the search text box and then press Enter.
- The ScreenTip for some buttons displays with the hyperlinked text Tell me more. Click this hyperlink (or press F1) and the Excel Help window opens with information about the button feature.
- Some dialog boxes and backstage areas contain a help button you can click to display information specific to the dialog box or backstage area.

Commands Review

FEATURE	RIBBON TAB, GROUP/OPTION	BUTTON	KEYBOARD SHORTCUT
Accounting format	HOME, Number	$ ▾	
AutoSum	HOME, Editing	Σ	Alt + =
close Excel		✕	Alt + F4
close workbook	FILE, *Close*		Ctrl + F4
Comma format	HOME, Number	,	
decrease decimal places	HOME, Number	.00 →.0	
Excel Help window		?	F1
Go To dialog box	HOME, Editing	🔍	Ctrl + G
increase decimal places	HOME, Number	←.0 .00	
merge and center cells	HOME, Alignment	▦	
Open backstage area	FILE, *Open*		Ctrl + O
Percent format	HOME, Number	%	Ctrl + Shift + %
Print backstage area	FILE, *Print*		Ctrl + P
Save As backstage area	FILE, *Save As*	💾	Ctrl + S

Concepts Check   Test Your Knowledge   SNAP

Completion: In the space provided at the right, indicate the correct term, symbol, or command.

1. The horizontal and vertical lines that define the cells in a worksheet area are referred to as this.   _____

2. Columns in a worksheet are labeled with these.   _____

3. Rows in a worksheet are labeled with these.   _____

4. Press this key on the keyboard to move the insertion point to the next cell.   _____

5. Press these keys on the keyboard to move the insertion point to the previous cell. _____

6. Data being typed in a cell displays in the cell as well as here. _____

7. If a number entered in a cell is too long to fit inside the cell, the number is changed to this. _____

8. This feature automatically inserts words, numbers, or formulas in a series. _____

9. This is the name of the small black square that displays in the bottom right corner of the active cell. _____

10. Use this button in the Editing group on the HOME tab to insert a formula in a cell. _____

11. With this function, a range of cells are added together and then divided by the number of cell entries. _____

12. To select nonadjacent columns using the mouse, hold down this key on the keyboard while clicking the column headers. _____

13. Click this button to merge selected cells and center data within the merged cells. _____

14. The Accounting Number Format button is located in this group on the HOME tab. _____

15. Press this function key to display the Excel Help window. _____

Skills Check   Assess Your Performance

Assessment

1   CREATE A WORKSHEET USING AUTOCOMPLETE

1. Create the worksheet shown in Figure 1.12 with the following specifications:
   a. To create the © symbol in cell A1, type (c).
   b. Type the misspelled words as shown and let the AutoCorrect feature correct them. Use the AutoComplete feature to insert the second occurrence of *Category, Available,* and *Balance.*
   c. Merge and center cells A1 and B1.
2. Save the workbook and name it **EL1-C1-A1-Plan**.
3. Print and then close **EL1-C1-A1-Plan.xlsx**.

Figure 1.12 Assessment 1

	A	B	C
1	Premiere Plan©		
2	Plan A	Catagory	
3		Availalbe	
4		Balence	
5	Plan B	Category	
6		Available	
7		Balance	
8			

Assessment

2 CREATE AND FORMAT A WORKSHEET

1. Create the worksheet shown in Figure 1.13 with the following specifications:
   a. Merge and center cells A1 through C1.
   b. After typing the data, automatically adjust the width of column A.
   c. Insert in cell B8 the sum of cells B3 through B7 and insert in cell C8 the sum of cells C3 through C7.
   d. Apply accounting formatting and decrease the decimal point by two positions to cells B3, C3, B8, and C8.
   e. Apply comma formatting and decrease the decimal point by two positions to cells B4 through C7.
   f. If any of the number amounts display as number symbols (###), automatically adjust the width of the appropriate columns.
2. Save the workbook and name it **EL1-C1-A2-Exp**.
3. Print and then close **EL1-C1-A2-Exp.xlsx**.

Figure 1.13 Assessment 2

	A	B	C	D
1	Construction Project			
2	Expense	Original	Current	
3	Material	129000	153000	
4	Labor	97000	98500	
5	Equipment rental	14500	11750	
6	Permits	1200	1350	
7	Tax	1950	2145	
8	Total			
9				

Assessment

3 CREATE A WORKSHEET USING THE FILL HANDLE

1. Type the worksheet data shown in Figure 1.14 with the following specifications:
   a. Type **Monday** in cell B2 and then use the fill handle to fill in the remaining days of the week.
   b. Type **350** in cell B3 and then use the fill handle to fill in the remaining numbers in the row.
   c. Merge and center cells A1 through G1.
2. Insert in cell G3 the sum of cells B3 through F3 and insert in cell G4 the sum of cells B4 through F4.
3. After typing the data, select cells B3 through G4 and then apply accounting formatting with two places past the decimal point.
4. If necessary, adjust column widths.
5. Save the workbook and name it **EL1-C1-A3-Invest**.
6. Print and then close **EL1-C1-A3-Invest.xlsx**.

Figure 1.14 Assessment 3

	A	B	C	D	E	F	G	H
1			CAPITAL INVESTMENTS					
2		Monday	Tuesday	Wednesday	Thursday	Friday	Total	
3	Budget	350	350	350	350	350		
4	Actual	310	425	290	375	400		
5								

Assessment

4 INSERT FORMULAS IN A WORKSHEET

1. Open **DIAnalysis.xlsx** and then save the workbook with Save As and name it **EL1-C1-A4-DIAnalysis**.
2. Insert a formula in cell B15 that totals the amounts in cells B4 through B14.
3. Use the fill handle to copy relatively the formula in cell B15 to cell C15.
4. Insert a formula in cell D4 that finds the average of the amounts in cells B4 and C4.
5. Use the fill handle to copy relatively the formula in cell D4 down to cells D5 through D14.
6. Select cells D5 through D14 and then apply comma formatting with no places past the decimal point.
7. Save, print, and then close **EL1-C1-A4-DIAnalysis.xlsx**.

Visual Benchmark Demonstrate Your Proficiency

CREATE, FORMAT, AND INSERT FORMULAS IN A WORKSHEET

1. At a blank workbook, create the worksheet shown in Figure 1.15 with the following specifications:
   a. Type the data in cells, as shown in the figure. Use the fill handle when appropriate, merge and center the text *Personal Expenses - July through December*, and automatically adjust column widths.

b. Insert formulas to determine averages and totals.

c. Apply accounting formatting with no places past the decimal point to the amounts in cells B4 through H4 and cells B12 through H12.

d. Apply comma formatting with no places past the decimal point to the amounts in cells B5 through H11.

2. Save the workbook and name it **EL1-C1-VB-PersExps**.

3. Print and then close **EL1-C1-VB-PersExps.xlsx**.

Figure 1.15 Visual Benchmark

	A	B	C	D	E	F	G	H	I
1									
2				Personal Expenses - July through December					
3	Expense	July	August	September	October	November	December	Average	
4	Rent	850	850	850	850	850	850		
5	Rental insurance	55	55	55	55	55	55		
6	Health insurance	120	120	120	120	120	120		
7	Electricity	129	135	110	151	168	173		
8	Utilities	53	62	49	32	55	61		
9	Telephone	73	81	67	80	82	75		
10	Groceries	143	137	126	150	147	173		
11	Gasoline	89	101	86	99	76	116		
12	Total								
13									

Case Study   Apply Your Skills

Part 1

You are the office manager for Deering Industries. One of your responsibilities is to create a monthly calendar containing information on staff meetings, training, and due dates for time cards. Open **DICalendar.xlsx** and then insert the following information:

- Type the text **November, 2015** in cell A2.
- Insert the days of the week (*Sunday, Monday, Tuesday, Wednesday, Thursday, Friday,* and *Saturday*) in cells A3 through G3. (Use the fill handle to fill in the days of the week and fill without formatting.)
- Insert the numbers *1* through *7* in cells A4 through G4.
- Insert in the calendar the remaining numbers of the days (numbers *8* through *14* in cells A6 through G6, numbers *15* through *21* in cells A8 through G8, numbers *22* through *28* in cells A10 through G10, and numbers *29* and *30* in cells A12 and B12. If you use the fill handle, fill without formatting.
- Excel training will be held Thursday, November 5, from 9:00 to 11:00 a.m. Insert this information in cell E5. (Insert the text on two lines by typing **Excel Training**, pressing Alt + Enter to move the insertion point to the next line, and then typing **9-11 a.m.**)
- A staff meeting is held the second and fourth Monday of each month from 9:00 to 10:00 a.m. Insert this information in cell B7 and cell B11.

- Time cards are due the first and third Fridays of the month. Insert in cells F5 and F9 information indicating that time cards are due.
- A production team meeting is scheduled for Tuesday, November 24, from 1:00 to 3:00 p.m. Insert this information in cell C11.

Save the workbook and name it **EL1-C1-CS-DICalendar**. Print and then close the workbook.

Part 2

The manager of the purchasing department has asked you to prepare a worksheet containing information on quarterly purchases. Open **DIExpenditures.xlsx** and then insert the data as shown in Figure 1.16. After typing the data, insert in the appropriate cells formulas to calculate averages and totals. Apply comma formatting to cells F5 through F8. Save the workbook and name it **EL1-C1-CS-DIExpenditures**. Print and then close the workbook.

Figure 1.16 Case Study, Part 2

	A	B	C	D	E	F	G
1			DEERING INDUSTRIES				
2			PURCHASING DEPARTMENT · EXPENDITURES				
3	Category					Average	
4	Supplies	$ 645.75	$ 756.25	$ 534.78	$ 78,950.00		
5	Equipment	4,520.55	10,789.35	3,825.00	12,890.72		
6	Furniture	458.94	2,490.72	851.75	743.20		
7	Training	1,000.00	250.00	1,200.00	800.00		
8	Software	249.00	1,574.30	155.45	3,458.70		
9	Total						
10							

Part 3

The manager of the purchasing department has asked you to prepare a note to the finances coordinator, Jennifer Strauss. In Word, type a note to Jennifer Strauss explaining that you have prepared an Excel worksheet with the purchasing department expenditures. You are including the cells from the worksheet containing the expenditure information. In Excel, open **EL1-C1-CS-DIExpenditures.xlsx**, copy cells A3 through F9, and then paste them in the Word document. Make any corrections to the table so the information is readable. Save the document and name it **EL1-C1-CS-DINotetoJS**. Print and then close the document. Close **EL1-C1-CS-DIExpenditures.xlsx**.

Part 4

You will be ordering copy machines for several departments in the company and have decided to research prices. Using the Internet, find three companies that sell copiers and write down information on different copier models. Open **DICopiers.xlsx** and then type the company, model number, and price in the designated cells. Save the completed workbook and name it **EL1-C1-CS-DICopiers**. Print and then close **EL1-C1-CS-DICopiers.xlsx**.

MICROSOFT® EXCEL®

Inserting Formulas in a Worksheet

PERFORMANCE OBJECTIVES

Upon successful completion of Chapter 2, you will be able to:

- Write formulas with mathematical operators
- Type a formula in the Formula bar
- Copy a formula
- Use the Insert Function feature to insert a formula in a cell
- Write formulas with the AVERAGE, MAX, MIN, COUNT, NOW, and TODAY functions
- Create absolute and mixed cell references

Tutorials

2.1 Performing Calculations Using Formulas

2.2 Copying and Testing Formulas

2.3 Using Statistical Functions

2.4 Writing Formulas with Date Functions and Dates

2.5 Displaying Formulas in a Worksheet

2.6 Creating Formulas and Absolute Addressing

Excel is a powerful decision-making tool containing data that can be manipulated to answer "What if?" situations. Insert a formula in a worksheet and then manipulate the data to make projections, answer specific questions, and plan for the future. For example, the owner of a company might prepare a worksheet on production costs and then determine the impact on company revenues if production is increased or decreased. Insert a formula in a worksheet to perform calculations on values. A formula contains a mathematical operator, value, cell reference, cell range, and function. Formulas can be written that add, subtract, multiply, and/or divide values. Formulas can also be written that calculate averages, percentages, minimum and maximum values, and much more. As you learned in Chapter 1, Excel includes an AutoSum button in the Editing group on the HOME tab that inserts a formula to calculate the total of a range of cells and also includes some commonly used formulas. Along with the AutoSum button, Excel includes a FORMULAS tab that offers a variety of functions to create formulas. Model answers for this chapter's projects appear on the following pages.

Excel
EL1C2

Note: Before beginning the projects, copy to your storage medium the EL1C2 subfolder from the EL1 folder on the CD that accompanies this textbook and make EL1C2 the active folder.

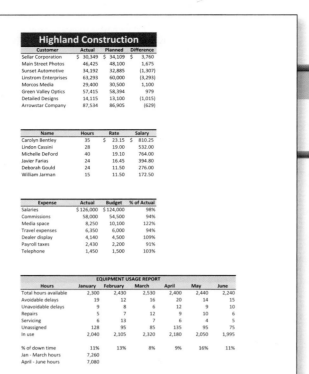

Highland Construction

Customer	Actual	Planned	Difference
Sellar Corporation	$ 30,349	$ 34,109	$ 3,760
Main Street Photos	46,425	48,100	1,675
Sunset Automotive	34,192	32,885	(1,307)
Linstrom Enterprises	63,293	60,000	(3,293)
Morcos Media	29,400	30,500	1,100
Green Valley Optics	57,415	58,394	979
Detailed Designs	14,115	13,100	(1,015)
Arrowstar Company	87,534	86,905	(629)

Name	Hours	Rate	Salary
Carolyn Bentley	35	$ 23.15	$ 810.25
Lindon Cassini	28	19.00	532.00
Michelle DeFord	40	19.10	764.00
Javier Farias	24	16.45	394.80
Deborah Gould	24	11.50	276.00
William Jarman	15	11.50	172.50

Expense	Actual	Budget	% of Actual
Salaries	$126,000	$124,000	98%
Commissions	58,000	54,500	94%
Media space	8,250	10,100	122%
Travel expenses	6,350	6,000	94%
Dealer display	4,140	4,500	109%
Payroll taxes	2,430	2,200	91%
Telephone	1,450	1,500	103%

EQUIPMENT USAGE REPORT						
Hours	January	February	March	April	May	June
Total hours available	2,300	2,430	2,530	2,400	2,440	2,240
Avoidable delays	19	12	16	20	14	15
Unavoidable delays	9	8	6	12	9	10
Repairs	5	7	12	9	10	6
Servicing	6	13	7	6	4	5
Unassigned	128	95	85	135	95	75
In use	2,040	2,105	2,320	2,180	2,050	1,995
% of down time	11%	13%	8%	9%	16%	11%
Jan - March hours	7,260					
April - June hours	7,080					

Project 1 Insert Formulas in a Worksheet

EL1-C2-P1-HCReports.xlsx

Dollar Wise
Financial Services

Technical Support Department

Employee	Test 1	Test 2	Test 3	Average
Arnson, Patrick	91%	87%	82%	87%
Barclay, Jeanine	76%	74%	72%	74%
Calahan, Jack	67%	71%	65%	68%
Cumpston, Kurt	86%	91%	90%	89%
Donovan, Nancy	85%	89%	78%	84%
Fisher-Edwards, Teri	70%	70%	70%	70%
Flanery, Stephanie	70%	70%	72%	71%
Herbertson, Wynn	91%	80%	85%	85%
Jewett, Troy	97%	94%	92%	94%
Leibrand, Maxine	72%	63%	65%	67%
Markovits, Claude	68%	93%	70%	77%
Nyegaard, Curtis	90%	89%	88%	89%
Pherson, Douglas	72%	82%	55%	70%

Highest Test Average	94%
Lowest Test Average	67%
Average of All Tests	79%
Test 2 Completed	13
Test 3 Completed	13

Prepared by:
Student Name
9/18/2015 14:05

Project 2 Insert Formulas with Statistical Functions

EL1-C2-P2-DWTests.xlsx

Dollar Wise
Financial Services

Technical Support Department

Employee	Test 1	Test 2
Arnson, Patrick	0.91	0.87
Barclay, Jeanine	0.76	0.74
Calahan, Jack	0.67	0.71
Cumpston, Kurt	0.86	0.91
Donovan, Nancy	0.85	0.89
Fisher-Edwards, Teri	0.7	0.7
Flanery, Stephanie	0.7	0.7
Herbertson, Wynn	0.91	0.8
Jewett, Troy	0.97	0.94
Leibrand, Maxine	0.72	0.63
Markovits, Claude	0.68	0.93
Nyegaard, Curtis	0.9	0.89
Pherson, Douglas	0.72	0.82

Highest Test Average	=MAX(E4:E16)
Lowest Test Average	=MIN(E4:E16)
Average of All Tests	=AVERAGE(E4:E16)
Test 2 Completed	=COUNT(C4:C16)
Test 3 Completed	=COUNT(D4:D16)

Prepared by:
Student Name
=NOW()

Page 1

Test 3	Average
0.82	=AVERAGE(B4:D4)
0.72	=AVERAGE(B5:D5)
0.65	=AVERAGE(B6:D6)
0.9	=AVERAGE(B7:D7)
0.78	=AVERAGE(B8:D8)
0.7	=AVERAGE(B9:D9)
0.72	=AVERAGE(B10:D10)
0.85	=AVERAGE(B11:D11)
0.92	=AVERAGE(B12:D12)
0.65	=AVERAGE(B13:D13)
0.7	=AVERAGE(B14:D14)
0.88	=AVERAGE(B15:D15)
0.55	=AVERAGE(B16:D16)

Page 2

EL1-C2-P2-DWTests.xlsx, Formulas

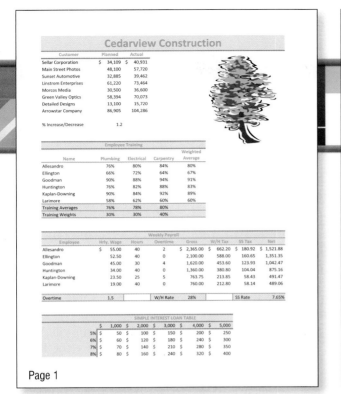

Cedarview Construction

Customer	Planned	Actual
Sellar Corporation	$ 34,109	$ 40,931
Main Street Photos	48,100	57,720
Sunset Automotive	32,885	39,462
Linstrom Enterprises	61,220	73,464
Morcos Media	30,500	36,600
Green Valley Optics	58,394	70,073
Detailed Designs	13,100	15,720
Arrowstar Company	86,905	104,286
% Increase/Decrease	1.2	

Employee Training

Name	Plumbing	Electrical	Carpentry	Weighted Average
Allesandro	76%	80%	84%	80%
Ellington	66%	72%	64%	67%
Goodman	90%	88%	94%	91%
Huntington	76%	82%	88%	83%
Kaplan-Downing	90%	84%	92%	89%
Larimore	58%	62%	60%	60%
Training Averages	76%	78%	80%	
Training Weights	30%	30%	40%	

Weekly Payroll

Employee	Hrly. Wage	Hours	Overtime	Gross	W/H Tax	SS Tax	Net
Allesandro	$ 55.00	40	2	$ 2,365.00	662.20	180.92	$ 1,521.88
Ellington	52.50	40	0	2,100.00	588.00	160.65	1,351.35
Goodman	45.00	30	4	1,620.00	453.60	123.93	1,042.47
Huntington	34.00	40	0	1,360.00	380.80	104.04	875.16
Kaplan-Downing	23.50	25	5	763.75	213.85	58.43	491.47
Larimore	19.00	40	0	760.00	212.80	58.14	489.06
Overtime	1.5		W/H Rate	28%		SS Rate	7.65%

SIMPLE INTEREST LOAN TABLE

	$ 1,000	$ 2,000	$ 3,000	$ 4,000	$ 5,000
5%	$ 50	$ 100	$ 150	$ 200	$ 250
6%	$ 60	$ 120	$ 180	$ 240	$ 300
7%	$ 70	$ 140	$ 210	$ 280	$ 350
8%	$ 80	$ 160	$ 240	$ 320	$ 400

Page 1

9%	$ 90	$ 180	$ 270	$ 360	$ 450
10%	$ 100	$ 200	$ 300	$ 400	$ 500
11%	$ 110	$ 220	$ 330	$ 440	$ 550
12%	$ 120	$ 240	$ 360	$ 480	$ 600
13%	$ 130	$ 260	$ 390	$ 520	$ 650
14%	$ 140	$ 280	$ 420	$ 560	$ 700
15%	$ 150	$ 300	$ 450	$ 600	$ 750

Page 2

Project 3 Insert Formulas Using Absolute and Mixed Cell References   EL1-C2-P3-CCReports.xlsx

---

Project 1   Insert Formulas in a Worksheet   4 Parts

You will open a worksheet containing data and then insert formulas to calculate differences, salaries, and percentages of budgets.

Writing Formulas with Mathematical Operators ■ ■ ■ ■ ■ ■

As you learned in Chapter 1, the AutoSum button in the Editing group on the HOME tab creates the formula for you. You can also write your own formulas using *mathematical operators*. Commonly used mathematical operators and their functions are displayed in Table 2.1. When writing your own formula, begin the formula with the equals sign (=). For example, to create a formula that divides the contents of cell B2 by the contents of cell C2 and inserts the result in cell D2, you would make D2 the active cell and then type =B2/C2.

HINT

After typing a formula in a cell, press the Enter key, the Tab key, Shift + Tab, or click Formula bar.

Table 2.1 Mathematical Operators

Operator	Function	Operator	Function
+	addition	/	division
-	subtraction	%	percentage
*	multiplication	^	exponentiation

Copying a Formula with Relative Cell References

▼ **Quick Steps**

Copy a Formula Relatively
1. Insert formula in cell.
2. Select cell containing formula and all cells you want to contain formula.
3. Click Fill button.
4. Click desired direction.

Fill

In many worksheets, the same basic formula is used repetitively. In a situation where a formula is copied to other locations in a worksheet, use a *relative cell reference*. Copy a formula containing relative cell references and the cell references change. For example, if you enter the formula *=SUM(A2:C2)* in cell D2 and then copy it relatively to cell D3, the formula in cell D3 displays as *=SUM(A3:C3)*. (Additional information on cell references is discussed later in this chapter in the "Using an Absolute Cell Reference in a Formula" section.)

To copy a formula relatively in a worksheet, use the Fill button or the fill handle. (You used the fill handle to copy a formula in Chapter 1.) To use the Fill button, select the cell containing the formula as well as the cells to which you want the formula copied and then click the Fill button in the Editing group on the HOME tab. At the Fill button drop-down list, click the desired direction. For example, if you are copying the formula down cells, click the *Down* option.

Project 1a **Finding Differences by Inserting and Copying a Formula** **Part 1 of 4**

1. Open **HCReports.xlsx**.
2. Save the workbook with Save As and name it **EL1-C2-P1-HCReports**.
3. Insert a formula by completing the following steps:
   a. Make cell D3 active.
   b. Type the formula **=C3-B3**.
   c. Press Enter.
4. Copy the formula to cells D4 through D10 by completing the following steps:
   a. Select cells D3 through D10.
   b. Click the Fill button in the Editing group on the HOME tab and then click *Down* at the drop-down list.
5. Save **EL1-C2-P1-HCReports.xlsx**.
6. With the worksheet open, make the following changes to cell contents:
   B4: Change *48,290* to *46425*
   C6: Change *61,220* to *60000*
   B8: Change *55,309* to *57415*
   B9: Change *12,398* to *14115*
7. Make cell D3 active, apply Accounting formatting, and then decrease the places past the decimal point to none.
8. Save **EL1-C2-P1-HCReports.xlsx**.

Step 4b

As you learned in Chapter 1, you can use the fill handle to copy a formula up, down, left, or right within a worksheet. To use the fill handle, insert the desired data in the cell (text, value, formula, etc.). With the cell active, position the mouse pointer on the fill handle until the mouse pointer turns into a thin, black cross. Hold down the left mouse button, drag and select the desired cells, and then release the mouse button. If you are dragging a cell containing a formula, a relative version of the formula is copied to the selected cells.

Use the fill handle to copy a relative version of a formula.

Checking Cell References in a Formula

To verify if a formula is using the correct cell references, double-click in a cell containing a formula and the cells referenced in the formula display with a colored border and shading in the worksheet. This feature makes identifying which cells are being referenced in a formula easy and is helpful when trying to identify errors that may occur in a formula.

Project 1b Calculating Salary by Inserting and Copying a Formula with the Fill Handle

Part 2 of 4

1. With **EL1-C2-P1-HCReports.xlsx** open, insert a formula by completing the following steps:
   a. Make cell D15 active.
   b. Click in the Formula bar text box and then type **=C15*B15**.
   c. Click the Enter button on the Formula bar.
2. Copy the formula to cells D16 through D20 by completing the following steps:
   a. Make sure cell D15 is still the active cell.
   b. Position the mouse pointer on the fill handle that displays at the lower right corner of cell D15 until the pointer turns into a thin, black cross.
   c. Hold down the left mouse button, drag down to cell D20, and then release the mouse button.
3. Save **EL1-C2-P1-HCReports.xlsx**.
4. Double-click in cell D20 to display the formula with cell references color coded to ensure the formula was copied relatively.
5. Make the following changes to cell contents in the worksheet:
   - B16: Change *20* to *28*
   - C17: Change *18.75* to *19.10*
   - B19: Change *15* to *24*
6. Select cells D16 through D20 and then apply Comma formatting.
7. Save **EL1-C2-P1-HCReports.xlsx**.

Step 1c

Step 1b

| IF | × ✓ fx | =C15*B15 |

	A	B	C	D
1	**Highland Construction**			
2	Customer	Actual	Planned	Difference
3	Sellar Corporation	$ 30,349	$ 34,109	$ 3,760
4	Main Street Photos	46,425	48,100	1,675
5	Sunset Automotive	34,192	32,885	(1,307)
6	Linstrom Enterprises	63,293	60,000	(3,293)
7	Morcos Media	29,400	30,500	1,100
8	Green Valley Optics	57,415	58,394	979
9	Detailed Designs	14,115	13,100	(1,015)
10	Arrowstar Company	87,534	86,905	(629)
11				
12				
13				
14	Name	Hours	Rate	Salary
15	Carolyn Bentley	35	$ 23.15	=C15*B15
16	Lindon Cassini	20	19.00	

	A	B	C	D
13				
14	Name	Hours	Rate	Salary
15	Carolyn Bentley	35	$ 23.15	$ 810.25
16	Lindon Cassini	20	19.00	$ 380.00
17	Michelle DeFord	40	18.75	$ 750.00
18	Javier Farias	24	16.45	$ 394.80
19	Deborah Gould	15	11.50	$ 172.50
20	William Jarman	15	11.50	$ 172.50
21				

Step 2c

Writing a Formula by Pointing

Quick Steps

Write a Formula by Pointing
1. Click cell that will contain formula.
2. Type equals sign.
3. Click cell you want to reference in formula.
4. Type desired mathematical operator.
5. Click next cell reference.
6. Press Enter.

In Project 1a and Project 1b, you wrote formulas using cell references such as =C3-B3. Another method for writing a formula is to "point" to the specific cells that are to be part of the formula. Creating a formula by pointing is more accurate than typing the cell reference since a mistake can happen when typing the cell reference.

To write a formula by pointing, click in the cell that will contain the formula, type the equals sign to begin the formula, and then click in the cell you want to reference in the formula. This inserts a moving border around the cell and also changes the mode from Enter to Point. (The word *POINT* displays at the left side of the Status bar.) Type the desired mathematical operator and then click the next cell reference. Continue in this manner until all cell references are specified and then press the Enter key. This ends the formula and inserts the result of the calculation of the formula in the active cell. When writing a formula by pointing, you can also select a range of cells you want included in the formula.

Project 1c — **Writing a Formula by Pointing that Calculates Percentage of Actual Budget**   Part 3 of 4

1. With **EL1-C2-P1-HCReports.xlsx** open, enter a formula by pointing that calculates the percentage of actual budget by completing the following steps:
   a. Make cell D25 active.
   b. Type the equals sign (=).
   c. Click in cell C25. (This inserts a moving border around the cell and changes the mode from Enter to Point.)
   d. Type the forward slash symbol (/).
   e. Click in cell B25.
   f. Make sure the formula in D25 is *=C25/B25* and then press Enter.
2. Make cell D25 active, position the mouse pointer on the fill handle, drag down to cell D31, and then release the mouse button.
3. Save **EL1-C2-P1-HCReports.xlsx**.

	A	B	C	D
23				
24	**Expense**	**Actual**	**Budget**	**% of Actual**
25	Salaries	$ 126,000	$ 124,000	=C25/B25
26	Commissions	58,000	54,500	
27	Media space	8,250	10,100	
28	Travel expenses	6,350	6,000	
29	Dealer display	4,140	4,500	
30	Payroll taxes	2,430	2,200	
31	Telephone	1,450	1,500	

Steps 1a-1e

C	D
Budget	**% of Actual**
$ 124,000	98%
54,500	94%
10,100	122%
6,000	94%
4,500	109%
2,200	91%
1,500	103%

Step 2

Determining the Order of Operations

If a formula contains two or more operators, Excel uses the same *order of operations* used in algebra. From left to right in a formula, this order is negations (negative number—a number preceded by -) first, then percentages (%), then exponentiations (^), followed by multiplications (*), divisions (/), additions (+), and subtractions (-). If you want to change the order of operations, use parentheses around the part of the formula you want calculated first. For example, suppose you want to create a formula using cells A1, B1, and C1, and each cell contains the value 5. If the formula is written as =A1+B1*C1, the result would be 30 (because 5*5=25 and 5+25=30). However, if you place parentheses around the first two cell references so the formula displays as =(A1+B1)*C1, the result would be 50 (because 5+5=10 and 10*5=50).

Excel requires each left parenthesis to be paired with a right parenthesis. If a formula is missing a left or right parenthesis, a message box will display explaining that an error exists in the formula and providing a possible correction, which you can accept or decline. This feature is useful when creating a formula that contains multiple layers of parentheses (called **nested parentheses**) because it will identify any missing left or right parentheses in the formula. Parentheses can also be used in various functions to further determine the order of operations in the function.

Using the Trace Error Button

As you are working in a worksheet, you may occasionally notice a button pop up near the active cell. The general term for this button is **smart tag**. The display of the smart tag button varies depending on the action performed. In Project 1d, you will insert a formula that will cause a smart tag button, named the Trace Error button, to appear. When the Trace Error button appears, a small, dark green triangle also displays in the upper left corner of the cell. Click the Trace Error button and a drop-down list displays with options for updating the formula to include specific cells, getting help with the error, ignoring the error, editing the error in the Formula bar, and completing an error check. In Project 1d, two of the formulas you insert return the desired results. You will click the Trace Error button, read information on what Excel perceives as the error, and then tell Excel to ignore the error.

Trace Error

Identifying Common Formula/Function Errors in Excel

Excel is a sophisticated program that requires data input and formula creation to follow strict guidelines in order to function properly. When guidelines that specify how data or formulas are entered are not followed, Excel will display one of many **error codes**. When an error is identified with a code, determining and then fixing the problem is easier than if no information is provided. Table 2.2 lists some common error codes.

Most errors in Excel are the result of the user incorrectly inputting data into a worksheet. However, most error messages will not display until the data is used in a formula or function. Common mistakes made while inputting data include placing text in a cell that requires a number, entering data in the wrong location, and entering numbers in an incorrect format. Other errors are the result of entering a formula or function improperly. A formula will often display an error message if it is trying to divide a number by zero or it contains a circular reference (that is, when a formula within a cell uses the results of that formula in the same cell). Functions tend to display error messages if the arguments of a particular function are not correctly defined or if a function name is typed incorrectly.

Table 2.2 Common Error Codes

Error Code	Meaning
#DIV/O	A formula is attempting to divide a number by zero.
#N/A	An argument parameter has been left out of a function.
#NAME?	A function name is not entered correctly.
#NUM!	An argument parameter does not meet a function's requirements.
#REF!	A referenced cell no longer exists within a worksheet.
#VALUE	The data entered is the wrong type (for example, text instead of numbers).

1. With **EL1-C2-P1-HCReports.xlsx** open, enter a formula by pointing that computes the percentage of equipment down time by completing the following steps:
   a. Make cell B45 active.
   b. Type the equals sign followed by the left parenthesis (=().
   c. Click in cell B37. (This inserts a moving border around the cell and changes the mode from Enter to Point.)
   d. Type the minus symbol (-).
   e. Click in cell B43.
   f. Type the right parenthesis followed by the forward slash ()/).
   g. Click in cell B37.
   h. Make sure the formula in cell B45 is *=(B37-B43)/B37* and then press Enter.

2. Make cell B45 active, position the mouse pointer on the fill handle, drag across to cell G45, and then release the mouse button.

3. Enter a formula by dragging through a range of cells by completing the following steps:
   a. Click in cell B46 and then click the AutoSum button in the Editing group on the HOME tab.
   b. Select cells B37 through D37.
   c. Click the Enter button on the Formula bar. (This inserts *7,260* in cell B46.)

4. Click in cell B47 and then complete steps similar to those in Step 3 to create a formula that totals hours available from April through June (cells E37 through G37). (This inserts *7,080* in cell B47.)

5. Click in cell B46 and notice the Trace Error button that displays. Complete the following steps to read about the error and then tell Excel to ignore the error:
   a. Click the Trace Error button.
   b. At the drop-down list that displays, click the *Help on this error* option.
   c. Read the information that displays in the Excel Help window and then close the window.
   d. Click the Trace Error button again and then click *Ignore Error* at the drop-down list.

6. Remove the dark green triangle from cell B47 by completing the following steps:
   a. Click in cell B47.
   b. Click the Trace Error button and then click *Ignore Error* at the drop-down list.

7. Save, print, and then close **EL1-C2-P1-HCReports.xlsx**.

<table>
<tr><td>**Project** **2**</td><td>**Insert Formulas with Statistical Functions**</td><td>**4 Parts**</td></tr>
</table>

You will use the AVERAGE function to determine average test scores, use the MINIMUM and MAXIMUM functions to determine lowest and highest averages, use the COUNT function to count the number of students taking a test, and display a formula in a cell rather than the result of the formula.

Inserting Formulas with Functions ▪■▪■▪■▪■▪■▪▪■▪■▪

In Project 2b in Chapter 1, you used the AutoSum button to insert the formula *=SUM(B2:B5)* in a cell. The beginning section of the formula, *=SUM*, is called a *function*, and it is a built-in formula. Using a function takes fewer keystrokes when creating a formula. For example, using the *=SUM* function saved you from having to type each cell to be included in the formula with the plus (+) symbol between cell entries.

Excel provides other functions for writing formulas. A function operates on what is referred to as an *argument*. An argument may consist of a constant, a cell reference, or another function. In the formula *=SUM(B2:B5)*, the cell range *(B2:B5)* is an example of a cell reference argument. An argument may also contain a *constant*. A constant is a value entered directly into the formula. For example, if you enter the formula *=SUM(B3:B9,100)*, the cell range *B3:B9* is a cell reference argument and *100* is a constant. In this formula, 100 is always added to the sum of the cells.

When a value calculated by the formula is inserted in a cell, this process is referred to as *returning the result*. The term *returning* refers to the process of calculating the formula and the term *result* refers to inserting the value in the cell.

You can type a function in a cell in a worksheet or you can use the Insert Function button on the Formula bar or on the FORMULAS tab to help you write the formula. Figure 2.1 displays the FORMULAS tab, which provides the Insert Function button as well as other buttons for inserting functions in a worksheet. The Function Library group on the FORMULAS tab contains a number of buttons for inserting functions from a variety of categories, such as *Financial*, *Logical*, *Text*, and *Date & Time*.

Click the Insert Function button on the Formula bar or on the FORMULAS tab and the Insert Function dialog box displays, as shown in Figure 2.2. At the Insert Function dialog box, the most recently used functions display in the *Select a function* list box. Choose a function category by clicking the down-pointing arrow

fx

Insert Function

Figure 2.1 FORMULAS Tab

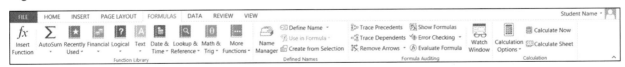

Figure 2.2 Insert Function Dialog Box

The most recently used functions display in this list box.

Click this down-pointing arrow to display a list of categories.

at the right side of the *Or select a category* option box and then clicking the desired category at the drop-down list. Use the *Search for a function* search box to locate a specific function.

With the desired function category selected, choose a function in the *Select a function* list box and then click OK. This displays a Function Arguments palette like the one shown in Figure 2.3. At this palette, enter in the *Number1* text box the range of cells you want included in the formula, any constants that are to be included as part of the formula, or another function. You can either type a cell reference or a range of cells in an argument text box or you can point to a cell or select a range of cells with the mouse pointer. Pointing to cells or selecting a range of cells using the mouse pointer is the preferred method of entering data into an argument text box because there is less chance of making errors. After entering a range of cells, a constant, or another function, click the OK button. You can include more than one argument in a function. If the function you are creating contains more than one argument, press the Tab key to move the insertion point to the *Number2* text box and then enter the second argument. If you need to display a specific cell or cells behind the function palette, move the palette by clicking and dragging it.

Figure 2.3 Example of a Function Arguments Palette

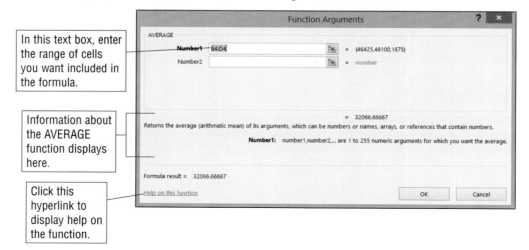

In this text box, enter the range of cells you want included in the formula.

Information about the AVERAGE function displays here.

Click this hyperlink to display help on the function.

Excel performs over 300 functions that are divided into these 13 categories: *Financial, Date & Time, Math & Trig, Statistical, Lookup & Reference, Database, Text, Logical, Information, Engineering, Cube, Compatibility,* and *Web.* Clicking the AutoSum button in the Function Library group on the FORMULAS tab or the Editing group on the HOME tab automatically adds numbers with the SUM function. The SUM function is included in the *Math & Trig* category. In some projects in this chapter, you will write formulas with functions in other categories, including *Statistical* and *Date & Time.*

Excel includes the Formula AutoComplete feature that displays a drop-down list of functions. To use this feature, click in the desired cell or click in the Formula bar text box, type the equals sign (=), and then type the first letter of the desired function. This displays a drop-down list with functions that begin with the letter. Double-click the desired function, enter the cell references, and then press Enter.

Writing Formulas with Statistical Functions

In this section, you will learn to write formulas with the statistical functions AVERAGE, MAX, MIN, and COUNT. The AVERAGE function returns the average (arithmetic mean) of the arguments. The MAX function returns the largest value in a set of values, and the MIN function returns the smallest value in a set of values. Use the COUNT function to count the number of cells that contain numbers within the list of arguments.

Finding Averages

A common function in a formula is the ***AVERAGE function***. With this function, a range of cells is added together and then divided by the number of cell entries. In Project 2a, you will use the AVERAGE function, which will add all of the test scores for a student and then divide that number by the total number of tests. You will use the Insert Function button to simplify the creation of the formula containing an AVERAGE function.

One of the advantages to using formulas in a worksheet is that you can easily manipulate data to answer certain questions. In Project 2a, you will learn the impact of retaking certain tests on the final average score.

| Project 2a | Averaging Test Scores in a Worksheet | Part 1 of 4 |

1. Open **DWTests.xlsx**.
2. Save the workbook with Save As and name it **EL1-C2-P2-DWTests**.
3. Use the Insert Function button to find the average of test scores by completing the following steps:
   a. Make cell E4 active.
   b. Click the Insert Function button on the Formula bar.

c. At the Insert Function dialog box, click the down-pointing arrow at the right side of the *Or select a category* option box and then click *Statistical* at the drop-down list.

d. Click *AVERAGE* in the *Select a function* list box.

e. Click OK.

f. At the Function Arguments palette, make sure *B4:D4* displays in the *Number1* text box. (If not, type **B4:D4** in the *Number1* text box.)

g. Click OK.

Step 3c

Step 3d

Step 3f

4. Copy the formula by completing the following steps:

   a. Make sure cell E4 is still active.

   b. Position the mouse pointer on the fill handle until the pointer turns into a thin black cross.

   c. Hold down the left mouse button, drag down to cell E16, and then release the mouse button.

5. Save and then print **EL1-C2-P2-DWTests.xlsx**.

6. After viewing the averages of test scores, you notice that a couple of students have low averages. You decide to see what happens to these average scores if students make up the tests on which they scored the lowest. You decide that a student can score a maximum of 70% on a retake of the test. Make the following changes to test scores to see how the changes will affect the test averages:

   B9: Change *50* to *70*
   C9: Change *52* to *70*
   D9: Change *60* to *70*
   B10: Change *62* to *70*
   B14: Change *0* to *70*
   D14: Change *0* to *70*
   D16: Change *0* to *70*

7. Save and then print **EL1-C2-P2-DWTests.xlsx**. (Compare the test averages of Teri Fisher-Edwards, Stephanie Flanery, Claude Markovits, and Douglas Pherson to see how retaking the tests affected their final test averages.)

tment	
Test 3	Average
82%	87%
72%	74%
65%	68%
90%	89%
78%	84%
60%	54%
72%	68%
85%	85%
92%	94%
65%	67%
0%	31%
88%	89%
0%	51%

Step 4c

When a formula such as the AVERAGE formula calculates cell entries, it ignores certain cell entries. The AVERAGE function will ignore text in cells and blank cells (not zeros). For example, in the worksheet containing test scores, a couple of cells contained a *0%* entry. This entry was included in the averaging of the test scores. To prevent including that particular test in the average, enter text in the cell such as *N/A* (for *not applicable*) or leave the cell blank.

Finding Maximum and Minimum Values

The **MAX** *function* in a formula returns the maximum value in a cell range and the **MIN** *function* returns the minimum value in a cell range. As an example, you could use the MAX and MIN functions in a worksheet containing employee hours to determine which employee worked the most number of hours and which worked the least. In a worksheet containing sales commissions, you could use the MAX and MIN functions to determine the salesperson who earned the most commission dollars and the one who earned the least.

Insert a MAX or a MIN function into a formula in the same manner as an AVERAGE function. In Project 2b, you will use the Formula AutoComplete feature to insert the MAX function in cells to determine the highest test score average and the Insert Function button to insert the MIN function to determine the lowest test score average.

Project 2b **Finding Maximum and Minimum Values in a Worksheet** Part 2 of 4

1. With **EL1-C2-P2-DWTests.xlsx** open, type the following in the specified cells:
   A19: **Highest Test Average**
   A20: **Lowest Test Average**
   A21: **Average of All Tests**
2. Insert a formula to identify the highest test score average by completing the following steps:
   a. Make cell B19 active.
   b. Type =M. (This displays the Formula AutoComplete list.)
   c. Double-click *MAX* in the Formula AutoComplete list.
   d. Type E4:E16) and then press Enter.
3. Insert a formula to identify the lowest test score average by completing the following steps:
   a. Make sure cell B20 is active.
   b. Click the Insert Function button on the Formula bar.
   c. At the Insert Function dialog box, make sure *Statistical* is selected in the *Or select a category* option box, and then click *MIN* in the *Select a function* list box. (You will need to scroll down the list to display *MIN*.)
   d. Click OK.
   e. At the Function Arguments palette, type E4:E16 in the *Number1* text box.
   f. Click OK.

Step 2c

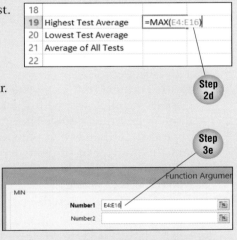

Step 2d

Step 3e

4. Insert a formula to determine the average of all test scores by completing the following steps:
   a. Make cell B21 active.
   b. Click the FORMULAS tab.
   c. Click the Insert Function button in the Function Library group.
   d. At the Insert Function dialog box, make sure *Statistical* is selected in the *Or select a category* option box and then click *AVERAGE* in the *Select a function* list box.
   e. Click OK.
   f. At the Function Arguments palette, make sure the insertion point is positioned in the *Number1* text box with existing text selected, use the mouse pointer to select the range E4:E16 in the worksheet, (you may need to move the palette to display the cells) and then click OK.

Step 4b

Step 4c

FILE HOME INSERT PAGE LAYOUT FORMULAS DATA

fx Σ Insert Function AutoSum Recently Used Financial Logical Text Date & Time Lookup & R Function Library

5. Save and then print **EL1-C2-P2-DWTests.xlsx**.
6. Change the *70%* values (which were previously *0%*) in cells B14, D14, and D16 to *N/A*. (This will cause the average test scores for Claude Markovits and Douglas Pherson to increase and will change the minimum number and average of all test scores.)
7. Save and then print **EL1-C2-P2-DWTests.xlsx**.

Counting Numbers in a Range

Use the **COUNT** *function* to count the numeric values in a range. For example, in a range of cells containing cells with text and cells with numbers, you can count how many cells in the range contain numbers. In Project 2c, you will use the COUNT function to specify the number of students taking Test 2 and Test 3. In the worksheet, the cells containing the text N/A are not counted by the COUNT function.

Project 2c	Counting the Number of Students Taking Tests	Part 3 of 4

1. With **EL1-C2-P2-DWTests.xlsx** open, make cell A22 active.
2. Type **Test 2 Completed**.
3. Make cell B22 active.
4. Insert a formula counting the number of students who have taken Test 2 by completing the following steps:
   a. With cell B22 active, click in the Formula bar text box.
   b. Type **=C**.
   c. At the Formula AutoComplete list that displays, scroll down the list until *COUNT* displays and then double-click *COUNT*.
   d. Type **C4:C16)** and then press Enter.
5. Count the number of students who have taken Test 3 by completing the following steps:
   a. Make cell A23 active.
   b. Type **Test 3 Completed**.
   c. Make cell B23 active.
   d. Click the Insert Function button on the Formula bar.
   e. At the Insert Function dialog box, make sure *Statistical* is selected in the *Or select a category* option box.
   f. Scroll down the list of functions in the *Select a function* list box until *COUNT* is visible and then double-click *COUNT*.
   g. At the formula palette, type **D4:D16** in the *Value1* text box and then click OK.
6. Save and then print **EL1-C2-P2-DWTests.xlsx**.
7. Add the test scores by completing the following steps:
   a. Make cell B14 active and then type **68**.
   b. Make cell D14 active and then type **70**.
   c. Make cell D16 active and then type **55**.
   d. Press Enter.
8. Save and then print **EL1-C2-P2-DWTests.xlsx**.

Step 4c

Step 4d

Writing Formulas with the NOW and TODAY Functions

The NOW and TODAY functions are part of the *Date & Time* category of functions. The **NOW function** returns the current date and time in a date and time format. The **TODAY function** returns the current date in a date format. Both the NOW and TODAY functions automatically update when a workbook is opened. To access the NOW and TODAY functions, click the Date & Time button in the Function Library group on the FORMULAS tab. You can also access these functions at the Insert Function dialog box.

Date & Time

The NOW and TODAY functions can also be updated without closing and then reopening the workbook. To update a workbook that contains a NOW or TODAY function, click the Calculate Now button in the Calculation group on the FORMULAS tab or press the F9 function key.

Calculate Now

Displaying Formulas

In some situations, you may need to display the formulas in a worksheet rather than the results of the formula. For instance, you may want to turn on formulas for auditing purposes or to check formulas for accuracy. Display all formulas in a worksheet, rather than the results, by clicking the FORMULAS tab and then clicking the Show Formulas button in the Formula Auditing group. You can also turn on the display of formulas with the keyboard shortcut Ctrl + `. (This is the grave accent, generally located to the left of the 1 key on the keyboard.) Press Ctrl + ` to turn off the display of formulas or click the Show Formulas button on the FORMULAS tab.

H I N T

Press Ctrl + ` to display formulas in a worksheet rather than the results.

Show Formulas

Project 2d **Using a NOW Function and Displaying Formulas** Part 4 of 4

1. With **EL1-C2-P2-DWTests.xlsx** open, make cell A26 active and then type **Prepared by:**.
2. Make cell A27 active and then type your first and last names.
3. Insert the current date and time by completing the following steps:
   a. Make cell A28 active.
   b. Click the Date & Time button in the Function Library group on the FORMULAS tab and then click *NOW* at the drop-down list.
   c. At the Function Arguments palette telling you that the function takes no argument, click OK.
4. Update the time in cell A28 by completing the following steps:
   a. Wait for 1 minute.
   b. Click the Calculate Now button in the Calculations group on the FORMULAS tab.
5. Click the Show Formulas button in the Formula Auditing group to turn on the display of formulas.
6. Print the worksheet with the formulas. (The worksheet will print on two pages.)
7. Press Ctrl + ` to turn off the display of formulas.
8. Save, print, and then close **EL1-C2-P2-DWTests.xlsx**.

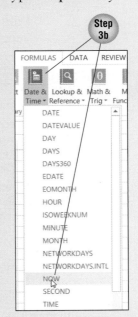

Step 3b

You will insert a formula containing an absolute cell reference that determines the effect on earnings with specific increases, insert a formula with multiple absolute cell references that determine the weighted average of scores, and use mixed cell references to determine simple interest.

Using Absolute and Mixed Cell References in Formulas ▪▪

A reference identifies a cell or a range of cells in a worksheet and can be relative, absolute, or mixed. A ***relative cell reference*** refers to a cell relative to a position in a formula. An ***absolute cell reference*** refers to a cell in a specific location. When a formula is copied, a relative cell reference adjusts while an absolute cell reference remains constant. A ***mixed cell reference*** does both: either the column remains absolute and the row is relative or the column is relative and the row remains absolute. Distinguish among relative, absolute, and mixed cell references using the dollar sign ($). Type a dollar sign before the column and/or row cell reference in a formula to specify that the column or row is an absolute cell reference.

Using an Absolute Cell Reference in a Formula

In this chapter, you have learned to copy a relative formula. For example, if the formula *=SUM(A2:C2)* in cell D2 is copied relatively to cell D3, the formula changes to *=SUM(A3:C3)*. In some situations, you may want a formula to contain an absolute cell reference, which always refers to a cell in a specific location. In Project 3a, you will add a column for projected job earnings and then perform "What if?" situations using a formula with an absolute cell reference. To identify an absolute cell reference, insert a $ sign before the row and the column. For example, the absolute cell reference C12 would be typed as *$C$12* in a formula.

Project 3a Inserting and Copying a Formula with an Absolute Cell Reference   **Part 1 of 4**

1. Open **CCReports.xlsx**.
2. Save the workbook with Save As and name it **EL1-C2-P3-CCReports**.
3. Determine the effect on actual job earnings with a 10% increase by completing the following steps:
   a. Make cell C3 active, type the formula =B3*$B$12, and then press Enter.
   b. Make cell C3 active and then use the fill handle to copy the formula to cells C4 through C10.
   c. Make cell C3 active, click the Accounting Number Format button on the HOME tab, and then click the Decrease Decimal button twice.

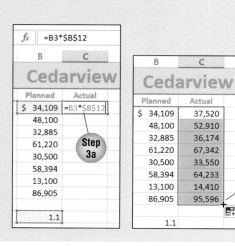

---

4. Save and then print **EL1-C2-P3-CCReports.xlsx**.
5. With the worksheet still open, determine the effect on actual job earnings with a 10% decrease by completing the following steps:
   a. Make cell B12 active.
   b. Type **0.9** and then press Enter.
6. Save and then print the **EL1-C2-P3-CCReports.xlsx**.
7. Determine the effects on actual job earnings with a 20% increase. (To do this, type **1.2** in cell B12 and then press Enter.)
8. Save and then print **EL1-C2-P3-CCReports.xlsx**.

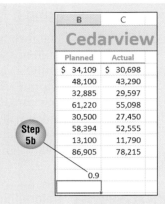

B	C
Cedarview	
Planned	Actual
$ 34,109	$ 30,698
48,100	43,290
32,885	29,597
61,220	55,098
30,500	27,450
58,394	52,555
13,100	11,790
86,905	78,215
0.9	

Step 5b

   In Project 3a, you created a formula with one absolute cell reference. You can also create a formula with multiple absolute cell references. For example, in Project 3b. you will create a formula that contains both relative and absolute cell references to determine the average of training scores based on specific weight percentages. In a weighted average, some scores have more value (weight) than others. For example, in project 3b, you will create a formula that determines the weighted average of training scores that gives more weight to the Carpentry percentages then the Plumbing or Electrical percentages.

Project 3b Inserting and Copying a Formula with Multiple Absolute Cell References   Part 2 of 4

1. With **EL1-C2-P3-CCReports.xlsx** open, insert the following formulas:
   a. Insert a formula in cell B23 that averages the percentages in cells B17 through B22.
   b. Copy the formula in cell B23 to the right to cells C23 and D23.
2. Insert a formula that determines the weighted average of training scores by completing the following steps:
   a. Make cell E17 active.
   b. Type the following formula:
      =$B$24*B17+$C$24*C17+$D$24*D17
   c. Press the Enter key.
   d. Copy the formula in cell E17 down to cells E18 through E22.
   e. With cells E17 through E22 selected, click the Decrease Decimal button three times.
3. Save and then print **EL1-C2-P3-CCReports.xlsx**.
4. With the worksheet still open, determine the effect on weighted training scores if the weighted values change by completing the following steps:
   a. Make cell B24 active, type **30**, and then press Enter.
   b. Make cell D24 active, type **40**, and then press Enter.
5. Save and then print **EL1-C2-P3-CCReports.xlsx**.

Employee Training				
Name	Plumbing	Electrical	Carpentry	Weighted Average
Allesandro	76%	80%	84%	80%
Ellington	66%	72%	64%	67%
Goodman	90%	88%	94%	91%
Huntington	76%	82%	88%	83%
Kaplan-Downing	90%	84%	92%	89%
Larimore	58%	62%	60%	60%
Training Averages	76%	78%	80%	
Training Weights	30%	30%	40%	

Step 4a   Step 4b

Using a Mixed Cell Reference in a Formula

The formula you created in Step 3a in Project 3a contained a relative cell reference (B3) and an absolute cell reference ($B$12). A formula can also contain a mixed cell reference. As stated earlier, in a mixed cell reference, either the column remains absolute and the row is relative or the column is relative and the row remains absolute. In Project 3c, you will insert a number of formulas—two of which will contain mixed cell references. You will insert the formula *=E29*E$26* to calculate withholding tax and *=E29*H$36* to calculate social security tax. The dollar sign before each row indicates that the row is an absolute cell reference.

| Project 3c | Determining Payroll Using Formulas with Absolute and Mixed Cell References | Part 3 of 4 |

1. With **EL1-C2-P3-CCReports.xlsx** open, make cell E29 active and then type the following formula that calculates the gross pay, including overtime (press Enter after typing each of the formulas):
   =(B29*C29+(B29*$B$36*D29))
2. Copy the formula in cell E29 down to cells E30 through E34.
3. Make cell F29 active and then type the following formula that calculates the amount of withholding tax:
   =E29*E$36
4. Copy the formula in cell F29 down to cells F30 through F34.
5. Make cell G29 active and then type the following formula that calculates the amount of social security tax:
   =E29*H$36
6. Copy the formula in cell G29 down to cells G30 through G34.
7. Make cell H29 active and then type the following formula that calculates net pay:
   =E29-(F29+G29)
8. Copy the formula in cell H29 down to cells H30 through H34.
9. Select cells E29 through H29 and then click the Accounting Number Format button.
10. Save **EL1-C2-P3-CCReports.xlsx**.

As you learned in Project 3c, a formula can contain a mixed cell reference. In Project 3d, you will create the formula *=$A41*B$40*. In the first cell reference in the formula, *$A41*, the column is absolute and the row is relative. In the second cell reference, *B$40*, the column is relative and the row is absolute. The formula containing the mixed cell reference allows you to fill in the column and row data using only one formula.

Identify an absolute or mixed cell reference by typing a dollar sign before the column and/or row reference or press the F4 function key to cycle through the various cell references. For example, type *=A41* in a cell, press F4, and the cell reference changes to *=$A$41*. Press F4 again and the cell reference changes to *=A$41*. The next time you press F4, the cell reference changes to *=$A41* and if you press it again, the cell reference changes back to *=A41*.

1. With **EL1-C2-P3-CCReports.xlsx** open, make cell B41 the active cell and then insert a formula containing mixed cell references by completing the following steps:
   a. Type =A41 and then press the F4 function key three times. (This changes the cell reference to *$A41*.)
   b. Type *B40 and then press the F4 function key twice. (This changes the cell reference to *B$40*.)
   c. Make sure the formula displays as =*$A41*B$40* and then press Enter.

Step
1c

2. Copy the formula to the right by completing the following steps:
   a. Make cell B41 active and then use the fill handle to copy the formula right to cell F41.
   b. With cells B41 through F41 selected, use the fill handle to copy the formula down to cell F51.

	B	C	D	E	F
	SIMPLE INTEREST LOAN TABLE				
	$ 1,000	$ 2,000	$ 3,000	$ 4,000	$ 5,000
5%	$ 50	$ 100	$ 150	$ 200	$ 250
6%					

Step
2a

	B	C	D	E	F
	SIMPLE INTEREST LOAN TABLE				
	$ 1,000	$ 2,000	$ 3,000	$ 4,000	$ 5,000
5%	$ 50	$ 100	$ 150	$ 200	$ 250
6%	$ 60	$ 120	$ 180	$ 240	$ 300
7%	$ 70	$ 140	$ 210	$ 280	$ 350
8%	$ 80	$ 160	$ 240	$ 320	$ 400
9%	$ 90	$ 180	$ 270	$ 360	$ 450
10%	$ 100	$ 200	$ 300	$ 400	$ 500
11%	$ 110	$ 220	$ 330	$ 440	$ 550
12%	$ 120	$ 240	$ 360	$ 480	$ 600
13%	$ 130	$ 260	$ 390	$ 520	$ 650
14%	$ 140	$ 280	$ 420	$ 560	$ 700
15%	$ 150	$ 300	$ 450	$ 600	$ 750

Step
2b

3. Save, print, and then close **EL1-C2-P3-CCReports.xlsx**.

Chapter Summary

- Type a formula in a cell and the formula displays in the cell as well as in the Formula bar. If cell entries are changed, a formula automatically recalculates the values and inserts the result in the cell.

- Create your own formula with commonly used operators, such as addition (+), subtraction (-), multiplication (*), division (/), percentage (%), and exponentiation (^). When writing a formula, begin with the equals sign (=).

- Excel uses the same order of operations as algebra and that order can be modified by adding parentheses around certain parts of a formula.

- Copy a formula to other cells in a row or column with the Fill button in the Editing group on the HOME tab or with the fill handle that displays in the bottom right corner of the active cell.

- Double-click in a cell containing a formula and the cell references will display with a colored border and cell shading.

- Another method for writing a formula is to point to specific cells that are part of the formula as the formula is being built.

- If Excel detects an error in a formula, a Trace Error button appears and a dark green triangle displays in the upper left corner of the cell containing the formula.

- Excel displays different error codes for different formula errors. An error code helps identify an error in a formula by providing information on the specific issue.

- Excel performs over 300 functions that are divided into 13 categories.

- A function operates on an argument, which may consist of a cell reference, a constant, or another function. When a value calculated by a formula is inserted in a cell, this is referred to as returning the result.

- The AVERAGE function returns the average (arithmetic mean) of the arguments. The MAX function returns the largest value in a set of values and the MIN function returns the smallest value in a set of values. The COUNT function counts the number of cells containing numbers within the list of arguments.

- The NOW function returns the current date and time and the TODAY function returns the current date.

- Turn on the display of formulas in a worksheet with the Show Formulas button on the FORMULAS tab or with the keyboard shortcut Ctrl + ` (grave accent).

- A reference identifies a cell or a range of cells in a worksheet and can be relative, absolute, or mixed. Identify an absolute cell reference by inserting a dollar sign ($) before the column and row. Cycle through the various cell reference options by typing the cell reference and then pressing F4.

Commands Review

FEATURE	RIBBON TAB, GROUP	BUTTON	KEYBOARD SHORTCUT
display formulas	FORMULAS, Formula Auditing		Ctrl + `
cycle through cell references			F4
Insert Function dialog box	FORMULAS, Function Library	fx	Shift + F3
SUM function	HOME, Editing OR FORMULAS, Function Library	Σ	Alt + =
update formulas	FORMULAS, Calculation		F9

Concepts Check   Test Your Knowledge

Completion: In the space provided at the right, indicate the correct term, symbol, or command.

1. When typing a formula, begin the formula with this sign.   _____

2. This is the operator for division that is used when writing a formula.   _____

3. This is the operator for multiplication that is used when writing a formula.   _____

4. As an alternative to the fill handle, use this button to copy a formula relatively in a worksheet.   _____

5. To display cell references for a formula, perform this action on a cell containing a formula.   _____

6. A formula's order of operations can be modified with these.   _____

7. Excel inserts this symbol in a cell that may contain a possible error.   _____

8. A function operates on this, which may consist of a constant, a cell reference, or another function.   _____

9. This function returns the largest value in a set of values.   _____

10. This is the keyboard shortcut to display formulas in a worksheet.   _____

11. This function returns the current date and time.   _____

12. To identify an absolute cell reference, type this symbol before the column and row.   _____

Skills Check Assess Your Performance

Assessment

1 INSERT AVERAGE, MAX, AND MIN FUNCTIONS

1. Open **DISalesAnalysis.xlsx**.
2. Save the workbook with Save As and name it **EL1-C2-A1-DISalesAnalysis**.
3. Use the AVERAGE function to determine the monthly sales (cells H4 through H9).
4. Apply accounting formatting with no places past the decimal point to cell H4.
5. Total each monthly column, including the *Average* column (cells B10 through H10).
6. Use the MAX function to determine the highest monthly total (for cells B10 through G10) and insert the amount in cell B11.
7. Use the MIN function to determine the lowest monthly total (for cells B10 through G10) and insert the amount in cell B12.
8. Save, print, and then close **EL1-C2-A1-DISalesAnalysis.xlsx**.

Assessment

2 INSERT THE SUM FUNCTION AND ENTER FORMULAS WITH MATHEMATICAL OPERATORS

1. Open **CMQrtlyIncome.xlsx**.
2. Save the workbook with Save As and name it **EL1-C2-A2-CMQrtlyIncome**.
3. The manager of Capstan Marine needs a condensed quarterly statement of income for the third quarter. Insert each of the following formulas by typing the formula, using the pointing method, or using the AutoSum button.
   a. In cell B7, subtract cost of goods sold from sales by entering **=B5-B6**.
   b. In cell B12, add the three expenses by entering **=SUM(B9:B11)**.
   c. In cell B14, subtract total expenses from gross margin by entering **=B7-B12**.
   d. In cell B15, multiply net income before taxes by 22% and then subtract that value from net income before taxes by entering **=B14-(B14*22%)**.
4. Relatively copy the formulas in column B to columns C and D using the fill handle as follows.
   a. Fill the formula in cell B7 to cells C7 and D7 .
   b. Fill the formula in cell B12 to cells C12 and D12.
   c. Fill the formula in cell B14 to C14 and D14.
   d. Fill the formula in cell B15 to C15 and D15.
5. Insert the total in cell E5 by using the AutoSum button to add the range B5:D5.
6. Fill the SUM function in cell E5 to the range E6:E15. (Cells E8 and E13 will contain hyphens.)
7. Apply accounting formatting with a dollar sign and one place past the decimal point to cells B5 through E5.
8. Insert a TODAY function in cell A18.
9. Save, print, and then close **EL1-C2-A2-CMQrtlyIncome.xlsx**.

Assessment

3 WRITE FORMULAS WITH ABSOLUTE CELL REFERENCES

1. Open **CCQuotas.xlsx**.
2. Save the workbook with Save As and name it **EL1-C2-A3-CCQuotas**.
3. Make the following changes to the worksheet:
   a. Insert a formula using an absolute reference to determine the projected quotas with a 10% increase from the current quota.
   b. Save and then print **EL1-C2-A3-CCQuotas.xlsx**.
   c. Determine the projected quotas with a 15% increase from the current quota by changing cell A15 to *15% Increase* and cell B15 to *1.15*.
   d. Save and then print **EL1-C2-A3-CCQuotas.xlsx**.
   e. Determine the projected quotas with a 20% increase from the current quota.
4. Apply accounting formatting with no places after the decimal point to cell C4.
5. Save, print, and then close **EL1-C2-A3-CCQuotas.xlsx**.

Assessment

4 WRITE FORMULAS WITH MIXED CELL REFERENCES

1. Open **AASMileageChart.xlsx**.
2. Save the workbook with Save As and name it **EL1-C2-A4-AASMileageChart**.
3. Determine the mileage range of vehicles that have differing miles per gallon and fuel tank capacities by following these steps:
   a. In cell C5, multiply vehicle fuel tank capacity by vehicle miles per gallon rating by entering =B5*C4.
   b. Change the cell references in the formula so when it is copied, it will multiply the correct values in the chart. Either type dollar signs in the formula or press the F4 function key until the correct mixed cell references display. ***Hint: Refer to Project 3d for assistance.***
   c. Use the fill handle to complete the chart (fill without formatting).
4. Save, print, and then close **EL1-C2-A4-AASMileageChart.xlsx**.

Assessment

5 USE HELP TO LEARN ABOUT EXCEL OPTIONS

1. Learn more about using parentheses within formulas by completing the following steps:
   a. At a blank workbook, display the Excel Help window, click in the search text box, type **overview of formulas**, and then press Enter.
   b. Click the <u>Overview of formulas</u> article hyperlink and then scroll down approximately one-third of the article to the heading *Use of parentheses*.
   c. Read the information about using parentheses in formulas.
   d. Close the Excel Help window.
2. Open **ParenFormulas.xlsx**.
3. Save the workbook with Save As and name it **EL1-C2-A5-ParenFormulas**.
4. Change the results of the formulas individually (do not use the fill handle) in the range B6:B10 by editing the formulas to include parentheses. Consider writing the formulas on paper before inserting them in the cells. ***Note: The last formula will require nested parentheses.***

5. Once the formulas have been edited, compare the new results to the values in column C.
6. Make sure that YES displays in column D for each formula.
7. Turn on the display of formulas.
8. Save, print, and then close **EL1-C2-A5-ParenFormulas.xlsx**.

Visual Benchmark   Demonstrate Your Proficiency

CREATE A WORKSHEET AND INSERT FORMULAS

1. At a blank workbook, type the data in the cells indicated in Figure 2.4 but **do not** type the data in the following cells. Instead, insert the formulas as indicated:

   - Cells D3 through D9: Insert a formula that calculates the salary.
   - Cells D14 through D19: Insert a formula that calculates the differences.
   - Cells B29 through D29: Insert a formula that calculates the averages.
   - Cells E24 through E28: Insert a formula that calculates the weighted average of test scores. *Hint: Refer to Project 3b, Step 2, for assistance on writing a formula with weighted averages.*

   The results of your formulas should match the results you see in the figure.

2. Apply any other formatting so your worksheet looks similar to the worksheet shown in Figure 2.4.
3. Save the workbook and name it **EL1-C2-VB-Formulas**.
4. Print **EL1-C2-VB-Formulas.xlsx**.
5. Press Ctrl + ` to turn on the display of formulas and then print the worksheet again.
6. Turn off the display of formulas and then close the workbook.

Figure 2.4 Visual Benchmark

	A	B	C	D	E	F
1		Weekly Payroll				
2	Employee	Hours	Rate	Salary		
3	Alvarez, Rita	40	$ 22.50	$ 900.00		
4	Campbell, Owen	15	22.50	337.50		
5	Heitmann, Luanne	25	19.00	475.00		
6	Malina, Susan	40	18.75	750.00		
7	Parker, Kenneth	40	18.75	750.00		
8	Reitz, Collette	20	15.00	300.00		
9	Shepard, Gregory	15	12.00	180.00		
10						
11						
12		Construction Projects				
13	Project	Projected	Actual	Difference		
14	South Cascade	$145,000	$ 141,597	$ (3,403)		
15	Rogue River Park	120,000	124,670	4,670		
16	Meridian	120,500	99,450	(21,050)		
17	Lowell Ridge	95,250	98,455	3,205		
18	Walker Canyon	70,000	68,420	(1,580)		
19	Nettleson Creek	52,000	49,517	(2,483)		
20						
21						
22		Test Scores				
23	Employee	Test No. 1	Test No. 2	Test No. 3	Wgt. Avg.	
24	Coffey, Annette	62%	64%	76%	70%	
25	Halverson, Ted	88%	96%	90%	91%	
26	Kohler, Jeremy	80%	76%	82%	80%	
27	McKnight, Carol	68%	72%	78%	74%	
28	Parkhurst, Jody	98%	96%	98%	98%	
29	Test Averages	79%	81%	85%		
30	Test Weights	25%	25%	50%		
31						

Case Study   Apply Your Skills

Part 1

You are the office manager for Allenmore Auto Sales and are responsible for preparing the monthly sales worksheet. Open **AASFebSales.xlsx** and then save the workbook with Save As and name it **EL1-C2-CS-AASFebSales**. Complete the workbook by inserting the following formulas:

- In column F, insert a formula that displays the gross profit, which is the price minus the dealer cost.
- In column H, insert a formula that multiplies the gross profit by the commission percentage.
- In column I, insert a formula that displays the net profit, which is the gross profit minus the total commission.
- Apply accounting formatting with a dollar sign to the amounts in cells D4, E4, F4, H4, and I4.

Save the workbook, print the workbook (it will print on two pages), and then close the workbook.

Part 2

The sales manager at Allenmore Auto Sales has asked you to determine the percentage of total commissions each salesperson has earned for the month of February. Open **AASFebCommissions.xlsx** and then save the workbook with Save As and name it **EL1-C2-CS-AASFebCommissions**. Insert a formula in cell C5 that divides B5 by the amount in cell C3. Use an absolute cell reference for cell C3 when writing the formula. Copy the formula down to cells C6 through C12. Save, print, and then close the workbook.

Part 3

You have created a workbook for automobile trade-ins for the month of February. The sales manager wants used automobiles to be wholesaled if they are not sold within a specific period of time. She wants you to determine the date each February trade-in is to be wholesaled. She wants any used automobile older than 2010 to be wholesaled after 45 days and any automobile newer than 2009 to be wholesaled after 60 days. Open **AASFebTradeIns.xlsx** and then save the workbook with Save As and name it **EL1-C2-CS-AASFebTradeIns**. Insert a formula in column G that adds 45 days to the date in column B for trade-ins 2009 and older and adds 60 days to trade-ins 2010 and newer. Save, print, and then close the workbook.

Part 4

The sales manager has asked you to locate at least two websites that provide estimates on the value of used automobiles (such as Kelley Blue Book (kbb.com) and Edmunds.com). She wants you to add at least two hyperlinks to the February trade-ins workbook. Sales people can use the hyperlinks in the worksheet to quickly determine the value of a used automobile. Use the Help feature to learn how to create hyperlinks in Excel. Open the **EL1-C2-CS-AASFebTradeIns.xlsx** workbook and save it with Save As and name it **EL1-C2-CS-AASFebTradeIns-2**. Add at least two hyperlinks to the workbook that link to websites that provide estimates on the value of used automobiles. Save, print, and then close the workbook.

MICROSOFT® EXCEL®

CHAPTER 3

Formatting an Excel Worksheet

PERFORMANCE OBJECTIVES

Upon successful completion of Chapter 3, you will be able to:

- Change column widths
- Change row heights
- Insert rows and columns in a worksheet
- Delete cells, rows, and columns in a worksheet
- Clear data in cells
- Apply formatting to data in cells
- Apply formatting to selected data using the Mini toolbar
- Apply a theme and customize the theme font and color
- Format numbers
- Repeat the last action
- Automate formatting with Format Painter
- Hide and unhide rows and columns

Tutorials

3.1 Adjusting Column Width and Row Height

3.2 Inserting and Deleting Columns and Rows

3.3 Applying Font Formatting

3.4 Applying Alignment Formatting

3.5 Applying Cell Styles and Themes

3.6 Formatting Numbers

3.7 Adding Borders and Shading to Cells

3.8 Using Format Painter

3.9 Hiding and Unhiding Columns and/or Rows

The appearance of a worksheet on the screen and how it looks when printed is called the *format*. In Chapter 1, you learned how to apply basic formatting to cells in a worksheet. Additional types of formatting you may want to apply to a worksheet include changing column width and row height; applying character formatting such as bold, italic, and underlining; specifying number formatting; inserting and deleting rows and columns; and applying borders, shading, and patterns to cells. You can also apply formatting to a worksheet with a theme. A theme is a set of formatting choices that include colors and fonts. Model answers for this chapter's projects appear on the following page.

Excel
EL1C3

Note: Before beginning the projects, copy to your storage medium the EL1C3 subfolder from the EL1 folder on the CD that accompanies this textbook and then make EL1C3 the active folder.

Capstan Marine Products
Purchasing Department

Company	Product #	Price	Number	Total
RD Manufacturing	240-490-B	$ 85.75	7	$ 600.25
	443-22-0	148.50	8	1,188.00
	855-495	42.75	5	213.75
Ray Enterprises	S894-T	4.99	30	149.70
	B-3448	25.50	12	306.00
	43-GB-39	45.00	20	900.00
Sunrise Corporation	341-453	19.99	8	159.92
	CT-342	304.75	5	1,523.75
	83-492	9.75	35	341.25
	L-756-M	95.40	4	381.60
Geneva Systems	340-19	15.99	20	319.80
	T-3491-S	450.50	5	2,252.50
	900-599	35.95	15	539.25
	43-49CE	120.00	5	600.00
	Total			$9,475.77

Project 1 Format a Product Pricing Worksheet

EL1-C3-P1-CMProducts.xlsx

Stanton & Barnett Associates

Employee	Hrly. Rate	Hours	Weekly Payroll Overtime	Gross	W/H Tax	SS Tax	Net
Lowell	$ 40.00	40	1	$ 1,660.00	$ 464.80	$ 126.99	$ 1,068.21
McIntyre	$ 40.00	40	3	$ 1,780.00	$ 498.40	$ 136.17	$ 1,145.43
Rawlings	$ 37.50	30	0	$ 1,125.00	$ 315.00	$ 86.06	$ 723.94
Fratzke	$ 32.00	40	2	$ 1,376.00	$ 385.28	$ 105.26	$ 885.46
Singleton	$ 25.00	25	0	$ 625.00	$ 175.00	$ 47.81	$ 402.19
Gleason	$ 22.00	40	1	$ 913.00	$ 255.64	$ 69.84	$ 587.52

Overtime	1.5		W/H Rate	28%		SS Rate	7.65%

Project 2 Apply a Theme to a Payroll Worksheet

EL1-C3-P2-SBAPayroll.xlsx

REAL PHOTOGRAPHY
Invoices

Invoice #	Client #	Service	Amount	Tax	Amount Due
2930	03-392	Family Portraits	$ 450.00	8.5%	$ 488.25
2942	02-498	Wedding Portraits	$ 1,075.00	8.8%	$ 1,169.60
2002	11-279	Development	$ 225.00	0.0%	$ 225.00
2007	04-325	Sports Portraits	$ 750.00	8.5%	$ 813.75
2376	03-392	Senior Portraits	$ 850.00	8.5%	$ 922.25
2129	11-279	Development	$ 350.00	0.0%	$ 350.00
2048	11-325	Wedding Portraits	$ 875.00	8.5%	$ 949.38
2054	04-325	Sports Portraits	$ 750.00	8.5%	$ 813.75
2064	05-665	Family Portraits	$ 560.00	8.8%	$ 609.28
2077	11-279	Development	$ 400.00	0.0%	$ 400.00
2079	04-325	Sports Portraits	$ 600.00	8.5%	$ 651.00
2908	55-340	Senior Portraits	$ 725.00	8.8%	$ 788.80
3001	11-279	Development	$ 310.00	8.8%	$ 337.28

Project 3 Format an Invoices Worksheet

EL1-C3-P3-RPInvoices.xlsx

Harris & Briggs
Construction

Preferred Customer	Job #	Projected	Actual	Difference
Sellar Corporation	2130	$ 34,109	$ 30,349	$ (3,760)
Main Street Photos	1201	$ 48,100	$ 48,290	$ 190
Sunset Automotive	318	$ 32,885	$ 34,192	$ 1,307
Linstrom Enterprises	1009	$ 61,220	$ 63,293	$ 2,073
Morcos Media	676	$ 30,500	$ 29,400	$ (1,100)
Green Valley Optics	2117	$ 52,394	$ 55,309	$ 2,915
Detailed Designs	983	$ 13,100	$ 12,398	$ (702)
Summit Services	899	$ 12,000	$ 11,734	$ (266)
Arrowstar Company	786	$ 88,905	$ 87,534	$ (1,371)

Project 4 Format a Company Budget Worksheet

EL1-C3-P4-HBCJobs.xlsx

Project 1   Format a Product Pricing Worksheet   7 Parts

You will open a workbook containing a worksheet with product pricing data and then format the worksheet by changing column widths and row heights, inserting and deleting rows and columns, and clearing data in cells. You will also apply font and alignment formatting to data in cells.

Changing Column Width ■■■■■■■■■■■■■■■■■■■■■■■■■■

Columns in a worksheet are the same width by default. In some worksheets, you may want to change column widths to accommodate more or less data. Change column width using the mouse on column boundaries or at a dialog box.

Changing Column Width Using Column Boundaries

As you learned in Chapter 1, you can adjust the width of a column by dragging the column boundary line or adjust a column width to the longest entry by double-clicking the boundary line. When you drag a column boundary, the column width displays in a box above the mouse pointer. The column width number that displays represents the average number of characters in the standard font that can fit in a cell.

HINT

To change the width of all columns in a worksheet, click the Select All button and then drag a column boundary to the desired position.

You can change the width of selected adjacent columns at the same time. To do this, select the columns and then drag one of the column boundaries within the selected columns. As you drag the boundary, the column width changes for all selected columns. To select adjacent columns, position the cell pointer on the first desired column header (the mouse pointer turns into a black, down-pointing arrow), hold down the left mouse button, drag the cell pointer to the last desired column header, and then release the mouse button.

Project 1a   Changing Column Width Using a Column Boundary   Part 1 of 7

1. Open **CMProducts.xlsx**.
2. Save the workbook with Save As and name it **EL1-C3-P1-CMProducts**.
3. Insert a formula in cell D2 that multiplies the price in cell B2 with the number in cell C2. Copy the formula in cell D2 down to cells D3 through D14.
4. Change the width of column D by completing the following steps:
   a. Position the mouse pointer on the column boundary in the column header between columns D and E until it turns into a double-headed arrow pointing left and right.
   b. Hold down the left mouse button, drag the column boundary to the right until *Width: 11.00 (106 pixels)* displays in the box, and then release the mouse button.

Step 4b

5. Make cell D15 active and then insert the sum of cells D2 through D14.
6. Change the width of columns A and B by completing the following steps:
   a. Select columns A and B. To do this, position the cell pointer on the column A header, hold down the left mouse button, drag the cell pointer to the column B header, and then release the mouse button.

b. Position the cell pointer on the column boundary between columns A and B until it turns into a double-headed arrow pointing left and right.

c. Hold down the left mouse button, drag the column boundary to the right until *Width: 10.33 (100 pixels)* displays in the box, and then release the mouse button.

7. Adjust the width of column C to accommodate the longest entry by double-clicking on the column boundary between columns C and D.

8. Save **EL1-C3-P1-CMProducts.xlsx**.

Step 6c

Changing Column Width at the Column Width Dialog Box

Quick Steps

Change Column Width

Drag column boundary line.
OR
Double-click column boundary.
OR
1. Click Format button.
2. Click *Column Width* at drop-down list.
3. Type desired width.
4. Click OK.

Format

At the Column Width dialog box, shown in Figure 3.1, you can specify a column width number. Increase the column width number to make the column wider or decrease the column width number to make the column narrower.

To display the Column Width dialog box, click the Format button in the Cells group on the HOME tab and then click *Column Width* at the drop-down list. At the Column Width dialog box, type the number representing the average number of characters in the standard font that you want to fit in the column and then press Enter or click OK.

Figure 3.1 Column Width Dialog Box

Type the column width in this text box.

Project 1b **Changing Column Width at the Column Width Dialog Box** Part 2 of 7

1. With **EL1-C3-P1-CMProducts.xlsx** open, change the width of column A by completing the following steps:
   a. Make any cell in column A active.
   b. Click the Format button in the Cells group on the HOME tab and then click *Column Width* at the drop-down list.
   c. At the Column Width dialog box, type 12.7 in the *Column width* text box.
   d. Click OK to close the dialog box.
2. Make any cell in column B active and then change the width of column B to *12.5* by completing steps similar to those in Step 1.
3. Make any cell in column C active and then change the width of column C to *8* by completing steps similar to those in Step 1.
4. Save **EL1-C3-P1-CMProducts.xlsx**.

Step 1c

Step 1d

Changing Row Height ■■■■■■■■■■■■■■■■■■■■■■■■

Row height can be changed in much the same manner as column width. For example, you can change the row height using the mouse on a row boundary or at the Row Height dialog box. Change row height using a row boundary in the same manner as you learned to change column width. To do this, position the cell pointer on the boundary between rows in the row header until it turns into a double-headed arrow pointing up and down, hold down the left mouse button, drag up or down until the row is the desired height, and then release the mouse button.

The height of selected rows that are adjacent can be changed at the same time. (The height of nonadjacent rows will not all change at the same time.) To do this, select the rows and then drag one of the row boundaries within the selected rows. As the boundary is being dragged, the row height changes for all selected rows.

As a row boundary is being dragged, the row height displays in a box above the mouse pointer. The row height number that displays represents a point measurement. A vertical inch contains approximately 72 points. Increase the point size to increase the row height; decrease the point size to decrease the row height.

At the Row Height dialog box, shown in Figure 3.2, you can specify a row height number. To display the Row Height dialog box, click the Format button in the Cells group on the HOME tab and then click *Row Height* at the drop-down list.

Quick Steps

Change Row Height
Drag row boundary line.
OR
1. Click Format button.
2. Click *Row Height* at drop-down list.
3. Type desired height.
4. Click OK.

HINT

To change the height of all rows in a worksheet, click the Select All button and then drag a row boundary to the desired position.

HINT

Excel measures row height in points and column width in characters.

Figure 3.2 Row Height Dialog Box

Type the row height in this text box.

Project 1c **Changing Row Height**   **Part 3 of 7**

1. With **EL1-C3-P1-CMProducts.xlsx** open, change the height of row 1 by completing the following steps:
   a. Position the cell pointer in the row header on the row boundary between rows 1 and 2 until it turns into a double-headed arrow pointing up and down.
   b. Hold down the left mouse button, drag the row boundary down until *Height: 19.80 (33 pixels)* displays in the box, and then release the mouse button.
2. Change the height of rows 2 through 14 by completing the following steps:
   a. Select rows 2 through 14. To do this, position the cell pointer on the number 2 in the row header, hold down the left mouse button, drag the cell pointer to the number 14 in the row header, and then release the mouse button.
   b. Position the cell pointer on the row boundary between rows 2 and 3 until it turns into a double-headed arrow pointing up and down.

c. Hold down the left mouse button, drag the row boundary down until *Height: 16.80 (28 pixels)* displays in the box, and then release the mouse button.

3. Change the height of row 15 by completing the following steps:
   a. Make cell A15 active.
   b. Click the Format button in the Cells group on the HOME tab and then click *Row Height* at the drop-down list.
   c. At the Row Height dialog box, type 20 in the *Row height* text box and then click OK.

4. Save **EL1-C3-P1-CMProducts.xlsx**.

Inserting and Deleting Cells, Rows, and Columns ■■■■■■

When you insert cells, rows, or columns in a worksheet, all references affected by the insertion are automatically adjusted.

New data may need to be included in an existing worksheet. For example, a row or several rows of new data may need to be inserted into a worksheet or data may need to be removed from a worksheet.

Inserting Rows

After you create a worksheet, you can add (insert) rows to the worksheet. Insert a row with the Insert button in the Cells group on the HOME tab or with options at the Insert dialog box. By default, a row is inserted above the row containing the active cell. To insert a row in a worksheet, select the row below where the row is to be inserted and then click the Insert button. If you want to insert more than one row, select the number of rows in the worksheet that you want inserted and then click the Insert button.

You can also insert a row by making a cell active in the row below where the row is to be inserted, clicking the Insert button arrow, and then clicking *Insert Sheet Rows*. Another method for inserting a row is to click the Insert button arrow and then click *Insert Cells*. This displays the Insert dialog box, as shown in Figure 3.3. At the Insert dialog box, click *Entire row*. This inserts a row above the active cell.

Quick Steps

Insert a Row
Click Insert button.
OR
1. Click Insert button arrow.
2. Click *Insert Sheet Rows* at drop-down list.
OR
1. Click Insert button arrow.
2. Click *Insert Cells*.
3. Click *Entire row* in dialog box.
4. Click OK.

Insert

Figure 3.3 Insert Dialog Box

1. With **EL1-C3-P1-CMProducts.xlsx** open, insert two rows at the beginning of the worksheet by completing the following steps:

   a. Make cell A1 active.
   b. Click the Insert button arrow in the Cells group on the HOME tab.
   c. At the drop-down list that displays, click *Insert Sheet Rows*.
   d. With cell A1 active, click the Insert button arrow and then click *Insert Sheet Rows* at the drop-down list.
2. Type the text **Capstan Marine Products** in cell A1.
3. Make cell A2 active and then type **Purchasing Department**.
4. Change the height of row 1 to *42.00 (70 pixels)*.
5. Change the height of row 2 to *21.00 (35 pixels)*.
6. Insert two rows by completing the following steps:

   a. Select rows 7 and 8 in the worksheet.
   b. Click the Insert button in the Cells group on the HOME tab.
7. Type the following data in the specified cells. For the cells that contain money amounts, you do not need to type the dollar sign:
   > A7: 855-495
   > B7: 42.75
   > C7: 5
   > A8: ST039
   > B8: 12.99
   > C8: 25
8. Make cell D6 active and then use the fill handle to copy the formula down to cells D7 and D8.
9. Save **EL1-C3-P1-CMProducts.xlsx**.

Inserting Columns

Insert columns in a worksheet in much the same way as rows. Insert a column with options from the Insert button drop-down list or with options at the Insert dialog box. By default, a column is inserted immediately to the left of the column containing the active cell. To insert a column in a worksheet, make a cell active in the column immediately to the right of where the new column is to be inserted, click the Insert button arrow, and then click *Insert Sheet Columns* at the drop-down list. If you want to insert more than one column, select the number of columns in the worksheet that you want inserted, click the Insert button arrow, and then click *Insert Sheet Columns*.

You also can insert a column by making a cell active in the column immediately to the right of where the new column is to be inserted, clicking the Insert button arrow, and then clicking *Insert Cells* at the drop-down list. At the Insert dialog box that displays, click *Entire column*. This inserts an entire column immediately to the left of the active cell.

Excel includes an especially helpful and time-saving feature related to inserting columns. When you insert columns in a worksheet, all references affected by the insertion are automatically adjusted.

▼ **Quick Steps**

Insert a Column
Click Insert button.
OR
1. Click Insert button arrow.
2. Click *Insert Sheet Columns* at drop-down list.
OR
1. Click Insert button arrow.
2. Click *Insert Cells.*
3. Click *Entire column.*
4. Click OK.

1. With **EL1-C3-P1-CMProducts.xlsx** open, insert a column by completing the following steps:
   a. Click in any cell in column A.
   b. Click the Insert button arrow in the Cells group on the HOME tab and then click *Insert Sheet Columns* at the drop-down list.
2. Type the following data in the specified cell:
   A3: **Company**
   A4: **RD Manufacturing**
   A8: **Smithco, Inc.**
   A11: **Sunrise Corporation**
   A15: **Geneva Systems**
3. Make cell A1 active and then adjust the width of column A to accommodate the longest entry.
4. Insert another column by completing the following steps:
   a. Make cell B1 active.
   b. Click the Insert button arrow and then click *Insert Cells* at the drop-down list.
   c. At the Insert dialog box, click *Entire column*.
   d. Click OK.
5. Type **Date** in cell B3 and then press Enter.
6. Save **EL1-C3-P1-CMProducts.xlsx**.

Deleting Cells, Rows, or Columns

Delete

You can delete specific cells in a worksheet or rows or columns in a worksheet. To delete a row, select the row and then click the Delete button in the Cells group on the HOME tab. To delete a column, select the column and then click the Delete button. Delete a specific cell by making the cell active, clicking the Delete button arrow, and then clicking *Delete Cells* at the drop-down list. This displays the Delete dialog box, shown in Figure 3.4. At the Delete dialog box, specify what you want deleted and then click OK. You can also delete adjacent cells by selecting the cells and then displaying the Delete dialog box.

Display the Delete dialog box by positioning the cell pointer in the worksheet, clicking the right mouse button, and then clicking *Delete* at the shortcut menu.

Figure 3.4 Delete Dialog Box

Choose the option that deletes the desired cell.

Clearing Data in Cells

If you want to delete the cell contents but not the cell, make the cell active or select desired cells and then press the Delete key. A quick method for clearing the contents of a cell is to right-click in the cell and then click *Clear Contents* at the shortcut menu. Another method for deleting cell content is to make the cell active or select desired cells, click the Clear button in the Editing group on the HOME tab, and then click *Clear Contents* at the drop-down list.

With the options at the Clear button drop-down list, you can clear the contents of the cell or selected cells as well as the formatting and comments. Click the *Clear Formats* option to remove formatting from cells or selected cells while leaving the data. You can also click the *Clear All* option to clear the contents of the cell or selected cells as well as the formatting.

▼ **Quick Steps**

Clear Data in Cells
1. Select desired cells.
2. Press Delete key.
OR
1. Select desired cells.
2. Click Clear button.
3. Click *Clear Contents* at drop-down list.

Clear

Project 1f **Deleting and Clearing Rows in a Worksheet** **Part 6 of 7**

1. With **EL1-C3-P1-CMProducts.xlsx** open, delete column B in the worksheet by completing the following steps:
   a. Click in any cell in column B.
   b. Click the Delete button arrow in the Cells group on the HOME tab and then click *Delete Sheet Columns* at the drop-down list.
2. Delete row 5 by completing the following steps:
   a. Select row 5.
   b. Click the Delete button in the Cells group.
3. Clear row contents by completing the following steps:
   a. Select rows 7 and 8.
   b. Click the Clear button in the Editing group on the HOME tab and then click *Clear Contents* at the drop-down list.
4. Type the following data in the specified cell:
   A7: **Ray Enterprises**
   B7: **S894-T**
   C7: **4.99**
   D7: **30**
   B8: **B-3448**
   C8: **25.50**
   D8: **12**
5. Make cell E6 active and then copy the formula down to cells E7 and E8.
6. Save **EL1-C3-P1-CMProducts.xlsx**.

Step 1b

Step 3b

Step 4

6			855-495	$	42.75	5	$	213.75
7	Ray Enterprises		S894-T	$	4.99	30		
8			B-3448	$	25.50	12		
9			43-GB-39	$	45.00	20	$	900.00

Applying Formatting ▪■■■■■■■■■■■■■■■■■■■■■■

With many of the groups on the HOME tab, you can apply formatting to text in the active cell or selected cells. Use buttons in the Font group to apply font formatting to text and use buttons in the Alignment group to apply alignment formatting to text.

Figure 3.5 Font Group

Use buttons in the Font group to apply formatting to cells or data in cells.

Applying Font Formatting

Apply a variety of formatting to cells in a worksheet with buttons in the Font group on the HOME tab. With buttons in the Font group, shown in Figure 3.5, you can change the font, font size, and font color; bold, italicize, and underline data in cells; change the text color; and apply a border or add fill to cells.

Use the Font button in the Font group to change the font of text in a cell and use the Font Size button to specify the size for the text. Apply bold formatting to text in a cell with the Bold button, italic formatting with the Italic button, and underlining with the Underline button.

Click the Increase Font Size button and the text in the active cell or selected cells increases to the next font size in the Font Size button arrow drop-down gallery. Click the Decrease Font Size button and text in the active cell or selected cells decreases in point size.

With the Borders button in the Font group, you can insert a border on any or all sides of the active cell or any or all sides of selected cells. The name of the button changes depending on the most recent border applied to a cell or selected cells. Use the Fill Color button to insert color in the active cell or in selected cells. With the Font Color button, you can change the color of text within a cell.

Formatting with the Mini Toolbar

Double-click in a cell and then select data within the cell and the Mini toolbar displays above the selected data. The Mini toolbar also displays when you right-click in any cell. The Mini toolbar contains buttons for applying font formatting such as font, font size, and font color, as well as bold and italic formatting. Click a button on the Mini toolbar to apply formatting to selected text.

Applying Alignment Formatting

The alignment of data in cells depends on the type of data entered. Enter words or text combined with numbers in a cell and the text is aligned at the left edge of the cell. Enter numbers in a cell and the numbers are aligned at the right side of the cell. Use options in the Alignment group to align text at the left, center, or right side of the cell; align text at the top, center, or bottom of the cell; increase and/or decrease the indent of text; and change the orientation of text in a cell.

As you learned in Chapter 1, you can merge selected cells by clicking the Merge & Center button. If you merged cells, you can split the merged cell into the original cells by selecting the cell and then clicking the Merge & Center button. If you click the Merge & Center button arrow, a drop-down list of options displays. Click the *Merge & Center* option to merge all of the selected cells and change to center cell alignment. Click the *Merge Across* option to merge each row of the selected cells. For example, if you select three cells and two rows, clicking the *Merge Across* option will merge the three cells in the first row and merge the three cells in the second row so you end up with two cells. Click the *Merge Cells* option to merge all selected cells but not change to center cell alignment. Use the last option, *Unmerge Cells* to split cells that were previously merged. If you select and merge cells containing data, only the data in the upper left cell will remain. Data in any other cells in the merged cells is deleted.

Click the Orientation button to rotate data in a cell. Click the Orientation button and a drop-down list displays with options for rotating text in a cell. If data typed in a cell is longer than the cell, it overlaps the next cell to the right. If you want data to remain in a cell and wrap to the next line within the same cell, click the Wrap Text button in the Alignment group.

Orientation

Wrap Text

Project 1g   **Applying Font and Alignment Formatting**   **Part 7 of 7**

1. With **EL1-C3-P1-CMProducts.xlsx** open, make cell B1 active and then click the Wrap Text button in the Alignment group on the HOME tab. (This wraps the company name within the cell.)
2. Select cells B1 through C2, click the Merge & Center button arrow in the Alignment group on the HOME tab, and then click *Merge Across* at the drop-down list.
3. After looking at the merged cells, you decide to merge additional cells and horizontally and vertically center text in the cells by completing the following steps:
   a. With cells B1 through C2 selected, click the Merge & Center button arrow and then click *Unmerge Cells* at the drop-down list.
   b. Select cells A1 through E2.
   c. Click the Merge & Center button arrow and then click the *Merge Across* option at the drop-down list.
   d. Click the Middle Align button in the Alignment group and then click the Center button.

4. Rotate text in the third row by completing the following steps:
   a. Select cells A3 through E3.
   b. Click the Orientation button in the Alignment group and then click *Angle Counterclockwise* at the drop-down list.
   c. After looking at the rotated text, you decide to return the orientation back to horizontal by clicking the Undo button on the Quick Access toolbar.
5. Change the font, font size, and font color for text in specific cells by completing the following steps:
   a. Make cell A1 active.
   b. Click the Font button arrow in the Font group, scroll down the drop-down gallery, and then click *Bookman Old Style*.
   c. Click the Font Size button arrow in the Font group and then click *22* at the drop-down gallery.

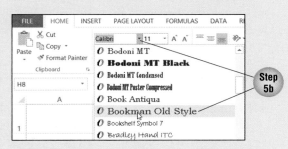

d. Click the Font Color button arrow and then click the *Dark Blue* option (ninth option in the *Standard Colors* section).

6. Make cell A2 active and then complete steps similar to those in Step 5 to change the font to Bookman Old Style, the font size to 16 points, and the font color to Dark Blue.

7. Select cells A3 through E3 and then click the Center button in the Alignment group.

8. With cells A3 through E3 still selected, click the Bold button in the Font group and then click the Italic button.

9. Select cells A3 through E18 and then change the font to Bookman Old Style.

10. Use the Mini toolbar to apply formatting to selected data by completing the following steps:
    a. Double-click in cell A4.
    b. Select the letters *RD*. (This displays the Mini toolbar above the selected word.)
    c. Click the Increase Font Size button on the Mini toolbar.
    d. Double-click in cell A14.
    e. Select the word *Geneva* and then click the Italic button on the Mini toolbar.

11. Adjust columns A through E to accommodate the longest entry in each column. To do this, select columns A through E and then double-click any selected column boundary.

12. Select cells D4 through D17 and then click the Center button in the Alignment group.

13. Add a double-line bottom border to cell A2 by completing the following steps:
    a. Make cell A2 active.
    b. Click the Borders button arrow in the Font group. (The name of this button varies depending on the last option selected.)
    c. Click the *Bottom Double Border* option at the drop-down list.

14. Add a single-line bottom border to cells A3 through E3 by completing the following steps:
    a. Select cells A3 through E3.
    b. Click the Borders button arrow and then click the *Bottom Border* option.

15. Apply fill color to specific cells by completing the following steps:
    a. Select cells A1 through E3.
    b. Click the Fill Color button arrow in the Font group.
    c. Click the *Blue, Accent 5, Lighter 80%* color option (ninth column, second row in the *Theme Colors* section).

16. Select cells C5 through C17 and then click the Comma Style button.

17. Select cells E5 through E17 and then click the Comma Style button.

18. Save, print, and then close **EL1-C3-P1-CMProducts.xlsx**.

Project 2   Apply a Theme to a Payroll Worksheet   1 Part

You will open a workbook containing a worksheet with payroll information and then insert text, apply formatting to cells and cell contents, apply a theme, and then change the theme font and colors.

Applying a Theme ■■■■■■■■■■■■■■■■■■■■■■■■■■■■

Excel provides a number of themes you can use to format text and cells in a worksheet. A ***theme*** is a set of formatting choices that includes a color theme (a set of colors), a font theme (a set of heading and body text fonts), and an effects theme (a set of lines and fill effects). To apply a theme, click the PAGE LAYOUT tab and then click the Themes button in the Themes group. At the drop-down gallery that displays, click the desired theme. Position the mouse pointer over a theme and the ***live preview*** feature will display the worksheet with the theme formatting applied. With the live preview feature, you can see how the theme formatting affects your worksheet before you make your final choice.

H I N T

Apply a theme to give your worksheet a professional look.

Themes

Project 2   Applying a Theme   Part 1 of 1

1. Open **SBAPayroll.xlsx** and then save it with Save As and name it **EL1-C3-P2-SBAPayroll**.
2. Make cell G4 active and then insert a formula that calculates the amount of social security tax. (Multiply the gross pay amount in cell E4 with the social security rate in cell H11; you will need to use the mixed cell reference H$11 when writing the formula.)
3. Copy the formula in cell G4 down to cells G5 through G9.
4. Make H4 the active cell and then insert a formula that calculates the net pay (gross pay minus withholding and social security tax).
5. Copy the formula in cell H4 down to cells H5 through H9.
6. Increase the height of row 1 to 36.00 points.
7. Make cell A1 active, click the Middle Align button in the Alignment group, click the Font Size button arrow, click *18* at the drop-down list, and then click the Bold button.
8. Type **Stanton & Barnett Associates** in cell A1.
9. Select cells A2 through H3 and then click the Bold button in the Font group.
10. Apply a theme and customize the font and colors by completing the following steps:
    a. Make cell A1 active.
    b. Click the PAGE LAYOUT tab.
    c. Click the Themes button in the Themes group and then click *Wisp* at the drop-down gallery. (You might want to point the mouse to individual themes to see how each theme's formatting affects the worksheet.)

d. Click the Colors button in the Themes group and then click *Red Orange* at the drop-down gallery.
e. Click the Fonts button in the Themes group, scroll down the drop-down gallery, and then click *TrebuchetMS*.

11. Select columns A through H and adjust the width of the columns to accommodate the longest entries.
12. Save, print, and then close **EL1-C3-P2-SBAPayroll.xlsx**.

Project 3   Format an Invoices Worksheet   2 Parts

You will open a workbook containing an invoice worksheet and apply number formatting to numbers in cells.

Formatting Numbers ■■■■■■■■■■■■■■■■■■■■■■■■■

Numbers in a cell, by default, are aligned at the right and decimals and commas do not display unless they are typed in the cell. Change the format of numbers with buttons in the Number group on the HOME tab or with options at the Format Cells dialog box with the Number tab selected.

Formatting Numbers Using Number Group Buttons

The format symbols you can use to format numbers include a percent sign (%), comma (,), and dollar sign ($). For example, if you type the number *$45.50* in a cell, Excel automatically applies currency formatting to the number. If you type *45%*, Excel automatically applies percent formatting to the number. The Number group on the HOME tab contains five buttons you can use to format numbers in cells. You learned about these buttons in Chapter 1.

Specify the formatting for numbers in cells in a worksheet before typing the numbers or format existing numbers in a worksheet. The Increase Decimal and Decrease Decimal buttons in the Number group on the HOME tab will change the number of places after the decimal point for existing numbers only.

The Number group on the HOME tab also contains the Number Format button. Click the Number Format button arrow and a drop-down list displays of common number formats. Click the desired format at the drop-down list to apply the number formatting to the cell or selected cells.

General	▾

Number Format

Project 3a **Formatting Numbers with Buttons in the Number Group** Part 1 of 2

1. Open **RPInvoices.xlsx**.
2. Save the workbook with Save As and name it **EL1-C3-P3-RPInvoices**.
3. Make the following changes to column widths:
   a. Change the width of column C to 17.00 characters.
   b. Change the width of column D to 10.00 characters.
   c. Change the width of column E to 7.00 characters.
   d. Change the width of column F to 12.00 characters.
4. Select row 1 and then click the Insert button in the Cells group on the HOME tab.
5. Change the height of row 1 to 42.00 points.
6. Select cells A1 through F1 and then make the following changes:
   a. Click the Merge & Center button in the Alignment group on the HOME tab.
   b. With cell A1 active, change the font size to 24 points.
   c. Click the Fill Color button arrow in the Font group and then click *Green, Accent 6, Lighter 80%* (last column, second row in the *Theme Colors* section).
   d. Click the Borders button arrow in the Font group and then click the *Top and Thick Bottom Border* option.
   e. With cell A1 active, type **REAL PHOTOGRAPHY** and then press Enter.

7. Change the height of row 2 to 24.00 points.
8. Select cells A2 through F2 and then make the following changes:
   a. Click the Merge & Center button in the Alignment group.
   b. With cell A2 active, change the font size to 18 points.
   c. Click the Fill Color button in the Font group. (This will fill the cell with green color.)
   d. Click the Borders button arrow in the Font group and then click the *Bottom Border* option.

9. Make the following changes to row 3:
   a. Change the height of row 3 to 18.00 points.
   b. Select cells A3 through F3, click the Bold button in the Font group, and then click the Center button in the Alignment group.
   c. With the cells still selected, click the Borders button arrow and then click the *Bottom Border* option.

10. Make the following number formatting changes:
   a. Select cells E4 through E16 and then click the Percent Style button in the Number group on the HOME tab.
   b. With the cells still selected, click once on the Increase Decimal button in the Number group. (The percentages should include one place after the decimal point.)

Step 10a   Step 10b

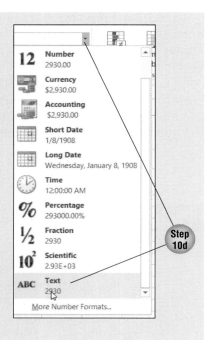

Step 10d

   c. Select cells A4 through B16.
   d. Click the Number Format button arrow, scroll down the drop-down list, and then click *Text*.
   e. With cells A4 through B16 still selected, click the Center button in the Alignment group.
11. Save **EL1-C3-P3-RPInvoices.xlsx**.

Formatting Numbers Using the Format Cells Dialog Box

Along with buttons in the Number group, you can format numbers with options at the Format Cells dialog box with the Number tab selected, as shown in Figure 3.6. Display this dialog box by clicking the Number group dialog box launcher or by clicking the Number Format button arrow and then clicking *More Number Formats* at the drop-down list. The left side of the dialog box displays

Figure 3.6 Format Cells Dialog Box with Number Tab Selected

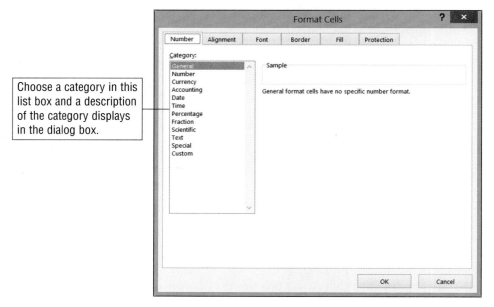

Choose a category in this list box and a description of the category displays in the dialog box.

number categories with a default category of *General*. At this setting, no specific formatting is applied to numbers except right alignment in the cells. The other number categories are described in Table 3.1.

Table 3.1 Number Categories at the Format Cells Dialog Box

Click this category	To apply this number formatting
Number	Specify the number of places after the decimal point and whether a thousand separator should be used; choose the display of negative numbers; right-align numbers in the cell.
Currency	Apply general monetary values; add a dollar sign as well as commas and decimal points, if needed; right-align numbers in the cell.
Accounting	Line up the currency symbols and decimal points in a column; add a dollar sign and two places after the decimal point; right-align numbers in the cell.
Date	Display the date as a date value; specify the type of formatting desired by clicking an option in the *Type* list box; right-align the date in the cell.
Time	Display the time as a time value; specify the type of formatting desired by clicking an option in the *Type* list box; right-align the time in the cell.
Percentage	Multiply the cell value by 100 and display the result with a percent symbol; add a decimal point followed by two places by default; change the number of digits with the *Decimal places* option; right-align numbers in the cell.
Fraction	Specify how a fraction displays in the cell by clicking an option in the *Type* list box; right-align a fraction in the cell.
Scientific	Use for very large or very small numbers; use the letter *E* to tell Excel to move the decimal point a specified number of places.
Text	Treat a number in the cell as text; the number is displayed in the cell exactly as typed.
Special	Choose a number type, such as *Zip Code*, *Phone Number*, or *Social Security Number*, in the *Type* option list box; useful for tracking list and database values.
Custom	Specify a numbering type by choosing an option in the *Type* list box.

Project 3b **Formatting Numbers at the Format Cells Dialog Box** Part 2 of 2

1. With **EL1-C3-P3-PRInvoices.xlsx** open, make cell F4 active, insert the formula =(D4*E4)+D4, and then press Enter.
2. Make cell F4 active and then copy the formula down to cells F5 through F16.
3. Apply accounting formatting by completing the following steps:
   a. Select cells D4 through D16.
   b. Click the Number group dialog box launcher.

Step 3b

c. At the Format Cells dialog box with the Number tab selected, click *Accounting* in the *Category* list box.

d. Make sure a *2* displays in the *Decimal places* option box and a *$* (dollar sign) displays in the *Symbol* option box.

e. Click OK.

4. Apply accounting formatting to cells F4 through F16 by completing actions similar to those in Step 3.

5. Save, print, and then close **EL1-C3-P3-RPInvoices.xlsx**.

Project 4 Format a Company Budget Worksheet   6 Parts

You will open a workbook containing a company budget worksheet and then apply formatting to cells with options at the Format Cells dialog box, use the Format Painter to apply formatting, and hide and unhide rows and columns in the worksheet.

Formatting Cells Using the Format Cells Dialog Box ■■■

In the previous section, you learned how to format numbers with options at the Format Cells dialog box with the Number tab selected. This dialog box also contains a number of other tabs you can select to format cells.

Aligning and Indenting Data

Align and indent data in cells using buttons in the Alignment group on the HOME tab or with options at the Format Cells dialog box with the Alignment tab selected, as shown in Figure 3.7. Display this dialog box by clicking the Alignment group dialog box launcher.

In the *Orientation* section, you can choose to rotate data. A portion of the *Orientation* section shows points on an arc. Click a point on the arc to rotate the text along that point. You can also type a rotation degree in the *Degrees* measurement box. Type a positive number to rotate selected text from the lower left to the upper right of the cell. Type a negative number to rotate selected text from the upper left to the lower right of the cell.

If data typed in a cell is longer than the cell, it overlaps the next cell to the right. If you want data to remain in a cell and wrap to the next line within the same cell, insert a check mark in the *Wrap text* check box in the *Text control* section of the dialog box. Insert a check mark in the *Shrink to fit* check box if you want to reduce the size of the text font so all selected data fits within the column. Insert a check mark in the *Merge cells* check box to combine two or more selected cells into a single cell.

If you want to enter data on more than one line within a cell, enter the data on the first line and then press Alt + Enter. Pressing Alt + Enter moves the insertion point to the next line within the same cell.

Figure 3.7 Format Cells Dialog Box with Alignment Tab Selected

Specify horizontal and vertical alignment with options in this section.

Use options in this section to control how text fits in a cell.

Rotate text in a cell by clicking a point on the arc or by entering a number in the *Degrees* measurement box.

Project 4a | **Aligning and Rotating Data in Cells** | Part 1 of 6

1. Open **HBCJobs.xlsx**.
2. Save the workbook with Save As and name it **EL1-C3-P4-HBCJobs**.
3. Make the following changes to the worksheet:
   a. Insert a new row at the beginning of the worksheet.
   b. Change the height of row 1 to 66.00 points.
   c. Merge and center cells A1 through E1.
   d. Type **Harris & Briggs** in cell A1 and then press Alt + Enter. (This moves the insertion point down to the next line in the same cell.)
   e. Type **Construction** and then press Enter.
   f. With cell A2 active, type **Preferred**, press Alt + Enter, type **Customer**, and then press Enter.
   g. Change the width of column A to 22.00 characters.
   h. Change the width of column B to 7.00 characters.
   i. Change the widths of columns C, D, and E to 10.00 characters.
4. Change number formatting for specific cells by completing the following steps:
   a. Select cells C3 through E11.
   b. Click the Number group dialog box launcher.
   c. At the Format Cells dialog box with the Number tab selected, click *Accounting* in the *Category* list box.
   d. Click the down-pointing arrow at the right side of the *Decimal places* measurement box until *0* displays.
   e. Make sure a *$* (dollar sign) displays in the *Symbol* option box.
   f. Click OK.
5. Make cell E3 active and then insert the formula =D3-C3. Copy this formula down to cells E4 through E11.

6. Change the orientation of data in cells by completing the following steps:
   a. Select cells B2 through E2.
   b. Click the Alignment group dialog box launcher.
   c. At the Format Cells dialog box with the Alignment tab selected, select *0* in the *Degrees* measurement box and then type *45*.
   d. Click OK.

Step 6c

7. Change the vertical alignment of text in cells by completing the following steps:
   a. Select cells A1 through E2.
   b. Click the Alignment group dialog box launcher.
   c. At the Format Cells dialog box with the Alignment tab selected, click the down-pointing arrow at the right side of the *Vertical* option box.
   d. Click *Center* at the drop-down list.
   e. Click OK.

Step 7c

Step 7d

8. Change the horizontal alignment of text in cells by completing the following steps:
   a. Select cells A2 through E2.
   b. Click the Alignment group dialog box launcher.
   c. At the Format Cells dialog box with the Alignment tab selected, click the down-pointing arrow at the right side of the *Horizontal* option box.
   d. Click *Center* at the drop-down list.
   e. Click OK.

Step 8c

Step 8d

9. Change the horizontal alignment and indent of text in cells by completing the following steps:
   a. Select cells B3 through B11.
   b. Click the Alignment group dialog box launcher.
   c. At the Format Cells dialog box with the Alignment tab selected, click the down-pointing arrow at the right side of the *Horizontal* option box and then click *Right (Indent)* at the drop-down list.
   d. Click once on the up-pointing arrow at the right side of the *Indent* measurement box. (This displays *1*.)
   e. Click OK.

Step 9d

Step 9c

10. Save **EL1-C3-P4-HBCJobs.xlsx**.

Changing the Font at the Format Cells Dialog Box

As you learned earlier in this chapter, the Font group on the HOME tab contains buttons for applying font formatting to data in cells. You can also change the font for data in cells with options at the Format Cells dialog box with the Font tab selected, as shown in Figure 3.8. At the Format Cells dialog box with the Font tab selected, you can change the font, font style, font size, and font color. You can also change the underlining method and add effects such as superscript and subscript. Click the Font group dialog box launcher to display this dialog box.

Figure 3.8 Format Cells Dialog Box with Font Tab Selected

Choose a typeface in this list box. Use the scroll bar at the right side of the box to view available typefaces.

Choose a typestyle in this list box. The options in the box may vary depending on the selected typeface.

Choose a type size in this list box or select the current measurement in the top box and then type the desired measurement.

Apply font effects to text by inserting a check mark in the check box next to the desired effect.

This area displays a preview of the text with the selected formatting applied.

Project 4b **Applying Font Formatting at the Format Cells Dialog Box** Part 2 of 6

1. With **EL1-C3-P4-HBCJobs.xlsx** open, change the font and font color by completing the following steps:
   a. Select cells A1 through E11.
   b. Click the Font group dialog box launcher.
   c. At the Format Cells dialog box with the Font tab selected, click *Garamond* in the *Font* list box. (You will need to scroll down the list to make this font visible.)
   d. Click *12* in the *Size* list box.
   e. Click the down-pointing arrow at the right of the *Color* option box.
   f. At the palette of color choices that displays, click the *Dark Red* color (first option in the *Standard Colors* section).
   g. Click OK to close the dialog box.
2. Make cell A1 active and then change the font to 24-point Garamond and apply bold formatting.
3. Select cells A2 through E2 and then apply bold formatting.
4. Save and then print **EL1-C3-P4-HBCJobs.xlsx**.

Step 1c

Step 1d

Step 1e

Step 1f

Step 1g

Adding Borders to Cells

⬇ Quick Steps

Add Borders to Cells
1. Select cells.
2. Click Borders button arrow.
3. Click desired border.
OR
1. Select cells.
2. Click Borders button arrow.
3. Click *More Borders.*
4. Use options in dialog box to apply desired border.
5. Click OK.

The gridlines that display in a worksheet do not print. As you learned earlier in this chapter, you can use the Borders button in the Font group to add borders to cells that will print. You can also add borders to cells with options at the Format Cells dialog box with the Border tab selected, as shown in Figure 3.9. Display this dialog box by clicking the Borders button arrow in the Font group and then clicking *More Borders* at the drop-down list.

With options in the *Presets* section, you can remove borders with the *None* option, add only outside borders with the *Outline* option, or click the *Inside* option to add borders to the inside of selected cells. In the *Border* section of the dialog box, specify the side of the cell or selected cells to which you want to apply a border. Choose the style of line desired for the border with the options that display in the *Style* list box. Add color to border lines with choices from the color palette that displays when you click the down-pointing arrow at the right side of the *Color* option box.

Figure 3.9 Format Cells Dialog Box with Border Tab Selected

Click the sides, top, and/or bottom of this preview area to insert or remove one or more borders.

Project 4c   **Adding Borders to Cells**   **Part 3 of 6**

1. With **EL1-C3-P4-HBCJobs.xlsx** open, remove the 45 degrees orientation you applied in Project 4a by completing the following steps:
   a. Select cells B2 through E2.
   b. Click the Alignment group dialog box launcher.
   c. At the Format Cells dialog box with the Alignment tab selected, select *45* in the *Degrees* measurement box and then type **0**.
   d. Click OK.
2. Change the height of row 2 to 33.00 points.

Step 1c

3. Add a thick, Dark Red border line to cells by completing the following steps:
   a. Select cells A1 through E11 (cells containing data).
   b. Click the Borders button arrow in the Font group and then click the *More Borders* option at the drop-down list.
   c. At the Format Cells dialog box with the Border tab selected, click the down-pointing arrow at the right side of the *Color* option box and then click the *Dark Red* color (first option in the *Standard Colors* section).
   d. Click the thick, single-line option in the *Style* list box in the *Line* section (sixth option in the second column).
   e. Click the *Outline* option in the *Presets* section.
   f. Click OK.

4. Add borders above and below cells by completing the following steps:
   a. Select cells A2 through E2.
   b. Click the Borders button arrow in the Font group and then click *More Borders* at the drop-down list.
   c. At the Format Cells dialog box with the Border tab selected, make sure the color is still Dark Red.
   d. Make sure the thick, single-line option is still selected in the *Style* list box in the *Line* section.
   e. Click the top border of the sample cell in the *Border* section of the dialog box.
   f. Click the double-line option in the *Style* list box (last option in the second column).
   g. Click the bottom border of the sample cell in the *Border* section of the dialog box.
   h. Click OK.
5. Save **EL1-C3-P4-HBCJobs.xlsx**.

Adding Fill and Shading to Cells

▼ **Quick Steps**

Add Fill and Shading to Cells
1. Select cells.
2. Click Fill Color button arrow.
3. Click desired color.
OR
1. Select cells.
2. Click Format button.
3. Click *Format Cells* at drop-down list.
4. Click Fill tab.
5. Use options in dialog box to apply desired shading.
6. Click OK.

Repeat Last Action
1. Apply formatting.
2. Move to desired location.
3. Press F4 or Ctrl + Y.

To enhance the visual display of cells and data within cells, consider adding fill and/or shading to cells. As you learned earlier in this chapter, you can add fill color to cells with the Fill Color button in the Font group. You can also add fill color and/or shading to cells in a worksheet with options at the Format Cells dialog box with the Fill tab selected, as shown in Figure 3.10. Display the Format Cells dialog box by clicking the Format button in the Cells group and then clicking *Format Cells* at the drop-down list. You can also display the dialog box by clicking the Font group, Alignment group, or Number group dialog box launcher. At the Format Cells dialog box, click the Fill tab or right-click in a cell and then click *Format Cells* at the shortcut menu.

Choose a fill color for a cell or selected cells by clicking a color choice in the *Background Color* section. To add shading to a cell or selected cells, click the Fill Effects button and then click the desired shading style at the Fill Effects dialog box.

Repeating the Last Action

If you want to apply other types of formatting, such as number, border, or shading formatting to other cells in a worksheet, use the Repeat command by pressing F4 or Ctrl + Y. The Repeat command repeats the last action performed.

Figure 3.10 Format Cells Dialog Box with Fill Tab Selected

Click a color in this color palette to apply a background color to a cell or selected cells.

Click this button to display the Fill Effects dialog box where you can choose a shading style.

Apply a pattern style and/or color with these two options.

1. With **EL1-C3-P4-HBCJobs.xlsx** open, add fill color to cell A1 and repeat the formatting by completing the following steps:
   a. Make cell A1 active.
   b. Click the Format button in the Cells group and then click *Format Cells* at the drop-down list.
   c. At the Format Cells dialog box, click the Fill tab.
   d. Click the light gold color in the *Background Color* section (eighth column, second row—see image below).

   e. Click OK.
   f. Select cells A2 through E2 and then press the F4 function key. (This repeats the light gold fill.)
2. Select row 2, insert a new row, and then change the height of the new row to 12.00 points.
3. Add shading to cells by completing the following steps:
   a. Select cells A2 through E2.
   b. Click the Format button in the Cells group and then click *Format Cells* at the drop-down list.
   c. At the Format Cells dialog box, if necessary, click the Fill tab.
   d. Click the Fill Effects button.
   e. At the Fill Effects dialog box, click the down-pointing arrow at the right side of the *Color 2* option box and then click *Gold, Accent 4* in the *Theme Colors* section (eighth column, top row).
   f. Click OK to close the Fill Effects dialog box.
   g. Click OK to close the Format Cells dialog box.
4. Save **EL1-C3-P4-HBCJobs.xlsx**.

Formatting with Format Painter ■■■■■■■■■■■■■■■

Quick Steps

Format with Format Painter
1. Select cells with desired formatting.
2. Double-click Format Painter button.
3. Select desired cells.
4. Click Format Painter button.

Format
Painter

Use the Format Painter button in the Clipboard group on the HOME tab to copy formatting to different locations in the worksheet. To use the Format Painter button, make active a cell or selected cells that contain the desired formatting, click the Format Painter button, and then click in the cell or selected cells to which you want the formatting applied.

When you click the Format Painter button, the mouse pointer displays with a paintbrush attached. If you want to apply formatting a single time, click the Format Painter button once. If you want to apply the formatting in more than one location in the worksheet, double-click the Format Painter button, selected the desired cells, and then click the Format Painter button to turn off the feature.

Project 4e   **Formatting with Format Painter**   Part 5 of 6

1. With **EL1-C3-P4-HBCJobs.xlsx** open, select cells A5 through E5.
2. Click the Font group dialog box launcher.
3. At the Format Cells dialog box, click the Fill tab.
4. Click the light green color in the *Background Color* section (last column, second row).
5. Click OK to close the dialog box.
6. Use Format Painter to "paint" formatting to rows by completing the following steps:
   a. With cells A5 through E5 selected, double-click the Format Painter button in the Clipboard group.
   b. Select cells A7 through E7.
   c. Select cells A9 through E9.
   d. Select cells A11 through E11.
   e. Turn off Format Painter by clicking the Format Painter button.
7. Save and then print **EL1-C3-P4-HBCJobs.xlsx**.

Step 3

Step 4

Hiding and Unhiding Columns and Rows ■■■■■■■■■■■

Quick Steps

Hide Columns
1. Select columns.
2. Click Format button.
3. Point to *Hide & Unhide*.
4. Click *Hide Columns*.

Hide Rows
1. Select rows.
2. Click Format button.
3. Point to *Hide & Unhide*.
4. Click *Hide Rows*.

If a worksheet contains columns and/or rows of sensitive data or data that you are not using or do not want to view, consider hiding the columns and/or rows. To hide columns in a worksheet, select the columns to be hidden, click the Format button in the Cells group on the HOME tab, point to *Hide & Unhide*, and then click *Hide Columns*. To hide selected rows, click the Format button in the Cells group, point to *Hide & Unhide*, and then click *Hide Rows*. To make a hidden column visible, select the column to the left and the column to the right of the hidden column, click the Format button in the Cells group, point to *Hide & Unhide*, and then click *Unhide Columns*. To make a hidden row visible, select the row above and the row below the hidden row, click the Format button in the Cells group, point to *Hide & Unhide*, and then click *Unhide Rows*.

If the first row or column is hidden, use the Go To feature to make the row or column visible. To do this, click the Find & Select button in the Editing group on the HOME tab and then click *Go To* at the drop-down list. At the Go To dialog box, type *A1* in the *Reference* text box and then click OK. At the worksheet, click the Format button in the Cells group, point to *Hide & Unhide*, and then click *Unhide Columns* or click *Unhide Rows*.

You can also unhide columns or rows using the mouse. If a column or row is hidden, the light gray boundary line in the column or row header displays as a slightly thicker gray line. To unhide a column, position the mouse pointer on the slightly thicker gray line that displays in the column header until the mouse pointer changes into a left-and-right-pointing arrow with a double line in the middle. (Make sure the mouse pointer displays with two lines between the arrows. If a single line displays, you will simply change the size of the visible column.) Hold down the left mouse button, drag to the right until the column displays at the desired width, and then release the mouse button. Unhide a row in a similar manner. Position the mouse pointer on the slightly thicker gray line in the row header until the mouse pointer changes into an up-and-down-pointing arrow with a double line in the middle. Drag down to display the row and then release the mouse button. If two or more adjacent columns or rows are hidden, you will need to unhide each column or row separately.

HINT
Set the column width to zero and the column is hidden. Set the row height to zero and the row is hidden.

Project 4f **Hiding and Unhiding Columns and Rows**   **Part 6 of 6**

1. With **EL1-C3-P4-HBCJobs.xlsx** open, hide the row for Linstrom Enterprises and the row for Summit Services by completing the following steps:
   a. Click the row 7 header to select the entire row.
   b. Hold down the Ctrl key and then click the row 11 header to select the entire row.
   c. Click the Format button in the Cells group on the HOME tab, point to *Hide & Unhide*, and then click *Hide Rows*.
2. Hide the column containing the actual amounts by completing the following steps:
   a. Click in cell D3 to make it the active cell.
   b. Click the Format button in the Cells group, point to *Hide & Unhide*, and then click *Hide Columns*.
3. Save and then print **EL1-C3-P4-HBCJobs.xlsx**.
4. Unhide the rows by completing the following steps:
   a. Select rows 6 through 12.
   b. Click the Format button in the Cells group, point to *Hide & Unhide*, and then click *Unhide Rows*.
   c. Click in cell A4.
5. Unhide column D by completing the following steps:
   a. Position the mouse pointer on the thicker gray line that displays between columns C and E in the column header until the pointer turns into a left-and-right-pointing arrow with a double line in the middle.
   b. Hold down the left mouse button, drag to the right until *Width: 9.56 (93 pixels)* displays in a box above the mouse pointer, and then release the mouse button.

6. Save, print, and then close **EL1-C3-P4-HBCJobs.xlsx**.

Chapter Summary

- Change column width using the mouse on column boundaries or with options at the Column Width dialog box.
- Change row height using the mouse on row boundaries or with options at the Row Height dialog box.
- Insert a row in a worksheet with the Insert button in the Cells group on the HOME tab or with options at the Insert dialog box.
- Insert a column in a worksheet with the Insert button in the Cells group or with options at the Insert dialog box.
- Delete a specific cell by clicking the Delete button arrow and then clicking *Delete Cells* at the drop-down list. At the Delete dialog box, specify if you want to delete just the cell or an entire row or column.
- Delete a selected row(s) or column(s) by clicking the Delete button in the Cells group.
- Delete cell contents by pressing the Delete key or clicking the Clear button in the Editing group on the HOME tab and then clicking *Clear Contents* at the drop-down list.
- Apply font formatting with buttons in the Font group on the HOME tab.
- Use the Mini toolbar to apply font formatting to selected data in a cell.
- Apply alignment formatting with buttons in the Alignment group on the HOME tab.
- Use the Themes button in the Themes group on the PAGE LAYOUT tab to apply a theme to cells in a worksheet that applies formatting such as color, font, and effects. Use the other buttons in the Themes group to customize the theme.
- Format numbers in cells with buttons in the Number group on the HOME tab or with options at the Format Cells dialog box with the Number tab selected.
- Apply formatting to cells in a worksheet with options at the Format Cells dialog box. This dialog box includes the following tabs for formatting cells: Number, Alignment, Font, Border, and Fill.
- Press F4 or Ctrl + Y to repeat the last action performed.
- Use the Format Painter button in the Clipboard group on the HOME tab to apply formatting to different locations in a worksheet.
- Hide selected columns or rows in a worksheet by clicking the Format button in the Cells group on the HOME tab, pointing to *Hide & Unhide*, and then clicking *Hide Columns* or *Hide Rows*.
- To make a hidden column visible, select the columns to the left and right, click the Format button in the Cells group, point to *Hide & Unhide*, and then click *Unhide Columns*.
- To make a hidden row visible, select the rows above and below, click the Format button in the Cells group, point to *Hide & Unhide*, and then click *Unhide Rows*.

Commands Review

FEATURE	RIBBON TAB, GROUP	BUTTON	KEYBOARD SHORTCUT
bold text	HOME, Font	**B**	Ctrl + B
borders	HOME, Font		
bottom-align (in row)	HOME, Alignment		
center-align (in column)	HOME, Alignment		
clear cell or cell contents	HOME, Editing		
decrease font size	HOME, Font	A˅	
decrease indent	HOME, Alignment		Ctrl + Alt + Shift + Tab
delete cells, rows, or columns	HOME, Cells		
fill color	Home, Font		
font	HOME, Font	Calibri	
font color	Home, Font	A˅	
font size	HOME, Font	11	
format	HOME, Cells		
Format Painter	HOME, Clipboard		
increase font size	HOME, Font	A˄	
increase indent	HOME, Alignment		Ctrl + Alt + Tab
insert cells, rows, or columns	HOME, Cells		
italicize text	HOME, Font	*I*	Ctrl + I
left-align (in column)	HOME, Alignment		
merge and center cells	HOME, Alignment		
middle-align (in row)	HOME, Alignment		
number format	HOME, Number	General	
orientation	HOME, Alignment		
repeat last action			F4 or Ctrl + Y
right-align (in column)	HOME, Alignment		
themes	PAGE LAYOUT, Themes		

FEATURE	RIBBON TAB, GROUP	BUTTON	KEYBOARD SHORTCUT
top-align (in row)	HOME, Alignment	≡	
underline text	HOME, Font	U ▾	Ctrl + U
wrap text	HOME, Alignment	🗏	

Concepts Check   Test Your Knowledge

Completion: In the space provided at the right, indicate the correct term, symbol, or command.

1. By default, a column is inserted on this side of the column containing the active cell.

2. To delete a row, select the row and then click the Delete button in this group on the HOME tab.

3. Use the options at this button's drop-down list to clear the contents of the cell or selected cells.

4. Use this button to insert color in the active cell or selected cells.

5. Select data in a cell and this displays above the selected text.

6. By default, numbers are aligned at this side of a cell.

7. Click this button in the Alignment group on the HOME tab to rotate data in a cell.

8. The Themes button is located on this tab.

9. If you type a number with a dollar sign, such as *$50.25*, Excel automatically applies this formatting to the number.

10. If you type a number with a percent sign, such as *25%*, Excel automatically applies this formatting to the number.

11. Align and indent data in cells using buttons in the Alignment group on the HOME tab or with options at this dialog box with the Alignment tab selected.

12. You can repeat the last action performed by pressing Ctrl + Y or this function key.

13. The Format Painter button is located in this group on the HOME tab.

14. To hide a column, select the column, click this button in the Cells group on the HOME tab, point to *Hide & Unhide*, and then click *Hide Columns*.

Skills Check   Assess Your Performance

Assessment

1   FORMAT A SALES WORKSHEET

1. Open **NSPSales.xlsx**.
2. Save the workbook with Save As and name it **EL1-C3-A1-NSPSales**.
3. Change the width of columns as follows:
   - Column A: 14.00
   - Columns B–E: 10.00
4. Select row 2 and then insert a new row.
5. Merge and center cells A2 through E2.
6. Type **Sales Department** in cell A2 and then press Enter.
7. Increase the height of row 1 to 33.00 points.
8. Increase the height of row 2 to 21.00 points.
9. Increase the height of row 3 to 18.00 points.
10. Make the following formatting changes to the worksheet:
    a. Make cell A1 active, change the font size to 18 points, and turn on bold formatting.
    b. Make cell A2 active, change the font size to 14 points, and turn on bold formatting.
    c. Select cells A3 through E3, click the Bold button in the Font group, and then click the Center button in the Alignment group.
    d. Select cells A1 through E3 and change the vertical alignment to *Middle Align*.
11. Insert the following formulas in the worksheet:
    a. Insert a formula in cell D4 that adds the amounts in cells B4 and C4. Copy the formula down to cells D5 through D11.
    b. Insert a formula in cell E4 that averages the amounts in cells B4 and C4. Copy the formula down to cells E5 through E11.
12. Make the following changes to the worksheet:
    a. Select cells B4 through E4 and then apply accounting formatting with a dollar sign and no places past the decimal point.
    b. Select cells B5 through E11 and then apply comma formatting and change the number of places past the decimal point to zero.
    c. Apply the Facet theme to the worksheet.
    d. Add a double-line border outline around cells A1 through E11.
    e. Select cells A1 and A2 and then apply Blue-Gray, Text 2, Lighter 80% fill color (fourth column, second row in the *Theme Colors* section).
    f. Select cells A3 through E3 and then apply Blue-Gray, Text 2, Lighter 60% fill color (fourth column, third row in the *Theme Colors* section).
13. Save, print, and then close **EL1-C3-A1-NSPSales.xlsx**.

2 FORMAT AN OVERDUE ACCOUNTS WORKSHEET

1. Open **CCorpAccts.xlsx**.
2. Save the workbook with Save As and name it **EL1-C3-A2-CCorpAccts**.
3. Change the width of columns as follows:
   - Column A: 21.00 characters
   - Column B: 10.00 characters
   - Column C: 12.00 characters
   - Column D: 13.00 characters
   - Column E: 7.00 characters
   - Column F: 12.00 characters
4. Make cell A1 active and then insert a new row.
5. Merge and center cells A1 through F1.
6. Type **Compass Corporation** in cell A1 and then press Enter.
7. Increase the height of row 1 to 42.00 points.
8. Increase the height of row 2 to 24.00 points.
9. Make the following formatting changes to the worksheet:
   a. Select cells A1 through F11 and then change the font to 10-point Cambria.
   b. Make cell A1 active, change the font size to 24 points, and turn on bold formatting.
   c. Make cell A2 active, change the font size to 18 points, and turn on bold formatting.
   d. Select cells A3 through F3, click the Bold button in the Font group, and then click the Center button in the Alignment group.
   e. Select cell A1 and then click the Middle Align button in the Alignment group.
   f. Select cells B4 through B11 and then click the Center button in the Alignment group.
   g. Select cells E4 through E11 and then click the Center button in the Alignment group.
10. Enter a formula in cell F4 that inserts the due date (the purchase date plus the number of days in the *Terms* column). Copy the formula down to cells F5 through F11.
11. Apply the following borders and fill color:
    a. Add a thick line outline border around cells A1 through F11.
    b. Make cell A2 active and then add a double-line border at the top and the bottom of the cell.
    c. Select cells A3 through F3 and then add a single line border to the bottom of the cells.
    d. Select cells A1 and A2 and then apply Blue, Accent 1, Lighter 80% fill color (fifth column, second row in the *Theme Colors* section).
12. Save, print, and then close **EL1-C3-A2-CCorpAccts.xlsx**.

3 FORMAT A SUPPLIES AND EQUIPMENT WORKSHEET

1. Open **OEBudget.xlsx**.
2. Save the workbook with Save As and name it **EL1-C3-A3-OEBudget**.
3. Select and then merge across cells A1 through D2. *Hint: Use the* **Merge Across** *option at the Merge & Center button drop-down list.*

4. With cells A1 and A2 selected, click the Middle Align button in the Alignment group and then click the Center button.
5. Make cell A1 active and then change the font size to 22 points and turn on bold formatting.
6. Make cell A2 active and then change the font size to 12 points and turn on bold formatting.
7. Change the height of row 1 to 36.00 points.
8. Change the height of row 2 to 21.00 points.
9. Change the width of column A to 15.00 characters.
10. Select cells A3 through A17, turn on bold, and then click the Wrap Text button in the Alignment group.
11. Make cell B3 active and then apply currency formatting with no places past the decimal point.
12. Select cells C6 through C19 and then apply percentage formatting with one place past the decimal point.
13. Make cell D6 active and then type a formula that multiplies the absolute cell reference $B$3 with the percentage in cell C6. Copy the formula down to cells D7 through D19.
14. With cells D6 through D19 selected, apply currency formatting with no places past the decimal point.
15. Make cell D8 active and then clear the cell contents. Use the Repeat command, F4, to clear the contents from cells D11, D14, and D17.
16. Select cells A1 through D19, change the font to Constantia, and then change the font color to Dark Blue (in the *Standard Colors* section).
17. Add Green, Accent 6, Lighter 80% green fill color (last column, second row in the *Theme Colors* section) to the following cells: A1, A2, A5–D5, A8–D8, A11–D11, A14–D14, and A17–D17.
18. Automatically adjust the width of column B.
19. Save, print, and then close **EL1-C3-A3-OEBudget.xlsx**.

Assessment

4 FORMAT A FINANCIAL ANALYSIS WORKSHEET

1. At a blank workbook, display the Format Cells dialog box with the Alignment tab selected and then experiment with the options in the *Text control* section.
2. Open **FinAnalysis.xlsx**.
3. Save the workbook with Save As and name it **EL1-C3-A4-FinAnalysis**.
4. Make cell B9 active and then insert a formula that averages the percentages in cells B3 through B8. Copy the formula to the right to cells C9 and D9.
5. Select cells B3 through D9, display the Format Cells dialog box with the Alignment tab selected, change the horizontal alignment to *Right (Indent)* and the indent to *2*, and then close the dialog box.
6. Select cells A1 through D9 and then change the font size to 14 points.
7. Select cells B2 through D2 and then change the orientation to 45 degrees.
8. Save, print, and then close **EL1-C3-A4-FinAnalysis.xlsx**.

Visual Benchmark · Demonstrate Your Proficiency

CREATE A WORKSHEET AND INSERT FORMULAS

1. At a blank workbook, type the data in the cells indicated in Figure 3.11 but **do not** type the data in the following cells: B8:D8, B14:D14, B20:D20, B22:D22, and B25:D25. For these cells, enter the appropriate formulas so your results match what you see in the figure.
2. Apply formatting so your worksheet looks similar to the worksheet shown in Figure 3.11.
3. Save the workbook and name it **EL1-C3-VB-BTBookings**.
4. Print **EL1-C3-VB-BTBookings.xlsx**.
5. Press Ctrl + ` to turn on the display of formulas and then print the worksheet again.
6. Turn off the display of formulas and then close the workbook.

Figure 3.11 Visual Benchmark

	A	B	C	D	E
1		**Bayside Travel**			
2		**First Quarter Booking Totals**			
3		January	February	March	
4	**Los Angeles**				
5	Tours	$ 65,395	$ 62,103	$ 58,450	
6	Cruises	48,525	43,218	54,055	
7	Other	29,329	26,398	30,391	
8	**Total**	143,249	131,719	142,896	
9					
10	**San Francisco**				
11	Tours	41,438	39,493	56,461	
12	Cruises	23,147	18,530	40,530	
13	Other	18,642	14,320	17,305	
14	**Total**	83,227	72,343	114,296	
15					
16	**Toronto**				
17	Tours	50,229	42,519	52,403	
18	Cruises	49,260	41,490	39,230	
19	Other	31,322	21,579	27,430	
20	**Total**	130,811	105,588	119,063	
21					
22	TOTAL	$357,287	$309,650	$376,255	
23					
24	**Gross Profit Factor**	26%			
25	**Estimated Gross Profit**	$ 92,895	$ 80,509	$ 97,826	

Case Study   Apply Your Skills

Part 1

You are the office manager for HealthWise Fitness Center and decide to prepare an Excel worksheet that displays the various plans offered by the health club. In this worksheet, you want to include yearly dues for each plan as well as quarterly and monthly payments. Open the **HFCDues.xlsx** workbook and then save it with Save As and name it **EL1-C3-CS-HFCDues-1**. Make the following changes to the worksheet:

- Select cells B3 through D8 and then apply accounting formatting with two places past the decimal point and without dollar signs.
- Make cell B3 active and then insert *500.00*.
- Make cell B4 active and then insert a formula that adds the amount in cell B3 with the product (multiplication) of cell B3 multiplied by 10%. (The formula should look like this: **=B3+(B3*10%)**. The Economy plan is the base plan and each additional plan costs 10% more than the previous plan.)
- Copy the formula in cell B4 down to cells B5 through B8.
- Insert a formula in cell C3 that divides the amount in cell B3 by 4 and then copy the formula down to cells C4 through C8.
- Insert a formula in cell D3 that divides the amount in cell B3 by 12 and then copy the formula down to cells D4 through D8.
- Apply formatting to enhance the visual display of the worksheet.

Save and print the completed worksheet.

With **EL1-C3-CS-HFCDues-1.xlsx** open, save the workbook with Save As and name it **EL1-C3-CS-HFCDues-2** and then make the following changes:

- You have been informed that the base rate for yearly dues has increased from $500.00 to $600.00. Change this amount in cell B3 of the worksheet.
- If clients are late with their quarterly or monthly dues payments, a late fee is charged. You decide to add the late fee information to the worksheet. Insert a new column to the right of column C. Type **Late Fees** in cell D2 and also in cell F2.
- Insert a formula in cell D3 that multiplies the amount in C3 by 5%. Copy this formula down to cells D4 through D8.
- Insert a formula in cell F3 that multiplies the amount in cell E3 by 7%. Copy this formula down to cells F4 through F8. If necessary, apply accounting formatting to cells F3 through F8 with two places after the decimal point and without dollar signs.
- Select cells B3 through F3 and change the accounting formatting to include dollar signs.
- Select cells B8 through F8 and change the accounting formatting to include dollar signs.
- Apply formatting to enhance the visual display of the worksheet.

Save, print, and then close **EL1-C3-CS-HFCDues-2.xlsx**.

Prepare a payroll sheet for the employees of the fitness center using the information in Figure 3.12, and include the following information:

Insert a formula in the *Overtime Pay* column that multiples the hourly wage by the overtime rate, which is 1.5, and then multiple that amount by the number of overtime hours. (Make sure you include parentheses around the first part of the formula.)

Insert a formula in the *Weekly Salary* column that multiplies the hourly wage by the number of hours plus the overtime pay. (Make sure you include parentheses in the first part of the formula.)

Apply formatting to enhance the visual display of the worksheet. Save the workbook and name it **EL1-C3-CS-HFCPayroll**. Press Ctrl + ` to turn on the display of formulas, print the worksheet, and then turn off the display of formulas.

Make the following changes to the worksheet:

- Change the hourly wage for Amanda Turney to *$22.00*.
- Increase the hours for Daniel Joyner to *20*.
- Remove the row for Grant Baker.
- Insert a row between Jean Overmeyer and Bonnie Haddon and then type the following information in the cells in the new row: *Employee:* **McGuire, Tonya**; *Hourly Wage:* **$17.50**; *Hours:* **15**; *Overtime Hours:* **0**.

Save and then print **EL1-C3-CS-HFCPayroll.xlsx**. Press Ctrl + ` to turn on the display of formulas, print the worksheet again, and then turn off the display of formulas. Save and close **EL1-C3-CS-HFCPayroll.xlsx**.

Figure 3.12 Case Study Part 2

HealthWise Fitness Center
Weekly Payroll

Employee	Hourly Wage	Hours	Overtime Hours	Overtime Pay	Weekly Salary
Heaton, Kelly	$26.50	40	2		
Severson, Joel	$25.00	40	0		
Turney, Amanda	$20.00	15	0		
Walters, Leslie	$19.65	30	0		
Overmeyer, Jean	$18.00	20	0		
Haddon, Bonnie	$16.00	40	3		
Baker, Grant	$15.00	40	0		
Calveri, Shannon	$12.00	15	0		
Dugan, Emily	$10.50	40	4		
Joyner, Daniel	$10.50	10	0		
Lee, Alexander	$10.50	10	0		

Part 3

Your boss is interested in ordering new equipment for the health club. She is interested in ordering three elliptical machines, three recumbent bikes, and three upright bikes. She has asked you to use the Internet to research models and prices for this new equipment. She then wants you to prepare a worksheet with the information. Using the Internet, search for information about the following equipment:

- Search for elliptical machines for sale. Locate two different models and, if possible, find at least two companies that sell each model. Make a note of the company names, model numbers, and prices.
- Search for recumbent bikes for sale. Locate two different models and, if possible, find at least two companies that sell each model. Make a note of the company names, model numbers, and prices.
- Search for upright bikes for sale. Locate two different models and, if possible, find at least two companies that sell each model. Make a note of the company names, model numbers, and prices.

Using the information you found on the Internet, prepare an Excel worksheet with the following information:

- Company name
- Equipment name
- Equipment model
- Price
- A column that multiplies the price by the number required (which is 3)

Include the fitness center name, HealthWise Fitness Center, and any other information you think is necessary to the worksheet. Apply formatting to enhance the visual display of the worksheet. Save the workbook and name it **EL1-C3-CS-HFCEquip**. Print and then close **EL1-C3-CS-HFCEquip.xlsx**.

Part 4

When a prospective client contacts HealthWise about joining, you send a letter containing information about the fitness center, the plans offered, and the dues amounts. Use a letter template in Word to create a letter to send to a prospective client. (You determine the client's name and address). Copy the cells in **EL1-C3-CS-HFCDues-02.xlsx** containing data and paste them into the body of the letter. Make formatting changes to make the data readable. Save the document and name it **HFCLetter**. Print and then close **HFCLetter.docx**.

MICROSOFT EXCEL

Enhancing a Worksheet

CHAPTER 4

PERFORMANCE OBJECTIVES

Upon successful completion of Chapter 4, you will be able to:

- Change worksheet margins
- Center a worksheet horizontally and vertically on the page
- Insert a page break in a worksheet
- Print gridlines and row and column headings
- Set and clear a print area
- Insert headers and footers
- Customize print jobs
- Complete a spelling check on a worksheet
- Find and replace data and cell formatting in a worksheet
- Sort data in cells in ascending and descending order
- Filter a list using AutoFilter

Tutorials

4.1 Changing Page Layout Options
4.2 Formatting a Worksheet Page for Printing
4.3 Using Page Break Preview
4.4 Inserting Headers and Footers
4.5 Formatting and Printing Multiple Worksheets
4.6 Completing a Spelling Check
4.7 Using Undo and Redo
4.8 Using Find and Replace
4.9 Finding and Replacing Text and Formatting
4.10 Sorting Data
4.11 Filtering Data Using a Custom AutoFilter

Excel contains features you can use to enhance and control the formatting of a worksheet. In this chapter, you will learn how to change worksheet margins, orientation, size, and scale; print column and row titles; print gridlines; and center a worksheet horizontally and vertically on the page. You will also learn how to complete a spelling check on text in a worksheet, find and replace specific data and formatting in a worksheet, sort and filter data, and plan and create a worksheet. Model answers for this chapter's projects appear on the following pages.

Note: Before beginning the projects, copy to your storage medium the EL1C4 subfolder from the EL1 folder on the CD that accompanies this textbook and make EL1C4 the active folder.

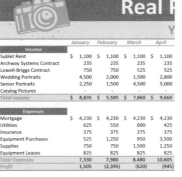

	January	February	March	April
Income				
Sublet Rent	$ 1,100	$ 1,100	$ 1,100	$ 1,100
Archway Systems Contract	235	235	235	235
Lowell-Briggs Contract	750	750	525	525
Wedding Portraits	4,500	2,000	1,500	2,800
Senior Portraits	2,250	1,500	4,500	5,000
Catalog Pictures	-	-	-	-
Total Income	$ 8,835	$ 5,585	$ 7,860	$ 9,660
Expenses				
Mortgage	$ 4,230	$ 4,230	$ 4,230	$ 4,230
Utilities	625	550	600	425
Insurance	375	375	375	375
Equipment Purchases	525	1,250	950	3,500
Supplies	750	750	1,500	1,250
Equipment Leases	825	825	825	825
Total Expenses	7,330	7,980	8,480	10,605
Profit	1,505	(2,395)	(620)	(945)

May	June	July	August	September	October
$ 1,100	$ 1,100	$ 1,100	$ 1,100	$ 1,100	$ 1,100
235	235	235	235	235	235
-	-	450	450	450	575
4,000	8,250	7,500	6,850	4,500	3,500
3,250	1,000	300	500	650	650
500	500	500	500	500	-
$ 9,085	$ 11,085	$ 10,085	$ 9,635	$ 7,435	$ 6,060
$ 4,230	$ 4,230	$ 4,230	$ 4,230	$ 4,230	$ 4,230
400	500	650	700	700	500
375	375	375	375	375	375
-	-	-	-	-	-
1,500	2,500	2,250	1,750	950	850
825	825	825	825	825	825
7,330	8,430	8,330	7,880	7,080	6,780
1,755	2,655	1,755	1,755	355	(720)

Student Name

November	December	Total
$ 1,100	$ 1,100	$ 13,200
235	235	2,820
575	575	5,625
3,500	7,000	55,900
400	400	20,400
-	-	2,500
$ 5,810	$ 9,310	$ 100,445
$ 4,230	$ 4,230	$ 50,760
550	650	6,850
375	375	4,500
-	-	6,225
850	2,000	16,900
825	825	9,900
6,830	8,080	95,135
(1,020)	1,230	5,310

Student Name

Project 1 Format a Yearly Budget Worksheet

EL1-C4-P1-RPBudget.xlsx

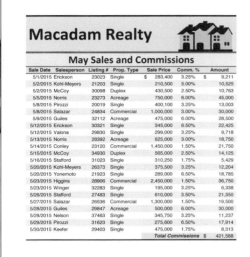

Macadam Realty

May Sales and Commissions

Sale Date	Salesperson	Listing #	Prop. Type	Sale Price	Comm. %	Amount
5/1/2015	Erickson	23023	Single	$ 283,400	3.25%	$ 9,211
5/2/2015	Kohl-Meyers	21203	Single	210,500	5.00%	10,525
5/2/2015	McCoy	30098	Duplex	430,500	2.50%	10,763
5/5/2015	Norris	23273	Acreage	750,000	6.00%	45,000
5/8/2015	Pirozzi	20019	Single	400,100	3.25%	13,003
5/8/2015	Salazar	24834	Commercial	1,000,000	3.00%	30,000
5/9/2015	Guiles	32112	Acreage	475,000	6.00%	28,500
5/12/2015	Erickson	30321	Single	345,000	6.50%	22,425
5/12/2015	Valona	29830	Single	299,000	3.25%	9,718
5/13/2015	Norris	28392	Acreage	625,000	3.00%	18,750
5/14/2015	Conley	23120	Commercial	1,450,000	1.50%	21,750
5/15/2015	McCoy	34930	Duplex	565,000	2.50%	14,125
5/16/2015	Stafford	31023	Single	310,250	1.75%	5,429
5/20/2015	Kohl-Meyers	26373	Single	375,500	3.25%	12,204
5/20/2015	Yonemoto	21923	Single	289,000	6.50%	18,785
5/23/2015	Higgins	28906	Commercial	2,450,000	1.50%	36,750
5/23/2015	Winger	32283	Single	195,000	3.25%	6,338
5/26/2015	Stafford	27483	Single	610,000	3.50%	21,350
5/27/2015	Salazar	26536	Commercial	1,300,000	1.50%	19,500
5/28/2015	Guiles	29847	Acreage	500,000	6.00%	30,000
5/28/2015	Nelson	37463	Single	345,750	3.25%	11,237
5/29/2015	Pirozzi	31623	Single	275,600	6.50%	17,914
5/30/2015	Keefer	29403	Single	475,000	1.75%	8,313
					Total Commissions	$ 421,588

Project 2 Format a May Sales and Commissions Worksheet

EL1-C4-P2-MRSales.xlsx

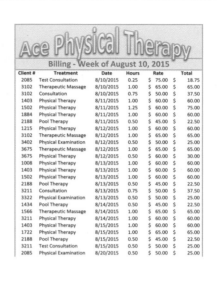

Ace Physical Therapy

Billing - Week of August 10, 2015

Client #	Treatment	Date	Hours	Rate	Total
2085	Test Consultation	8/10/2015	0.25	$ 75.00	$ 18.75
3102	Therapeutic Massage	8/10/2015	1.00	$ 65.00	65.00
3102	Consultation	8/10/2015	0.75	$ 50.00	37.50
1403	Physical Therapy	8/11/2015	1.00	$ 60.00	60.00
1502	Physical Therapy	8/11/2015	1.25	$ 60.00	75.00
1884	Physical Therapy	8/11/2015	1.00	$ 60.00	60.00
2188	Pool Therapy	8/11/2015	0.50	$ 45.00	22.50
1215	Physical Therapy	8/12/2015	1.00	$ 60.00	60.00
3102	Therapeutic Massage	8/12/2015	1.00	$ 65.00	65.00
3402	Physical Examination	8/12/2015	0.50	$ 50.00	25.00
3675	Therapeutic Massage	8/12/2015	1.00	$ 65.00	65.00
3675	Physical Therapy	8/12/2015	0.50	$ 60.00	30.00
1008	Physical Therapy	8/13/2015	1.00	$ 60.00	60.00
1403	Physical Therapy	8/13/2015	1.00	$ 60.00	60.00
1502	Physical Therapy	8/13/2015	1.00	$ 60.00	60.00
2188	Pool Therapy	8/13/2015	0.50	$ 45.00	22.50
3211	Consultation	8/13/2015	0.75	$ 50.00	37.50
3322	Physical Examination	8/13/2015	0.50	$ 50.00	25.00
1434	Pool Therapy	8/14/2015	0.50	$ 45.00	22.50
1566	Therapeutic Massage	8/14/2015	1.00	$ 65.00	65.00
3211	Physical Therapy	8/14/2015	1.00	$ 60.00	60.00
1403	Physical Therapy	8/15/2015	1.00	$ 60.00	60.00
1722	Physical Therapy	8/15/2015	1.00	$ 65.00	65.00
2188	Pool Therapy	8/15/2015	0.50	$ 45.00	22.50
3211	Test Consultation	8/15/2015	0.50	$ 50.00	25.00
2085	Physical Examination	8/20/2015	0.50	$ 50.00	25.00

Project 3 Format a Billing Worksheet

EL1-C4-P3-APTBilling.xlsx

Project 1 Format a Yearly Budget Worksheet — 12 Parts

You will format a yearly budget worksheet by inserting formulas; changing margins, page orientation, and page size; inserting a page break; printing column headings on multiple pages; scaling data to print on one page; inserting a background picture; inserting headers and footers; and identifying a print area and customizing a print job.

Formatting a Worksheet Page

An Excel worksheet contains default page formatting. For example, a worksheet contains left and right margins of 0.7 inch and top and bottom margins of 0.75 inch. In addition, a worksheet prints in portrait orientation and the worksheet page size is 8.5 inches by 11 inches. These defaults, along with additional settings, can be changed and/or controlled with options on the PAGE LAYOUT tab.

Changing Margins

The Page Setup group on the PAGE LAYOUT tab contains buttons for changing the margins and the page orientation and size, as well as buttons for establishing a print area, inserting a page break, applying a picture background, and printing titles.

Change the worksheet margins by clicking the Margins button in the Page Setup group on the PAGE LAYOUT tab. This displays a drop-down list of

Margins

▼ **Quick Steps**

Change Worksheet Margins
1. Click PAGE LAYOUT tab.
2. Click Margins button.
3. Click desired predesigned margin.
OR
1. Click PAGE LAYOUT tab.
2. Click Margins button.
3. Click *Custom Margins* at drop-down list.
4. Change the top, left, right, and/or bottom measurements.
5. Click OK.

predesigned margin choices. If one of the predesigned choices is what you want to apply to the worksheet, click the option. If you want to customize the margins, click the *Custom Margins* option at the bottom of the Margins button drop-down list. This displays the Page Setup dialog box with the Margins tab selected, as shown in Figure 4.1.

A worksheet page showing the cells and margins displays in the dialog box. As you increase or decrease the top, bottom, left, or right margin measurements, the sample worksheet page reflects the change. You can also increase or decrease the measurement from the top of the page to the header with the *Header* measurement box or the measurement from the footer to the bottom of the page with the *Footer* measurement box. (You will learn about headers and footers later in this chapter.)

Figure 4.1 Page Setup Dialog Box with Margins Tab Selected

Changes made to margin measurements are reflected in the sample worksheet page.

▼ **Quick Steps**

Center a Worksheet Horizontally and/or Vertically
1. Click PAGE LAYOUT tab.
2. Click Margins button.
3. Click *Custom Margins* at drop-down list.
4. Click *Horizontally* option and/or click *Vertically* option.
5. Click OK.

Centering a Worksheet Horizontally and/or Vertically

By default, a worksheet prints in the upper left corner of the page. You can center a worksheet on the page by changing the margins. However, an easier method for centering a worksheet is to use the *Horizontally* and/or *Vertically* options that display in the Page Setup dialog box with the Margins tab selected. If you choose one or both of these options, the worksheet page in the preview section displays how the worksheet will print on the page.

Project 1a · **Changing Margins and Horizontally and Vertically Centering a Worksheet**   Part 1 of 12

1. Open **RPBudget.xlsx**.
2. Save the workbook with Save As and name it **EL1-C4-P1-RPBudget**.
3. Insert the following formulas in the worksheet:
   a. Insert formulas in column N, rows 5 through 10 that sum the totals for each income item.
   b. Insert formulas in row 11, columns B through N that sum the income as well as the total for all income items.

c. Insert formulas in column N, rows 14 through 19 that sum the totals for each expense item.

d. Insert formulas in row 20, columns B through N that sum the expenses as well as the total of expenses.

e. Insert formulas in row 21, columns B through N that subtract the total expenses from the income. (To begin the formula, make cell B21 active and then type the formula =B11-B20. Copy this formula to columns C through N.)

f. Apply the Accounting format with no places past the decimal point to cells N5 and N14.

4. Click the PAGE LAYOUT tab.

5. Click the Margins button in the Page Setup group and then click *Custom Margins* at the drop-down list.

6. At the Page Setup dialog box with the Margins tab selected, click the up-pointing arrow at the right side of the *Top* measurement box until *3.5* displays.

7. Click the up-pointing arrow at the right side of the *Bottom* measurement box until *1.5* displays.

8. Preview the worksheet by clicking the Print Preview button located toward the bottom of the Page Setup dialog box. The worksheet appears to be a little low on the page so you decide to horizontally and vertically center it by completing the following steps:

a. Click the Page Setup hyperlink that displays below the galleries in the *Settings* category in the Print backstage area.

b. Click the Margins tab at the Page Setup dialog box.

c. Change the *Top* and *Bottom* measurements to *1*.

d. Click the *Horizontally* check box.

e. Click the *Vertically* check box.

f. Click OK to close the dialog box.

g. Look at the preview of the worksheet and then click the Back button to return to the worksheet.

9. Save **EL1-C4-P1-RPBudget.xlsx**.

Changing Page Orientation

Click the Orientation button in the Page Setup group and a drop-down list displays with two choices: *Portrait* and *Landscape*. The two choices are represented by sample pages. A sample page that is taller than it is wide shows how the default orientation (*Portrait*) prints data on the page. The other choice, *Landscape*, rotates the data and prints it on a page that is wider than it is tall.

Changing the Page Size

An Excel worksheet page size, by default, is set at 8.5 inches × 11 inches. You can change this default page size by clicking the Size button in the Page Setup group. At the drop-down list that displays, notice that the default setting is *Letter* and that the measurement *8.5" × 11"* displays below *Letter*. This drop-down list also contains a number of page sizes, such as *Executive* and *Legal*, and a number of envelope sizes.

Project 1b   Changing Page Orientation and Size   **Part 2 of 12**

1. With **EL1-C4-P1-RPBudget.xlsx** open, click the Orientation button in the Page Setup group on the PAGE LAYOUT tab and then click *Landscape* at the drop-down list.
2. Click the Size button in the Page Setup group and then click *Legal* at the drop-down list.
3. Preview the worksheet by clicking the FILE tab and then clicking the *Print* option. After viewing the worksheet in the Print backstage area, press the Esc key to return to the worksheet.
4. Save **EL1-C4-P1-RPBudget.xlsx**.

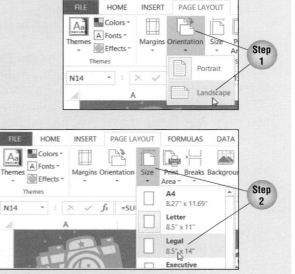

Inserting and Removing Page Breaks

The default left and right margins of 0.7 inch allow approximately 7 inches of cells across the page (8.5 inches minus 1.4 inches equals 7.1 inches). If a worksheet contains more than 7 inches of cells across the page, a page break is inserted and the remaining columns are moved to the next page. A page break displays as a broken line along cell borders. Figure 4.2 shows the page break in **EL1-C4-P1-RPBudget.xlsx** when the paper size is set to *Letter*.

A page break also displays horizontally in a worksheet. By default, a worksheet can contain approximately 9.5 inches of cells vertically down the page. This is because the paper size is set by default at 11 inches. With the default top and bottom margins of 0.75 inch, this allows 9.5 inches of cells to print on one page.

Figure 4.2 Page Break

	A	B	C	D	E	F	G	H	I	J	K	L	M	N	O	P
1																
2																
3		January	February	March	April	May	June	July	August	September	October	November	December	Total		
4	Income															
5	Sublet Rent	$ 1,100	$ 1,100	$ 1,100	$ 1,100	$ 1,100	$ 1,100	$ 1,100	$ 1,100	$ 1,100	$ 1,100	$ 1,100	$ 1,100	$ 13,200		
6	Archway Systems Contract	235	235	235	235	235	235	235	235	235	235	235	235	2,820		
7	Lowell-Briggs Contract	750	750	525	525	-	-	450	450	450	575	575	575	5,625		
8	Wedding Portraits	4,500	2,000	1,500	2,800	4,000	8,250	7,500	6,850	4,500	3,500	3,500	7,000	55,900		
9	Senior Portraits	2,250	1,500	4,500	5,000	3,250	1,000	300	500	650	650	400	400	20,400		
10	Catalog Pictures	-	-	-	-	500	500	500	500	500	-	-	-	2,500		
11	Total Income	$ 8,835	$ 5,585	$ 7,860	$ 9,660	$ 9,085	$ 11,085	$ 10,085	$ 9,635	$ 7,435	$ 6,060	$ 5,810	$ 9,310	$ 100,445		
12																
13	Expenses															
14	Mortgage	$ 4,230	$ 4,230	$ 4,230	$ 4,230	$ 4,230	$ 4,230	$ 4,230	$ 4,230	$ 4,230	$ 4,230	$ 4,230	$ 4,230	$ 50,760		
15	Utilities	625	550	600	425	400	500	650	700	700	500	550	650	6,850		
16	Insurance	375	375	375	375	375	375	375	375	375	375	375	375	4,500		
17	Equipment Purchases	525	1,250	950	3,500	-	-	-	-	-	-	-	-	6,225		
18	Supplies	750	750	1,500	1,250	1,500	2,500	2,250	1,750	950	850	850	2,000	16,900		

Real Photography
Yearly Budget

page break

Sheet1 +

Excel automatically inserts page breaks in a worksheet. Insert your own page break if you would like more control over what cells print on a page. To insert your own page break, select the column or row, click the Breaks button in the Page Setup group on the PAGE LAYOUT tab, and then click *Insert Page Break* at the drop-down list. A page break is inserted immediately left of the selected column or immediately above the selected row.

Breaks

If you want to insert both horizontal and vertical page breaks at the same time, make a cell active, click the Breaks button in the Page Setup group, and then click *Insert Page Break*. This causes a horizontal page break to be inserted immediately above the active cell and a vertical page break to be inserted at the left side of the active cell. To remove a page break, select the column or row or make the desired cell active, click the Breaks button in the Page Setup group, and then click *Remove Page Break* at the drop-down list.

A page break automatically inserted by Excel may not be visible initially in a worksheet. One way to display the page break is to display the worksheet in the Print backstage area. When you return to the worksheet, the page break will display in the worksheet.

Excel provides a page break view that displays worksheet pages and page breaks. To display this view, click the Page Break Preview button located in the view area at the right side of the Status bar or click the VIEW tab and then click the Page Break Preview button in the Workbook Views group. This causes the worksheet to display similar to the worksheet shown in Figure 4.3. The word *Page* along with the page number displays in gray behind the cells in the worksheet. A dashed blue line indicates a page break inserted by Excel and a solid blue line indicates a page break inserted manually.

Page Break
Preview

You can edit a worksheet in Page Break Preview.

Move a page break by positioning the arrow pointer on the blue line, holding down the left mouse button, dragging the line to the desired location, and then releasing the mouse button. To return to the Normal view, click the Normal button in the view area on the Status bar or click the VIEW tab and then click the Normal button in the Workbook Views group.

Normal

Figure 4.3 Worksheet in Page Break Preview

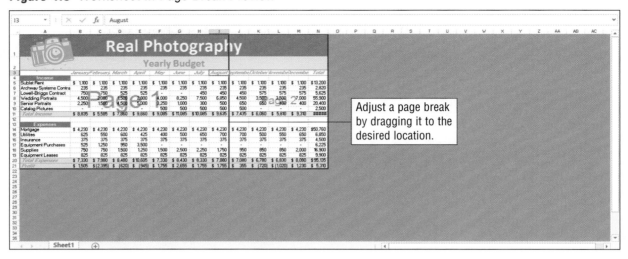

Adjust a page break by dragging it to the desired location.

Project 1c   **Inserting a Page Break in a Worksheet**   Part 3 of 12

1. With **EL1-C4-P1-RPBudget.xlsx** open, click the Size button in the Page Setup group on the PAGE LAYOUT tab and then click *Letter* at the drop-down list.
2. Click the Margins button and then click *Custom Margins* at the drop-down list.
3. At the Page Setup dialog box with the Margins tab selected, click in the *Horizontally* check box to remove the check mark, click in the *Vertically* check box to remove the check mark, and then click OK to close the dialog box.
4. Insert a page break between columns I and J by completing the following steps:
   a. Select column J.
   b. Click the Breaks button in the Page Setup group and then click *Insert Page Break* at the drop-down list. Click in any cell in column I.
5. View the worksheet in Page Break Preview by completing the following steps:
   a. Click the Page Break Preview button located in the view area on the Status bar.
   b. View the pages and page breaks in the worksheet.
   c. You decide to include the first six months of the year on one page. To do this, position the arrow pointer on the vertical blue line until the arrow pointer displays as a left-and-right-pointing arrow, hold down the left mouse button, drag the line to the left so it is between columns G and H, and then release the mouse button.

Step 4b

Step 5a

Step 5c

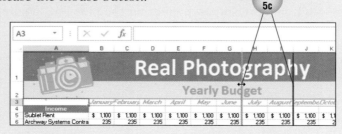

d. Click the Normal button located in
   the view area on the Status bar.
6. Save **EL1-C4-P1-RPBudget.xlsx**.

Step
5d

Printing Column and Row Titles on Multiple Pages

The columns and rows in a worksheet are usually titled. For example, in
EL1-C4-P1-RPBudget.xlsx, the column titles include *Income, Expenses, January,
February, March,* and so on. The row titles include the income and expenses
categories. If a worksheet prints on more than one page, having column and/or
row titles printing on each page can be useful. To do this, click the Print Titles
button in the Page Setup group on the PAGE LAYOUT tab. This displays the Page
Setup dialog box with the Sheet tab selected, as shown in Figure 4.4.

At the Page Setup dialog box with the Sheet tab selected, specify the range of
row cells you want to print on every page in the *Rows to repeat at top* text box. Type
a cell range using a colon. For example, if you want cells A1 through J1 to print
on every page, type *A1:J1* in the *Rows to repeat at top* text box. Type the range of
column cells you want to print on every page in the *Columns to repeat at left* text
box. To make rows and columns easier to identify on the printed page, specify that
row and/or column headings print on each page.

Figure 4.4 Page Setup Dialog Box with Sheet Tab Selected

Type the row range
in this text box.

Type the column
range in this text box.

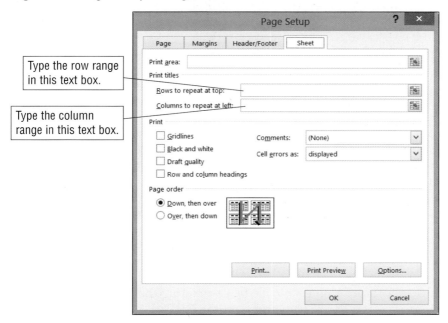

1. With **EL1-C4-P1-RPBudget.xlsx** open, click the PAGE LAYOUT tab and then click the Print Titles button in the Page Setup group.
2. At the Page Setup dialog box with the Sheet tab selected, click in the *Columns to repeat at left* text box.
3. Type **A1:A21**.
4. Click OK to close the dialog box.
5. Save and then print **EL1-C4-P1-RPBudget.xlsx**.

Scaling Data

Width

Using buttons in the Scale to Fit group on the PAGE LAYOUT tab, you can adjust the printed output by a percentage to fit the number of pages specified. For example, if a worksheet contains too many columns to print on one page, click the down-pointing arrow at the right side of the *Width* option box in the Scale to Fit group on the PAGE LAYOUT tab and then click *1 page*. This causes the data to shrink so all columns display and print on one page.

1. With **EL1-C4-P1-RPBudget.xlsx** open, click the down-pointing arrow at the right side of the *Width* option box in the Scale to Fit group on the PAGE LAYOUT tab.
2. At the drop-down list that displays, click the *1 page* option.
3. Display the Print backstage area, notice that all cells containing data display on one page in the worksheet, and then return to the worksheet.
4. Change margins by completing the following steps:
   a. Click the Margins button in the Page Setup group and then click *Custom Margins* at the drop-down list.
   b. At the Page Setup dialog box with the Margins tab selected, select the current number in the *Top* measurement box and then type **3.5**.
   c. Select the current number in the *Left* measurement box and then type **0.3**.
   d. Select the current number in the *Right* measurement box and then type **0.3**.
   e. Click OK to close the Page Setup dialog box.
5. Specify that you want row titles to print on each page by completing the following steps:
   a. Click the Print Titles button in the Page Setup group on the PAGE LAYOUT tab.
   b. At the Page Setup dialog box with the Sheet tab selected, select and then delete the text that displays in the *Columns to repeat at left* text box.

c. Click in the *Rows to repeat at top* text box and then type **A3:N3**.
d. Click OK to close the dialog box.
6. Save and then print **EL1-C4-P1-RPBudget.xlsx**. (The worksheet will print on two pages with the row titles repeated on the second page.)
7. At the worksheet, return to the default margins by clicking the PAGE LAYOUT tab, clicking the Margins button, and then clicking the *Normal* option at the drop-down list.
8. Prevent titles from printing on second and subsequent pages by completing the following steps:
   a. Click the Print Titles button in the Page Setup group.
   b. At the Page Setup dialog box with the Sheet tab selected, select and then delete the text that displays in the *Rows to repeat at top* text box.
   c. Click OK to close the dialog box.
9. Change the scaling back to the default by completing the following steps:
   a. Click the down-pointing arrow at the right side of the *Width* option box in the Scale to Fit group and then click *Automatic* at the drop-down list.
   b. Click the up-pointing arrow at the right side of the *Scale* measurement box until *100%* displays in the box.
10. Save **EL1-C4-P1-RPBudget.xlsx**.

Step 5c

Step 9a

Step 9b

Inserting a Background Picture

Using the Background button in the Page Setup group on the PAGE LAYOUT tab, you can insert a picture as a background to the worksheet. The picture displays only on the screen and does not print. To insert a picture, click the Background button in the Page Setup group and then click the Browse button at the Insert Pictures window. At the Sheet Background dialog box, navigate to the folder containing the desired picture and then double-click the picture. To remove the picture from the worksheet, click the Delete Background button.

▼ Quick Steps

Insert a Background Picture
1. Click PAGE LAYOUT tab.
2. Click Background button.
3. Navigate to desired picture and double-click picture.

Background

Project 1f **Inserting a Background Picture** **Part 6 of 12**

1. With **EL1-C4-P1-RPBudget.xlsx** open, insert a background picture by completing the following steps:
   a. Click the Background button in the Page Setup group on the PAGE LAYOUT tab.
   b. At the Insert Pictures window, click the Browse button.
   c. At the Sheet Background dialog box, navigate to the EL1C4 folder and then double-click **Ship.jpg**.
   d. Scroll down the worksheet to display the ship.
2. Display the Print backstage area, notice that the picture does not display in the preview worksheet, and then return to the worksheet.
3. Remove the picture by clicking the Delete Background button in the Page Setup group on the PAGE LAYOUT tab.
4. Save **EL1-C4-P1-RPBudget.xlsx**.

Step 1c

Printing Gridlines and Row and Column Headings

By default, the gridlines that create the cells in a worksheet and the row numbers and column letters that label the cells do not print. The Sheet Options group on the PAGE LAYOUT tab contain check boxes for gridlines and headings. The *View* check boxes for gridlines and headings contain check marks. At these settings, gridlines and row and column headings display on the screen but do not print. If you want them to print, insert check marks in the *Print* check boxes. Complex worksheets may be easier to read with the gridlines printed.

You can also control the display and printing of gridlines and headings with options at the Page Setup dialog box with the Sheet tab selected. Display this dialog box by clicking the Sheet Options dialog box launcher. To print gridlines and headings, insert check marks in the check boxes located in the *Print* section of the dialog box. The *Print* section contains two additional options: *Black and white* and *Draft quality*. If you are printing with a color printer, you can print the worksheet in black and white by inserting a check mark in the *Black and white* check box. Insert a check mark in the *Draft quality* option if you want to print a draft of the worksheet. With this option checked, some formatting, such as shading and fill, does not print.

Project 1g   Printing Gridlines and Row and Column Headings   Part 7 of 12

1. With **EL1-C4-P1-RPBudget.xlsx** open, click in the *Print* check box below *Gridlines* in the Sheet Options group on the PAGE LAYOUT tab to insert a check mark.
2. Click in the *Print* check box below *Headings* in the Sheet Options group to insert a check mark.
3. Click the Margins button in the Page Setup group and then click *Custom Margins* at the drop-down list.
4. At the Page Setup dialog box with the Margins tab selected, click in the *Horizontally* check box to insert a check mark.
5. Click in the *Vertically* check box to insert a check mark.
6. Click OK to close the dialog box.
7. Save and then print **EL1-C4-P1-RPBudget.xlsx**.
8. Click in the *Print* check box below *Headings* in the Sheet Options group to remove the check mark.
9. Click in the *Print* check box below *Gridlines* in the Sheet Options group to remove the check mark.
10. Save **EL1-C4-P1-RPBudget.xlsx**.

Printing a Specific Area of a Worksheet

Print Area

Use the Print Area button in the Page Setup group on the PAGE LAYOUT tab to select and print specific areas in a worksheet. To do this, select the cells you want to print, click the Print Area button in the Page Setup group, and then click *Set Print Area* at the drop-down list. This inserts a border around the selected cells. Display the Print backstage area and click the Print button and the cells within the border are printed.

You can specify more than one print area in a worksheet. To do this, select the first group of cells, click the Print Area button in the Page Setup group, and then click *Set Print Area*. Select the next group of cells, click the Print Area button, and then click *Add to Print Area*. Clear a print area by clicking the Print Area button in the Page Setup group and then clicking *Clear Print Area* at the drop-down list.

Each area specified as a print area will print on a separate page. If you want nonadjacent print areas to print on the same page, consider hiding columns and/or rows in the worksheet to bring the areas together.

Project 1h **Printing Specific Areas**   **Part 8 of 12**

1. With **EL1-C4-P1-RPBudget.xlsx** open, print the first half of the year's income and expenses by completing the following steps:
   a. Select cells A3 through G21.
   b. Click the Print Area button in the Page Setup group on the PAGE LAYOUT tab and then click *Set Print Area* at the drop-down list.
   c. With the border surrounding the cells A3 through G21, click the FILE tab, click the *Print* option, and then click the Print button at the Print backstage area.
   d. Clear the print area by clicking the Print Area button in the Page Setup group and then clicking *Clear Print Area* at the drop-down list.
2. Suppose you want to print the income and expenses information as well as the totals for the month of April. To do this, hide columns and select a print area by completing the following steps:
   a. Select columns B through D.
   b. Click the HOME tab.
   c. Click the Format button in the Cells group, point to *Hide & Unhide*, and then click *Hide Columns*.
   d. Click the PAGE LAYOUT tab.
   e. Select cells A3 through E21. (Columns A and E are now adjacent.)
   f. Click the Print Area button in the Page Setup group and then click *Set Print Area* at the drop-down list.
3. Click the FILE tab, click the *Print* option, and then click the Print button.
4. Clear the print area by ensuring cells A3 through E21 are selected, clicking the Print Area button in the Page Setup group, and then clicking *Clear Print Area* at the drop-down list.
5. Unhide the columns by completing the following steps:
   a. Click the HOME tab.
   b. Select columns A and E. (These columns are adjacent.)
   c. Click the Format button in the Cells group, point to *Hide & Unhide*, and then click *Unhide Columns*.
   d. Deselect the text by clicking in any cell containing data in the worksheet.
6. Save **EL1-C4-P1-RPBudget.xlsx**.

Inserting Headers and Footers ■■■■■■■■■■■■■■■■■■

▼ Quick Steps

Insert a Header or Footer
1. Click INSERT tab.
2. Click Header & Footer button.
3. Click Header button and then click predesigned header or click Footer button and then click predesigned footer.
OR
1. Click INSERT tab.
2. Click Header & Footer button.
3. Click desired header or footer elements.

Header & Footer

Text that prints at the top of each worksheet page is called a *header* and text that prints at the bottom of each worksheet page is called a *footer*. Create a header and/or footer with the Header & Footer button in the Text group on the INSERT tab, in Page Layout View, or with options at the Page Setup dialog box with the Header/Footer tab selected.

To create a header with the Header & Footer button, click the INSERT tab and then click the Header & Footer button in the Text group. This displays the worksheet in Page Layout view and displays the HEADER & FOOTER TOOLS DESIGN tab. Use buttons on this tab, shown in Figure 4.5, to insert predesigned headers and/or footers or insert header and footer elements such as page numbers, date, time, path name, and file name. You can also create a different header or footer on the first page of the worksheet or create a header or footer for even pages and another for odd pages.

At the Print backstage area, you can preview your headers and footers before printing. Click the FILE tab and then the *Print* option to display the Print backstage area. A preview of the worksheet displays at the right side of the backstage area. If your worksheet will print on more than one page, you can view the different pages by clicking the Next Page button or the Previous Page button. These buttons are located below and to the left of the preview worksheet at the Print backstage area. Two buttons display in the bottom right corner of the Print backstage area. Click the Zoom to Page button to zoom in or out of the preview of the worksheet. Click the Show Margins button in the Print backstage area and margin guidelines and handles display on the preview page. The handles display as black squares that you can use to increase or decrease the page margins and column widths. To do this, position the mouse pointer on the desired handle, hold down the left mouse button, and then drag to the desired position.

Figure 4.5 HEADER & FOOTER TOOLS DESIGN Tab

Project 1i	Inserting a Header in a Worksheet	Part 9 of 12

1. With **EL1-C4-P1-RPBudget.xlsx** open, create a header by completing the following steps:
   a. Click the INSERT tab.
   b. Click the Header & Footer button in the Text group.

c. Click the Header button located at the left side of the HEADER & FOOTER TOOLS DESIGN tab and then click *Page 1, EL1-C4-P1-RPBudget.xlsx* at the drop-down list. (This inserts the page number in the middle header box and the workbook name in the right header box.)

2. Preview the worksheet by completing the following steps:

a. Click the FILE tab and then click the *Print* option.

b. At the Print backstage area, look at the preview worksheet that displays at the right side of the backstage area.

c. View the next page of the worksheet by clicking the Next Page button that displays below and to the left of the preview worksheet.

Step 1c

Step 2c

d. View the first page by clicking the Previous Page button that displays left of the Next Page button.

e. Click the Zoom to Page button in the lower right corner of the backstage area. (Notice that the preview page has zoomed in on the worksheet.)

f. Click the Zoom to Page button.

g. Click the Page Margins button in the lower right corner of the backstage area. (Notice the guidelines and handles that display on the preview page.)

Step 2g

h. Click the Page Margins button to remove the guidelines and handles.

i. Click the Back button to return to the workbook.

3. Save **EL1-C4-P1-RPBudget.xlsx**.

You also can insert a header and/or footer by switching to Page Layout view. In Page Layout view, the top of the worksheet page displays with the text *Click to add header*. Click this text and the insertion point is positioned in the middle header box. Type the desired header in this box or click in the left box or the right box and then type the header. Create a footer in a similar manner. Scroll down the worksheet until the bottom of the page displays and then click the text *Click to add footer*. Type the footer in the center footer box or click the left or right box and then type the footer.

1. With **EL1-C4-P1-RPBudget.xlsx** open, make sure the workbook displays in Page Layout view.
2. Scroll down the worksheet until the text *Click to add footer* displays and then click the text.

Step 2

3. Type your first and last names.
4. Click in the left footer box, click the HEADER & FOOTER TOOLS DESIGN tab, and then click the Current Date button in the Header & Footer Elements group. (This inserts a date code. The date will display when you click outside the footer box.)
5. Click in the right footer box and then click the Current Time button in the Header & Footer Elements group. (This inserts the time as a code. The time will display when you click outside the footer box.)
6. View the header and footer at the Print backstage area and then return to the worksheet.
7. Modify the header by completing the following steps:
   a. Scroll to the beginning of the worksheet and display the header text.
   b. Click the page number in the middle header box. (This displays the HEADER & FOOTER TOOLS DESIGN tab, changes the header to a field, and selects the field.)
   c. Press the Delete key to delete the header.
   d. Click the header text that displays in the right header box and then press the Delete key.
   e. With the insertion point positioned in the right header box, insert the page number by clicking the HEADER & FOOTER TOOLS DESIGN tab and then clicking the Page Number button in the Header & Footer Elements group.
   f. Click in the left header box and then click the File Name button in the Header & Footer Elements group.

Step 7f

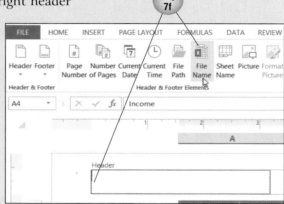

8. Click in any cell in the worksheet that contains data.
9. View the header and footer at the Print backstage area and then return to the worksheet.
10. Save **EL1-C4-P1-RPBudget.xlsx**.

In addition to selecting options on the HEADER & FOOTER TOOLS DESIGN tab, you can insert and customize headers and footers with options at the Page Setup dialog box with the Header/Footer tab selected, as shown in Figure 4.6. Display this dialog box by clicking the PAGE LAYOUT tab and then clicking the Page Setup group dialog box launcher. At the Page Setup dialog box, click the Header/Footer tab. If your worksheet contains headers or footers, they will display in the dialog box. With the check box options that display in

Figure 4.6 Page Setup Dialog Box with Header/Footer Tab Selected

Insert a check mark in this check box if you want to create different headers and/or footers for odd pages and even pages.

Insert a check mark in this check box if you want to create different headers and/or footers on the first page.

Click this button to display the Header dialog box where you can create the header.

Click this button to display the Footer dialog box where you can create the footer.

the lower left corner of the dialog box, you can specify that you want to insert different odd and even page headers and/or footers or insert a different first page header and/or footer. The bottom two check box options are active by default. These defaults scale the header and footer text with the worksheet text and align the header and footer with the page margins.

To create different odd and even page headers, click the *Different odd and even pages* check box to insert a check mark and then click the Custom Header button. This displays the Header dialog box with the Odd Page Header tab selected. Type or insert the desired odd page header data in the *Left section, Center section*, or *Right section* text box and then click the Even Page Header tab. Type or insert the desired even page header data in the desired section text box and then click OK. Use the buttons that display above the section boxes to format the header text and insert information such as the page number, current date, current time, file name, worksheet name, and so on. Complete similar steps to create different odd and even page footers and a different first page header or footer.

Project 1k Creating Different Odd and Even Page Headers and Footers and a Different First Page Header and Footer   Part 11 of 12

1. With **EL1-C4-P1-RPBudget.xlsx** open, remove the page break by clicking the PAGE LAYOUT tab, clicking the Breaks button in the Page Setup group, and then clicking *Reset All Page Breaks* at the drop-down list.
2. Change the margins by completing the following steps:
   a. Click the Margins button in the Page Setup group on the PAGE LAYOUT tab and then click *Custom Margins* at the drop-down list.
   b. At the Page Setup dialog box with the Margins tab selected, select the current number in the *Left* measurement box and then type 3.
   c. Select the current number in the *Right* measurement box and then type 3.
   d. Click OK to close the dialog box.
3. Click the Page Setup group dialog box launcher on the PAGE LAYOUT tab.

4. At the Page Setup dialog box, click the Header/Footer tab.
5. At the Page Setup dialog box with the Header/Footer tab selected, click the *Different odd and even pages* check box to insert a check mark and then click the Custom Header button.
6. At the Header dialog box with the Odd Page Header tab selected, click the Format Text button (located above the *Left section* text box). At the Font dialog box, click *12* in the *Size* list box box and then click OK.
7. At the Header dialog box, type **Yearly Budget** in the *Left section* text box.

8. Click the Even Page Header tab, click in the *Left section* text box, and then click the Insert Page Number button.
9. Click in the *Right section* text box and then type **Yearly Budget**.
10. Select the text *Yearly Budget*, click the Format Text button, click *12* in the *Size* list box box, and then click OK.
11. Click OK to close the Header dialog box.
12. Click the Custom Footer button and at the Footer dialog box with the Odd Page Footer tab selected, delete the data in the *Left section* text box and select and delete the data in the *Right section* text box. (The footer should contain only your name.)
13. Select your name, click the Format Text button, click *12* in the *Size* list box box, and then click OK.
14. Click the Even Page Footer tab, type your name in the *Center section* text box, select your name, and then change the font size to 12 points.
15. Click OK to close the Footer dialog box and then click OK to close the Page Setup dialog box. (View the header and footer in the Print backstage area and then return to the worksheet.)
16. Click the Page Setup group dialog box launcher on the PAGE LAYOUT tab.
17. At the Page Setup dialog box, click the Header/Footer tab.
18. At the Page Setup dialog box with the Header/Footer tab selected, click the *Different odd and even pages* check box to remove the check mark.
19. Click the *Different first page* check box to insert a check mark and then click the Custom Header button.
20. At the Header dialog box with the Header tab selected, click the First Page Header tab.
21. Click in the *Right section* text box and then click the Insert Page Number button located above the section boxes.

22. Click OK to close the Header dialog box and then click OK to close the Page Setup dialog box.
23. View the header and footer in the Print backstage area and then return to the worksheet.
24. Save **EL1-C4-P1-RPBudget.xlsx**.

Customizing Print Jobs ■■■■■■■■■■■■■■■■■■■■■■■■

As you learned earlier in this chapter, you can preview worksheets in the Print backstage area. Use options in the *Settings* category at the Print backstage area, to specify what you want printed. By default, the active worksheet prints. You can change this by clicking the first gallery that displays in the *Settings* category. At the drop-down list that displays, you can specify to print the entire workbook (which is useful when a workbook contains more than one worksheet) or only selected cells. With the other galleries in the *Settings* category, you can specify if you want pages printed on one side or both sides (this is dependent on your printer) and collated. You can also specify the worksheet orientation, size, and margins and whether you want the worksheet scaled to fit all columns or rows on one page.

With the *Pages* text boxes in the *Settings* category, specify the pages of your worksheet you want printed. For example, if you want to print pages 2 and 3 of your active worksheet, type *2* in the measurement box immediately right of the word *Pages* in the *Settings* category and then type *3* in the measurement box immediately right of the word *to*. You can also use the up- and down-pointing arrows to insert page numbers.

Project 1I	Printing Specific Pages of a Worksheet	Part 12 of 12

1. With **EL1-C4-P1-RPBudget.xlsx** open, print the first two pages of the worksheet by completing the following steps:
   a. Click the FILE tab and then click the *Print* option.
   b. At the Print backstage area, click in the measurement box immediately right of *Pages* and below the first gallery in the *Settings* category and then type 1.
   c. Click in the measurement box immediately right of *to* in the *Settings* category and then type 2.
   d. Click the Print button.

2. Print selected cells by completing the following steps:
   a. Display the worksheet in Normal view.
   b. Select cells A3 through D11.
   c. Click the FILE tab and then the *Print* option.
   d. At the Print backstage area, select and then delete the numbers in the *Pages* measurement boxes. (These are the numbers you inserted in Steps 1b and 1c.)
   e. Click the first gallery in the *Settings* category (displays with *Print Active Sheets*) and then click *Print Selection* at the drop-down list.
   f. Click the Print button.
3. Save and then close **EL1-C4-P1-RPBudget.xlsx**.

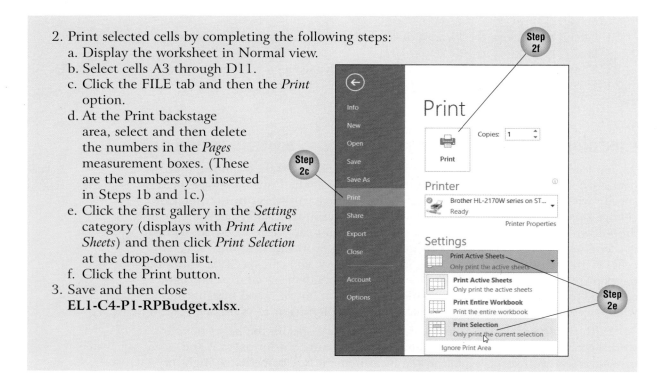

Project 2   Format a May Sales and Commissions Worksheet   3 Parts

You will format a sales commission worksheet by inserting a formula, completing a spelling check, and finding and replacing data and cell formatting.

▼ **Quick Steps**

Complete a Spelling Check
1. Click REVIEW tab.
2. Click Spelling button.
3. Replace or ignore selected words.

Spelling

HINT

Customize spell checking options at the Excel Options dialog box with *Proofing* selected.

Undo   Redo

Completing a Spelling Check ■■■■■■■■■■■■■■■■■■■■

Excel includes a spelling checker you can use to verify the spelling of text in a worksheet. The spelling checker uses an electronic dictionary to identity misspelled words and suggest alternatives. Before checking the spelling in a worksheet, make the first cell active. The spelling checker reviews the worksheet from the active cell to the last cell in the worksheet that contains data.

To use the spelling checker, click the REVIEW tab and then click the Spelling button. Figure 4.7 displays the Spelling dialog box. At this dialog box, you can click a button to tell Excel to ignore a word or you can replace a misspelled word with a word from the *Suggestions* list box.

Using Undo and Redo ■■■■■■■■■■■■■■■■■■■■■

Excel includes an Undo button on the Quick Access toolbar that will reverse certain commands or delete the last data typed in a cell. For example, if you apply formatting to selected cells in a worksheet and then decide you want the formatting removed, click the Undo button on the Quick Access toolbar. If you decide you want the formatting back again, click the Redo button on the Quick Access toolbar.

Figure 4.7 Excel Spelling Dialog Box

A word in the worksheet not found in the spelling check dictionary displays here.

Suggested spellings display in the *Suggestions* list box.

Excel maintains actions in temporary memory. If you want to undo an action, click the down-pointing arrow at the right side of the Undo button and a drop-down list displays containing the actions performed on the worksheet. Click the desired action at the drop-down list. Any actions preceding a chosen action are also undone. You can do the same with the Redo drop-down list. Multiple actions must be undone or redone in sequence.

HINT

Ctrl + Z is the keyboard shortcut to undo a command.

Project 2a **Spell Checking and Formatting a Worksheet** Part 1 of 3

1. Open **MRSales.xlsx**.
2. Save the workbook with Save As and name it **EL1-C4-P2-MRSales**.
3. Complete a spelling check on the worksheet by completing the following steps:
   a. Make cell A1 active.
   b. Click the REVIEW tab.
   c. Click the Spelling button in the Proofing group.
   d. Click the Change button as needed to correct misspelled words in the worksheet. (When the spelling check stops at the proper names *Pirozzi* and *Yonemoto*, click the Ignore All button.)

   e. At the message telling you the spelling check is complete, click OK.
4. Insert a formula and then copy the formula without the formatting by completing the following steps:
   a. Make cell G4 active and then insert a formula that multiplies the sale price by the commission percentage.
   b. Copy the formula down to cells G5 through G26.
   c. Some of the cells contain shading that you do not want removed, so click the Auto Fill Options button that displays at the bottom right of the selected cells and then click the *Fill Without Formatting* option at the drop-down list.

5. Make cell G27 active and then insert the sum of cells G4 through G26.
6. Apply accounting formatting with no places past the decimal point and add a dollar sign to cells G4 and G27.
7. Apply a theme by clicking the PAGE LAYOUT tab, clicking the Themes button, and then clicking *Ion* at the drop-down gallery.
8. After looking at the worksheet with the Ion theme applied, you decide you want to return to the original formatting. To do this, click the Undo button on the Quick Access toolbar.

9. Save **EL1-C4-P2-MRSales.xlsx**.

Finding and Replacing Data and
Cell Formatting in a Worksheet

▼ Quick Steps

Find Data
1. Click Find & Select button.
2. Click *Find* at drop-down list.
3. Type data in *Find what* text box.
4. Click Find Next button.

Find & Select

Excel provides a Find feature you can use to look for specific data and either replace it with nothing or replace it with other data. This feature is particularly helpful for finding data quickly in a large worksheet. Excel also includes a find and replace feature. Use this tool to look for specific data in a worksheet and replace it with other data.

To find specific data in a worksheet, click the Find & Select button located in the Editing group on the HOME tab and then click *Find* at the drop-down list. This displays the Find and Replace dialog box with the Find tab selected, as shown in Figure 4.8. Type the data you want to find in the *Find what* text box and then click the Find Next button. Continue clicking the Find Next button to move to the next occurrence of the data. If the Find and Replace dialog box obstructs your view of the worksheet, use the mouse pointer on the title bar to drag the dialog box to a different location.

Figure 4.8 Find and Replace Dialog Box with Find Tab Selected

To find specific data in a worksheet and replace it with other data, click the Find & Select button in the Editing group on the HOME tab and then click *Replace* at the drop-down list. This displays the Find and Replace dialog box with the Replace tab selected, as shown in Figure 4.9. Enter the data you want to find in the *Find what* text box. Press the Tab key or click in the *Replace with* text box and then enter the data that is to replace the data in the *Find what* text box.

Click the Find Next button to tell Excel to find the next occurrence of the data. Click the Replace button to replace the data and find the next occurrence. If you know that you want to replace all occurrences of the data in the *Find what* text box with the data in the *Replace with* text box, click the Replace All button. Click the Close button to close the Replace dialog box.

Display additional find and replace options by clicking the Options button. This expands the dialog box, as shown in Figure 4.10. By default, Excel will look for any data that contains the same characters as the data in the *Find what* text box, without concern for the characters before or after the entered data. For example, in Project 2b, you will look for sale prices of $450,000 and replace them with sale prices of $475,000. If you do not specify to Excel that you want to find cells that contain only *450000,* Excel will stop at any cell containing *450000.* In this example, Excel will stop at a cell containing *$1,450,000* and a cell containing *$2,450,000.* To specify that the only data that should be contained in the cell is what is entered in the *Find what* text box, click the Options button to expand the dialog box and then insert a check mark in the *Match entire cell contents* check box.

▼ Quick Steps

Find and Replace Data
1. Click Find & Select button.
2. Click *Replace* at drop-down list.
3. Type data in *Find what* text box.
4. Type data in *Replace with* text box.
5. Click Replace button or Replace All button.

Figure 4.9 Find and Replace Dialog Box with Replace Tab Selected

Type the data you want to find in this text box.

Type the data that is to replace the data in the *Find what* text box.

Figure 4.10 Expanded Find and Replace Dialog Box

Use these two Format buttons to search for specific cell formatting and replace it with other cell formatting.

Search the active worksheet or the entire workbook with the *Within* option box.

With this option, you can search by rows or by columns.

If the *Match case* option is active (contains a check mark), Excel will look for only that data that matches the case of the data entered in the *Find what* text box. Remove the check mark from this check box if you do not want Excel to find exact case matches. Excel will search in the current worksheet. If you want Excel to search an entire workbook, change the *Within* option to *Workbook*. Excel, by default, searches by rows in a worksheet. You can change this to *By Columns* with the *Search* option.

| Project 2b | Finding and Replacing Data | Part 2 of 3 |

1. With **EL1-C4-P2-MRSales.xlsx** open, find all occurrences of *Land* in the worksheet and replace with *Acreage* by completing the following steps:
   a. Click the Find & Select button in the Editing group on the HOME tab and then click *Replace* at the drop-down list.
   b. At the Find and Replace dialog box with the Replace tab selected, type **Land** in the *Find what* text box.
   c. Press the Tab key. (This moves the insertion point to the *Replace with* text box.)
   d. Type **Acreage**.
   e. Click the Replace All button.
   f. At the message telling you that four replacements were made, click OK.
   g. Click the Close button to close the Find and Replace dialog box.

2. Find all occurrences of *$450,000* and replace them with *$475,000* by completing the following steps:
   a. Click the Find & Select button in the Editing group and then click *Replace* at the drop-down list.
   b. At the Find and Replace dialog box with the Replace tab selected, type **450000** in the *Find what* text box.
   c. Press the Tab key.
   d. Type **475000**.
   e. Click the Options button to display additional options. (If additional options already display, skip this step.)
   f. Click the *Match entire cell contents* check box to insert a check mark.
   g. Click the Replace All button.
   h. At the message telling you that two replacements were made, click OK.
   i. At the Find and Replace dialog box, click the *Match entire cell contents* check box to remove the check mark.
   j. Click the Close button to close the Find and Replace dialog box.
3. Save **EL1-C4-P2-MRSales.xlsx**.

Use the Format buttons at the expanded Find and Replace dialog box (see Figure 4.10) to search for specific cell formatting and replace it with other formatting. Click the down-pointing arrow at the right side of the Format button and a drop-down list displays. Click the *Format* option and the Find Format dialog box displays with the Number, Alignment, Font, Border, Fill, and Protection tabs. Specify formatting at this dialog box. Click the *Choose Format From Cell* option from the Format button drop-down list or click the Choose Format From Cell button in the Find Format dialog box and the mouse pointer displays with a pointer tool attached. Click in the cell containing the desired formatting and the formatting displays in the *Preview* box to the left of the Format button. Click the *Clear Find Format* option at the Find button drop-down list and any formatting in the *Preview* box is removed.

Project 2c   **Finding and Replacing Cell Formatting**   **Part 3 of 3**

1. With **EL1-C4-P2-MRSales.xlsx** open, search for a light turquoise fill color and replace it with a light green fill color by completing the following steps:
   a. Click the Find & Select button in the Editing group on the HOME tab and then click *Replace* at the drop-down list.
   b. At the Find and Replace dialog box with the Replace tab selected, make sure the dialog box is expanded. (If not, click the Options button.)
   c. Select and then delete any text that displays in the *Find what* text box.
   d. Select and then delete any text that displays in the *Replace with* text box.
   e. Make sure the boxes immediately preceding the two Format buttons display with the text *No Format Set*. (If not, click the down-pointing arrow at the right of the Format button, and then click the *Clear Find Format* option at the drop-down list. Do this for each Format button.)
   f. Click the top Format button.
   g. At the Find Format dialog box, click the Fill tab.
   h. Click the More Colors button.
   i. At the Colors dialog box with the Standard tab selected, click the light turquoise color shown at the right.
   j. Click OK to close the Colors dialog box.
   k. Click OK to close the Find Format dialog box.
   l. Click the bottom Format button.
   m. At the Replace Format dialog box with the Fill tab selected, click the light green color (last column, second row), as shown at the right.
   n. Click OK to close the dialog box.
   o. At the Find and Replace dialog box, click the Replace All button.
   p. At the message telling you that 10 replacements were made, click OK.

Step 1f

Step 1i

Step 1m

2. Search for a light gray fill color and replace it with a light yellow fill color by completing the following steps:
   a. At the Find and Replace dialog box, click the top Format button.
   b. At the Find Format dialog box with the Fill tab selected, click the light gray color (fourth column, second row), as shown at the right.
   c. Click OK to close the Find Format dialog box.
   d. Click the bottom Format button.
   e. At the Replace Format dialog box with the Fill tab selected, click the yellow color (eighth column, second row), as shown below and to the right.
   f. Click OK to close the dialog box.
   g. At the Find and Replace dialog box, click the Replace All button.
   h. At the message telling you that 78 replacements were made, click OK.

Step 2b

Step 2e

3. Search for 11-point Calibri formatting and replace it with 10-point Arial formatting by completing the following steps:
   a. With the Find and Replace dialog box open, clear formatting from the top Format button by clicking the down-pointing arrow at the right side of the top Format button and then clicking the *Clear Find Format* option at the drop-down list.
   b. Clear formatting from the bottom Format button by clicking the down-pointing arrow at the right side of the bottom Format button and then clicking *Clear Replace Format*.
   c. Click the top Format button.
   d. At the Find Format dialog box, click the Font tab.
   e. Scroll down the *Font* list box and then click *Calibri*.
   f. Click *11* in the *Size* list box.
   g. Click OK to close the dialog box.
   h. Click the bottom Format button.
   i. At the Replace Format dialog box with the Font tab selected, scroll down the *Font* list box and then click *Arial*.
   j. Click *10* in the *Size* list box.
   k. Click OK to close the dialog box.
   l. At the Find and Replace dialog box, click the Replace All button.
   m. At the message telling you that 174 replacements were made, click OK.
   n. At the Find and Replace dialog box, remove formatting from both Format buttons.
   o. Click the Close button to close the Find and Replace dialog box.
4. Save, print, and then close **EL1-C4-P2-MRSales.xlsx**.

Step 3a

Project 3 Format a Billing Worksheet   4 Parts

You will insert a formula in a weekly billing worksheet and then sort and filter specific data in the worksheet.

Sorting Data ■■■■■■■■■■■■■■■■■■■■■■■■■■■■■

Excel is primarily a spreadsheet program, but it also includes some basic database functions. With a database program, you can alphabetize information or arrange numbers numerically. Data can even be sorted by columns in a worksheet. To sort data in a worksheet, use the Sort & Filter button in the Editing group on the HOME tab.

To sort data in a worksheet, select the cells containing the data you want to sort, click the Sort & Filter button in the Editing group, and then click the option representing the desired sort. The sort option names vary depending on the data in selected cells. For example, if the first column of selected cells contains text, the sort options in the drop-down list display as *Sort A to Z* and *Sort Z to A*. If the selected cells contain dates, the sort options in the drop-down list display as *Sort Oldest to Newest* and *Sort Newest to Oldest*, and if the cells contain numbers or values, the sort options display as *Sort Smallest to Largest* and *Sort Largest to Smallest*. If you select more than one column in a worksheet, Excel will sort the data in the first selected column.

▼ Quick Steps

Sort Data
1. Select cells.
2. Click Sort & Filter button.
3. Click desired sort option at drop-down list.

Sort & Filter

H I N T

If you are not satisfied with the results of the sort, immediately click the Undo button.

Project 3a   **Sorting Data**   Part 1 of 4

1. Open **APTBilling.xlsx** and save it with Save As and name it **EL1-C4-P3-APTBilling**.
2. Insert a formula in cell F4 that multiplies the rate by the hours. Copy the formula down to cells F5 through F29.
3. Sort the data in the first column in descending order by completing the following steps:
   a. Make cell A4 active.
   b. Click the Sort & Filter button in the Editing group on the HOME tab.
   c. Click the *Sort Largest to Smallest* option at the drop-down list.
4. Sort in ascending order by clicking the Sort & Filter button and then clicking *Sort Smallest to Largest* at the drop-down list.
5. Save **EL1-C4-P3-APTBilling.xlsx**.

Completing a Custom Sort

If you want to sort data in a column other than the first column, use the Sort dialog box. If you select just one column in a worksheet, click the Sort & Filter button, and then click the desired sort option, only the data in that column is sorted. If this data is related to data to the left or right of the data in the sorted column, that relationship is broken. For example, if you sort cells C4 through C29 in EL1-C4-P3-APTBilling.xlsx, the client number, treatment, hours, and total no longer match the date.

Use the Sort dialog box to sort data and maintain the relationship among all cells. To sort using the Sort dialog box, select the cells you want sorted, click the Sort & Filter button, and then click *Custom Sort*. This displays the Sort dialog box, shown in Figure 4.11.

▼ Quick Steps

Complete a Custom Sort
1. Select cells.
2. Click Sort & Filter button.
3. Click *Custom Sort* at drop-down list.
4. Specify options at Sort dialog box.
5. Click OK.

Figure 4.11 Sort Dialog Box

Click this button to specify a second column for sorting.

Click this down-pointing arrow and then specify if you are sorting on values, cell color, font color, or cell icon.

Click this down-pointing arrow and then specify the sort order.

Click this down-pointing arrow and then click the desired column in the drop-down list.

The data displayed in the *Sort by* option box will vary depending on what you have selected. Generally, the data that displays is the title of the first column of selected cells. If the selected cells do not have a title, the data may display as *Column A*. Use this option to specify what column you want sorted. Using the Sort dialog box to sort data in a column maintains the relationship among the data.

Project 3b **Sorting Data Using the Sort Dialog Box** Part 2 of 4

1. With **EL1-C4-P3-APTBilling.xlsx** open, sort the rates in cells E4 through E29 in descending order and maintain the relationship to the other data by completing the following steps:
   a. Select cells A3 through F29.
   b. Click the Sort & Filter button and then click *Custom Sort*.
   c. At the Sort dialog box, click the down-pointing arrow at the right of the *Sort by* option box and then click *Rate* at the drop-down list.
   d. Click the down-pointing arrow at the right of the *Order* option box and then click *Largest to Smallest* at the drop-down list.

Step 1c

Step 1d

   e. Click OK to close the Sort dialog box.
   f. Deselect the cells.
2. Sort the dates in ascending order (oldest to newest) by completing steps similar to those in Step 1.
3. Save and then print **EL1-C4-P3-APTBilling.xlsx**.

Sorting More Than One Column

When sorting data in cells, you can sort in more than one column. For example, in Project 3c, you will sort the dates from oldest to newest and the client numbers from lowest to highest. In this sort, the dates are sorted first and then the client numbers are sorted in ascending order within the same date.

To sort in more than one column, select all columns in the worksheet that need to remain relative and then display the Sort dialog box. At the Sort dialog box, specify the first column you want sorted in the *Sort by* option box, click the *Add Level* button, and then specify the second column in the first *Then by* option box. In Excel, you can sort on multiple columns. Add additional *Then by* option boxes by clicking the *Add Level* button.

Project 3c **Sorting Data in Two Columns**   Part 3 of 4

1. With **EL1-C4-P3-APTBilling.xlsx** open, select cells A3 through F29.
2. Click the Sort & Filter button and then click *Custom Sort*.
3. At the Sort dialog box, click the down-pointing arrow at the right side of the *Sort by* option box and then click *Date* in the drop-down list. (Skip this step if *Date* already displays in the *Sort by* option box.)
4. Make sure *Oldest to Newest* displays in the *Order* option box.
5. Click the Add Level button.
6. Click the down-pointing arrow at the right of the *Then by* option box and then click *Client #* in the drop-down list.
7. Click OK to close the dialog box.
8. Deselect the cells.
9. Save and then print **EL1-C4-P3-APTBilling.xlsx**.

Filtering Data ■■■■■■■■■■■■■■■■■■■■■■■■■■■■■

You can place a restriction, called a ***filter***, on data in a worksheet to temporarily isolate specific data. To turn on filtering, make a cell containing data active, click the Sort & Filter button in the Editing group on the HOME tab, and then click *Filter* at the drop-down list. This turns on filtering and causes a filter arrow to appear with each column label in the worksheet, as shown in Figure 4.12. You do not need to select data before turning on filtering because Excel automatically searches for column labels in a worksheet.

To filter data in a worksheet, click the filter arrow in the heading you want to filter. This causes a drop-down list to display with options to filter all records, create a custom filter, or select an entry that appears in one or more of the cells in the column. When you filter data, the filter arrow changes to a funnel icon. The funnel icon indicates that rows in the worksheet have been filtered. To turn off filtering, click the Sort & Filter button and then click *Filter*.

If a column contains numbers, click the filter arrow and point to *Number Filters* and a side menu displays with options for filtering numbers. For example, you can filter numbers that are equal to, greater than, or less than a number you specify; filter the top ten numbers; and filter numbers that are above or below a specified number.

▼ Quick Steps

Filter a List
1. Select cells.
2. Click Sort & Filter button.
3. Click *Filter* at drop-down list.
4. Click down-pointing arrow of heading to filter.
5. Click desired option at drop-down list.

Figure 4.12 Filtering Data

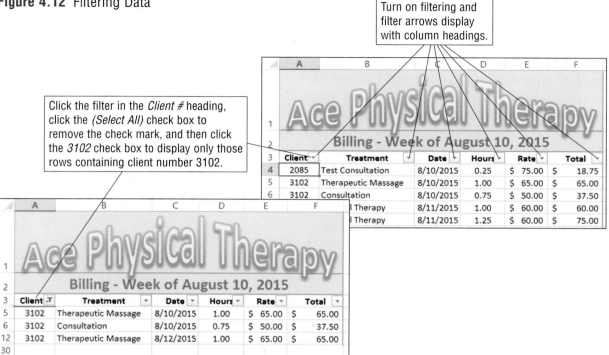

Turn on filtering and filter arrows display with column headings.

Click the filter in the *Client #* heading, click the *(Select All)* check box to remove the check mark, and then click the *3102* check box to display only those rows containing client number 3102.

Project 3d **Filtering Data** Part 4 of 4

1. With **EL1-C4-P3-APTBilling.xlsx** open, click in cell A4.
2. Turn on filtering by clicking the Sort & Filter button in the Editing group on the HOME tab and then clicking *Filter* at the drop-down list.
3. Filter rows for client number 3102 by completing the following steps:
   a. Click the filter arrow in the *Client #* heading.
   b. Click the *(Select All)* check box to remove the check mark.
   c. Scroll down the list box and then click *3102* to insert a check mark in the check box.
   d. Click OK.
4. Redisplay all rows containing data by completing the following steps:
   a. Click the funnel icon in the *Client #* heading.
   b. Click the *(Select All)* check box to insert a check mark. (This also inserts check marks for all items in the list.)
   c. Click OK.

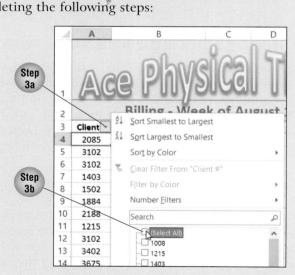

5. Filter a list of clients receiving physical therapy by completing the following steps:
   a. Click the filter arrow in the *Treatment* heading.
   b. Click the *(Select All)* check box.
   c. Click the *Physical Therapy* check box.
   d. Click OK.
6. Redisplay all rows containing data by completing the following steps:
   a. Click the funnel icon in the *Treatment* heading.
   b. Click the *Clear Filter From "Treatment"* option.
7. Display the top two highest rates by completing the following steps:
   a. Click the filter arrow in the *Rate* heading.
   b. Point to *Number Filters* and then click *Top 10* at the side menu.
   c. At the Top 10 AutoFilter dialog box, select the *10* that displays in the middle measurement box and then type *2*.
   d. Click OK to close the dialog box.

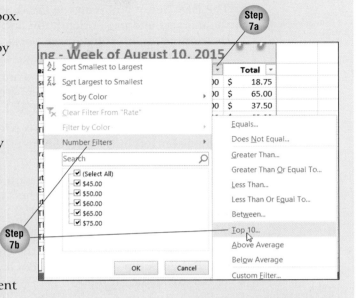

8. Redisplay all rows that contain data by completing the following steps:
   a. Click the funnel icon in the *Rate* heading.
   b. Click the *Clear Filter From "Rate"* option.
9. Display totals greater than $60 by completing the following steps:
   a. Click the filter arrow in the *Total* heading.
   b. Point to *Number Filters* and then click *Greater Than*.
   c. At the Custom AutoFilter dialog box, type *60* and then click OK.

10. Print the worksheet by clicking the FILE tab, clicking the *Print* option, and then clicking the Print button.
11. Turn off the filtering feature by clicking the Sort & Filter button and then clicking *Filter* at the drop-down list.
12. Save, print, and then close **EL1-C4-P3-APTBilling.xlsx**.

Chapter Summary

- The Page Setup group on the PAGE LAYOUT tab contains buttons for changing the margins and page orientation and size, as well as buttons for establishing the print area, inserting a page break, applying a picture background, and printing titles.

- The default left and right margins are 0.7 inch and the default top and bottom margins are 0.75 inch. Change these default margins with the Margins button in the Page Setup group on the PAGE LAYOUT tab.

- Display the Page Setup dialog box with the Margins tab selected by clicking the Margins button in the Page Setup group on the PAGE LAYOUT tab and then clicking *Custom Margins* at the drop-down list.

- Center a worksheet on the page with the *Horizontally* and *Vertically* options at the Page Setup dialog box with the Margins tab selected.

- Click the Orientation button in the Page Setup group on the PAGE LAYOUT tab to display the two orientation choices: *Portrait* and *Landscape*.

- Insert a page break by selecting the column or row, clicking the Breaks button in the Page Setup group on the PAGE LAYOUT tab, and then clicking *Insert Page Break* at the drop-down list.

- To insert both horizontal and vertical page breaks at the same time, make a cell active, click the Breaks button, and then click *Insert Page Break* at the drop-down list.

- Preview the page breaks in a worksheet by clicking the Page Break Preview button in the view area on the Status bar or clicking the VIEW tab and then clicking the Page Break Preview button in the Workbook Views group.

- Use options at the Page Setup dialog box with the Sheet tab selected to specify printing column and/or row titles on each page. Display this dialog box by clicking the Print Titles button in the Page Setup group on the PAGE LAYOUT tab.

- Use options in the Scale to Fit group on the PAGE LAYOUT tab to scale data to fit on a specific number of pages.

- Use the Background button in the Page Setup group on the PAGE LAYOUT tab to insert a worksheet background picture. A background picture displays on the screen but does not print.

- Use options in the Sheet Options group on the PAGE LAYOUT tab to specify whether to view and/or print gridlines and headings.

- Specify the print area by selecting the desired cells, clicking the Print Area button in the Page Setup group on the PAGE LAYOUT tab, and then clicking *Set Print Area* at the drop-down list. Add another print area by selecting the desired cells, clicking the Print Area button, and then clicking *Add to Print Area* at the drop-down list.

- Create a header and/or footer with the Header & Footer button in the Text group on the INSERT tab, in Page Layout view, or with options at the Page Setup dialog box with the Header/Footer tab selected.

- Customize a print job with options at the Print backstage area.

- To check spelling in a worksheet, click the REVIEW tab and then click the Spelling button.

- Click the Undo button on the Quick Access toolbar to reverse the most recent action and click the Redo button to redo a previously reversed action.
- Use options at the Find and Replace dialog box with the Find tab selected to find specific data and/or formatting in a worksheet.
- Use options at the Find and Replace dialog box with the Replace tab selected to find specific data and/or formatting and replace it with other data and/or formatting.
- Sort data in a worksheet with options from the Sort & Filter button in the Editing group on the HOME tab.
- Create a custom sort with options at the Sort dialog box. Display this dialog box by clicking the Sort & Filter button and then clicking *Custom Sort* at the drop-down list.
- Use filtering to temporarily isolate specific data. Turn on the filter feature by clicking the Sort & Filter button in the Editing group on the HOME tab and then clicking *Filter* at the drop-down list. This inserts filter arrows with each column label. Click a filter arrow and then use options at the drop-down list that displays to specify the filter data.

Commands Review

FEATURE	RIBBON TAB, GROUP	BUTTON, OPTION	KEYBOARD SHORTCUT
background picture	PAGE LAYOUT, Page Setup		
filter data	HOME, Editing		
Find and Replace dialog box with Find tab selected	HOME, Editing	, *Find*	Ctrl + F
Find and Replace dialog box with Replace tab selected	HOME, Editing	, *Replace*	Ctrl + H
header and footer	INSERT, Text		
insert page break	PAGE LAYOUT, Page Setup	, *Insert Page Break*	
margins	PAGE LAYOUT, Page Setup		
orientation	PAGE LAYOUT, Page Setup		
Page Layout view	VIEW, Workbook Views		
Page Setup dialog box with Margins tab selected	PAGE LAYOUT, Page Setup	, *Custom Margins*	
Page Setup dialog box with Sheet tab selected	PAGE LAYOUT, Page Setup		
preview page break	VIEW, Workbook Views		

FEATURE	RIBBON TAB, GROUP	BUTTON, OPTION	KEYBOARD SHORTCUT
print area	PAGE LAYOUT, Page Setup		
remove page break	PAGE LAYOUT, Page Setup	, *Remove Page Break*	
scale height	PAGE LAYOUT, Scale to Fit		
scale to fit	PAGE LAYOUT, Scale to Fit		
scale width	PAGE LAYOUT, Scale to Fit		
size	PAGE LAYOUT, Page Setup		
sort data	HOME, Editing		
spelling checker	REVIEW, Proofing		F7

Concepts Check Test Your Knowledge

Completion: In the space provided at the right, indicate the correct term, symbol, or command.

1. This is the default left and right margin measurement. _____

2. This is the default top and bottom margin measurement. _____

3. The Margins button is located on this tab. _____

4. By default, a worksheet prints in this orientation on a page. _____

5. Click the Print Titles button in the Page Setup group on the PAGE LAYOUT tab and the Page Setup dialog box displays with this tab selected. _____

6. Use options in this group on the PAGE LAYOUT tab to adjust the printed output by a percentage to fit the number of pages specified. _____

7. Use this button in the Page Setup group on the PAGE LAYOUT tab to select and print specific areas in a worksheet. _____

8. Click the Header & Footer button in the Text group on the INSERT tab and the worksheet displays in this view. _____

9. This tab contains options for formatting and customizing a header and/or footer. _____

10. Click this tab to display the Spelling button. _____

11. The Undo and Redo buttons are located on this toolbar. _____

12. Click this button in the Find and Replace dialog box to expand the dialog box. _____

13. Use these two buttons at the expanded Find and Replace dialog box to search for specific cell formatting and replace it with other formatting. _____

14. Use this button in the Editing group on the HOME tab to sort data in a worksheet. _____

15. Use this feature to temporarily isolate specific data in a worksheet. _____

Skills Check Assess Your Performance

Assessment

1 **FORMAT A DATA ANALYSIS WORKSHEET**

1. Open **DISemiSales.xlsx**.
2. Save the workbook with Save As and name it **EL1-C4-A1-DISemiSales**.
3. Make the following changes to the worksheet:
    a. Insert a formula in cell H4 that averages the amounts in cells B4 through G4.
    b. Copy the formula in cell H4 down to cells H5 through H9.
    c. Insert a formula in cell B10 that adds the amounts in cells B4 through B9.
    d. Copy the formula in cell B10 over to cells C10 through H10. (Click the Auto Fill Options button and then click *Fill Without Formatting* at the drop-down list.)
    e. Apply accounting formatting to cell H4.
    f. Change the orientation of the worksheet to landscape.
    g. Change the top margin to 3 inches and the left margin to 1.5 inches.
4. Save and then print **EL1-C4-A1-DISemiSales.xlsx**.
5. Make the following changes to the worksheet:
    a. Change the orientation back to portrait.
    b. Change the top margin to 1 inch and the left margin to 0.7 inch.
    c. Horizontally and vertically center the worksheet on the page.
    d. Scale the worksheet so it fits on one page.
6. Save, print, and then close **EL1-C4-A1-DISemiSales.xlsx**.

Assessment

2 FORMAT A TEST RESULTS WORKSHEET

1. Open **CMTests.xlsx**.
2. Save the workbook with Save As and name it **EL1-C4-A2-CMTests**.
3. Make the following changes to the worksheet:
   a. Insert a formula in cell N4 that averages the test scores in cells B4 through M4.
   b. Copy the formula in cell N4 down to cells N5 through N21.
   c. Type **Average** in cell A22.
   d. Insert a formula in cell B22 that averages the test scores in cells B4 through B21.
   e. Copy the formula in cell B22 across to cells C22 through N22.
   f. Insert a page break between columns G and H.
4. View the worksheet using Page Break Preview.
5. Change back to the Normal view.
6. Specify that the column titles (A3 through A22) are to print on each page.
7. Create a header that prints the page number at the right side of the page.
8. Create a footer that prints your name at the left side of the page and the workbook file name at the right side of the page.
9. Display the worksheet in Normal view.
10. Save and then print the worksheet.
11. Set a print area for cells N3 through N22 and then print the cells.
12. Clear the print area.
13. Save and then close **EL1-C4-A2-CMTests.xlsx**.

Assessment

3 FORMAT AN EQUIPMENT RENTAL WORKSHEET

1. Open **HERInvoices.xlsx**.
2. Save the workbook with Save As and name it **EL1-C4-A3-HERInvoices**.
3. Insert a formula in cell H3 that multiplies the rate in cell G3 by the hours in cell F3. Copy the formula in cell H3 down to cells H4 through H16.
4. Insert a formula in cell H17 that sums the amounts in cells H3 through H16.
5. Complete the following find and replaces:
   a. Find all occurrences of cells containing *75* and replace them with *90*.
   b. Find all occurrences of cells containing *55* and replace them with *60*.
   c. Find all occurrences of *Barrier Concrete* and replace them with *Lee Sand and Gravel*.
   d. Find all occurrences of 11-point Calibri and replace them with 10-point Cambria.
   e. After completing the find and replaces, clear all formatting from the Format buttons.
6. Insert a header that prints the date at the left side of the page and the time at the right side of the page.
7. Insert a footer that prints your name at the left side of the page and the workbook file name at the right side of the page.
8. Print the worksheet horizontally and vertically centered on the page.
9. Save and then close **EL1-C4-A3-HERInvoices.xlsx**.

4   FORMAT AN INVOICES WORKSHEET

1. Open **RPInvoices.xlsx**.
2. Save the workbook with Save As and name it **EL1-C4-A4-RPInvoices**.
3. Insert a formula in G4 that multiplies the amount in E4 with the percentage in F4 and then adds the product to cell E4. (If you write the formula correctly, the result in G4 will display as *$488.25*.)
4. Copy the formula in cell G4 down to cells G5 through G17, click the Auto Fill Options button, and then click the *Fill Without Formatting* option.
5. Complete a spelling check on the worksheet.
6. Find all occurrences of *Picture* and replace them with *Portrait*. (Do not type a space after *Picture* or *Portrait* because you want to find occurrences that end with an *s*. Make sure the *Match entire cell contents* check box does not contain a check mark.)
7. Sort the records by invoice number in ascending order (smallest to largest).
8. Complete a new sort that sorts the records by client number in ascending order (A to Z).
9. Complete a new sort that sorts by date in ascending order (oldest to newest).
10. Insert a footer in the worksheet that prints your name at the left side of the page and the current date at the right side of the page.
11. Display the worksheet in Normal view.
12. Center the worksheet horizontally and vertically on the page.
13. Save and then print **EL1-C4-A4-RPInvoices.xlsx**.
14. Select cells A3 through G3 and then turn on the filter feature and complete the following filters:
    a. Filter and then print a list of rows containing client number 11-279 and then clear the filter.
    b. Filter and then print a list of rows containing the top three highest amounts due and then clear the filter.
    c. Filter and then print a list of rows containing amounts due that are less than $500 and then clear the filter.
15. Save and then close **EL1-C4-A4-RPInvoices.xlsx**.

5   CREATE A WORKSHEET CONTAINING KEYBOARD SHORTCUTS

1. Use Excel's Help feature to learn about keyboard shortcuts in Excel. After reading the information presented, create a worksheet with the following features:
   - Create a title for the worksheet.
   - Include at least 10 keyboard shortcuts along with an explanation of each shortcut.
   - Set the data in cells in a typeface other than Calibri and change the data color.
   - Add borders to the cells. (You determine the border style.)
   - Add a color of shading to cells. (You determine the color; make it complement the data color.)
   - Create a header that prints the date at the right margin and create a footer that prints your name at the left margin and the file name at the right margin.
2. Save the workbook and name it **EL1-C4-A5-KeyboardShortcuts**.
3. Print and then close **EL1-C4-A5-KeyboardShortcuts.xlsx**.

Visual Benchmark Demonstrate Your Proficiency

CREATE AND FORMAT AN EXPENSE WORKSHEET

1. At a blank workbook, type the data in the cells as indicated in Figure 4.13 on the next page, but **do not** type the data in the cells noted below. Instead, insert the formulas as indicated:

   - Cells N3 through N8: Insert a formula that sums the monthly expenses for the year.
   - Cells B9 through N9: Insert a formula that sums the monthly expenses for each month and the entire year.

   (The results of your formulas should match the results you see in the figure.)

2. Change the left and right margins to 0.45 inch and change the top margin to 1.5 inches.

3. Apply formatting so your worksheet looks similar to the worksheet shown in Figure 4.13. (Set the heading in 26-point Cambria and set the remaining data in 10-point Cambria. Apply bold formatting as shown in the figure.)

4. Save the workbook and name it **EL1-C4-VB-HERExpenses**.

5. Look at the printing of the worksheet shown in Figure 4.14 and then make the following changes:

   - Insert a page break between columns G and H.
   - Insert the headers and footer as shown.
   - Specify that the column titles print on the second page, as shown in Figure 4.14.

6. Save and then print **EL1-C4-VB-HERExpenses.xlsx**. (Your worksheet should print on two pages and appear as shown in Figure 4.14 on the next page.)

7. Close **EL1-C4-VB-HERExpenses.xlsx**.

Figure 4.13 Visual Benchmark Data

	A	B	C	D	E	F	G	H	I	J	K	L	M	N
1					**Hilltop Equipment Rental**									
2	**Expenses**	**January**	**February**	**March**	**April**	**May**	**June**	**July**	**August**	**September**	**October**	**November**	**December**	**Total**
3	Lease	$ 3,250	$ 3,250	$ 3,250	$ 3,250	$ 3,250	$ 3,250	$ 3,250	$ 3,250	$ 3,250	$ 3,250	$ 3,250	$ 3,250	$ 39,000
4	Utilities	3,209	2,994	2,987	2,500	2,057	1,988	1,845	1,555	1,890	2,451	2,899	3,005	29,380
5	Payroll	10,545	9,533	11,542	10,548	11,499	12,675	13,503	13,258	12,475	10,548	10,122	9,359	135,607
6	Insurance	895	895	895	895	895	895	895	895	895	895	895	895	10,740
7	Maintenance	2,439	1,856	2,455	5,410	3,498	3,110	2,479	3,100	1,870	6,105	4,220	3,544	40,086
8	Supplies	341	580	457	330	675	319	451	550	211	580	433	601	5,528
9	*Total Expenses*	$ 20,679	$ 19,108	$ 21,586	$ 22,933	$ 21,874	$ 22,237	$ 22,423	$ 22,608	$ 20,591	$ 23,829	$ 21,819	$ 20,654	$ 260,341
10														

Figure 4.14 Visual Benchmark Printed Pages

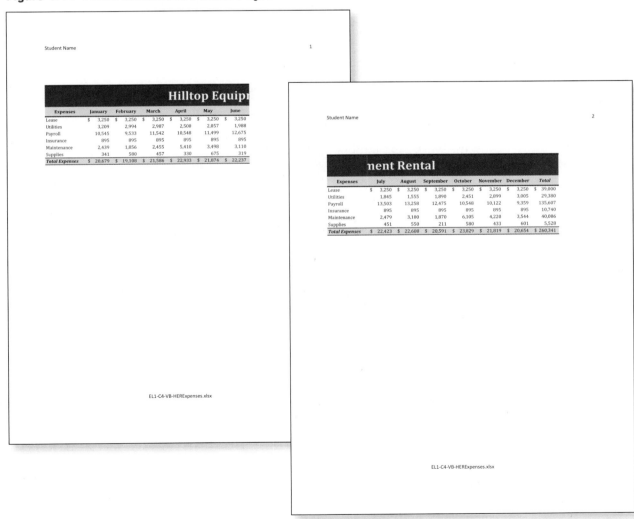

Case Study   Apply Your Skills

You are a sales associate for Macadam Realty. Your supervisor has asked you to complete a form that she started containing information on sample mortgages. She wants to display the form in the reception area display rack. She has already inserted a formula (in cell G4) that calculates monthly payments using the PMT function. (You will learn more about this function in Chapter 5.) Open **MRMortgages.xlsx** and then save it with Save As and name it **EL1-C4-CS-MRMortgages-01**. Add the following information and make the following changes:

- In column C, insert a formula that determines the down payment amount.
- In column D, insert a formula that determines the loan amount.
- In column G, drag the formula in cell G4 down to cells G5 through G47.
- Insert the date and time as a header and your name and the workbook name (**EL1-C4-CS-MRMortgages-01.xlsx**) as a footer.
- Find 11-point Calibri formatting and replace it with 11-point Candara formatting.
- Scale the worksheet so it prints on one page.

Save and then print **EL1-C4-CS-MRMortgages-01.xlsx**. After looking at the printed worksheet, you decide that you need to make the following changes:

- Sort the values in the *Price of Home* column from smallest to largest.
- Change the percentage amount in column E from 6% to 7%.
- Shade the cells in row 4 that contain data in the light gold color that matches the fill in cell A2. Copy this shading to every other row of cells in the worksheet (stopping at row 46). *Apply accounting formatting with a dollar sign and no places past the decimal point to cells A4, C4, D4, and G4.

Save the edited worksheet with Save As and name it **EL1-C4-CS-MRMortgages-02**. Make sure the worksheet prints on one page. Save, print, and then close **EL1-C4-CS-MRMortgages-02.xlsx**.

You are responsible for preparing a worksheet containing sales and commissions for the year. You will print the worksheet for distribution to staff members who attend an upcoming meeting. You have created the worksheet and included the sales and commission totals and now need to insert formulas and format the worksheet. Open **MRSalesComms.xlsx** and then save the workbook with Save As and name it **EL1-C4-CS-MRSalesComms**. Make the following changes to the worksheet:

- Calculate the sales and commissions and insert the totals in the appropriate locations in the worksheet.
- Calculate the total sales and total commissions and insert the totals in the appropriate locations in the worksheet.
- Apply appropriate number formatting.
- Apply formatting so the worksheet is formatted similar to the worksheet you prepared in Part 1.
- Change the left margin to 1.2 inches and the top margin to 1.5 inches.
- Include a header that prints the page number and a footer that prints your name.

Save the worksheet and then print it so that the row titles (A4:A14) print on both pages. After looking at the worksheet, you decide to make the following changes:

- Remove the header containing the page number.
- Edit the footer so the date prints at the left margin and your name prints at the right margin.
- Change the orientation to landscape.
- Scale the worksheet so it prints on one page.

Print, save, and then close **EL1-C4-CS-MRSalesComms.xlsx**.

Part 3

You have clients living in Canada that are interested in purchasing real estate in the United States. For those clients, you like to keep a dollar conversion worksheet available. Using the Internet, search for a site that converts the US dollar to the Canadian dollar. Determine the current currency exchange rate for the Canadian dollar and then create a worksheet with the following specifications:

- Apply formatting that is similar to the formatting in the worksheets you worked with in the first two parts of the case study.
- Create a column for home prices in US dollars with home amounts that begin with $100,000, increment every $50,000, and end with $1,000,000.
- Create a column for home prices converted to Canadian dollars.
- Apply any other formatting you feel is necessary to improve the worksheet.

Save the completed workbook and name it **EL1-C4-CS-CanadaPrices**. Display formulas and then print the worksheet. Turn off the display of formulas and then save and close the workbook.

MICROSOFT® EXCEL® Performance Assessment

Excel
Excel L1U1

Note: Before beginning unit assessments, copy to your storage medium the EL1U1 subfolder from the EL1U1 folder on the CD that accompanies this textbook and then make EL1U1 the active folder.

Assessing Proficiency ■■■■■■■■■■■■■■■■

In this unit, you have learned to create, save, print, edit, and format Excel worksheets; create and insert formulas; and enhance worksheets with features such as headers and footers, page numbering, sorting, and filtering.

Assessment 1 Calculate Total, Maximum, Minimum, and Average Yearly Sales

1. Open **DI2015Sales.xlsx** and then save the workbook with Save As and name it **EL1-U1-A1-DI2015Sales**.
2. Insert in cells D4 through D14 the appropriate sales totals.
3. Insert in cells B15, C15, and D15 the appropriate first half, second half, and total sales, respectively. (If you use the fill handle to copy the formula in cell B15 to cells C15 and D15, you will need to fill without formatting so the right border remains in cell D15.)
4. Insert in cell B17 a formula that inserts the maximum total sales amount from cells D4 through D14.
5. Insert in cell B18 a formula that inserts the minimum total sales amount from cells D4 through D14.
6. Insert in cell B19 a formula that inserts the average of total sales in cells D4 through D14.
7. Apply accounting formatting to cell D4 with a dollar sign. (Make sure the places after the decimal point remain set at zero.)
8. Save, print, and then close **EL1-U1-A1-DI2015Sales.xlsx**.

Assessment 2 Create Worksheet with AutoFill and Calculate Hours and Gross Pay

1. Create the Excel worksheet shown in Figure U1.1. Use AutoFill to fill in the days of the week and some of the hours.
2. Insert a formula in cells H4 through H10 that calculates the total hours.
3. Insert a formula in cells J4 through J10 that calculates the gross pay (total hours multiplied by pay rate).
4. Insert a formula in cells B11 through J11 that totals the hours, total hours, pay rate, and gross pay.

5. Apply formatting to the cells as shown in the figure.
6. Change the page orientation to landscape.
7. Save the worksheet and name it **EL1-U1-A2-CPPayroll**.
8. Turn on the display of formulas, print the worksheet (prints on two pages), and then turn off the display of formulas.
9. Save and then close **EL1-U1-A2-CPPayroll.xlsx**.

Figure U1.1 Assessment 2

	A	B	C	D	E	F	G	H	I	J
1				**Capstan Products**						
2				**Payroll - Week Ended: March 14, 2015**						
3	**Employee**	**Monday**	**Tuesday**	**Wednesday**	**Thursday**	**Friday**	**Saturday**	**Total Hours**	**Pay Rate**	**Gross Pay**
4	Loftus, Maureen	8	8	8	8	8	0	40	$ 28.50	$1,140.00
5	Banyai, Robert	3	3	3	3	0	8	20	15.35	307.00
6	Martinez, Michelle	0	8	8	8	8	8	40	19.00	760.00
7	Wilhelm, Marshall	0	5	5	5	5	8	28	13.50	378.00
8	Ziegler, Cathleen	0	0	0	0	4	4	8	22.45	179.60
9	Hope, Trevor	0	0	0	0	4	4	8	13.50	108.00
10	Anthony, Charles	0	4	4	4	4	4	20	13.50	270.00
11	**Total**	11	28	28	28	33	36	164	$ 125.80	$3,142.60

Assessment 3 Sales Bonuses Workbook

1. Create the Excel worksheet shown in Figure U1.2. Format the cells as you see them in the figure.
2. Insert a formula in cells D4 through D11 that calculates the bonus amount (sales times bonus).
3. Insert a formula in cells E4 through E11 that calculates the net sales (sales minus bonus amount).
4. Insert the sum of cells B4 through B11 in cell B12, the sum of cells D4 through D11 in cell D12, and the sum of cells E4 through E11 in cell E12.
5. Apply accounting formatting with no places after the decimal point and no dollar sign to cells B5 through B11 and cells D5 through E11.
6. Apply accounting formatting with a dollar sign and no places after the decimal point to cells B4, D4, E4, B12, D12, and E12.
7. Insert a footer that contains your first and last names and the current date.
8. Print the worksheet horizontally and vertically centered on the page.
9. Save the workbook and name it **EL1-U1-A3-SBASales**.
10. Close **EL1-U1-A3-SBASales.xlsx**.

Figure U1.2 Assessment 3

	A	B	C	D	E	F
1	Stanton & Barnet Associates					
2	Sales Department					
3	Associate	Sales	Bonus	Bonus Amount	Net Sales	
4	Conway, Amanda	$101,450	5%			
5	Eckhart, Geneva	94,375	2%			
6	Farris, Edward	73,270	0%			
7	Greenwood, Wayne	110,459	5%			
8	Hagen, Chandra	120,485	5%			
9	Logan, Courtney	97,520	2%			
10	Pena, Geraldo	115,850	5%			
11	Rubin, Alex	76,422	0%			
12	Total					
13						

Assessment 4 Format a Department Budget

1. Open **CMDeptBudgets.xlsx** and then save the workbook with Save As and name it **EL1-U1-A4-CMDeptBudgets**.
2. Insert a formula using an absolute cell reference to determine the projected budget with an increase of 10% over the current budget. (Use the number *1.1* in cell B3 when writing the formula.)
3. Insert formulas to total the budget amounts and the projected budget amounts.
4. Make cell A15 active and then use the NOW function to insert the current date and time.
5. Save and then print the worksheet.
6. Determine the projected budget with an increase of 5% over the current budget by changing the text in cell A3 to *5% Increase* and the number in cell B3 to *1.05*.
7. Save, print, and then close **EL1-U1-A4-CMDeptBudgets.xlsx**.

Assessment 5 Format Weekly Payroll Workbook

1. Open **CCPayroll.xlsx** and then save the workbook with Save As and name it **EL1-U1-A5-CCPayroll**.
2. Insert a formula in cell E3 that multiplies the hourly rate by the hours and then adds that to the multiplication of the hourly rate by the overtime pay rate (1.5) and then overtime hours. (Use parentheses in the formula and use an absolute cell reference for the overtime pay rate. Refer to Chapter 2, Project 3c.) Copy the formula down to cells E4 through E16.
3. Insert a formula in cell F3 that multiplies the gross pay by the withholding tax rate (W/H Rate). (Use an absolute cell reference for the cell containing the withholding rate. Refer to Chapter 2, Project 3c.) Copy the formula down to cells F4 through F16.

4. Insert a formula in cell G3 that multiplies the gross pay by the social security rate (SS Rate). Use an absolute cell reference for the cell containing the social security rate. (Refer to Chapter 2, Project 3c.) Copy the formula down to cells G4 through G16.
5. Insert a formula in cell H4 that adds together the social security tax and the withholding tax and subtracts that sum from the gross pay. (Refer to Chapter 2, Project 3c.) Copy the formula down to cells H4 through H16.
6. Sort the employee last names alphabetically in ascending order (A to Z).
7. Center the worksheet horizontally and vertically on the page.
8. Insert a footer that prints your name at the left side of the page and the file name at the right side of the page.
9. Save, print, and then close **EL1-U1-A5-CCPayroll.xlsx**.

Assessment 6 Format Customer Sales Analysis Workbook

1. Open **DIAnnualSales.xlsx** and then save the workbook with Save As and name it **EL1-U1-A6-DIAnnualSales**.
2. Insert formulas and drag formulas to complete the worksheet. After dragging the total formula in row 10, specify that you want to fill without formatting. (This retains the right border in cell N10.) Do this with the Auto Fill Options button.
3. Insert in cell B11 the highest total from cells B10 through M10. Insert in cell B12 the lowest total from cells B10 through M10.
4. Change the orientation to landscape.
5. Insert a header that prints the page number at the right side of the page.
6. Insert a footer that prints your name at the right side of the page.
7. Horizontally and vertically center the worksheet on the page.
8. Specify that the column headings in cells A3 through A12 print on both pages.
9. Save, print, and then close **EL1-U1-A6-DIAnnualSales.xlsx**.

Assessment 7 Format Invoices Workbook

1. Open **RPInvoices.xlsx** and then save the workbook with Save As and name it **EL1-U1-A7-RPInvoices**.
2. Insert a formula in cell G4 that multiplies the amount in cell E4 by the percentage in cell F4 and then adds that total to the amount in cell E4. (Use parentheses in this formula.)
3. Copy the formula in cell G4 down to cells G5 through G18.
4. Apply accounting formatting with two places after the decimal point and a dollar sign to cell G4, and then apply comma formatting with two places after the decimal point to cells G5 through G18.
5. Find all occurrences of cells containing *11-279* and replace them with *10-005*.
6. Find all occurrences of cells containing *8.5* and replace them with *9.0*.
7. Search for all occurrences of the Calibri font and replace them with the Candara font. (Do not specify a type size so that Excel replaces all sizes of Calibri with Candara.)
8. Print **EL1-U1-A7-RPInvoices.xlsx**.
9. Filter and then print a list of rows containing only the client number *04-325*. (After printing, return the list to *(Select All)*.)
10. Filter and then print a list of rows containing only the service *Development*. (After printing, return the list to *(Select All)*.)
11. Filter and then print a list of rows containing the three highest totals in the *Amount Due* column. (After printing, turn off the filter feature.)
12. Save and then close **EL1-U1-A7-RPInvoices.xlsx**.

Writing Activities ■■■■■■■■■■ ■■■■■■■■■

The following activities give you the opportunity to practice your writing skills along with demonstrating an understanding of some of the important Excel features you have mastered in this unit. Use correct grammar, appropriate word choices, and clear sentence construction.

Activity 1 Plan and Prepare Orders Summary Workbook

Plan and prepare a worksheet with the information shown in Figure U1.3. Apply formatting of your choosing to the worksheet. Save the completed worksheet and name it **EL1-U1-Act1-OrdersSumm**. Print and then close **EL1-U1-Act1-OrdersSumm.xlsx**.

Figure U1.3 Activity 1

Prepare a weekly summary of orders taken that itemizes the products coming into the company and the average order size. The products and average order size include:

Black and gold wall clock: $2,450 worth of orders, average order size of $125
Traveling alarm clock: $1,358 worth of orders, average order size of $195
Waterproof watch: $890 worth of orders, average order size of $90
Dashboard clock: $2,135 worth of orders, average order size of $230
Pyramid clock: $3,050 worth of orders, average order size of $375
Gold chain watch: $755 worth of orders, average order size of $80

In the worksheet, total the amount ordered and also calculate the average weekly order size. Sort the data in the worksheet by the order amount in descending order.

Activity 2 Prepare Depreciation Workbook

Assets within a company, such as equipment, can be depreciated over time. Several methods are available for determining the amount of depreciation, such as the straight-line depreciation method, the fixed-declining balance method, and the double-declining method. Use Excel's Help feature to learn about two depreciation methods: straight-line and double-declining depreciation. (The straight-line depreciation function, SLN, and the double-declining depreciation function, DDB, are located in the *Financial* category.) After reading about the two methods, create an Excel worksheet describing the methods with the following information:

- An appropriate title
- A heading for straight-line depreciation
- The straight-line depreciation function
- The name of and a description for each straight-line depreciation function argument category
- A heading for double-declining depreciation

- The double-declining depreciation function
- The name of and a description for each double-declining depreciation function argument category

Apply formatting of your choosing to the worksheet. Save the completed workbook and name it **EL1-U1-Act2-DepMethods**. Print the worksheet horizontally and vertically centered on the page. Close **EL1-U1-Act2-DepMethods.xlsx**.

Activity 3 Insert Straight-Line Depreciation Formula

Open **RPDepreciation.xlsx** and then save the workbook and name it **EL1-U1-Act3-RPDepreciation**. Insert the function to determine straight-line depreciation in cell E4. Copy the formula down to cells E5 through E9. Print the worksheet horizontally and vertically centered on the page. Save and then close **EL1-U1-Act3-RPDepreciation.xlsx**.

Optional: Briefly research straight-line and double-declining depreciation to find out why businesses depreciate their assets. What purpose does it serve? Locate information about the topics on the Internet or in your school library. Then use Word 2013 to write a half-page, single-spaced report explaining the financial reasons for using depreciation methods. Save the document and name it **EL1-U1-Act3-DepReport**. Print and then close the document.

Internet Research ■■■■■■■■■■■■■■■■■■■■

Create a Travel Planning Worksheet

Search for information on the Internet on traveling to a specific country that interests you. Find sites that provide cost information for airlines, hotels, meals, entertainment, and car rentals. Using the first week of the next month as the travel dates, create a travel planning worksheet for the country that includes the following:

- An appropriate title
- Appropriate headings
- Airline costs
- Hotel costs (off-season and in-season rates if available)
- Estimated meal costs
- Entertainment costs
- Car rental costs

Save the completed workbook and name it **EL1-U1-Act4-TrvlWksht**. Print and then close the workbook.

MICROSOFT®
EXCEL®

Level 1

Unit 2 ■ Enhancing the Display of Workbooks

MICROSOFT EXCEL

Moving Data within and between Workbooks

CHAPTER 5

PERFORMANCE OBJECTIVES

Upon successful completion of Chapter 5, you will be able to:

- **Create a workbook with multiple worksheets**
- **Move, copy, and paste cells within and between worksheets**
- **Split a worksheet into windows and freeze panes**
- **Name a range of cells and use a range in a formula**
- **Open multiple workbooks**
- **Arrange, size, and move workbooks**
- **Copy and paste data between workbooks**
- **Link data between worksheets**

Tutorials

Up to this point, the workbooks you have been working in have consisted of only single worksheets. In this chapter, you will learn to create a workbook with several worksheets and complete tasks such as copying and pasting data within and between worksheets. Moving and pasting or copying and pasting selected cells in and between worksheets is useful for rearranging data and saving time. You will also work with multiple workbooks and complete tasks such as arranging, sizing, and moving workbooks and opening and closing multiple workbooks. Model answers for this chapter's projects appear on the following pages.

Excel
EL1C5

Note: Before beginning the projects, copy to your storage medium the EL1C5 subfolder from the EL1 folder on the CD that accompanies this textbook and then make EL1C5 the active folder.

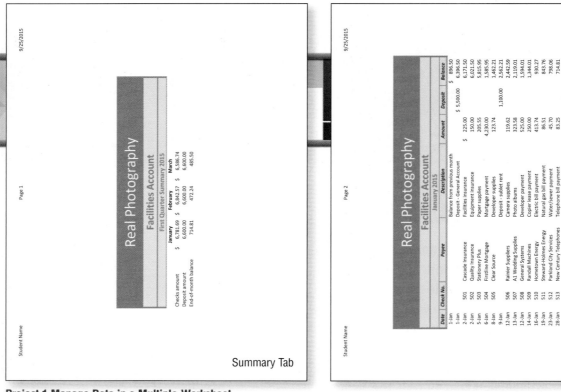

Project 1 Manage Data in a Multiple-Worksheet Account Workbook EL1-C5-P1-RPFacAccts.xlsx

Summary Tab

Real Photography
Facilities Account
First Quarter Summary 2015

	January	February	March
Checks amount	$ 6,781.69	$ 6,842.57	$ 6,586.74
Deposit amount	6,600.00	6,600.00	6,600.00
End-of-month balance	714.81	472.24	485.50

January Tab

Real Photography
Facilities Account
January 2015

Date	Check No.	Payee	Description	Amount	Deposit	Balance
1-Jan			Balance from previous month			$ 896.50
1-Jan			Deposit - General Account		$ 5,500.00	6,396.50
2-Jan	501	Cascade Insurance	Facilities insurance	$ 225.00		6,171.50
2-Jan	502	Quality Insurance	Equipment insurance	150.00		6,021.50
5-Jan	503	Stationery Plus	Paper supplies	205.55		5,815.95
6-Jan	504	Firstline Mortgage	Mortgage payment	4,230.00		1,585.95
8-Jan	505	Clear Source	Developer supplies	123.74		1,462.21
9-Jan			Deposit - sublet rent		1,100.00	2,562.21
12-Jan	506	Rainier Suppliers	Camera supplies	119.62		2,442.59
13-Jan	507	A1 Wedding Supplies	Photo albums	323.58		2,119.01
12-Jan	508	General Systems	Developer payment	525.00		1,594.01
14-Jan	509	Randall Machines	Copier lease payment	250.00		1,344.01
16-Jan	510	Hometown Energy	Electric bill payment	413.74		930.27
19-Jan	511	Steward-Holmes Energy	Natural gas bill payment	86.51		843.76
23-Jan	512	Parkland City Services	Water/sewer payment	45.70		798.06
28-Jan	513	New Century Telephones	Telephone bill payment	83.25		714.81
			Total	$ 6,781.69	$ 6,600.00	

February Tab

Real Photography
Facilities Account
February 2015

Date	Check No.	Payee	Description	Amount	Deposit	Balance
1-Feb			Balance from previous month			$ 714.81
2-Feb			Deposit - General Account		$ 5,500.00	6,214.81
3-Feb	514	Firstline Mortgage	Mortgage payment	$ 4,230.00		1,984.81
5-Feb	515	Cascade Insurance	Facilities insurance	225.00		1,759.81
10-Feb	516	Quality Insurance	Equipment insurance	150.00		1,609.81
11-Feb	517	Stationery Plus	Paper supplies	266.43		1,343.38
12-Feb	518	Clear Source	Developer supplies	123.74		1,219.64
13-Feb			Deposit - sublet rent		1,100.00	2,319.64
16-Feb	519	Rainier Suppliers	Camera supplies	119.62		2,200.02
17-Feb	520	A1 Wedding Supplies	Photo albums	323.58		1,876.44
17-Feb	521	General Systems	Developer payment	525.00		1,351.44
20-Feb	522	Randall Machines	Copier lease payment	250.00		1,101.44
20-Feb	523	Hometown Energy	Electric bill payment	413.74		687.70
23-Feb	524	Steward-Holmes Energy	Natural gas bill payment	86.51		601.19
24-Feb	525	Parkland City Services	Water/sewer payment	45.70		555.49
26-Feb	526	New Century Telephones	Telephone bill payment	83.25		472.24
			Total	$ 6,842.57	$ 6,600.00	

March Tab

Real Photography
Facilities Account
March 2015

Date	Check No.	Payee	Description	Amount	Deposit	Balance
1-Mar			Balance from previous month			$ 472.24
2-Mar			Deposit - General Account		$ 5,500.00	5,972.24
2-Mar			Deposit - sublet rent			5,972.24
4-Mar	527	Firstline Mortgage	Mortgage payment	$ 4,230.00		1,742.24
5-Mar	528	Cascade Insurance	Facilities insurance	225.00		1,517.24
6-Mar	529	Stationery Plus	Paper supplies	113.76		1,403.48
9-Mar	530	Clear Source	Developer supplies	251.90		1,151.58
9-Mar	531		Deposit - sublet rent		1,100.00	2,251.58
9-Mar	532	Rainier Suppliers	Camera supplies	119.62		2,131.96
9-Mar	533	A1 Wedding Supplies	Photo albums	323.58		1,808.38
12-Mar	534	General Systems	Developer payment	525.00		1,283.38
16-Mar	535	Randall Machines	Copier lease payment	250.00		1,033.38
17-Mar	536	Hometown Energy	Electric bill payment	326.42		706.96
23-Mar	537	Steward-Holmes Energy	Natural gas bill payment	92.51		614.45
24-Mar	538	Parkland City Services	Water/sewer payment	45.70		568.75
27-Mar	539	New Century Telephones	Telephone bill payment	83.25		485.50
			Total	$ 6,586.74	$ 6,600.00	

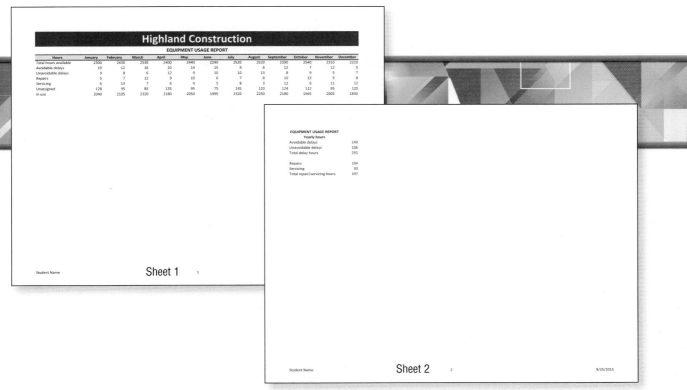

Highland Construction

EQUIPMENT USAGE REPORT

Hours	January	February	March	April	May	June	July	August	September	October	November	December
Total hours available	2300	2430	2530	2400	2440	2240	2520	2520	2390	2540	2310	2210
Avoidable delays	19	12	16	20	14	15	9	12	7	12	7	5
Unavoidable delays	9	8	6	12	9	10	10	13	8	9	5	7
Repairs	5	7	12	9	10	6	7	8	10	13	9	8
Servicing	6	13	7	6	4	5	8	3	12	6	11	12
Unassigned	128	95	85	135	95	75	145	120	124	112	95	120
In use	2040	2105	2320	2180	2050	1995	2320	2250	2190	1945	2005	1830

Student Name   Sheet 1   1

EQUIPMENT USAGE REPORT
Yearly hours

Avoidable delays	149
Unavoidable delays	106
Total delay hours	255
Repairs	104
Servicing	93
Total repair/servicing hours	197

Student Name   Sheet 2   2   9/25/2015

Project 2 Write Formulas Using Ranges in an Equipment Usage Workbook
EL1-C5-P2-HCEqpRpt.xlsx

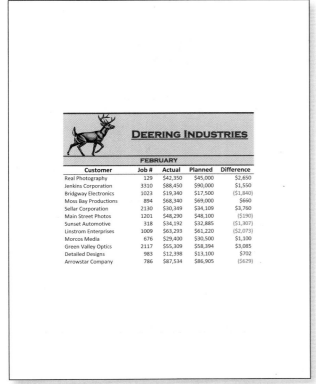

DEERING INDUSTRIES

FEBRUARY

Customer	Job #	Actual	Planned	Difference
Real Photography	129	$42,350	$45,000	$2,650
Jenkins Corporation	3310	$88,450	$90,000	$1,550
Bridgway Electronics	1023	$19,340	$17,500	($1,840)
Moss Bay Productions	894	$68,340	$69,000	$660
Sellar Corporation	2130	$30,349	$34,109	$3,760
Main Street Photos	1201	$48,290	$48,100	($190)
Sunset Automotive	318	$34,192	$32,885	($1,307)
Linstrom Enterprises	1009	$63,293	$61,220	($2,073)
Morcos Media	676	$29,400	$30,500	$1,100
Green Valley Optics	2117	$55,309	$58,394	$3,085
Detailed Designs	983	$12,398	$13,100	$702
Arrowstar Company	786	$87,534	$86,905	($629)

Project 3 Arrange, Size, and Copy Data between Workbooks
EL1-C5-P3-DIFebJobs.xlsx

Dollar Wise
Financial Services

First Quarter			
Expense	Actual	Budget	Variance
Salaries	$ 122,000.00	$ 128,000.00	$ 6,000.00
Commissions	58,000.00	56,000.00	(2,000.00)
Media space	8,250.00	10,100.00	1,850.00
Travel expenses	6,350.00	6,000.00	(350.00)
Dealer display	4,140.00	4,500.00	360.00
Payroll taxes	2,430.00	2,400.00	(30.00)
Telephone	1,450.00	1,500.00	50.00

1st Qtr Tab

Project 4 Linking and Copying Data within and between Worksheets and Word
EL1-C5-P4-DWQtrlyExp.xlsx

Dollar Wise Financial Services

Second Quarter			
Expense	*Actual*	*Budget*	*Variance*
Salaries	$ 98,200.00	$ 128,000.00	$ 29,800.00
Commissions	42,300.00	56,000.00	13,700.00
Media space	9,150.00	10,100.00	950.00
Travel expenses	6,350.00	6,000.00	(350.00)
Dealer display	3,140.00	4,500.00	1,360.00
Payroll taxes	1,675.00	2,400.00	725.00
Telephone	1,255.00	1,500.00	245.00

2nd Qtr Tab

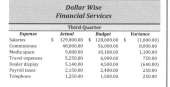

Dollar Wise Financial Services

Third Quarter			
Expense	*Actual*	*Budget*	*Variance*
Salaries	$ 129,000.00	$ 128,000.00	$ (1,000.00)
Commissions	48,000.00	56,000.00	8,000.00
Media space	9,000.00	10,100.00	1,100.00
Travel expenses	5,250.00	6,000.00	750.00
Dealer display	5,140.00	4,500.00	(640.00)
Payroll taxes	2,150.00	2,400.00	250.00
Telephone	1,250.00	1,500.00	250.00

3rd Qtr Tab

Dollar Wise Financial Services

Fourth Quarter			
Expense	*Actual*	*Budget*	*Variance*
Salaries	$ 125,200.00	$ 128,000.00	$ 2,800.00
Commissions	49,300.00	56,000.00	6,700.00
Media space	9,150.00	10,100.00	950.00
Travel expenses	5,850.00	6,000.00	150.00
Dealer display	3,240.00	4,500.00	1,260.00
Payroll taxes	1,975.00	2,400.00	425.00
Telephone	1,355.00	1,500.00	145.00

4th Qtr Tab

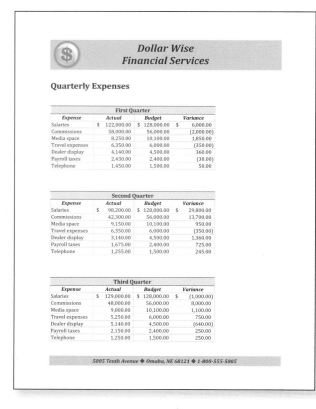

Dollar Wise Financial Services

Quarterly Expenses

First Quarter			
Expense	*Actual*	*Budget*	*Variance*
Salaries	$ 122,000.00	$ 128,000.00	$ 6,000.00
Commissions	58,000.00	56,000.00	(2,000.00)
Media space	8,250.00	10,100.00	1,850.00
Travel expenses	6,350.00	6,000.00	(350.00)
Dealer display	4,140.00	4,500.00	360.00
Payroll taxes	2,430.00	2,400.00	(30.00)
Telephone	1,450.00	1,500.00	50.00

Second Quarter			
Expense	*Actual*	*Budget*	*Variance*
Salaries	$ 98,200.00	$ 128,000.00	$ 29,800.00
Commissions	42,300.00	56,000.00	13,700.00
Media space	9,150.00	10,100.00	950.00
Travel expenses	6,350.00	6,000.00	(350.00)
Dealer display	3,140.00	4,500.00	1,360.00
Payroll taxes	1,675.00	2,400.00	725.00
Telephone	1,255.00	1,500.00	245.00

Third Quarter			
Expense	*Actual*	*Budget*	*Variance*
Salaries	$ 129,000.00	$ 128,000.00	$ (1,000.00)
Commissions	48,000.00	56,000.00	8,000.00
Media space	9,000.00	10,100.00	1,100.00
Travel expenses	5,250.00	6,000.00	750.00
Dealer display	5,140.00	4,500.00	(640.00)
Payroll taxes	2,150.00	2,400.00	250.00
Telephone	1,250.00	1,500.00	250.00

5005 Tenth Avenue ❖ Omaha, NE 68121 ❖ 1-800-555-5005

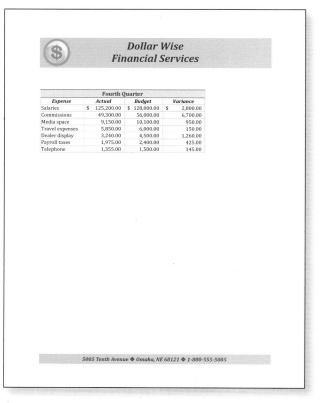

Dollar Wise Financial Services

Fourth Quarter			
Expense	*Actual*	*Budget*	*Variance*
Salaries	$ 125,200.00	$ 128,000.00	$ 2,800.00
Commissions	49,300.00	56,000.00	6,700.00
Media space	9,150.00	10,100.00	950.00
Travel expenses	5,850.00	6,000.00	150.00
Dealer display	3,240.00	4,500.00	1,260.00
Payroll taxes	1,975.00	2,400.00	425.00
Telephone	1,355.00	1,500.00	145.00

5005 Tenth Avenue ❖ Omaha, NE 68121 ❖ 1-800-555-5005

EL1-C5-P4-DWQtrlyRpt.docx

Project	1	Manage Data in a Multiple-Worksheet Account Workbook	7 Parts

You will open an account workbook containing multiple worksheets and then insert and delete worksheets and move, copy, and paste data between the worksheets. You will also hide and unhide worksheets and format and print multiple worksheets in the workbook.

Creating a Workbook with Multiple Worksheets ■■■■■■

An Excel workbook, by default, contains one worksheet, but you can add additional worksheets to it. Add additional worksheets to a workbook to store related data. For example, you might want to create a workbook with a worksheet for the expenses for each salesperson in the company and another worksheet for the monthly payroll for each department within the company. Another example is recording sales statistics for each quarter in individual worksheets within a workbook.

Creating multiple worksheets within a workbook is helpful for saving related data.

Inserting a New Worksheet

Insert a new worksheet in a workbook by clicking the New sheet button that displays to the right of the Sheet1 tab at the bottom of the worksheet area. You can also insert a new worksheet with the keyboard shortcut Shift + F11. A new worksheet tab is inserted to the right of the active tab. To move between worksheets, click the desired tab. The active worksheet tab displays with a white background and the worksheet name displays in green. Any inactive tabs display with a light gray background and gray text.

▼ **Quick Steps**
Insert a Worksheet
Click New sheet button.
OR
Press Shift + F11.

New sheet

Deleting a Worksheet

If you no longer need a worksheet in a workbook, delete the worksheet by clicking the desired worksheet tab, clicking the Delete button arrow in the Cells group on the HOME tab, and then clicking *Delete Sheet* at the drop-down list. You can also delete a worksheet by right-clicking the worksheet tab and then clicking *Delete* at the shortcut menu. When you click the Delete button or option, Excel displays a message telling you that you cannot undo deleting sheets. At this message, click the Delete button.

▼ **Quick Steps**
Delete a Worksheet
1. Click worksheet tab.
2. Click Delete button arrow.
3. Click *Delete Sheet*.
4. Click Delete button.

Selecting Multiple Worksheets

To work with more than one worksheet at a time, select the desired worksheets. You might want to select multiple worksheets to apply the same formatting to cells or to delete multiple worksheets. To select adjacent worksheet tabs, click the first tab, hold down the Shift key, and then click the last tab. To select nonadjacent worksheet tabs, click the first tab, hold down the Ctrl key, and then click any other tabs you want selected.

Copy

Cut

Paste

Copying, Cutting, and Pasting Cells

At times, you may need to copy cells or move cells to a different location within a worksheet or to another worksheet or workbook. You can move or copy cells in a worksheet or between worksheets or workbooks. Perform these actions by selecting cells and then using the Cut, Copy, and/or Paste buttons in the Clipboard group on the HOME tab.

Copying and Pasting Selected Cells

Quick Steps

Copy and Paste Cells
1. Select cells.
2. Click Copy button.
3. Click desired cell.
4. Click Paste button.

Ctrl + C is the keyboard shortcut to copy selected data.

Copying selected cells can be useful in worksheets that contain repetitive data. To copy cells, select the cells and then click the Copy button in the Clipboard group on the HOME tab. This causes a moving dashed line border (called a *marquee*) to display around the selected cells. If you are copying cells to another worksheet, click the worksheet tab. Click the cell where you want the first selected cell copied and then click the Paste button in the Clipboard group. Remove the moving marquee from selected cells by pressing the Esc key or double-clicking in any cell.

You can also copy selected cells in the same worksheet using the mouse and the Ctrl key. To do this, select the cells you want to copy and then position the mouse pointer on any border around the selected cells until the pointer turns into an arrow pointer. Hold down the Ctrl key and the left mouse button, drag the outline of the selected cells to the desired location, release the left mouse button, and then release the Ctrl key.

Project 1a   **Inserting, Deleting, Selecting, Copying, Pasting, and Formatting Worksheets**   Part 1 of 7

1. Open **RPFacAccts.xlsx** and then save the workbook with Save As and name it **EL1-C5-P1-RPFacAccts**.
2. Insert a new worksheet in the workbook by completing the following steps:
   a. Click the 2ndHalfSales worksheet tab to make it active.
   b. Click the New sheet button that displays to the right of the 2ndHalfSales worksheet tab. (This inserts a new worksheet to the right of the 2ndHalfSales worksheet with the name Sheet4.)

3. Delete two worksheet tabs by completing the following steps:
   a. Click the 1stHalfSales worksheet tab.
   b. Hold down the Shift key and then click the 2ndHalfSales worksheet tab. (These tabs must be adjacent. If they are not, hold down the Ctrl key when clicking the 2ndHalfSales worksheet tab.)
   c. With the two worksheet tabs selected, click the Delete button arrow in the Cells group on the HOME tab and then click *Delete Sheet* at the drop-down list.
   d. At the message that displays telling you that you cannot undo deleting sheets, click the Delete button.

---

4. Copy cells from Sheet1 to Sheet4 by completing the following steps:
   a. Click the Sheet1 tab to make it the active worksheet.
   b. Select cells A1 through A3 (the first three rows of data).
   c. Click the Copy button in the Clipboard group on the HOME tab.
   d. Click the Sheet4 tab to make it the active tab.
   e. With A1 the active cell, click the Paste button in the Clipboard group on the HOME tab.

5. Make the following changes to the new worksheet:
   a. Make cell A3 active and then type **First Quarter Summary 2015**.
   b. Change the width of column A to 20.00 characters.
   c. Change the widths of columns B, C, and D to 12.00 characters.
   d. Type the following text in the specified cells:
      B4: **January**
      C4: **February**
      D4: **March**
      A5: **Checks amount**
      A6: **Deposit amount**
      A7: **End-of-month balance**
   e. Select cells B4 through D4, click the Bold button in the Font group on the HOME tab, and then click the Center button in the Alignment group.
   f. Select cells B5 through D7 and then apply accounting formatting without dollar signs and with two places after the decimal point.
6. Apply formatting to cells in all four worksheets by completing the following steps:
   a. Click Sheet1 to make it active and then click in cell A1 to make it the active cell.
   b. Hold down the Shift key and then click Sheet4. (This selects all four worksheets.)
   c. With cell A1 active, change the row height to 51.00 points.
   d. Make cell A3 active.
   e. Change the font size to 14 points.
   f. Click each remaining worksheet tab (Sheet2, Sheet3, and Sheet4) and notice the formatting changes applied to all of the cells.
7. Change column widths for the three worksheets by completing the following steps:
   a. Click Sheet1 to make it active.
   b. Hold down the Shift key and then click Sheet3.
   c. Select columns E, F, and G and then change the column width to 10.00 characters.
   d. Click Sheet2 and then click Sheet 3. Notice that the widths of columns E, F, and G have changed to 10.00 characters. Click Sheet4 and notice that the column widths did not change.
8. Save **EL1-C5-P1-RPFacAccts.xlsx**.

Using Paste Options

When you paste cells in a worksheet, you can specify how you want the cells pasted by clicking the Paste button arrow and then clicking the desired paste option button at the drop-down list. You can also click the Paste button (not the button arrow) and a Paste Options button displays in the lower right corner of the pasted cell(s). Display a list of paste options by clicking the button or pressing

Paste Options

Figure 5.1 Paste Option Buttons

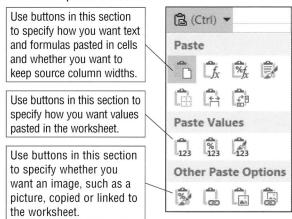

Use buttons in this section to specify how you want text and formulas pasted in cells and whether you want to keep source column widths.

Use buttons in this section to specify how you want values pasted in the worksheet.

Use buttons in this section to specify whether you want an image, such as a picture, copied or linked to the worksheet.

the Ctrl key. This causes a drop-down list to display, as shown in Figure 5.1. The same option buttons display when you click the Paste button arrow. Hover your mouse over a button in the drop-down list and the descriptive name of the button displays along with the keyboard shortcut. Use buttons in this drop-down list to specify what you want pasted.

Moving Selected Cells

▼ **Quick Steps**

Move and Paste Cells
1. Select cells.
2. Click Cut button.
3. Click desired cell.
4. Click Paste button.

Ctrl + X is the keyboard shortcut to cut selected data. Ctrl + V is the keyboard shortcut to paste data.

You can move selected cells and cell contents within and between worksheets. Move selected cells with the Cut and Paste buttons in the Clipboard group on the HOME tab or by dragging with the mouse.

To move selected cells with buttons on the HOME tab, select the cells and then click the Cut button in the Clipboard group. Click the cell where you want the first selected cell inserted and then click the Paste button in the Clipboard group.

To move selected cells with the mouse, select the cells and then position the mouse pointer on any border of the selected cells until the pointer turns into an arrow pointer with a four-headed arrow attached. Hold down the left mouse button, drag the outline of the selected cells to the desired location, and then release the mouse button.

Project 1b **Copying and Moving Cells and Pasting Cells Using Paste Options** **Part 2 of 7**

1. With **EL1-C5-P1-RPFacAccts.xlsx** open, copy cells from Sheet2 to Sheet3 using the Paste Options button by completing the following steps:
   a. Click the Sheet2 tab to make it active.
   b. Select cells C7 through E9.
   c. Click the Copy button in the Clipboard group.
   d. Click the Sheet3 tab.
   e. Make cell C7 active.
   f. Click the Paste button in the Clipboard group.

g. Click the Paste Options button that displays in the lower right corner of the pasted cells and then click the Keep Source Column Widths button at the drop-down list.

h. Make Sheet2 active and then press the Esc key to remove the moving marquee.

2. Make Sheet1 active.

3. You realize that the sublet rent deposit was recorded on the wrong day. The correct day is January 9. To move the cells containing information on the deposit, complete the following steps:

   a. Make cell A13 active and then insert a row. (The new row should display above the row containing information on *Rainier Suppliers*.)

   b. Select cells A7 through F7.

   c. Click the Cut button in the Clipboard group on the HOME tab.

   d. Click in cell A13 to make it active.

   e. Click the Paste button in the Clipboard group.

   f. Change the date of the deposit from January 1 to January 9.

   g. Select row 7 and then delete it.

4. Move cells using the mouse by completing the following steps:

   a. Click the Sheet2 tab.

   b. Make cell A13 active and then insert a new row.

   c. Using the mouse, select cells A7 through F7.

   d. Position the mouse pointer on any boundary of the selected cells until it turns into an arrow pointer with a four-headed arrow attached. Hold down the left mouse button, drag the outline of the selected cells to row 13, and then release the mouse button.

12	12-Feb	518	Clear Source	Developer supplies	123.74
13					
14	16-Feb	519	Rainier Su A13:F13	Camera supplies	119.62
15	17-Feb	520	A1 Wedding Supplies	Photo albums	323.58

Step 4d

   e. Change the date of the deposit to February 13.

   f. Delete row 7.

5. Save **EL1-C5-P1-RPFacAccts.xlsx**.

Copying and Pasting with the Clipboard Task Pane

Use the Clipboard task pane to copy and paste multiple items. To use the task pane, click the Clipboard task pane launcher. This button is located in the lower right corner of the Clipboard group on the HOME tab. The Clipboard task pane displays at the left side of the screen in a manner similar to what you see in Figure 5.2.

Select data or an object you want to copy and then click the Copy button in the Clipboard group. Continue selecting cells, text, or other items and clicking the Copy button. To paste an item into a worksheet, make the desired cell active and then click the item in the Clipboard task pane. If the copied item is text, the first 50 characters display in the task pane. If you want to paste all of the selected items into a single location, make the desired cell active and then click the Paste All button in the task pane. When all desired items have been pasted into the worksheet, click the Clear All button to remove any remaining items from the task pane.

▼ **Quick Steps**

Copy and Paste Multiple Items
1. Click Clipboard task pane launcher.
2. Select desired cells.
3. Click Copy button.
4. Repeat Steps 2 and 3 as desired.
5. Make desired cell active.
6. Click item in Clipboard task pane to be inserted in worksheet.
7. Repeat Step 6 as desired.

Figure 5.2 Clipboard Task Pane

Click this button to paste all items in the Clipboard task pane into the worksheet.

Click this button to clear all of the items from the Clipboard task pane.

Cut or copied items display in this list box.

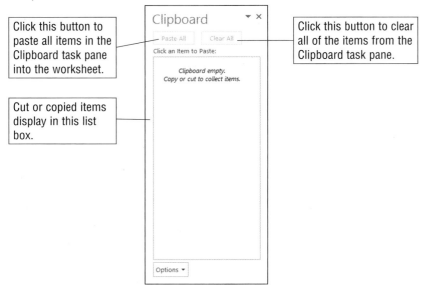

Project 1c Copying and Pasting Cells Using the Clipboard Task Pane Part 3 of 7

1. With **EL1-C5-P1-RPFacAccts.xlsx** open, select cells for copying by completing the following steps:
   a. Display the Clipboard task pane by clicking the Clipboard task pane launcher. (If the Clipboard task pane contains any copied data, click the Clear All button.)
   b. Click the Sheet1 tab.
   c. Select cells C15 through E16.
   d. Click the Copy button in the Clipboard group.
   e. Select cells C19 through E19.
   f. Click the Copy button in the Clipboard group.
2. Paste the copied cells by completing the following steps:
   a. Click the Sheet2 tab.
   b. Make cell C15 active.
   c. Click the item in the Clipboard task pane representing *General Systems Developer*.
   d. Click the Sheet3 tab.
   e. Make cell C15 active.
   f. Click the item in the Clipboard task pane representing *General Systems Developer*.
   g. Make cell C19 active.
   h. Click the item in the Clipboard task pane representing *Parkland City Services*.
3. Click the Clear All button located toward the top of the Clipboard task pane.
4. Close the Clipboard task pane by clicking the Close button (contains an X) located in the upper right corner of the task pane.
5. Save **EL1-C5-P1-RPFacAccts.xlsx**.

Pasting Values Only

When you paste cells containing a value as well as a formula, use button options from the Paste button or Paste Options button drop-down list to specify what you want pasted. With the buttons in the *Paste Values* section of the drop-down list, you can choose to insert the value only, the value with numbering formatting, or the value with the source formatting.

Project 1d   **Copying and Pasting Values**   **Part 4 of 7**

1. With **EL1-C5-P1-RPFacAccts.xlsx** open, make Sheet1 the active tab.
2. Make cell G6 active, type the formula =(F6-E6)+G5, and then press Enter.
3. Copy the formula in cell G6 down to cells G7 through G20.
4. Copy as a value (and not a formula) the final balance amount from Sheet1 to Sheet2 by completing the following steps:
   a. Make cell G20 active.
   b. Click the Copy button in the Clipboard group.
   c. Click the Sheet2 tab.
   d. Make cell G5 active and then click the Paste button arrow.
   e. At the drop-down list that displays, click the Values button in the *Paste Values* section of the drop-down list. (This inserts the value and not the formula.)
5. Make cell G6 active, insert a formula that determines the balance (see Step 2), and then copy the formula down to cells G7 through G20.
6. Copy the amount in cell G20 and then paste the value only in cell G5 in Sheet3. Apply accounting formatting with a dollar sign and two decimal places to the cell.
7. With Sheet3 active, make cell G6 active, insert a formula that determines the balance (see Step 2), and then copy the formula down to cells G7 through G20.
8. Insert formulas and apply formatting to cells in three worksheets by completing the following steps:
   a. Click Sheet1 to make it active.
   b. Hold down the Shift key and then click Sheet3.
   c. Make cell D21 active, click the Bold button in the Font group on the HOME tab, and then type **Total**.
   d. Make cell E21 active and then click once on the AutoSum button in the Editing group on the HOME tab. (This inserts the formula =SUM(E13:E20).)
   e. Change the formula to =SUM(E7:E20) and then press Enter.
   f. Make cell F21 active and then click once on the AutoSum button. (This inserts the formula =SUM(F12:F20).)
   g. Change the formula to =SUM(F6:F20) and then press Enter.
   h. Select cells E21 and F21 and then click the Accounting Number Format button. Make cell G5 active and then click the Accounting Number Format button. (Cell G5 in Sheet1 already contains accounting formatting but cells G5 in Sheet2 and Sheet3 do not.)
   i. Click the Sheet2 tab and notice the text and formulas inserted in the worksheet, click Sheet3 and notice the text and formulas, and then click Sheet4 (to deselect the tabs).
9. Copy values from Sheet1 to Sheet4 by completing the following steps:
   a. Make Sheet1 active.
   b. Make cell E21 active and then click the Copy button in the Clipboard group.
   c. Make Sheet4 active.
   d. Make cell B5 active and then click the Paste button in the Clipboard group.

e. Click the Paste Options button and then click the Values button in the *Paste Values* section of the drop-down list.

f. Make Sheet1 active.

g. Make cell F21 active and then click the Copy button.

h. Make Sheet4 active.

i. Make cell B6 active, click the Paste button arrow, and then click the Values button at the drop-down list.

j. Make Sheet1 active.

k. Make cell G20 active and then click the Copy button.

l. Make Sheet4 active.

m. Make cell B7 active, click the Paste button arrow, and then click the Values button at the drop-down list.

10. Complete steps similar to those in Step 9 to insert amounts and balances for February and March.

11. Select cells B5 through D5 and then click the Accounting Number Format button.

12. Save **EL1-C5-P1-RPFacAccts.xlsx**.

Managing Worksheets

Quick Steps

Move or Copy a Worksheet
1. Right-click sheet tab.
2. Click *Move or Copy*.
3. At Move or Copy dialog box, click desired worksheet name in *Before sheet* list box.
4. Click OK.
OR
Drag worksheet tab to desired position. (To copy, hold down Ctrl key while dragging.)

Right-click a sheet tab and a shortcut menu displays, as shown in Figure 5.3, with the options for managing worksheets. For example, remove a worksheet by clicking the *Delete* option. Move or copy a worksheet by clicking the *Move or Copy* option. Clicking this option causes a Move or Copy dialog box to display, in which you specify where you want to move or copy the selected sheet. By default, Excel names worksheets in a workbook *Sheet1, Sheet2, Sheet3,* and so on. To rename a worksheet, click the *Rename* option (which selects the default sheet name) and then type the desired name.

In addition to the shortcut menu options, you can use the mouse to move or copy worksheets. To move a worksheet, position the mouse pointer on the worksheet tab, hold down the left mouse button (a page icon displays next to the mouse pointer), drag the page icon to the desired position, and then release the mouse button. For example, to move the Sheet2 tab after the Sheet3 tab, position the mouse pointer on the Sheet2 tab, hold down the left mouse button, drag the page icon so it is positioned after the Sheet3 tab, and then release the mouse button. To copy a worksheet, hold down the Ctrl key while dragging the sheet tab.

Use the *Tab Color* option at the shortcut menu to apply a color to a worksheet tab. Right-click a worksheet tab, point to *Tab Color* at the shortcut menu, and then click the desired color at the color palette.

H I N T

Use the tab scroll button to bring into view any worksheet tabs not currently visible.

Quick Steps

Apply Color to a Sheet Tab
1. Right-click sheet tab.
2. Point to *Tab Color*.
3. Click desired color at color palette.

Figure 5.3 Sheet Tab Shortcut Menu

1. With **EL1-C5-P1-RPFacAccts.xlsx** open, move Sheet4 by completing the following steps:
   a. Right-click Sheet4 and then click *Move or Copy* at the shortcut menu.
   b. At the Move or Copy dialog box, make sure *Sheet1* is selected in the *Before sheet* list box, and then click OK.

2. Rename Sheet4 by completing the following steps:
   a. Right-click the Sheet4 tab and then click *Rename*.
   b. Type **Summary** and then press Enter.
3. Complete steps similar to those in Step 2 to rename Sheet1 to *January*, Sheet2 to *February*, and Sheet3 to *March*.
4. Change the color of the Summary sheet tab by completing the following steps:
   a. Right-click the Summary sheet tab.
   b. Point to *Tab Color* at the shortcut menu.
   c. Click the *Red* color option in the *Standard Colors* section (second color option).

5. Follow steps similar to those in Step 4 to change the January sheet tab to Blue (eighth color option in the *Standard Colors* section), the February sheet tab to Purple (last color option in the *Standard Colors* section), and the March sheet tab to Green (sixth color option in the *Standard Colors* section).
6. Save **EL1-C5-P1-RPFacAccts.xlsx**.

Figure 5.4 Unhide Dialog Box

▼ Quick Steps

Hide a Worksheet
1. Click Format button.
2. Point to *Hide & Unhide*.
3. Click *Hide Sheet*.
OR
1. Right-click worksheet tab.
2. Click *Hide* at shortcut menu.

Unhide a Worksheet
1. Click Format button.
2. Point to *Hide & Unhide*.
3. Click *Unhide Sheet*.
4. Double-click desired hidden worksheet in Unhide dialog box.
OR
1. Right-click worksheet tab.
2. Click *Unhide* at shortcut menu.
3. Double-click desired hidden worksheet in Unhide dialog box.

The names of hidden worksheets display in this list box.

Hiding a Worksheet in a Workbook

In a workbook containing multiple worksheets, you can hide a worksheet that may contain sensitive data or data you do not want to display or print with the workbook. To hide a worksheet in a workbook, click the Format button in the Cells group on the HOME tab, point to *Hide & Unhide*, and then click *Hide Sheet*. You can also hide a worksheet by right-clicking a worksheet tab and then clicking the *Hide* option at the shortcut menu. To make a hidden worksheet visible, click the Format button in the Cells group, point to *Hide & Unhide*, and then click *Unhide Sheet*, or right-click a worksheet tab and then click *Unhide* at the shortcut menu. At the Unhide dialog box, as shown in Figure 5.4, double-click the name of the hidden worksheet you want to display.

Format

Project 1f   **Hiding a Worksheet and Formatting Multiple Worksheets**   **Part 6 of 7**

1. With **EL1-C5-P1-RPFacAccts.xlsx** open, hide the Summary worksheet by completing the following steps:
   a. Click the Summary tab.
   b. Click the Format button in the Cells group on the HOME tab, point to *Hide & Unhide*, and then click *Hide Sheet*.

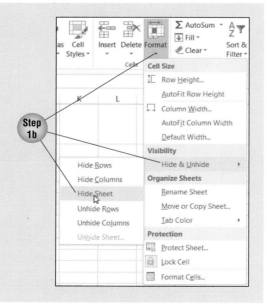

Step 1b

2. Unhide the worksheet by completing the following steps:
   a. Click the Format button in the Cells group, point to *Hide & Unhide*, and then click *Unhide Sheet*.
   b. At the Unhide dialog box, make sure *Summary* is selected and then click OK.

3. Insert a header for each worksheet by completing the following steps:
   a. With the Summary tab active, hold down the Shift key and then click the March tab. (This selects all four tabs.)
   b. Click the INSERT tab.
   c. Click the Header & Footer button in the Text group.
   d. Click the Header button in the Header & Footer group on the HEADER & FOOTER TOOLS DESIGN tab and then click the option at the drop-down list that prints your name at the left side of the page (if a name displays at the left side of the page, select the name and then type your first and last names), the page number in the middle, and the date at the right side.
4. With all the sheet tabs selected, horizontally and vertically center each worksheet on the page. ***Hint: Do this at the Page Setup dialog box with the Margins tab selected.***
5. With all of the sheet tabs still selected, change the page orientation to landscape. ***Hint: Do this with the Orientation button on the PAGE LAYOUT tab.***
6. Save **EL1-C5-P1-RPFacAccts.xlsx**.

Printing a Workbook Containing Multiple Worksheets

By default, Excel prints the currently displayed worksheet. If you want to print all of the worksheets in a workbook, display the Print backstage area, click the first gallery in the *Settings* category, click *Print Entire Workbook* at the drop-down list, and then click the Print button. You can also print specific worksheets in a workbook by selecting the tabs of the worksheets you want printed. With the desired worksheet tabs selected, display the Print backstage area and then click the Print button.

▼ **Quick Steps**

Print All Worksheets in a Workbook
1. Click FILE tab.
2. Click *Print* option.
3. Click first gallery in *Settings* category.
4. Click *Print Entire Workbook*.
5. Click Print button.

1. With **EL1-C5-P1-RPFacAccts.xlsx** open, click the FILE tab and then click the *Print* option.
2. At the Print backstage area, click the first gallery in the *Settings* category and then click *Print Entire Workbook* at the drop-down list.
3. Click the Print button.
4. Save and then close **EL1-C5-P1-RPFacAccts.xlsx**.

Project 2 Write Formulas Using Ranges in an Equipment Usage Workbook

2 Parts

You will open an equipment usage workbook, view the document at different zoom percentages, and then split the window and edit cells. You will also name ranges and then use the range names to write formulas in the workbook.

Using Zoom

Zoom

100%

Zoom to Selection

The VIEW tab contains a Zoom group with three buttons to change zoom settings. Click the Zoom button in the Zoom group to open the Zoom dialog box, which contains options for changing the zoom percentage. Click the 100% button in the Zoom group to return the view to 100%, which is the default. Select a range of cells and then click the Zoom to Selection button to cause Excel to scale the zoom setting so that the selected range fills the worksheet area.

Use the zoom slider bar that displays at the right side of the Status bar to change the zoom percentage. Click the Zoom Out button (displays with a minus symbol) to decrease the zoom percentage or click the Zoom In button (displays with a plus symbol) to increase the zoom percentage. Another method for increasing or decreasing zoom percentage is to click and drag the zoom slider bar button on the slider bar.

Splitting a Worksheet into Windows and Freezing and Unfreezing Panes

In some worksheets, not all cells display at one time in the worksheet area (for example, in **EL1-C5-P2-HCEqpRpt.xlsx**). When working in a worksheet with more cells than can display at one time, you may find splitting the worksheet window into panes helpful. Split the worksheet window into panes with the Split button in the Window group on the VIEW tab. When you click the Split button, the worksheet splits into four window panes, as shown in Figure 5.5. The windows are split by thick, light gray lines called *split lines*. To remove split lines from a worksheet, click the Split button to deactivate it.

A window pane will display the active cell. As the insertion point is moved through the pane, another active cell may display. This additional active cell displays when the insertion point passes over one of the split lines that creates the pane. As you move through a worksheet, you may see both active cells. If you make a change to one active cell, the change is made in the other as well. If you want only one active cell to display, freeze the window panes by clicking the Freeze Panes button in the Window group on the VIEW tab and then clicking *Freeze Panes* at the drop-down list. You can maintain the display of column headings while editing or typing text in cells by clicking the Freeze Panes button and then clicking *Freeze Top Row*. Maintain the display of row headings by clicking the Freeze Panes button and then clicking *Freeze First Column*. Unfreeze window panes by clicking the Freeze Panes button and then clicking *Unfreeze Panes* at the drop-down list.

Using the mouse, you can move the split lines that divide the window. To do this, position the mouse pointer on a split line until the pointer turns into a left-and-right-pointing arrow with a double line in the middle. Hold down the left mouse button, drag the outline of the split line to the desired location, and then release the mouse button. If you want to move both the horizontal and vertical split lines at the same time, position the mouse pointer on the intersection of the split lines until the pointer turns into a four-headed arrow. Hold down the left mouse button, drag the split lines to the desired direction, and then release the mouse button.

▼ Quick Steps

Split a Worksheet
1. Click VIEW tab.
2. Click Split button.

Split

Remove a split line by double-clicking anywhere on the split line that divides the panes.

Freeze Panes

Figure 5.5 Split Window

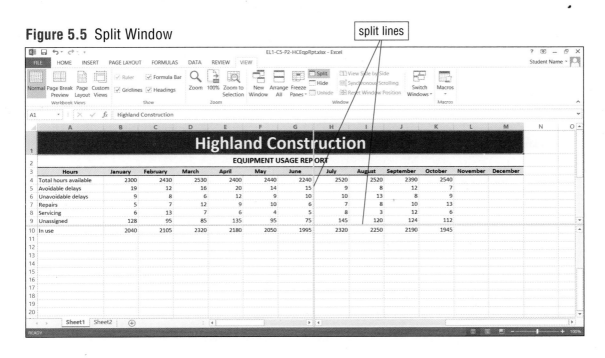

1. Open **HCEqpRpt.xlsx** and then save the workbook with Save As and name it **EL1-C5-P2-HCEqpRpt**.
2. Increase the Zoom percentage by clicking twice on the Zoom In button at the right side of the zoom slider bar.
3. Select cells G3 through I10, click the VIEW tab, and then click the Zoom to Selection button in the Zoom group.
4. Click the Zoom button in the Zoom group, click the *75%* option at the Zoom dialog box, and then click OK.
5. Click the 100% button in the Zoom group.
6. Make cell A1 active and then split the window by clicking the Split button in the Window group on the VIEW tab. (This splits the window into four panes.)
7. Drag the vertical split line by completing the following steps:
   a. Position the mouse pointer on the vertical split line until the pointer turns into a left-and-right-pointing arrow with a double line in the middle.
   b. Hold down the left mouse button, drag to the left until the vertical split line is immediately to the right of the first column, and then release the mouse button.

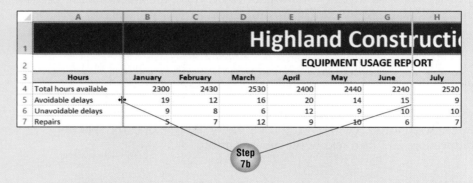

8. Freeze the window panes by clicking the Freeze Panes button in the Window group on the VIEW tab and then clicking *Freeze Panes* at the drop-down list.
9. Make cell L4 active and then type the following data in the specified cells:

L4: 2310	M4: 2210
L5: 12	M5: 5
L6: 5	M6: 7
L7: 9	M7: 8
L8: 11	M8: 12
L9: 95	M9: 120
L10: 2005	M10: 1830

10. Unfreeze the window panes by clicking the Freeze Panes button and then clicking *Unfreeze Panes* at the drop-down list.
11. Remove the panes by clicking the Split button in the Window group to deactivate it.
12. Save **EL1-C5-P2-HCEqpRpt.xlsx**.

Working with Ranges ■■■■■■■■■■■■■■■■■■■■■■■■■■■

A selected group of cells is referred to as a *range*. A range of cells can be formatted, moved, copied, or deleted. You can also name a range of cells and then move the insertion point to the range or use a named range as part of a formula.

To name a range, select the cells and then click in the Name box located at the left of the Formula bar. Type a name for the range (do not use a space) and then press Enter. To move the insertion point to a specific range and select the range, click the down-pointing arrow at the right side of the Name box and then click the range name.

You can also name a range using the Define Name button on the FORMULAS tab. To do this, click the FORMULAS tab and then click the Define Name button in the Defined Names group. At the New Name dialog box, type a name for the range and then click OK.

A range name can be used in a formula. For example, if a range is named *Profit* and you want to insert the average of all cells in the Profit range, make the desired cell active and then type =*AVERAGE(Profit)*. Use a named range in the current worksheet or in another worksheet within the workbook.

▼ **Quick Steps**

Name a Range
1. Select cells.
2. Click in Name box.
3. Type range name.
4. Press Enter.

Define Name

H I N T

Another method for moving to a range is to click the Find & Select button in the Editing group on the HOME tab and then click *Go To*. At the Go To dialog box, double-click the range name.

Project 2b **Naming a Range and Using a Range in a Formula**   **Part 2 of 2**

1. With **EL1-C5-P2-HCEqpRpt.xlsx** open, click the Sheet2 tab and then type the following text in the specified cells:
   - A1: EQUIPMENT USAGE REPORT
   - A2: Yearly hours
   - A3: Avoidable delays
   - A4: Unavoidable delays
   - A5: Total delay hours
   - A6: (leave blank)
   - A7: Repairs
   - A8: Servicing
   - A9: Total repair/servicing hours
2. Make the following formatting changes to the worksheet:
   a. Automatically adjust the width of column A.
   b. Center and bold the text in cells A1 and A2.
3. Select a range of cells in Sheet1, name the range, and use it in a formula in Sheet2 by completing the following steps:
   a. Click the Sheet1 tab.
   b. Select cells B5 through M5.
   c. Click in the Name box located to the left of the Formula bar.
   d. Type **adhours** (for Avoidable Delays Hours) and then press Enter.
   e. Click the Sheet2 tab.
   f. Make cell B3 active.
   g. Type the equation =SUM(adhours) and then press Enter.

4. Click the Sheet1 tab and then complete the following steps:
   a. Select cells B6 through M6.
   b. Click the FORMULAS tab.
   c. Click the Define Name button in the Defined Names group.
   d. At the New Name dialog box, type **udhours** and then click OK.
   e. Click the Sheet2 tab, make sure cell B4 is active, type the equation **=SUM(udhours)**, and then press Enter.

5. Click the Sheet1 tab and then complete the following steps:
   a. Select cells B7 through M7 and then name the range *rhours*.
   b. Click the Sheet2 tab, make cell B7 active, type the equation **=SUM(rhours)**, and then press Enter.
   c. Click the Sheet1 tab.
   d. Select cells B8 through M8 and then name the range *shours*.
   e. Click the Sheet2 tab, make sure cell B8 is active, type the equation **=SUM(shours)**, and then press Enter.
6. With Sheet2 still active, make the following changes:
   a. Make cell B5 active.
   b. Double-click the AutoSum button in the Editing group on the HOME tab.
   c. Make cell B9 active.
   d. Double-click the AutoSum button in the Editing group.
7. Click the Sheet1 tab and then move to the adhours range by clicking the down-pointing arrow at the right side of the Name box and then clicking *adhours* at the drop-down list.
8. Select both sheet tabs, change the orientation to landscape, scale the contents to fit on one page (by changing the width to *1 page* on the PAGE LAYOUT tab), and then insert a custom footer with your name, the page number, and the date.
9. With both worksheet tabs selected, print both worksheets in the workbook.
10. Save and then close **EL1-C5-P2-HCEqpRpt.xlsx**.

Project 3 Arrange, Size, and Copy Data between Workbooks   3 Parts

You will open, arrange, hide, unhide, size, and move multiple workbooks. You will also copy cells from one workbook and paste them in another workbook.

Working with Windows ■■■■■■■■■■■■■■■■■■■■■■■■■

You can open multiple workbooks in Excel, open a new window with the current workbook, and arrange the open workbooks in the Excel window. With multiple workbooks open, you can cut and paste or copy and paste cell entries from one workbook to another using the same techniques discussed earlier in this chapter with the exception that you make the destination workbook active before using the Paste command.

Opening Multiple Workbooks

With multiple workbooks open, or more than one version of the current workbook open, you can move or copy information between workbooks and compare the contents of several workbooks. When you open a new workbook or a new window of the current workbook, it is placed on top of the original workbook.

New Window

Open a new window of the current workbook by clicking the VIEW tab and then clicking the New Window button in the Window group. Excel adds a colon followed by the number *2* to the end of the workbook title and adds a colon followed by the number *1* to the end of the originating workbook name.

Open multiple workbooks at one time at the Open dialog box. Select adjacent workbooks by clicking the name of the first workbook to be opened, holding down the Shift key, clicking the name of the last workbook to be opened, and then clicking the Open button. If workbooks are nonadjacent, click the name of the first workbook to be opened, hold down the Ctrl key, and then click the names of any other workbooks you want to open.

Switch Windows

To see what workbooks are currently open, click the VIEW tab and then click the Switch Windows button in the Window group. The names of the open workbooks display in a drop-down list and the workbook name preceded by a check mark is the active workbook. To make one of the other workbooks active, click the desired workbook name at the drop-down list.

Another method for determining which workbooks are open is to hover your mouse over the Excel icon button that displays on the Taskbar. This causes a thumbnail to display of each open workbook. If you have more than one workbook open, the Excel button on the Taskbar displays additional layers in a cascaded manner. The layer behind the Excel button displays only a portion of the edge at the right side of the button. If you have multiple workbooks open, hovering the mouse over the Excel button on the Taskbar will cause thumbnails of all of the workbooks to display above the button. (This depends on your monitor size.) To change to the desired workbook, click the thumbnail that represents the workbook.

Arranging Workbooks

If you have more than one workbook open, you can arrange the workbooks at the Arrange Windows dialog box, shown in Figure 5.6. To display this dialog box, open several workbooks and then click the Arrange All button in the Window group on the VIEW tab. At the Arrange Windows dialog box, click *Tiled* to display a portion of each open workbook. Figure 5.7 displays four tiled workbooks.

Quick Steps

Arrange Workbooks
1. Click VIEW tab.
2. Click Arrange All button.
3. At Arrange Windows dialog box, click desired arrangement.
4. Click OK.

Arrange All

Figure 5.6 Arrange Windows Dialog Box

Use options at this dialog box to choose an arrange method.

Figure 5.7 Tiled Workbooks

Choose the *Horizontal* option at the Arrange Windows dialog box and the open workbooks display across the screen. The *Vertical* option displays the open workbooks up and down the screen. The last option, *Cascade*, displays the Title bar of each open workbook. Figure 5.8 shows four cascaded workbooks.

The option you select for displaying multiple workbooks depends on which part of the workbooks is most important to view simultaneously. For example, the tiled workbooks in Figure 5.7 allow you to view the company names and the first few rows and columns of each workbook.

Figure 5.8 Cascaded Workbooks

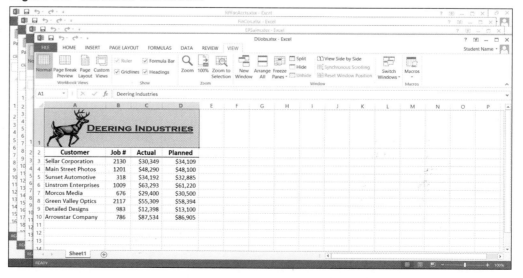

Hiding/Unhiding Workbooks

With the Hide button in the Window group on the VIEW tab, you can hide the active workbook. If a workbook has been hidden, redisplay it by clicking the Unhide button in the Window group. At the Unhide dialog box, make sure the desired workbook is selected in the list box and then click OK.

Hide   Unhide

Project 3a **Opening, Arranging, and Hiding/Unhiding Workbooks**   Part 1 of 3

1. Open several workbooks at the same time by completing the following steps:
   a. Display the Open dialog box with EL1C5 the active folder.
   b. Click the workbook named *DIJobs.xlsx*.
   c. Hold down the Ctrl key, click *EPSales.xlsx*, click *FinCon.xlsx*, and then click *RPFacAccts.xlsx*.
   d. Release the Ctrl key and then click the Open button in the dialog box.
2. Make **DIJobs.xlsx** the active workbook by clicking the VIEW tab, clicking the Switch Windows button, and then clicking *DIJobs.xlsx* at the drop-down list.

3. Tile the workbooks by completing the following steps:
   a. Click the VIEW tab and then click the Arrange All button in the Window group.
   b. At the Arrange Windows dialog box, make sure *Tiled* is selected and then click OK.
4. Cascade the workbooks by completing the following steps:
   a. Click the Arrange All button in the **DIJobs.xlsx** workbook.
   b. At the Arrange Windows dialog box, click *Cascade* and then click OK.

5. Hide and unhide workbooks by completing the following steps:
   a. Make sure **DIJobs.xlsx** is the active workbook. (The file name displays on top of each workbook file.)
   b. Click the Hide button in the Window group on the VIEW tab.
   c. Make sure **RPFacAccts.xlsx** is the active workbook. (The file name displays at the top of each workbook file.)
   d. Click the VIEW tab and then click the Hide button.
   e. At the active workbook, click the Unhide button.
   f. At the Unhide dialog box, click *RPFacAccts.xlsx* in the list box and then click OK.
   g. Click the Unhide button.
   h. At the Unhide dialog box, make sure **DIJobs.xlsx** is selected in the list box and then click OK. (If the workbook is not selected, click the **RPFacAccts.xlsx** title bar to make it active.)

6. Close all of the open workbooks (without saving changes) except **DIJobs.xlsx**.
7. Open a new window with the current workbook by clicking the New Window button in the Window group on the VIEW tab. (Notice that the new window contains the workbook name followed by a colon and the number *2*.)
8. Switch back and forth between the two versions of the workbook.
9. Make **DIJobs.xlsx:2** the active window and then close the workbook.

Sizing and Moving Workbooks

Maximize

Minimize

Close

Restore Down

Use the Maximize and Minimize buttons located in the upper right corner of the active workbook to change the size of the window. The Maximize button is the button in the upper right corner of the active workbook immediately to the left of the Close button. (The Close button is the button containing the *X*.) The Minimize button is located immediately to the left of the Maximize button.

If you arrange all open workbooks and then click the Maximize button in the active workbook, the active workbook expands to fill the screen. In addition, the Maximize button changes to the Restore Down button. To return the active workbook back to its original size, click the Restore Down button.

If you click the Minimize button in the active workbook, the workbook is reduced and displays as a layer behind the Excel button on the Taskbar. To maximize a workbook that has been minimized, click the Excel button on the Taskbar and then click the thumbnail representing the workbook.

Project 3b **Minimizing, Maximizing, and Restoring Workbooks** **Part 2 of 3**

1. Make sure **DIJobs.xlsx** is open.
2. Maximize **DIJobs.xlsx** by clicking the Maximize button located in the upper right corner of the screen immediately left of the Close button.
3. Open **EPSales.xlsx** and **FinCon.xlsx**.
4. Make the following changes to the open workbooks:
   a. Tile the workbooks.
   b. Click the **DIJobs.xlsx** Title bar to make it the active workbook.
   c. Minimize **DIJobs.xlsx** by clicking the Minimize button that displays at the right side of the Title bar.
   d. Make **EPSales.xlsx** the active workbook and then minimize it.
   e. Minimize **FinCon.xlsx**.
5. Click the Excel button on the Taskbar, click the **DIJobs.xlsx** thumbnail, and then close the workbook without saving changes.
6. Complete steps similar to Step 5 to close the other two workbooks.

Step 2

Step 4c

Moving, Linking, Copying, and Pasting Data ■■■■■■■■■

With more than one workbook open, you can move, link, copy, and/or paste data from one workbook to another. To move, link, copy, and/or paste data between workbooks, use the cutting and pasting options you learned earlier in this chapter together with the information about windows.

Moving and Copying Data

You can move or copy data within a worksheet, between worksheets, and between workbooks and other programs, such as Word, PowerPoint, and Access. The Paste Options button provides a variety of options for pasting data in a worksheet, another workbook, or another program. In addition to pasting data, you can also link data and paste data as an object or a picture object.

Project 3c	**Copying Selected Cells from One Open Worksheet to Another**	**Part 3 of 3**

1. Open **DIFebJobs.xlsx**.
2. If you just completed Project 3b, click the Maximize button so the worksheet fills the entire worksheet window.
3. Save the workbook with Save As and name it **EL1-C5-P3-DIFebJobs**.
4. With **EL1-C5-P3-DIFebJobs.xlsx** open, open **DIJobs.xlsx**.
5. Select and then copy text from **DIJobs.xlsx** to **EL1-C5-P3-DIFebJobs.xlsx** by completing the following steps:
    a. With **DIJobs.xlsx** the active workbook, select cells A3 through D10.
    b. Click the Copy button in the Clipboard group on the HOME tab.
    c. Click the Excel button on the Taskbar and then click the **EL1-C5-P3-DIFebJobs.xlsx** thumbnail.

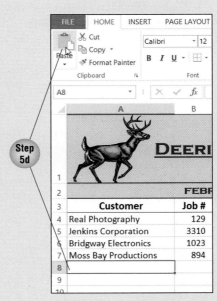

   d. Make cell A8 active and then click the Paste button in the Clipboard group.
   e. Make cell E7 active and then drag the fill handle down to cell E15.
6. Print **EL1-C5-P3-DIFebJobs.xlsx** horizontally and vertically centered on the page.
7. Save and then close **EL1-C5-P3-DIFebJobs.xlsx**.
8. Close **DIJobs.xlsx**.

Project 4   Linking and Copying Data within and between Worksheets and Word   2 Parts

You will open a workbook containing four worksheets with quarterly expenses data, copy and link cells between the worksheets, and then copy and paste the worksheets into Word as picture objects.

Linking Data

▼ **Quick Steps**

Link Data between Worksheets
1. Select cells.
2. Click Copy button.
3. Click desired worksheet tab.
4. Click in desired cell.
5. Click Paste button arrow.
6. Click *Paste Link* at drop-down list.

In some situations, you may want to copy and link data within or between worksheets or workbooks rather than copy and paste data. Linking data is useful when you need to maintain consistency and control over critical data in worksheets or workbooks. When data is linked, a change made in a linked cell is automatically made to the other cells in the link. You can make links with individual cells or with a range of cells. When linking data, the worksheet that contains the original data is called the *source worksheet* and the worksheet relying on the source worksheet for the data in the link is called the *dependent worksheet*.

To create a link, make active the cell containing the data to be linked (or select the cells) and then click the Copy button in the Clipboard group on the HOME tab. Make active the worksheet where you want to paste the cells, click the Paste button arrow, and then click the Paste Link button located in the *Other Paste Options* section in the drop-down list. You can also create a link by clicking the Paste button, clicking the Paste Options button, and then clicking the Paste Link button in the *Other Paste Options* section in the drop-down list.

Project 4a   **Linking Cells between Worksheets**   Part 1 of 2

1. Open **DWQtrlyExp.xlsx** and then save the workbook with Save As and name it **EL1-C5-P4-DWQtrlyExp**.
2. Link cells in the first quarter worksheet to the other three worksheets by completing the following steps:
   a. With the 1st Qtr tab active, select cells C4 through C10.
   b. Click the Copy button in the Clipboard group on the HOME tab.
   c. Click the 2nd Qtr tab.
   d. Make cell C4 active.
   e. Click the Paste button arrow and then click the Paste Link button located in the *Other Paste Options* section in the drop-down list.
   f. Click the 3rd Qtr tab and then make cell C4 active.
   g. Click the Paste button arrow and then click the Paste Link button.
   h. Click the 4th Qtr tab and then make cell C4 active.
   i. Click the Paste button.
   j. Click the Paste Options button and then click the Paste Link button in the *Other Paste Options* section in the drop-down list.

Step 2e

Step 2j

3. Click the 1st Qtr tab and then press the Esc key to remove the moving marquee.
4. Insert a formula in each worksheet that subtracts the budget amount from the variance amount by completing the following steps:
   a. Make sure the first quarter worksheet displays.
   b. Hold down the Shift key and then click the 4th Qtr tab. (This selects all four tabs.)
   c. Make cell D4 active and then type the formula =C4-B4 and press Enter.
   d. Copy the formula in cell D4 down to cells D5 through D10.
   e. Make cell D4 active and then apply accounting formatting with two places after the decimal point and a dollar sign.
   f. Click the 2nd Qtr tab and notice that the formula was inserted and copied in this worksheet.
   g. Click the other worksheet tabs and notice the amounts in column D.
   h. Click the 1st Qtr tab.
5. With the first quarter worksheet active, make the following changes to some of the linked cells:

   C4: Change *$126,000* to *$128,000*

   C5: Change *54,500* to *56,000*

   C9: Change *2,200* to *2,400*

6. Click the 2nd Qtr tab and notice that the values in cells C4, C5, and C9 automatically changed (because they were linked to the first quarter worksheet).
7. Click the other tabs and notice that the values changed.
8. Save **EL1-C5-P4-DWQtrlyExp.xlsx** and then print all four worksheets in the workbook.

quarter	
Budget	*Variance*
$ 126,000.00	4,000.00
54,500.00	(3,500.00)
10,100.00	1,850.00
6,000.00	(350.00)
4,500.00	360.00
2,200.00	(230.00)
1,500.00	50.00

Step 4d

Copying and Pasting Data between Programs

Microsoft Office is a suite that allows *integration*, which is the combining of data from two or more programs into one file. Integration can occur by copying and pasting data between programs. For example, you can create a worksheet in Excel, select specific data in the worksheet, and then copy it to a Word document. When pasting Excel data in a Word document, you can choose to keep the source formatting, use destination styles, link the data, insert the data as a picture, or keep the text only.

Project 4b **Copying and Pasting Excel Data into a Word Document** Part 2 of 2

1. With **EL1-C5-P4-DWQtrlyExp.xlsx** open, open the Word program.
2. In Word, open the document named **DWQtrlyRpt.docx** located in the EL1C5 folder on your storage medium.
3. Save the Word document with Save As and name it **EL1-C5-P4-DWQtrlyRpt**.
4. Click the Excel button on the Taskbar.
5. Copy the first quarter data into the Word document by completing the following steps:
   a. Click the 1st Qtr tab.
   b. Select cells A2 through D10.
   c. Click the Copy button in the Clipboard group on the HOME tab.
   d. Click the Word button on the Taskbar.

e. In the **EL1-C5-P4-DWQtrlyRpt.docx** document, press Ctrl + End to move the insertion point below the heading.
f. Click the Paste button arrow. (This displays a drop-down list of paste option buttons.)
g. Move your mouse over the various buttons in the drop-down list to see how each option will insert the data in the document.
h. Click the Picture button. (This inserts the data as a picture object.)
i. Press Ctrl + End and then press the Enter key twice. (This moves the insertion point below the data.)
j. Click the Excel button on the Taskbar.

6. Click the 2nd Qtr tab and then complete steps similar to those in Step 5 to copy and paste the second quarter data to the Word document.
7. Click the 3rd Qtr tab and then complete steps similar to those in Step 5 to copy and paste the third quarter data to the Word document.
8. Click the 4th Qtr tab and then complete steps similar to those in Step 5 to copy and paste the fourth quarter data to the Word document. (The data will display on two pages.)
9. Print the document by clicking the FILE tab, clicking the *Print* option, and then clicking the Print button at the Print backstage area.
10. Save and close **EL1-C5-P4-DWQtrlyRpt.docx** and then close Word.
11. In Excel, press the Esc key to remove the moving marquee and then make cell A1 active.
12. Save and then close **EL1-C5-P4-DWQtrlyExp.xlsx**.

Chapter Summary

- An Excel workbook, by default, contains one worksheet. Add a new worksheet to a workbook by clicking the New sheet button or with the keyboard shortcut Shift + F11.
- Delete a worksheet with the Delete button in the Cells group on the HOME tab or by right-clicking a worksheet tab and then clicking *Delete* at the shortcut menu.
- Manage more than one worksheet at a time by first selecting the worksheets. Use the mouse together with the Shift key to select adjacent worksheet tabs and use the mouse together with the Ctrl key to select nonadjacent worksheet tabs.
- Copy or move selected cells and cell contents in and between worksheets using the Cut, Copy, and Paste buttons in the Clipboard group on the HOME tab or by dragging with the mouse.
- Move selected cells with the mouse by dragging the outline of the selected cells to the desired position.
- Copy selected cells with the mouse by holding down the Ctrl key while dragging the cells to the desired position.
- When pasting data, specify how you want cells pasted by clicking the Paste button arrow or pasting the cells and then clicking the Paste Options button. Clicking either button causes a drop-down list of paste option buttons to display. Click the desired button in the drop-down list.

- Use the Clipboard task pane to copy and paste data within and between worksheets and workbooks. Display the Clipboard task pane by clicking the Clipboard task pane launcher.

- Perform maintenance activities, such as deleting and renaming, on worksheets within a workbook by clicking the right mouse button on a worksheet tab and then clicking the desired option at the shortcut menu.

- You can use the mouse to move or copy worksheets. To move a worksheet, drag the worksheet tab with the mouse. To copy a worksheet, hold down the Ctrl key and then drag the worksheet tab with the mouse.

- Use the *Tab Color* option at the worksheet tab shortcut menu to apply a color to a worksheet tab.

- Hide and unhide a worksheet by clicking the Format button in the Cells group and then clicking the desired option at the drop-down list or by right-clicking the worksheet tab and then clicking the desired option at the shortcut menu.

- To print all worksheets in a workbook, display the Print backstage area, click the first gallery in the *Settings* category, and then click *Print Entire Workbook* at the drop-down list. You can also print specific worksheets by selecting the tabs of the worksheets you want to print.

- Use buttons in the Zoom group on the VIEW tab or the zoom slider bar located at the right side of the Status bar to change the display zoom percentage.

- Split the worksheet window into panes with the Split button in the Window group on the VIEW tab. To remove a split from a worksheet, click the Split button to deactivate it.

- Freeze window panes by clicking the Freeze Panes button in the Window group on the VIEW tab and then clicking *Freeze Panes* at the drop-down list. Unfreeze window panes by clicking the Freeze Panes button and then clicking *Unfreeze Panes* at the drop-down list.

- A selected group of cells is referred to as a range. A range can be named and used in a formula. Name a range by typing the name in the Name box located to the left of the Formula bar or at the New Name dialog box.

- To open multiple workbooks that are adjacent, display the Open dialog box, click the first workbook, hold down the Shift key, click the last workbook, and then click the Open button. To open workbooks that are nonadjacent, click the first workbook, hold down the Ctrl key, click the desired workbooks, and then click the Open button.

- To see a list of open workbooks, click the VIEW tab and then click the Switch Windows button in the Window group.

- Arrange multiple workbooks in a window with options at the Arrange Windows dialog box.

- Hide the active workbook by clicking the Hide button and unhide a workbook by clicking the Unhide button in the Window group on the VIEW tab.

- Click the Maximize button located in the upper right corner of the active workbook to make the workbook fill the entire window area. Click the Minimize button to shrink the active workbook to a button on the Taskbar. Click the Restore Down button to return the workbook to its previous size.

- You can move, link, copy, and/or paste data between workbooks.

Commands Review

FEATURE	RIBBON TAB, GROUP	BUTTON, OPTION	KEYBOARD SHORTCUT
Arrange Windows dialog box	VIEW, Window	⊟	
Clipboard task pane	HOME, Clipboard	⌐	
copy selected cells	HOME, Clipboard	📋	Ctrl + C
cut selected cells	HOME, Clipboard	✂	Ctrl + X
freeze window panes	VIEW, Window	▦ , *Freeze Panes*	
hide worksheet	HOME, Cells	▢ , *Hide & Unhide, Hide Sheet*	
insert new worksheet		⊕	Shift + F11
maximize window		▢	
minimize window		—	
New Name dialog box	FORMULAS, Defined Names	⊡	
paste selected cells	HOME, Clipboard	📋	Ctrl + V
restore down		▱	
split window into panes	VIEW, Window	▤	
unfreeze window panes	VIEW, Window	▦ , *Unfreeze Panes*	
unhide worksheet	HOME, Cells	▢ , *Hide & Unhide, Unhide Sheet*	

Concepts Check   Test Your Knowledge

Completion: In the space provided at the right, indicate the correct term, symbol, or command.

1. By default, a workbook contains this number of worksheets.   _____

2. Click this button to insert a new worksheet in a workbook.   _____

3. To select nonadjacent worksheet tabs, click the first tab, hold down this key, and then click any other tabs you want selected.   _____

4. To select adjacent worksheet tabs, click the first tab, hold down this key, and then click the last tab.   _____

5. The Cut, Copy, and Paste buttons are located in this group on the HOME tab. _____

6. This button displays in the lower right corner of pasted cells. _____

7. Use this task pane to copy and paste multiple items. _____

8. Click this option at the worksheet tab shortcut menu to apply a color to a worksheet tab. _____

9. To print all of the worksheets in a workbook, display the Print backstage area, click the first gallery in the *Settings* category, and then click this option at the drop-down list. _____

10. The Split button is located on this tab. _____

11. Display the Arrange Windows dialog box by clicking this button in the Window group on the VIEW tab. _____

12. Click this button to make the active workbook expand to fill the screen. _____

13. Click this button to reduce the active workbook to a layer behind the Excel button on the Taskbar. _____

14. When linking data between worksheets, the worksheet containing the original data is called this. _____

Skills Check   Assess Your Performance

Assessment

1   COPY AND PASTE DATA BETWEEN WORKSHEETS IN A SALES WORKBOOK Grade It

1. Open **EPSales.xlsx** and then save the workbook with Save As and name it **EL1-C5-A1-EPSales**.
2. Turn on the display of the Clipboard task pane, click the Clear All button to clear any content, and then complete the following steps:
   a. Select and copy cells A7 through C7.
   b. Select and copy cells A10 through C10.
   c. Select and copy cells A13 through C13.
   d. Display the second worksheet, make cell A7 active, and then paste the *Avalon Clinic* cells.
   e. Make cell A10 active and then paste the *Stealth Media* cells.
   f. Make A13 active and then paste the *Danmark Contracting* cells.
   g. Make the third worksheet active and then complete similar steps to paste the cells in the same location as in the second worksheet.
   h. Clear the contents of the Clipboard task pane and then close the task pane.

3. Change the name of the Sheet1 tab to *2013 Sales*, the name of the Sheet2 tab to *2014 Sales*, and the name of the Sheet3 tab to *2015 Sales*.

4. Change the color of the 2013 Sales tab to Blue, the color of the 2014 Sales tab to Green, and the color of the 2015 Sales tab to Yellow.

5. Make 2013 Sales the active worksheet, select all three tabs, and then insert a formula in cell D4 that sums the amounts in cells B4 and C4. Copy the formula in cell D4 down to cells D5 through D14.

6. Make cell D15 active and then insert a formula that sums the amounts in cells D4 through D14.

7. Apply accounting formatting with a dollar sign and no places after the decimal point to cell D4 (on all three worksheets).

8. Insert a footer on all three worksheets that prints your name at the left side and the current date at the right.

9. Save **EL1-C5-A1-EPSales.xlsx**.

10. Print all three worksheets and then close **EL1-C5-A1-EPSales.xlsx**.

Assessment

2   COPY, PASTE, AND FORMAT WORKSHEETS IN AN INCOME STATEMENT WORKBOOK

1. Open **CMJanIncome.xlsx** and then save the workbook with Save As and name it **EL1-C5-A2-CMJanIncome**.

2. Copy cells A1 through B17 in Sheet1 and paste them into Sheet2. (Click the Paste Options button and then click the Keep Source Column Widths button at the drop-down list.)

3. Make the following changes to the Sheet2 worksheet:
   a. Adjust the row heights so they match the heights in the Sheet1 worksheet.
   b. Change the month from *January* to *February*.
   c. Change the amount in cell B4 to *97,655*.
   d. Change the amount in cell B5 to *39,558*.
   e. Change the amount in cell B11 to *1,105*.

4. Select both sheet tabs and then insert the following formulas:
   a. Insert a formula in cell B6 that subtracts the cost of sales from the sales revenue (*=B4-B5*).
   b. Insert a formula in cell B16 that sums the amounts in cells B8 through B15.
   c. Insert a formula in cell B17 that subtracts the total expenses from the gross profit (*=B6-B16*).

5. Change the name of the Sheet1 tab to *January* and the name of the Sheet2 tab to *February*.

6. Change the color of the January tab to Blue and the color of the February tab to Red.

7. Insert a custom header on both worksheets that prints your name at the left side, the date in the middle, and the file name at the right side.

8. Save, print, and then close **EL1-C5-A2-CMJanIncome.xlsx**.

3 FREEZE AND UNFREEZE WINDOW PANES IN A TEST SCORES WORKBOOK

1. Open **CMCertTests.xlsx** and then save the workbook with Save As and name it **EL1-C5-A3-CMCertTests**.
2. Make sure cell A1 is active and then split the window by clicking the VIEW tab and then clicking the Split button in the Window group. (This causes the window to split into four panes.)
3. Drag both the horizontal and vertical split lines up and to the left until the horizontal split line is immediately below the second row and the vertical split line is immediately to the right of the first column.
4. Freeze the window panes.
5. Add two rows immediately above row 18 and then type the following text in the specified cells:

A18: **Nauer, Sheryl**	A19: **Nunez, James**
B18: 75	B19: **98**
C18: 83	C19: **96**
D18: 85	D19: **100**
E18: 78	E19: **90**
F18: 82	F19: **95**
G18: 80	G19: **93**
H18: 79	H19: **88**
I18: 82	I19: **91**
J18: 92	J19: **89**
K18: 90	K19: **100**
L18: 86	L19: **96**
M18: 84	M19: **98**

6. Insert a formula in cell N3 that averages the percentages in cells B3 through M3 and then copy the formula down to cells N4 through N22.
7. Unfreeze the window panes.
8. Remove the split.
9. Change the orientation to landscape and then scale the worksheet to print on one page. *Hint: Do this with the* **Width** *option in the Scale to Fit group on the PAGE LAYOUT tab.*
10. Save, print, and then close **EL1-C5-A3-CMCertTests.xlsx**.

4 CREATE, COPY, PASTE, AND FORMAT CELLS IN AN EQUIPMENT USAGE WORKBOOK

1. Create the worksheet shown in Figure 5.9. (Change the width of column A to 21.00 characters.)
2. Save the workbook and name it **EL1-C5-A4-HCMachRpt**.
3. With **EL1-C5-A4-HCMachRpt.xlsx** open, open **HCEqpRpt.xlsx**.

4. Select and copy the following cells from **HCEqpRpt.xlsx** to **EL1-C5-A4-HCMachRpt.xlsx**:
   a. Copy cells A4 through G4 in **HCEqpRpt.xlsx** and paste them into **EL1-C5-A4-HCMachRpt.xlsx** beginning with cell A12.
   b. Copy cells A10 through G10 in **HCEqpRpt.xlsx** and paste them into **EL1-C5-A4-HCMachRpt.xlsx** beginning with cell A13.
5. With **EL1-C5-A4-HCMachRpt.xlsx** the active workbook, make cell A1 active and then apply the following formatting:
   a. Change the height of row 1 to 25.20 points.
   b. Change the font size of the text in cell A1 to 14 points.
   c. Apply the Blue, Accent 5, Lighter 80% fill color (ninth column, second row in the *Theme Colors* section) to cell A1.
6. Select cells A2 through G2 and apply the Blue, Accent 5, Darker 50% fill color (ninth column, last row in the *Theme Colors* section).
7. Select cells B2 through G2 and apply the White, Background 1 text color (first column, first row in the *Theme Colors* section). (Make sure the text in the cells is right-aligned.)
8. Select and then apply the Blue, Accent 5, Lighter 80% fill color (ninth column, second row in the *Theme Colors* section) to the following cells: A3 through G3, A7 through G7, and A11 through G11.
9. Print the worksheet centered horizontally and vertically on the page.
10. Save and then close **EL1-C5-A4-HCMachRpt.xlsx**.
11. Close **HCEqpRpt.xlsx** without saving the changes.

Figure 5.9 Assessment 4

	A	B	C	D	E	F	G	H
1			EQUIPMENT USAGE REPORT					
2		January	February	March	April	May	June	
3	Machine #12							
4	Total hours available	2200	2330	2430	2300	2340	2140	
5	In use	1940	2005	2220	2080	1950	1895	
6								
7	Machine #25							
8	Total hours available	2100	2240	2450	2105	2390	1950	
9	In use	1800	1935	2110	1750	2215	1645	
10								
11	Machine #30							
12								

Assessment

5 COPYING AND LINKING DATA IN A WORD DOCUMENT

1. In this chapter you learned how to link data in cells between worksheets. You can also copy data in an Excel worksheet and then paste and link the data in a file in another program such as Word. Use buttons in the Paste Options button drop-down list to link data or use options at the Paste Special dialog box. Open Word and then open the document named **DWLtr.docx** located in the EL1C5 folder. Save the document with Save As and name it **EL1-C5-A5-DWLtr**.

2. Click the Excel button on the Taskbar, open **DWMortgages.xlsx**, and then save the workbook with Save As and name it **EL1-C5-A5-DWMortgages**.
3. Select cells A2 through G10 and then click the Copy button.
4. Click the Word button on the Taskbar. (This displays **EL1-C5-A5-DWLtr.docx**.)
5. Move the insertion point between the two paragraphs of text.
6. Click the Paste button arrow and then click *Paste Special* at the drop-down list.
7. At the Paste Special dialog box, look at the options available and click the *Paste link* option, click *Microsoft Excel Worksheet Object* in the *As* list box, and then click OK.
8. Save, print, and then close **EL1-C5-A5-DWLtr.docx**.
9. Click the Excel button on the Taskbar.
10. Make cell A3 active and then change the number from *$300,000* to *$400,000*. Copy the number in cell A3 down to cells A4 through A10. (Cells A3 through A10 should now contain the amount *$400,000*.) Select cells A4 through A10 and then apply accounting formatting with no dollars signs and no places after the decimal point.
11. Save, print, and then close **EL1-C5-A5-DWMortgages.xlsx**.
12. Click the Word button on the Taskbar.
13. Open **EL1-C5-A5-DWLtr.docx**. At the message that displays asking if you want to update the data from the linked files, click Yes.
14. Save, print, and then close **EL1-C5-A5-DWLtr.docx**.
15. Close Word.

Visual Benchmark   Demonstrate Your Proficiency

CREATE AND FORMAT A SALES WORKSHEET USING FORMULAS

1. At a blank workbook, create the worksheet shown in Figure 5.10 with the following specifications:
   - Do not type the data in cells D4 through D9. Instead, enter a formula that totals the first-half and second-half yearly sales.
   - Apply the formatting shown in the figure, including changing font sizes, column widths, and row heights and inserting shading and border lines.
   - Rename the sheet tab and change the tab color as shown in the figure.
2. Copy cells A1 through D9 and then paste the cells in Sheet2.
3. Edit the cells and apply formatting so your worksheet matches the worksheet shown in Figure 5.11. Rename the sheet tab and change the tab color as shown in the figure.
4. Save the completed workbook and name it **EL1-C5-VB-CMSemiSales**.
5. Print both worksheets.
6. Close **EL1-C5-VB-CMSemiSales.xlsx**.

Figure 5.10 Sales 2014 Worksheet

	A	B	C	D	E
1	**Clearline Manufacturing**				
2	SEMIANNUAL SALES - 2014				
3	Customer	1st Half	2nd Half	Total	
4	Lakeside Trucking	$ 84,300	$ 73,500	$ 157,800	
5	Gresham Machines	33,000	40,500	73,500	
6	Real Photography	30,890	35,465	66,355	
7	Genesis Productions	72,190	75,390	147,580	
8	Landower Company	22,000	15,000	37,000	
9	Jewell Enterprises	19,764	50,801	70,565	
10					
11					
12					
13					
14					
15					
16					
17					
18					
19					
20					

Sales 2014 | Sales 2015 | (+)

Figure 5.11 Sales 2015 Worksheet

	A	B	C	D	E
1	**Clearline Manufacturing**				
2	SEMIANNUAL SALES - 2015				
3	Customer	1st Half	2nd Half	Total	
4	Lakeside Trucking	$ 84,300	$ 73,500	$ 157,800	
5	Gresham Machines	33,000	40,500	73,500	
6	Real Photography	20,750	15,790	36,540	
7	Genesis Productions	51,270	68,195	119,465	
8	Landower Company	22,000	15,000	37,000	
9	Jewell Enterprises	14,470	33,770	48,240	
10					
11					
12					
13					
14					
15					
16					
17					
18					
19					
20					

Sales 2014 | Sales 2015 | (+)

Case Study   Apply Your Skills

Part 1

You are an administrator for Gateway Global, an electronics manufacturing corporation. You are gathering information on money spent on supplies and equipment purchases. You have gathered information for the first quarter of the year and decide to create a workbook containing worksheets for monthly information. To do this, create a worksheet that contains the following information:

- Company name is Gateway Global.
- Create the title *January Expenditures*.
- Create the columns shown in Figure 5.12.

Figure 5.12 Case Study Part 1

Department	Supplies	Equipment	Total
Production	$25,425	$135,500	
Technical Support	$14,500	$65,000	
Finance	$5,790	$22,000	
Sales and Marketing	$35,425	$8,525	
Facilities	$6,000	$1,200	
Total			

- Insert a formula in the *Total* column that sums the amounts in the *Supplies* and *Equipment* columns and insert a formula in the *Total* row that sums the supplies amounts, equipment amounts, and total amounts.
- Apply formatting such as fill color, borders, font color, and shading to enhance the appearance of the worksheet.

After creating and formatting the worksheet, complete the following:

- Insert a new worksheet and then copy the data in Sheet1 to Sheet2.
- Insert a new worksheet and then copy the data in Sheet1 to Sheet3.
- Make the following changes to data in Sheet2:
  - Change *January Expenditures* to *February Expenditures*.
  - Change the Production department supplies amount to *$38,550* and the equipment amount to *$88,500*.
  - Change the Technical Support department equipment amount to *$44,250*.
  - Change the Finance department supplies amount to *$7,500*.
- Make the following changes to data in Sheet3:
  - Change *January Expenditures* to *March Expenditures*.
  - Change the Production department supplies amount to *$65,000* and the equipment amount to *$150,000*.
  - Change the Technical Support department supplies amount to *$21,750* and the equipment amount to *$43,525*.
  - Change the Facilities department equipment amount to *$18,450*.

Create a new worksheet that summarizes the supplies and equipment totals for January, February, and March. Apply the same formatting to the worksheet as you applied to the other three. Change the tab name for Sheet1 to *Jan. Expenditures*, the tab name for Sheet2 to *Feb. Expenditures*, the tab name for Sheet3 to *Mar. Expenditures*, and the tab name for Sheet4 to *Qtr. Summary*. Change the color of each tab. (You determine the colors.)

Insert a header that prints your name at the left side of each worksheet and the current date at the right side of each worksheet. Save the workbook and name it **EL1-C5-CS-GGExp**. Print all the worksheets in the workbook and then close the workbook.

Part

2

Help

Employees of Gateway Global have formed two intramural co-ed softball teams and you have volunteered to keep statistics for the players. Open **GGStats.xlsx** and then make the following changes to both worksheets in the workbook:

- Insert a formula that calculates a player's batting average (Hits / At Bats).
- Insert a formula that calculates a player's on-base percentage: (Walks + Hits) / (At Bats + Walks). Select cells E5 through F15 and then specify that you want to display three places after the decimal point.
- Insert the company name.
- Apply formatting to enhance the appearance of the worksheets.
- Horizontally and vertically center the worksheets.
- Insert a footer that prints on both worksheets and prints your name at the left side of the worksheet and the date at the right of the worksheet.

Use the Help feature to learn about applying cell styles or click the Cells Styles button in the Styles group on the HOME tab and then experiment with applying different styles. Apply the Good cell style to any cell in the *Batting Average* column with an average over .400. Apply this style to cells in both worksheets. Save the workbook and name it **EL1-C5-CS-GGStats**. Print both worksheets and then close **EL1-C5-CS-GGStats.xlsx**.

Part 3

Many of the suppliers for Gateway Global are international and use metric measurements. The purchasing manager has asked you to prepare a worksheet in Excel that converts length measurements..

Use the Internet to locate information on converting the following length measurements:

- 1 inch to centimeters
- 1 foot to centimeters
- 1 yard to meters
- 1 mile to kilometers

Locate a site on the Internet that provides the formula for converting Fahrenheit temperatures to Celsius temperatures and then create another worksheet in the workbook with the following information:

- Insert Fahrenheit temperatures beginning with 0 and continuing to 100 in increments of 5 (for example, 0, 5, 10, 15, and so on).
- Insert a formula that converts the Fahrenheit temperature to a Celsius temperature.

Include the company name, Gateway Global, in both worksheets. Apply additional formatting to improve the appearance of both worksheets. Rename both sheet names and apply a color to each tab. (You determine the names and colors.) Save the workbook and name it **EL1-C5-CS-GGConv**. Print both worksheets centered horizontally and vertically on the page and then close **EL1-C5-CS-GGConv.xlsx**.

Part 4

Open Microsoft Word and then create a letterhead document that contains the company name, *Gateway Global*; the address (you decide the street address, city, state, and ZIP code or street address, city, province, and postal code); and the telephone number (you decide). Apply formatting to improve the appearance of the letterhead. Save the document and name it **EL1-C5-CS-GGLtrhd**. Save the document again and name it **EL1-C5-CS-GGConvLtr**.

In Excel, open **EL1-C5-CS-GGConv.xlsx** (the workbook you created in Part 3). In the Fahrenheit conversion worksheet, copy the cells containing data and then paste the cells in **EL1-C5-CS-GGConvLtr.docx** as a picture object. Center the cells (picture object) between the left and right margins. Save, print, and then close **EL1-C5-CS-GGConvLtr.docx**. Close Microsoft Word and then in Excel close **EL1-C5-CS-GGConv.xlsx**.

EXCEL

Maintaining Workbooks

CHAPTER

6

PERFORMANCE OBJECTIVES

Upon successful completion of Chapter 6, you will be able to:

- Create and rename a folder
- Delete workbooks and folders
- Copy and move workbooks within and between folders
- Copy and move worksheets between workbooks
- Maintain consistent formatting with styles
- Insert, modify, and remove hyperlinks
- Create financial forms using templates

Tutorials

6.1 Maintaining Workbooks
6.2 Managing Folders
6.3 Managing the Recent Workbooks List
6.4 Managing Worksheets
6.5 Formatting with Cell Styles
6.6 Inserting Hyperlinks
6.7 Using Excel Templates

Once you have been working with Excel for a period of time, you will have accumulated several workbook files. You should organize your workbooks into folders to facilitate fast retrieval of information. Occasionally, you should perform file maintenance activities, such as copying, moving, renaming, and deleting workbooks, to ensure the workbook lists in your various folders are manageable. You will learn these file management tasks in this chapter, along with creating and applying styles to a workbook, inserting hyperlinks in a workbook, and using an Excel template to create a workbook. Model answers for this chapter's projects appear on the following pages.

Excel
EL1C6

Note: Before beginning the projects, copy to your storage medium the EL1C6 subfolder from the EL1 folder on the CD that accompanies this textbook and then make EL1C6 the active folder.

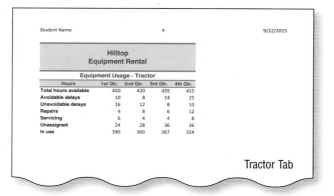

Student Name   1   9/22/2015

Hilltop Equipment Rental

Equipment	
Front Loader	
Hours available	1725
Hours in use	1446
Forklift	
Hours available	1730
Hours in use	1485
Tractor	
Hours available	1720
Hours in use	1441
Backhoe	
Hours available	1745
Hours In use	1422

Equipment Hours Tab

Project 2 Copy and Move Worksheets into an Equipment Rental Workbook
EL1-C6-P2-HEREquip.xlsx

Student Name   2   9/22/2015

Hilltop Equipment Rental

Equipment Usage - Front Loader

Hours	1st Qtr.	2nd Qtr.	3rd Qtr.	4th Qtr.
Total hours available	434	425	440	426
Avoidable delays	11	9	11	9
Unavoidable delays	8	14	7	11
Repairs	10	4	12	7
Servicing	5	10	8	11
Unassigned	32	24	36	40
In use	368	364	366	348

Front Loader Tab

Student Name   3   9/22/2015

Hilltop Equipment Rental

Equipment Usage - Forklift

Hours	1st Qtr.	2nd Qtr.	3rd Qtr.	4th Qtr.
Total hours available	436	440	428	426
Avoidable delays	12	8	5	8
Unavoidable delays	7	10	10	5
Repairs	4	9	12	3
Servicing	12	6	12	8
Unassigned	32	21	32	29
In use	369	386	357	373

Forklift Tab

Student Name   4   9/22/2015

Hilltop Equipment Rental

Equipment Usage - Tractor

Hours	1st Qtr.	2nd Qtr.	3rd Qtr.	4th Qtr.
Total hours available	450	420	435	415
Avoidable delays	10	8	14	25
Unavoidable delays	16	12	8	10
Repairs	4	8	6	12
Servicing	6	4	4	8
Unassigned	24	28	36	36
In use	390	360	367	324

Tractor Tab

Student Name   5   9/22/2015

Hilltop Equipment Rental

Equipment Usage - Backhoe

Hours	1st Qtr.	2nd Qtr.	3rd Qtr.	4th Qtr.
Total hours available	450	435	440	420
Avoidable delays	14	10	8	15
Unavoidable delays	12	8	12	12
Repairs	8	5	14	8
Servicing	10	8	10	4
Unassigned	62	32	26	45
In use	344	372	370	336

Backhoe Tab

O'Rourke Enterprises

Maintenance Department - Weekly Payroll

Employee	Hrly. Rate	Hours	Gross	W/H Tax	SS Tax	Net
Williams, Pamela	$ 43.00	40	$ 1,720.00	$ 481.60	$ 131.58	$ 1,106.82
Ternes, Reynaldo	41.50	40	1,660.00	464.80	126.99	1,068.21
Sinclair, Jason	38.00	30	1,140.00	319.20	87.21	733.59
Pierson, Rhea	38.00	40	1,520.00	425.60	116.28	978.12
Nyegaard, James	25.00	25	625.00	175.00	47.81	402.19
Lunde, Beverly	21.00	40	840.00	235.20	64.26	540.54

Withholding rate	28%
Social Security rate	7.65%

Weekly Payroll Tab

Project 3 Create and Apply Styles to a Payroll Workbook
EL1-C6-P3-OEPayroll.xlsx

O'Rourke Enterprises

Invoices

Invoice #	Customer #	Date	Amount	Tax	Amount Due
1001	34002	4/2/2012	$ 450.00	8.50%	$ 488.25
1002	12034	4/4/2012	1,075.00	8.80%	1,169.60
1003	40059	4/6/2012	225.00	0.00%	225.00
1004	23002	4/10/2012	750.00	8.50%	813.75
1005	59403	4/10/2012	350.00	0.00%	350.00
1006	80958	4/11/2012	875.00	8.50%	949.38
1007	23494	4/13/2012	750.00	8.50%	813.75
1008	45232	4/17/2012	560.00	8.80%	609.28
1009	76490	4/18/2012	400.00	0.00%	400.00
1010	45466	4/19/2012	600.00	8.50%	651.00
1011	34094	4/23/2012	95.00	0.00%	95.00
1012	45450	4/25/2012	2,250.00	8.50%	2,441.25
1013	23044	4/26/2012	225.00	8.80%	244.80
1014	48933	4/30/2012	140.00	0.00%	140.00

Invoices Tab

O'Rourke Enterprises
Overdue Accounts

Customer	Account #	Amount Due	Purchase Date	Terms	Due Date
Alliance Corporation	342	$ 8,540	4/2/2015	15	4/17/2015
Taylor-Brown Products	112	15,400	4/4/2015	30	5/4/2015
Meridian Center	543	1,525	4/11/2015	15	4/26/2015
Bower Consultants	322	3,000	4/14/2015	15	4/29/2015
Action Manufacturing	655	6,225	4/16/2015	30	5/16/2015
Summit Trading	223	2,500	4/23/2015	15	5/8/2015

Overdue Accounts Tab

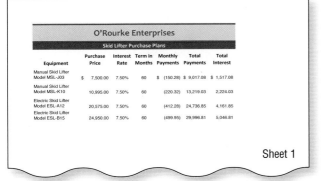

O'Rourke Enterprises
Skid Lifter Purchase Plans

Equipment	Purchase Price	Interest Rate	Term in Months	Monthly Payments	Total Payments	Total Interest
Manual Skid Lifter Model MSL-J03	$ 7,500.00	7.50%	60	(150.28)	$ 9,017.08	$ 1,517.08
Manual Skid Lifter Model MSL-K10	10,995.00	7.50%	60	(220.32)	13,219.03	2,224.03
Electric Skid Lifter Model ESL-A12	20,575.00	7.50%	60	(412.28)	24,736.85	4,161.85
Electric Skid Lifter Model ESL-B15	24,950.00	7.50%	60	(499.95)	29,996.81	5,046.81

Sheet 1

EL1-C6-P3-OEPlans.xlsx

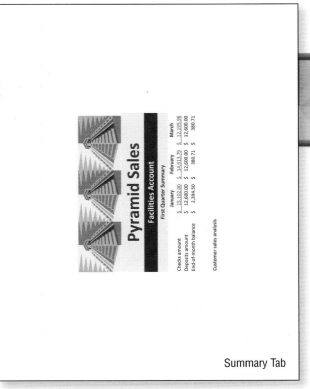

Summary Tab

Project 4 Insert, Modify, and Remove Hyperlinks

EL1-C6-P4-PSAccts.xlsx

Billing Statement

Project 5 Create a Billing Statement Workbook Using a Template

EL1-C6-P5-Billing.xlsx

Project 1 Manage Workbooks

8 Parts

You will perform a variety of file management tasks, including creating and renaming a folder; selecting and then deleting, copying, cutting, pasting, and renaming workbooks; deleting a folder; and opening, printing, and closing a workbook.

Maintaining Workbooks ■■■■■■■■■■■■■■■■■■■■■■■■■■

You can complete many workbook management tasks at the Open and Save As dialog boxes. These tasks include copying, moving, printing, and renaming workbooks; opening multiple workbooks; and creating and renaming new folders. Perform some file maintenance tasks, such as creating a folder and deleting files, with options from the Organize button drop-down list or a shortcut menu and navigate to folders using the Address bar. The elements of the Open dialog box are identified in Figure 6.1.

Figure 6.1 Open Dialog Box

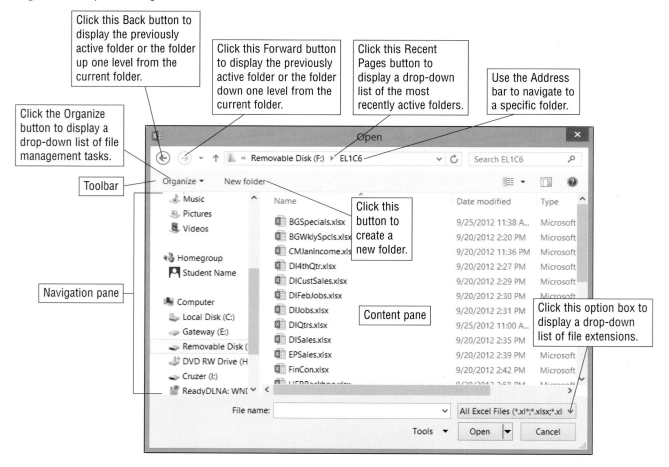

Click this Back button to display the previously active folder or the folder up one level from the current folder.

Click this Forward button to display the previously active folder or the folder down one level from the current folder.

Click this Recent Pages button to display a drop-down list of the most recently active folders.

Use the Address bar to navigate to a specific folder.

Click the Organize button to display a drop-down list of file management tasks.

Toolbar

Click this button to create a new folder.

Click this option box to display a drop-down list of file extensions.

Navigation pane

Content pane

Directions and projects in this chapter assume that you are managing workbooks and folders on a USB flash drive or your computer's hard drive. If you are using your OneDrive, some of the workbook and folder management tasks may vary.

Creating a Folder

In Excel, you should logically group and store workbooks in *folders*. For example, you could store all of the workbooks related to one department in one folder with the department name being the folder name. You can also create a folder within a folder (called a *subfolder*). If you create workbooks for a department by individuals, each individual name could have a subfolder within the department folder. The main folder on a disk or drive is called the root folder. You create additional folders as branches of this root folder.

At the Open dialog box and Save As dialog box, workbook file names display in the Content pane preceded by workbook icons and folder names display preceded by folder icons. Create a new folder by clicking the New folder button located in the toolbar at the Open dialog box or Save As dialog box. This inserts a new folder in the Content pane. Type the name for the folder and then press Enter.

A folder name can contain a maximum of 255 characters. Numbers, spaces, and symbols can be used in the folder name, except those symbols identified in the Saving a Workbook section in Chapter 1.

▼ **Quick Steps**

Create a Folder
1. Press Ctrl + F12 to display the Open dialog box.
2. Click New folder button.
3. Type folder name.
4. Press Enter.

New folder

New folder

HINT

Change the default folder with the *Default local file location* option at the Excel Options dialog box with *Save* selected in the left panel.

Project 1a   Creating a Folder   Part 1 of 8

1. With Excel open, create a folder named *Payroll* on your storage medium by completing the following steps:
   a. Press Ctrl + F12 to display the Open dialog box.
   b. At the Open dialog box, navigate to your storage medium.
2. Double-click the *EL1C6* folder name to make it the active folder.
3. Click the New folder button on the toolbar.
4. Type **Payroll** and then press Enter.
5. Close the Open dialog box.

Renaming a Folder

▼ **Quick Steps**

Rename a Folder
1. Display Open dialog box.
2. Click desired folder.
3. Click Organize button.
4. Click *Rename* at drop-down list.
5. Type new name.
6. Press Enter.
OR
1. Display Open dialog box.
2. Right-click folder name.
3. Click *Rename*.
4. Type new name.
5. Press Enter.

As you organize your files and folders, you may decide to rename a folder. Rename a folder using the Organize button in the Open dialog box or using a shortcut menu. To rename a folder using the Organize button, display the Open dialog box, click in the Content pane the folder you want to rename, click the Organize button located on the toolbar, and then click *Rename* at the drop-down list. This selects the folder name and inserts a border around the name. Type the new name for the folder and then press Enter. To rename a folder using a shortcut menu, display the Open dialog box, right-click the folder name in the Content pane, and then click *Rename* at the shortcut menu. Type a new name for the folder and then press Enter.

A tip to remember when you are organizing files and folders is to make sure your system is set up to display all of the files in a particular folder and not just the Excel files, for example. You can display all files in a folder in the Open dialog box by clicking the button to the right of the *File name* text box and then clicking *All Files (*.*)* at the drop-down list.

Organize

Project 1b **Renaming a Folder** Part 2 of 8

1. Press Ctrl + F12 to display the Open dialog box and make sure the EL1C6 folder is the active folder.
2. Right-click the *Payroll* folder name in the Content pane.
3. Click *Rename* at the shortcut menu.
4. Type **Finances** and then press Enter.

Selecting Workbooks

You can complete workbook management tasks on one workbook or selected workbooks. To select one workbook, display the Open dialog box and then click the desired workbook. To select several adjacent workbooks, click the first workbook, hold down the Shift key, and then click the last workbook. To select workbooks that are not adjacent, click the first workbook, hold down the Ctrl key, click any other desired workbooks, and then release the Ctrl key.

Deleting Workbooks and Folders

At some point, you may want to delete certain workbooks from your storage medium or any other drive or folder in which you may be working. To delete a workbook, display the Open or Save As dialog box, click the workbook in the Content pane, click the Organize button, and then click *Delete* at the drop-down list. If you are deleting a file from a removable storage medium such as a USB drive, a message will display asking you to confirm the deletion. At this message, click the Yes button. To delete a workbook using a shortcut menu, display the Open dialog box, right-click the workbook name in the Content pane, and then click *Delete* at the shortcut menu. If you are deleting a file from a removable storage medium such as a USB flash drive, click Yes at the confirmation dialog box.

Deleting to the Recycle Bin

Workbooks deleted from a removable drive are deleted permanently while workbooks deleted from the hard drive are automatically sent to the Windows Recycle Bin. You can easily restore a deleted workbook from the Recycle Bin. To free space on the drive, empty the Recycle Bin on a periodic basis. Restoring a workbook from or emptying the contents of the Recycle Bin is completed at the Windows desktop (not in Excel). To display the Recycle Bin, minimize the Excel window and then double-click the Recycle Bin icon located on the Windows desktop. At the Recycle Bin, you can restore file(s) and empty the Recycle Bin.

Project 1c	**Selecting and Deleting Workbooks**	**Part 3 of 8**

1. At the Open dialog box, open **RPFacAccts.xlsx** (located in the EL1C6 folder).
2. Save the workbook with Save As and name it **EL1-C6-P1-RPFacAccts**.
3. Close **EL1-C6-P1-RPFacAccts.xlsx**.
4. Delete **EL1-C6-P1-RPFacAccts.xlsx** by completing the following steps:
   a. Display the Open dialog box with the EL1C6 folder the active folder.
   b. Click ***EL1-C6-P1-RPFacAccts.xlsx*** to select it.
   c. Click the Organize button and then click *Delete* at the drop-down list.
   d. If a message displays asking if you are sure you want to delete the worksheet, click Yes.

Step 4c

5. Delete selected workbooks by completing the following steps:
   a. Click **DICustSales.xlsx** in the Content pane.
   b. Hold down the Shift key and then click **DIJobs.xlsx**.
   c. Position the mouse pointer on one of the selected workbooks and then click the right mouse button.
   d. At the shortcut menu that displays, click *Delete*.
   e. If a message displays asking if you are sure you want to delete the items, click Yes.
6. Close the Open dialog box.

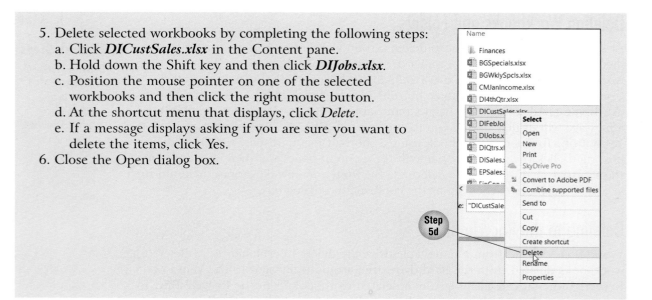

Step 5d

Copying Workbooks

In previous chapters, you have been opening a workbook from your storage medium and saving it with a new name in the same location. This process makes an exact copy of the workbook, preserving the original file on your storage medium. You can also copy a workbook into another folder.

Project 1d | **Saving a Copy of an Open Workbook to Another Folder** | Part 4 of 8

1. Open **EPSales.xlsx**.
2. Save the workbook with Save As and name it **TotalSales**. (Make sure the EL1C6 folder is the active folder.)
3. Save a copy of **TotalSales.xlsx** in the Finances folder you created in Project 1a (and renamed in Project 1b) by completing the following steps:
   a. With **TotalSales.xlsx** open, press F12 to display the Save As dialog box.
   b. At the Save As dialog box, change to the Finances folder. To do this, double-click *Finances* at the beginning of the Content pane. (Folders are listed before workbooks.)
   c. Click the Save button located in the lower right corner of the dialog box.
4. Close **TotalSales.xlsx**.
5. Change back to the EL1C6 folder by completing the following steps:
   a. Press Ctrl + F12 to display the Open dialog box.
   b. Click *EL1C6* that displays in the Address bar.
6. Close the Open dialog box.

Step 5b

You can copy a workbook to another folder without opening the workbook first. To do this, use the *Copy* and *Paste* options from the shortcut menu at the Open dialog box or the Save As dialog box. You can also copy a workbook or selected workbooks into the same folder. When you do this, Excel adds a hyphen followed by the word *Copy* to the end of the document name.

To move or copy files or folders on your OneDrive, go to onedrive.com, make sure you are logged in to your account, and then use the onedrive.com toolbar to move a workbook or folder to another location or copy and then move a workbook or folder to another location.

▼ **Quick Steps**
Copy a Workbook
1. Display Open or Save As dialog box.
2. Right-click workbook name.
3. Click *Copy*.
4. Navigate to desired folder.
5. Right-click blank area in Content pane.
6. Click *Paste*.

Project 1e   **Copying a Workbook at the Open Dialog Box**   **Part 5 of 8**

Note: If you are using your OneDrive, the steps for copying, cutting, and pasting workbooks will vary from the steps in Project 1e and 1f. Please check with your instructor.

1. Copy **CMJanIncome.xlsx** to the Finances folder. To begin, display the Open dialog box with the EL1C6 folder active.
2. Position the arrow pointer on **CMJanIncome.xlsx**, click the right mouse button, and then click *Copy* at the shortcut menu.
3. Change to the Finances folder by double-clicking *Finances* at the beginning of the Content pane.
4. Position the arrow pointer in any blank area in the Content pane, click the right mouse button, and then click *Paste* at the shortcut menu.
5. Change back to the EL1C6 folder by clicking *EL1C6* that displays in the Address bar.
6. Close the Open dialog box.

Sending Workbooks to a Different Drive or Folder

You can copy a workbook to another folder or drive without having to navigate to the new location. With the *Send to* option, you can send a copy of a workbook to another drive or folder. To use this option, position the arrow pointer on the workbook you want to copy, click the right mouse button, point to *Send to* (which causes a side menu to display), and then click the desired drive or folder.

Cutting and Pasting a Workbook

You can remove a workbook from one folder and insert it in another folder using the *Cut* and *Paste* options from the shortcut menu at the Open dialog box. To do this, display the Open dialog box, position the arrow pointer on the workbook to be removed (cut), click the right mouse button, and then click *Cut* at the shortcut menu. Change to the desired folder or drive, position the arrow pointer in any blank area in the Content pane, click the right mouse button, and then click *Paste* at the shortcut menu.

▼ **Quick Steps**
Move a Workbook
1. Display Open dialog box.
2. Right-click workbook name.
3. Click *Cut*.
4. Navigate to desired folder.
5. Right-click blank area in Content pane.
6. Click *Paste*.

1. Display the Open dialog box with the EL1C6 folder active.
2. Position the arrow pointer on **FinCon.xlsx**, click the right mouse button, and then click *Cut* at the shortcut menu.
3. Double-click *Finances* to make it the active folder.
4. Position the arrow pointer in any blank area in the Content pane, click the right mouse button, and then click *Paste* at the shortcut menu.
5. Click *EL1C6* that displays in the Address bar.

▼ Quick Steps

Renaming Workbooks

**Rename a
Workbook**
1. Display Open dialog box.
2. Click desired workbook.
3. Click Organize button.
4. Click *Rename*.
5. Type new name.
6. Press Enter.
OR
1. Display Open dialog box.
2. Right-click workbook name.
3. Click *Rename*.
4. Type new name.
5. Press Enter.

At the Open dialog box, use the *Rename* option from the Organize button drop-down list or the shortcut menu to give a workbook a different name. The *Rename* option changes the name of the workbook and keeps it in the same folder. To use *Rename*, display the Open dialog box, click once on the workbook to be renamed, click the Organize button, and then click *Rename* at the drop-down list. This causes a thin black border to surround the workbook name and the name to be selected. Type the new name and then press Enter.

You can also rename a workbook by right-clicking the workbook name at the Open dialog box and then clicking *Rename* at the shortcut menu. Type the new name for the workbook and then press the Enter key.

1. Make sure the Open dialog box displays with the EL1C6 folder the active folder.
2. Double-click *Finances* to make it the active folder.
3. Click once on **FinCon.xlsx** to select it.
4. Click the Organize button on the toolbar.
5. Click *Rename* at the drop-down list.
6. Type Analysis and then press the Enter key.

Step 4

Step 5

7. Complete steps similar to those in Steps 3 through 6 to rename **CMJanIncome.xlsx** to **CMJanProfits**.
8. Click the Back button (displays as *Back to EL1C6*) at the left side of the Address bar.

Deleting a Folder and Its Contents

As you learned earlier in this chapter, you can delete a workbook or selected workbooks. In addition to workbooks, you can delete a folder and all of its contents. Delete a folder in the same manner as you delete a workbook.

Project 1h	**Deleting a Folder and Its Contents**	**Part 8 of 8**

1. Make sure the Open dialog box displays with the EL1C6 folder active.
2. Right-click the *Finances* folder name in the Content pane.
3. Click *Delete* at the shortcut menu.
4. If you are deleting the folder from a removable drive, click Yes at the message that displays asking if you want to delete the folder.
5. Close the Open dialog box.

Project 2	**Copy and Move Worksheets into an Equipment Rental Workbook**	**3 Parts**

You will manage workbooks at the Open backstage area and then open multiple workbooks and copy and move worksheets between the workbooks.

Managing the Recent Workbooks List ■■■■■■■■■■■■

When you open and close workbooks, Excel keeps a list of the most recently opened workbooks. To view this list, click the FILE tab and then click the *Open* option. This displays the Open backstage area, similar to what you see in Figure 6.2. (Your workbook names may vary from what you see in the figure.) The most recently opened workbook names display in the Recent Workbooks list, which displays when the *Recent Workbooks* option is selected. The most recently accessed folder names display in the Recent Folders list, which displays when the *Computer* option is selected. Generally, the 25 most recently opened workbook names display in the Recent Workbooks list. To open a workbook, scroll down the list and then click the desired workbook name.

The Excel opening screen contains a Recent list that displays the most recently opened workbooks. The workbook names in the Recent list are the same that display in the Recent Workbooks list at the Open backstage area.

Figure 6.2 Open Backstage Area

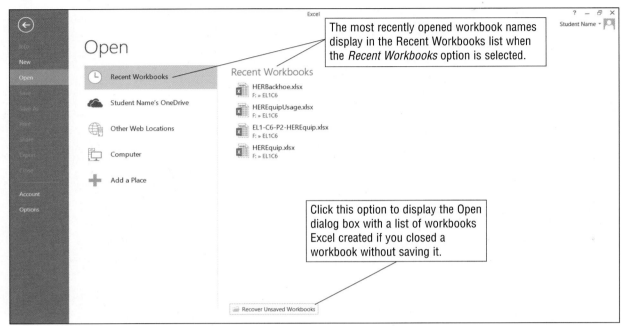

Pinning a Workbook

If you want a workbook name to remain at the top of the Recent Workbooks list, at the Open backstage area or the Recent list at the Excel opening screen "pin" the workbook name. To do this, click the gray pin that displays at the right side of the workbook name. This changes the left-pointing pin to a down-pointing pin. The next time you display the Open backstage area or the Excel opening screen, the workbook name you pinned displays at the top of the list. To "unpin" a workbook name, click the down-pointing pin to change it to a left-pointing pin. You can also pin a workbook name to the Recent Workbooks list or Recent list by right-clicking the workbook name and then clicking *Pin to list* at the shortcut menu. To unpin the workbook name, right-click the workbook name and then click *Unpin from list* at the shortcut menu.

Recovering an Unsaved Workbook

If you close a workbook without saving it, you can recover it with the *Recover Unsaved Workbooks* option located below the Recent Workbooks list. Click this option and the Open dialog box displays with workbook names that Excel automatically saved. At this dialog box, double-click the desired workbook name to open the workbook.

Clearing the Recent Workbooks List and the Recent List

Clear the contents (except pinned workbooks) of the Recent Workbooks list or Recent list by right-clicking a workbook name in the list and then clicking *Clear unpinned Workbooks* at the shortcut menu. At the message asking if you are sure you want to remove the items, click the Yes button. To clear a folder in the Recent Folders list, right-click a folder in the list and then click *Remove from list* at the shortcut menu.

Project 2a **Managing Workbooks at the Open Backstage Area** Part 1 of 3

1. Close any open workbooks.
2. Click the FILE tab and then click the *Open* option.
3. Make sure the *Recent Workbooks* option is selected. Notice the workbook names that display in the Recent Workbooks list.
4. Navigate to the EL1C6 folder on your storage medium, open **HEREquip.xlsx**, and then save the workbook with Save As and name it **EL1-C6-P2-HEREquip**.
5. Close **EL1-C6-P2-HEREquip.xlsx**.
6. Open **HEREquipUsage.xlsx** and then close it.
7. Open **HERBackhoe.xlsx** and then close it.
8. Pin the three workbooks to the Recent Workbooks list (you will use them in Project 2b) by completing the following steps:
   a. Click the FILE tab and then make sure the *Open* option is selected. (This displays the Open backstage area with the *Recent Workbooks* option selected.)
   b. Click the left-pointing pin that displays at the right side of **EL1-C6-P2-HEREquip.xlsx**. (This rotates the pin from left pointing to down pointing.)

   c. Click the left-pointing pin that displays at the right side of **HEREquipUsage.xlsx**.

d. Right-click **HERBackhoe.xlsx** and then click *Pin to list* at the shortcut menu.
e. Click the Back button to exit the Open backstage area.

9. Open **EL1-C6-P2-HEREquip.xlsx** by clicking the FILE tab and then clicking ***EL1-C6-P2-HEREquip.xlsx*** in the Recent Workbooks list. (After clicking the FILE tab, make sure the *Open* option is selected. This displays the Open backstage area with *Recent Workbooks* selected.)

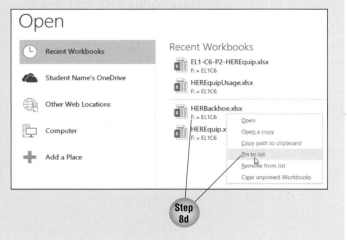

Step
8d

Managing Worksheets ▪▪▪▪▪▪▪▪▪▪▪▪▪▪▪▪▪▪▪▪▪

▼ **Quick Steps**

Copy a Worksheet to Another Workbook
1. Right-click desired sheet tab.
2. Click *Move or Copy.*
3. Select desired destination workbook.
4. Select desired worksheet location.
5. Click *Create a copy* check box.
6. Click OK.

You can move or copy individual worksheets within the same workbook or to another existing workbook. Exercise caution when moving sheets, since calculations or charts based on data in a worksheet might become inaccurate if you move the worksheet. To make a duplicate of a worksheet in the same workbook, hold down the Ctrl key and then drag the worksheet tab to the desired position.

Copying a Worksheet to Another Workbook

To copy a worksheet to another existing workbook, open both the source and the destination workbooks. Right-click the worksheet tab and then click *Move or Copy* at the shortcut menu. At the Move or Copy dialog box, shown in Figure 6.3, select the destination workbook name from the *To book* drop-down list, select the worksheet that you want the copied worksheet placed before in the *Before sheet* list box, click the *Create a copy* check box, and then click OK.

Figure 6.3 Move or Copy Dialog Box

Click a worksheet in this list box and the moved or copied worksheet is inserted before it.

Click this down-pointing arrow and then click the desired workbook.

Insert a check mark in this check box if you want to copy the worksheet.

1. With **EL1-C6-P2-HEREquip.xlsx** open, open **HEREquipUsage.xlsx**.
2. Copy the Front Loader worksheet by completing the following steps:
   a. With **HEREquipUsage.xlsx** the active workbook, right-click the Front Loader tab and then click *Move or Copy* at the shortcut menu.
   b. Click the down-pointing arrow next to the *To book* option box and then click *EL1-C6-P2-HEREquip.xlsx* at the drop-down list.
   c. Click *(move to end)* in the *Before sheet* list box.
   d. Click the *Create a copy* check box to insert a check mark.
   e. Click OK. (Excel switches to the **EL1-C6-P2-HEREquip.xlsx** workbook and inserts the copied Front Loader worksheet after Sheet1.)
3. Complete steps similar to those in Step 2 to copy the Tractor worksheet to the **EL1-C6-P2-HEREquip.xlsx** workbook.
4. Complete steps similar to those in Step 2 to copy the Forklift worksheet to the **EL1-C6-P2-HEREquip.xlsx** workbook and insert the Forklift worksheet before the Tractor worksheet.
5. Save **EL1-C6-P2-HEREquip.xlsx**.
6. Make **HEREquipUsage.xlsx** the active workbook and then close it.

Moving a Worksheet to Another Workbook

To move a worksheet to another existing workbook, open both the source and the destination workbooks. Make active the worksheet you want to move in the source workbook, right-click the worksheet tab, and then click *Move or Copy* at the shortcut menu. At the Move or Copy dialog box, shown in Figure 6.3, select the destination workbook name from the *To book* drop-down list, select the worksheet before which you want the worksheet placed in the *Before sheet* list box, and then click OK. If you need to reposition a worksheet tab, drag the tab to the desired position.

Be careful when moving a worksheet to another workbook file. If formulas exist in the source workbook that depend on the contents of the cells in the worksheet that is moved, they will no longer calculate properly.

▼ **Quick Steps**

Move a Worksheet to Another Workbook
1. Right-click desired worklsheet tab.
2. Click *Move or Copy*.
3. Select desired destination workbook.
4. Select desired worksheet location.
5. Click OK.

1. With **EL1-C6-P2-HEREquip.xlsx** open, open **HERBackhoe.xlsx**.
2. Move Sheet1 from **HERBackhoe.xlsx** to
   EL1-C6-P2-HEREquip.xlsx by completing the
   following steps:
   a. With **HERBackhoe.xlsx** the active workbook,
      right-click the Sheet1 tab and then click
      Move or Copy at the shortcut menu.
   b. Click the down-pointing arrow next to
      the *To book* option box and then click
      EL1-C6-P2-HEREquip.xlsx at the drop-down list.
   c. Click *(move to end)* in the *Before sheet* list box.
   d. Click OK.
3. With **EL1-C6-P2-HEREquip.xlsx** open, make the
   following changes:
   a. Rename Sheet1 as *Equipment Hours*.
   b. Rename Sheet1 (2) as *Backhoe*.
4. Create a range for the front loader total hours available by
   completing the following steps:
   a. Click the Front Loader tab.
   b. Select cells B4 through E4.
   c. Click in the Name box.
   d. Type FrontLoaderHours.
   e. Press Enter.
5. Complete steps similar to those in Step 4
   to create the following ranges:
   a. In the Front Loader worksheet, create a
      range with cells B10 through E10 and
      name it *FrontLoaderHoursInUse*.
   b. Click the Forklift tab and then create
      a range with cells B4 through E4 and
      name it *ForkliftHours* and create a range
      with cells B10 through E10 and name it
      ForkliftHoursInUse.
   c. Click the Tractor tab and then create a range with cells B4 through E4 and name it
      TractorHours and create a range with cells B10 through E10 and name it *TractorHoursInUse*.
   d. Click the Backhoe tab and then create a range with cells B4 through E4 and
      name it *BackhoeHours* and create a range with cells B10 through E10 and name it
      BackhoeHoursInUse.
6. Click the Equipment Hours tab to make it the active
   worksheet and then insert a formula that calculates
   the total hours for the front loader by completing the
   following steps:
   a. Make cell C4 active.
   b. Type =SUM(Fr.
   c. When you type *Fr*, a drop-down list displays with the
      front loader ranges. Double-click *FrontLoaderHours*.

d. Type) (the closing parenthesis).
e. Press Enter.

7. Complete steps similar to those in Step 6 to insert ranges in the following cells:

a. Make cell C5 active and then insert a formula that calculates the total in-use hours for the front loader.

b. Make cell C8 active and then insert a formula that calculates the total hours available for the forklift.

c. Make cell C9 active and then insert a formula that calculates the total in-use hours for the forklift.

d. Make cell C12 active and then insert a formula that calculates the total hours available for the tractor.

e. Make cell C13 active and then insert a formula that calculates the total in-use hours for the tractor.

f. Make cell C16 active and then insert a formula that calculates the total hours available for the backhoe.

g. Make cell C17 active and then insert a formula that calculates the total in-use hours for the backhoe.

8. Make the following changes to specific worksheets:

a. Click the Front Loader tab and then change the number in cell E4 from *415* to *426* and change the number in cell C6 from *6* to *14*.

b. Click the Forklift tab and then change the number in cell E4 from *415* to *426* and change the number in cell D8 from *4* to *12*.

9. Select all of the worksheet tabs and then create a header that prints your name at the left side of each worksheet, the page number in the middle, and the current date at the right side.

10. Save and then print all of the worksheets in **EL1-C6-P2-HEREquip.xlsx**.

11. Close the workbook. (Make sure all workbooks are closed.)

12. Make the following changes to the Open backstage area.

a. Click the FILE tab.

b. Make sure the *Open* option is selected and *Recent Workbooks* is selected.

c. Unpin **EL1-C6-P2-HEREquip.xlsx** from the Recent Workbooks list by clicking the down-pointing pin that displays at the right side of **EL1-C6-P2-HEREquip.xlsx**. (This changes the down-pointing pin to a left-pointing pin and moves the file down the list.)

d. Unpin **HERBackhoe.xlsx** and **HEREquipUsage.xlsx**.

e. Click the Back button to exit the Open backstage area.

Project 3   Create and Apply Styles to a Payroll Workbook   5 Parts

You will open a payroll workbook, define and apply styles, and then modify the styles. You will also copy the styles to another workbook and then apply the styles in the new workbook.

Formatting with Cell Styles ▪▪▪▪▪▪▪▪▪▪▪▪▪▪▪▪▪▪▪▪▪▪

In some worksheets, you may want to apply formatting to highlight or accentuate certain cells. You can apply formatting to a cell or selected cells with a cell style. A *style* is a predefined set of formatting attributes, such as font, font size, alignment, borders, shading, and so forth. You can use one of the predesigned styles from the Cell Styles drop-down gallery or create your own style.

▼ **Quick Steps**

Apply a Cell Style
1. Select desired cell(s).
2. Click Cell Styles button.
3. Click desired style.

Cell Styles

Applying a Style

To apply a style, select the desired cell(s), click the Cell Styles button in the Styles group on the HOME tab, and then click the desired option at the drop-down gallery shown in Figure 6.4. If you hover your mouse pointer over a style in the drop-down gallery, the cell or selected cells display with the formatting applied.

Figure 6.4 Cell Styles Drop-Down Gallery

Choose an option at this drop-down gallery to apply a predesigned style to a cell or selected cells in a worksheet.

| **Project 3a** | **Formatting with Cell Styles** | **Part 1 of 5** |

1. Open **OEPayroll.xlsx** and then save the workbook with Save As and name it **EL1-C6-P3-OEPayroll**.
2. With Sheet1 the active worksheet, insert the necessary formulas to calculate gross pay, withholding tax amount, social security tax amount, and net pay. *Hint: Refer to Project 3c in Chapter 2 for assistance.* Select cells D4 through G4 and then click the Accounting Number Format button to insert dollar signs.
3. Make Sheet2 active and then insert a formula that calculates the amount due. Make cell F4 active and then click the Accounting Number Format button to insert a dollar sign.

4. Make Sheet3 active and then insert a formula in the *Due Date* column that calculates the purchase date plus the number of days in the *Terms* column. **Hint: The formula in cell F4 will be =D4+E4**.

5. Apply cell styles to cells by completing the following steps:
   a. Make Sheet1 active and then select cells A11 and A12.
   b. Click the Cell Styles button in the Styles group on the HOME tab.
   c. At the drop-down gallery, hover your mouse over styles to see how the style formatting affects the selected cells.
   d. Click the *Check Cell* option in the *Data and Model* section.

6. Select cells B11 and B12, click the Cell Styles button, and then click the *Output* option in the *Data and Model* section (first column, second row in the *Data and Model* section).

7. Save **EL1-C6-P3-OEPayroll.xlsx**.

Defining a Cell Style

You can apply a style from the Cell Styles drop-down gallery or you can create your own style. Using a style to apply formatting has several advantages. A style helps to ensure consistent formatting from one worksheet to another. Once you define all attributes for a particular style, you do not have to redefine them again. If you need to change the formatting, change the style and all cells formatted with that style automatically reflect the change.

Two basic methods are available for defining your own cell style. You can define a style with formats already applied to a cell or you can display the Style dialog box, click the Format button, and then choose formatting options at the Format Cells dialog box. Styles you create are available only in the workbook in which they are created.

To define a style with existing formatting, select the cell or cells containing the desired formatting, click the Cell Styles button in the Styles group on the HOME tab, and then click the *New Cell Style* option located toward the bottom of the drop-down gallery. At the Style dialog box, shown in Figure 6.5, type a name for the new style in the *Style name* text box and then click OK to close the dialog box. The styles you create display at the top of the drop-down gallery in the *Custom* section when you click the Cell Styles button.

Figure 6.5 Style Dialog Box

Check boxes identify options set by current styles.

Project 3b **Defining and Applying a Style** **Part 2 of 5**

1. With **EL1-C6-P3-OEPayroll.xlsx** open, define a style named *C06Title* with the formatting in cell A1 by completing the following steps:
   a. Make sure Sheet1 is active and then make cell A1 active.
   b. Click the Cell Styles button in the Styles group on the HOME tab and then click the *New Cell Style* option located toward the bottom of the drop-down gallery.
   c. At the Style dialog box, type **C06Title** in the *Style name* text box.
   d. Click OK.

2. Even though cell A1 is already formatted, the style has not been applied to it. (Later, you will modify the style and the style must be applied to the cell for the change to affect it.) Apply the C06Title style to cell A1 by completing the following steps:
   a. Make sure cell A1 is the active cell.

b. Click the Cell Styles button in the Styles group on the HOME tab.

c. Click the *C06Title* style in the *Custom* section located toward the top of the drop-down gallery.

3. Apply the C06Title style to other cells by completing the following steps:
   a. Click the Sheet2 tab.
   b. Make cell A1 active.
   c. Click the Cell Styles button in the Styles group and then click the *C06Title* style at the drop-down gallery. (Notice that the style did not apply the row height formatting. The style applies only cell formatting.)
   d. Click the Sheet3 tab.
   e. Make cell A1 active.
   f. Click the Cell Styles button and then click the *C06Title* style at the drop-down gallery.
   g. Click the Sheet1 tab.

4. Save **EL1-C6-P3-OEPayroll.xlsx**.

In addition to defining a style based on cell formatting, you can also define a new style without first applying the formatting. To do this, you would display the Style dialog box, type a name for the new style, and then click the Format button. At the Format Cells dialog box, apply any desired formatting and then click OK to close the dialog box. At the Style dialog box, remove the check mark from any formatting that you do not want included in the style and then click OK to close the Style dialog box.

▼ **Quick Steps**

Define a Style
1. Click in blank cell.
2. Click Cell Styles button.
3. Click *New Cell Style*.
4. Type name for style.
5. Click Format button.
6. Choose formatting options.
7. Click OK.
8. Click OK.

Project 3c **Defining a Style without First Applying Formatting**   **Part 3 of 5**

1. With **EL1-C6-P3-OEPayroll.xlsx** open, define a new style named *C06Subtitle* without first applying the formatting by completing the following steps:
   a. With Sheet1 active, click in any empty cell.
   b. Click the Cell Styles button in the Styles group and then click *New Cell Style* at the drop-down gallery.
   c. At the Style dialog box, type C06Subtitle in the *Style name* text box.
   d. Click the Format button in the Style dialog box.
   e. At the Format Cells dialog box, click the Font tab.
   f. At the Format Cells dialog box with the Font tab selected, change the font to Candara, the font style to bold, the size to 12 points, and the color to White, Background 1.

g. Click the Fill tab.

h. Click the green option shown at the right (last column, fifth row in the palette).

i. Click the Alignment tab.

j. Change the horizontal alignment to center alignment.

k. Click OK to close the Format Cells dialog box.

l. Click OK to close the Style dialog box.

2. Apply the C06Subtitle style by completing the following steps:

   a. Make cell A2 active.

   b. Click the Cell Styles button and then click the *C06Subtitle* style located toward the top of the drop-down gallery in the *Custom* section.

   c. Click the Sheet2 tab.

   d. Make cell A2 active.

   e. Click the Cell Styles button and then click the *C06Subtitle* style.

   f. Click the Sheet3 tab.

   g. Make cell A2 active.

   h. Click the Cell Styles button and then click the *C06Subtitle* style.

   i. Click the Sheet1 tab.

3. Apply the following predesigned cell styles:

   a. Select cells A3 through G3.

   b. Click the Cell Styles button and then click the *Heading 3* style at the drop-down gallery.

   c. Select cells A5 through G5.

   d. Click the Cell Styles button and then click the *20% - Accent3* style.

   e. Apply the 20% - Accent3 style to cells A7 through G7 and cells A9 through G9.

   f. Click the Sheet2 tab.

   g. Select cells A3 through F3 and then apply the Heading 3 style.

   h. Select cells A5 through F5 and then apply the 20% - Accent3 style.

   i. Apply the 20% - Accent3 style to every other row of cells (cells A7 through F7, A9 through F9, and so on, finishing with cells A17 through F17).

   j. Click the Sheet3 tab.

   k. Select cells A3 through F3 and then apply the Heading 3 style.

   l. Apply the 20% - Accent3 style to cells A5 through F5, A7 through F7, and A9 through F9.

4. With Sheet3 active, change the height of row 1 to 36.00 points.

5. Make Sheet2 active and then change the height of row 1 to 36.00 points.

6. Make Sheet1 active.

7. Save **EL1-C6-P3-OEPayroll.xlsx** and then print only the first worksheet.

Modifying a Style

One of the advantages to formatting with a style is that you can modify the formatting of the style and all cells formatted with that style automatically reflect the change. You can modify a style you create or one of the predesigned styles provided by Excel. When you modify a predesigned style, only the style in the current workbook is affected. If you open a blank workbook, the cell styles available are the default styles.

To modify a style, click the Cell Styles button in the Styles group on the HOME tab and then right-click the desired style at the drop-down gallery. At the shortcut menu that displays, click *Modify*. At the Style dialog box, click the Format button. Make the desired formatting changes at the Format Cells dialog box and then click OK. Click OK to close the Style dialog box and any cells formatted with the specific style are automatically updated.

▼ **Quick Steps**
Modify a Style
1. Click Cell Styles button.
2. Right-click desired style at drop-down gallery.
3. Click *Modify*.
4. Click Format button.
5. Make desired formatting changes.
6. Click OK to close Format Cells dialog box.
7. Click OK to close Style dialog box.

Project 3d **Modifying Styles**   Part 4 of 5

1. With **EL1-C6-P3-OEPayroll.xlsx** open, modify the C06Title style by completing the following steps:
   a. Click in any empty cell.
   b. Click the Cell Styles button in the Styles group.
   c. At the drop-down gallery, right-click the *C06Title* style located toward the top of the gallery in the *Custom* section and then click *Modify*.
   d. At the Style dialog box, click the Format button.
   e. At the Format Cells dialog box, click the Font tab and then change the font to Candara.
   f. Click the Alignment tab.
   g. Click the down-pointing arrow to the right of the *Vertical* option box and then click *Center* at the drop-down list.
   h. Click the Fill tab.
   i. Click the light blue fill color as shown at the right (fifth column, third row in the palette).
   j. Click OK to close the Format Cells dialog box.
   k. Click OK to close the Style dialog box.

2. Modify the C06Subtitle style by completing the following steps:
   a. Click in any empty cell.
   b. Click the Cell Styles button in the Styles group.
   c. At the drop-down gallery, right-click on the *C06Subtitle* style located toward the top of the gallery in the *Custom* section and then click *Modify*.
   d. At the Style dialog box, click the Format button.
   e. At the Format Cells dialog box, click the Font tab and then change the font to Calibri.
   f. Click the Fill tab.
   g. Click the dark blue fill color as shown at the right (fifth column, sixth row in the palette).
   h. Click OK to close the Format Cells dialog box.
   i. Click OK to close the Style dialog box.
3. Modify the predefined 20% - Accent3 style by completing the following steps:
   a. Click the Cell Styles button in the Styles group.
   b. At the drop-down gallery, right-click on the *20% - Accent3* style and then click *Modify*.
   c. At the Style dialog box, click the Format button.
   d. At the Format Cells dialog box, make sure the Fill tab is active.
   e. Click the light blue fill color as shown at the right (fifth column, second row in the palette).
   f. Click OK to close the Format Cells dialog box.
   g. Click OK to close the Style dialog box.
4. Click each worksheet tab and notice the formatting changes made by the modified styles.
5. Change the name of Sheet1 to *Weekly Payroll*, the name of Sheet2 to *Invoices*, and the name of Sheet3 to *Overdue Accounts*.
6. Apply a different color to each of the three worksheet tabs.
7. Save and then print all the worksheets in **EL1-C6-P3-OEPayroll.xlsx**.

Copying Styles to Another Workbook

Quick Steps

Copy Styles to Another Workbook
1. Open workbook containing desired styles.
2. Open workbook to be modified.
3. Click Cell Styles button.
4. Click *Merge Styles* option.
5. Double-click name of workbook that contains styles.

Styles you define are saved with the workbook in which they are created. You can, however, copy styles from one workbook to another. To do this, open the workbook containing the styles you want to copy and open the workbook into which you want to copy the styles. Click the Cell Styles button in the Styles group on the HOME tab and then click the *Merge Styles* option located at the bottom of the drop-down gallery. At the Merge Styles dialog box, shown in Figure 6.6, double-click the name of the workbook that contains the styles you want to copy.

Figure 6.6 Merge Styles Dialog Box

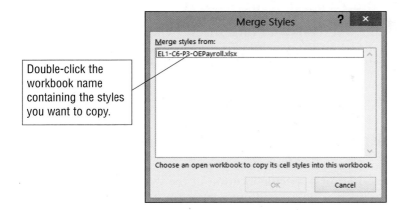

Double-click the workbook name containing the styles you want to copy.

HINT

The Undo command will not reverse the effects of the Merge Styles dialog box.

Quick Steps

Remove a Style
1. Select cells formatted with style to be removed.
2. Click Cell Styles button.
3. Click *Normal* at drop-down gallery.

Delete a Style
1. Click Cell Styles button.
2. Right-click style to be deleted.
3. Click *Delete* at shortcut menu.

Removing a Style

If you apply a style to text and then decide you do not want it applied, return the formatting to Normal, which is the default. To do this, select the cells formatted with the style you want to remove, click the Cell Styles button, and then click *Normal* at the drop-down gallery.

Deleting a Style

To delete a style, click the Cell Styles button in the Styles group on the HOME tab. At the drop-down gallery that displays, right-click the style you want to delete and then click *Delete* at the shortcut menu. Formatting applied by the deleted style is removed from cells in the workbook.

HINT

You cannot delete the Normal style.

Project 3e Copying Styles   Part 5 of 5

1. With **EL1-C6-P3-OEPayroll.xlsx** open, open **OEPlans.xlsx**.
2. Save the workbook with Save As and name it **EL1-C6-P3-OEPlans**.
3. Copy the styles in **EL1-C6-P3-OEPayroll.xlsx** into **EL1-C6-P3-OEPlans.xlsx** by completing the following steps:
   a. Click the Cell Styles button in the Styles group on the HOME tab.
   b. Click the *Merge Styles* option located toward the bottom of the drop-down gallery.
   c. At the Merge Styles dialog box, double-click **EL1-C6-P3-OEPayroll.xlsx** in the *Merge styles from* list box.
   d. At the message that displays asking if you want to merge styles that have the same names, click Yes.
4. Apply the C06Title style to cell A1 and the C06Subtitle style to cell A2.
5. Increase the height of row 1 to 36.00 points.
6. Save, print, and then close **EL1-C6-P3-OEPlans.xlsx**.
7. Close **EL1-C6-P3-OEPayroll.xlsx**.

Step 3c

Project **4** **Insert, Modify, and Remove Hyperlinks** **3 Parts**

You will open a facilities account workbook and then insert hyperlinks to a website, to cells in other worksheets in the workbook, and to another workbook. You will modify and edit hyperlinks and then remove a hyperlink from the workbook.

Inserting Hyperlinks ■■■■■■■■■■ ■■■■■■■■■■■

▼ Quick Steps

Insert Hyperlink
1. Click INSERT tab.
2. Click Hyperlink button.
3. Make desired changes at Insert Hyperlink dialog box.
4. Click OK.

Hyperlink

A hyperlink in a workbook can serve a number of purposes: Click it to navigate to a web page on the Internet or a specific location in the workbook, to display a different workbook, to open a file in a different program, to create a new document, or to link to an email address. Create a customized hyperlink by clicking the desired cell in a workbook, clicking the INSERT tab, and then clicking the Hyperlink button in the Links group. This displays the Insert Hyperlink dialog box, shown in Figure 6.7. At this dialog box, identify what you want to link to and the location of the link. Click the ScreenTip button to customize the hyperlink ScreenTip.

Linking to an Existing Web Page or File

Link to a web page on the Internet by typing a web address or with the Existing File or Web Page button in the *Link to* section. To link to an existing web page, type the address of the web page, such as *www.emcp.com*. By default, the automatic formatting of hyperlinks is turned on and the web address is formatted as a hyperlink. (The text is underlined and the color is changed to blue.)

You can turn off the automatic formatting of hyperlinks at the AutoCorrect dialog box. Display this dialog box by clicking the FILE tab, clicking *Options*, and then clicking *Proofing* in the left panel of the Excel Options dialog box. Click the AutoCorrect Options button to display the AutoCorrect dialog box. At this dialog

Figure 6.7 Insert Hyperlink Dialog Box

box, click the AutoFormat As You Type tab and then remove the check mark from the *Internet and network paths with hyperlinks* check box. To link to a web page at the Insert Hyperlink dialog box, display the dialog box, click the Existing File or Web Page button in the *Link to* section and then type the web address in the *Address* text box.

In some situations, you may want to provide information to your readers from a variety of sources. For example, you may want to provide additional information in an Excel workbook, a Word document, or a PowerPoint presentation. To link an Excel workbook to a workbook or file in another application, display the Insert Hyperlink dialog box and then click the Existing File or Web Page button in the *Link to* section. Use buttons in the *Look in* section to navigate to the folder containing the desired file and then click the file. Make other changes in the Insert Hyperlink dialog box as needed and then click OK.

Navigating Using Hyperlinks

Navigate to a hyperlinked location by clicking the hyperlink in the worksheet. Hover the mouse over the hyperlink and a ScreenTip displays with the address of the hyperlinked location. If you want specific information to display in the ScreenTip, click the ScreenTip button in the Insert Hyperlink dialog box, type the desired text in the Set Hyperlink ScreenTip dialog box, and then click OK.

Project 4a **Linking to a Website and Another Workbook** Part 1 of 3

1. Open **PSAccts.xlsx** and then save the workbook with Save As and name it **EL1-C6-P4-PSAccts**.
2. Insert a hyperlink to information about Pyramid Sales, a fictitious company (the hyperlink will connect to the publishing company website), by completing the following steps:
   a. Make cell A13 active.
   b. Click the INSERT tab and then click the Hyperlink button in the Links group.
   c. At the Insert Hyperlink dialog box, if necessary, click the Existing File or Web Page button in the *Link to* section.
   d. Type **www.emcp.com** in the *Address* text box.
   e. Select the text that displays in the *Text to display* text box and then type Company information.
   f. Click the ScreenTip button located in the upper right corner of the dialog box.

---

g. At the Set Hyperlink ScreenTip dialog box, type **View the company website.** and then click OK.

h. Click OK to close the Insert Hyperlink dialog box.

3. Navigate to the company website (in this case, the publishing company website) by clicking the <u>Company information</u> hyperlink in cell A13.

4. Close the Web browser.

5. Create a link to another workbook by completing the following steps:

 a. Make cell A11 active, type **Semiannual sales**, and then press the Enter key.

 b. Make cell A11 active and then click the Hyperlink button in the Links group on the INSERT tab.

 c. At the Insert Hyperlink dialog box, make sure the Existing File or Web Page button is selected.

 d. If necessary, click the down-pointing arrow at the right side of the *Look in* option box and then navigate to the EL1C6 folder on your storage medium.

 e. Double-click *PSSalesAnalysis.xlsx*.

6. Click the <u>Semiannual sales</u> hyperlink to open **PSSalesAnalysis.xlsx**.

7. Look at the information in the workbook and then close it.

8. Save **EL1-C6-P4-PSAccts.xlsx**.

Linking to a Place in the Workbook

To create a hyperlink to another location in the workbook, click the Place in This Document button in the *Link to* section in the Edit Hyperlink dialog box. If you are linking to a cell within the same worksheet, type the cell name in the *Type the cell reference* text box. If you are linking to another worksheet in the workbook, click the desired worksheet name in the *Or select a place in this document* list box.

Linking to a New Workbook

In addition to linking to an existing workbook, you can create a hyperlink to a new workbook. To do this, display the Insert Hyperlink dialog box and then click the Create New Document button in the *Link to* section. Type a name for the new workbook in the *Name of new document* text box and then specify if you want to edit the workbook now or later.

Linking Using a Graphic

You can use a graphic, such as a clip art image, picture, or text box, to hyperlink to a file or website. To hyperlink with a graphic, select the graphic, click the INSERT tab, and then click the Hyperlink button. You can also right-click the graphic and then click *Hyperlink* at the shortcut menu. At the Insert Hyperlink dialog box, specify the location you want to link to and the text you want to display in the hyperlink.

Linking to an Email Address

You can insert a hyperlink to an email address at the Insert Hyperlink dialog box. To do this, click the E-mail Address button in the *Link to* section, type the desired address in the *E-mail address* text box, and then type a subject for the email in the *Subject* text box. Click in the *Text to display* text box and then type the text you want to display in the worksheet.

Project 4b | **Linking to a Place in a Workbook, to Another Workbook, and Using a Graphic**

Part 2 of 3

1. With **EL1-C6-P4-PSAccts.xlsx** open, create a link from the checks amount in cell B6 to the checks amount in cell G20 in the January worksheet by completing the following steps:
   a. Make cell B6 active.
   b. Click the Hyperlink button in the Links group on the INSERT tab.
   c. At the Insert Hyperlink dialog box, click the Place in This Document button in the *Link to* section.
   d. Select the text in the *Type the cell reference* text box and then type G20.
   e. Click *January* in the *Or select a place in this document* list box.
   f. Click OK to close the Insert Hyperlink dialog box.
2. Make cell C6 active and then complete steps similar to those in Steps 1b through 1f except click *February* in the *Or select a place in this document* list box.
3. Make cell D6 active and then complete steps similar to those in Steps 1b through 1f except click *March* in the *Or select a place in this document* list box.
4. Click the hyperlinked amount in cell B6. (This makes cell G20 active in the January worksheet.)
5. Click the Summary worksheet tab.
6. Click the hyperlinked amount in cell C6. (This makes cell G20 active in the February worksheet.)
7. Click the Summary worksheet tab.
8. Click the hyperlinked amount in cell D6. (This makes cell G20 active in the March worksheet.)
9. Click the Summary worksheet tab.

10. Use the first pyramid graphic image in cell A1 to create a link to the company web page by completing the following steps:

a. Right-click the first pyramid graphic image in cell A1 and then click *Hyperlink* at the shortcut menu.

b. At the Insert Hyperlink dialog box, if necessary, click the Existing File or Web Page button in the *Link to* section.

c. Type **www.emcp.com** in the *Address* text box.

d. Click the ScreenTip button located in the upper right corner of the dialog box.

e. At the Set Hyperlink ScreenTip dialog box, type **View the company website.** and then click OK.

f. Click OK to close the Insert Hyperlink dialog box.

11. Make cell A5 active.

12. Navigate to the company website (the publishing company website) by clicking the first pyramid graphic image.

13. Close the Web browser.

14. Save **EL1-C6-P4-PSAccts.xlsx**.

Modifying, Editing, and Removing a Hyperlink

You can modify or change the hyperlink text or destination. To do this, right-click the hyperlink and then click *Edit Hyperlink* at the shortcut menu. At the Edit Hyperlink dialog box, make any desired changes and then close the dialog box. The Edit Hyperlink dialog box contains the same options as the Insert Hyperlink dialog box.

In addition to modifying the hyperlink, you can edit hyperlink text in a cell. To do this, make the cell active and then make the desired changes. For example, you can apply a different font or font size, change the text color, and apply a text effect. Remove a hyperlink from a workbook by right-clicking the cell containing the hyperlink and then clicking *Remove Hyperlink* at the shortcut menu.

| Project 4c | Modifying, Editing, and Removing a Hyperlink | Part 3 of 3 |

1. With **EL1-C6-P4-PSAccts.xlsx** open, modify the <u>Semiannual sales</u> hyperlink by completing the following steps:

a. Position the mouse pointer on the <u>Semiannual sales</u> hyperlink in cell A11, click the right mouse button, and then click *Edit Hyperlink* at the shortcut menu.

b. At the Edit Hyperlink dialog box, select the text *Semiannual sales* in the *Text to display* text box and then type **Customer sales analysis**.

c. Click the ScreenTip button located in the upper right corner of the dialog box.

d. At the Set Hyperlink ScreenTip dialog box, type **Click this hyperlink to display the workbook containing customer sales analysis.**

e. Click OK to close the Set Hyperlink ScreenTip dialog box.

f. Click OK to close the Edit Hyperlink dialog box.

2. Click the Customer sales analysis hyperlink.

3. After looking at the **PSSalesAnalysis.xlsx** workbook, close it.

4. With cell A11 active, edit the Customer sales analysis hyperlink text by completing the following steps:

a. Click the HOME tab.

b. Click the Font Color button arrow in the Font group and then click the *Dark Red* color option (first option in the *Standard Colors* section).

c. Click the Bold button.

d. Click the Underline button. (This removes underlining from the text.)

5. Remove the Company information hyperlink by right-clicking in cell A13 and then clicking *Remove Hyperlink* at the shortcut menu.

6. Press the Delete key to remove the contents of cell A13.

7. Save, print only the first worksheet (the Summary worksheet), and then close **EL1-C6-P4-PSAccts.xlsx**.

Project 5	**Create a Billing Statement Workbook Using a Template**	1 Part

You will open a Billing Statement template provided by Excel, add data, save it as an Excel workbook, and then print the workbook.

Using Excel Templates ■■■■■■■■■■■■■■■■■■■■■■■■■

Excel provides a number of template worksheet forms formatted for specific uses. With Excel templates, you can create a variety of worksheets with specialized formatting, such as balance sheets, billing statements, loan amortizations, sales invoices, and time cards. Display installed templates by clicking the FILE tab and then clicking the *New* option. This displays the New backstage area, as shown in Figure 6.8.

Click the desired template in the New backstage area and a preview of the template displays in a window. Click the Create button that displays below the template preview and a workbook based on the template opens and displays on the screen. Locations for personalized text display in placeholders in the worksheet. To enter information in the worksheet, position the mouse pointer (white plus sign) in the location you want to type data and then click the left mouse button. After typing the data, click the next location. You can also move the insertion point to another cell using the commands learned in Chapter 1. For example, press the Tab key to make the next cell active or press Shift + Tab to make the previous cell active. If you are connected to the Internet, you can download a number of predesigned templates offered by Microsoft.

Quick Steps

Use an Excel Template
1. Click FILE tab.
2. Click *New* option.
3. Double-click desired template.

Figure 6.8 New Backstage Area

Use this option to search for templates at Office.com.

The templates that display in this section of your New backstage area will vary from what you see in this figure.

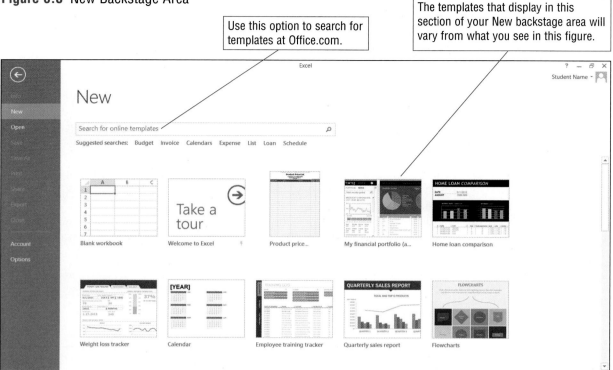

Project 5   **Preparing a Billing Statement Using a Template**   Part 1 of 1

1. Click the FILE tab and then click the *New* option.
2. At the New backstage area, type **billing statement** in the search text box and then press Enter.
3. Double-click the *Billing statement* template (first row, first column).

4. Click the Normal button in the view area on the Status bar.

5. With cell B1 active, type **IN-FLOW SYSTEMS**.
6. Click the text *Street Address* (cell B2) and then type **320 Milander Way**.
7. Click in each specified location (cell) and then type the text indicated:

    Address 2 (cell B3): **P.O. Box 2300**

    City, ST ZIP Code (cell B4): **Boston, MA 02188**

    Phone (cell F2): **(617) 555-3900**

    Fax (cell F3): **(617) 555-3945**

    Statement # (cell C8): **5432**

    Customer ID (cell C10): **25-345**

    Name (cell F8): **Aidan Mackenzie**

    Company Name (cell F9): **Stanfield Enterprises**

    Street Address (cell F10): **9921 South 42nd Avenue**

    Address 2 (cell F11): **P.O. Box 5540**

    City, ST ZIP Code (cell F12): **Boston, MA 02193**

    Date (cell B15): (insert current date in numbers as **##/##/####** and if necessary, adjust the width of the column)

    Type (cell C15): **System Unit**

    Invoice # (cell D15): **7452**

    Description (cell E15): **Calibration Unit**

    Amount (cell F15): **950**

    Payment (cell G15): **200**

    Customer Name (cell C21): **Stanfield Enterprises**

    Amount Enclosed (cell C26): **750**

Steps
5-7

8. Save the completed invoice and name it **EL1-C6-P5-Billing**.
9. Print and then close **EL1-C6-P5-Billing.xlsx**.

Chapter Summary

- Perform file management tasks, such as copying, moving, printing, and renaming workbooks and creating and renaming folders, at the Open dialog box or Save As dialog box.

- Create a new folder by clicking the New folder button located on the toolbar at the Open dialog box or Save As dialog box.

- Rename a folder with the *Rename* option from the Organize button drop-down list or with a shortcut menu.

- Use the Shift key to select adjacent workbooks in the Open dialog box and use the Ctrl key to select nonadjacent workbooks.

- To delete a workbook, use the *Delete* option from the Organize button drop-down list or use a shortcut menu option. Workbooks deleted from the hard drive are automatically sent to the Windows Recycle Bin, where they can be restored or permanently deleted.

- Use the *Copy* and *Paste* options from the shortcut menu at the Open dialog box or Save As dialog box to copy a workbook from one folder to another folder or drive.

- Use the *Send to* option from the shortcut menu to send a copy of a workbook to another drive or folder.

- Remove a workbook from a folder or drive and insert it in another folder or drive using the *Cut* and *Paste* options from the shortcut menu.

- Use the *Rename* option from the Organize button drop-down list or the shortcut menu to give a workbook a different name.

- To move or copy a worksheet to another existing workbook, open both the source workbook and the destination workbook and then open the Move or Copy dialog box.

- Use options from the Cell Styles button drop-down gallery to apply predesigned styles to a cell or selected cells.

- Automate the formatting of cells in a workbook by defining and then applying styles. A style is a predefined set of formatting attributes.

- Define a style with formats already applied to a cell or display the Style dialog box, click the Format button, and then choose formatting options at the Format Cells dialog box.

- To apply a style, select the desired cell or cells, click the Cell Styles button in the Styles group in the HOME tab, and then click the desired style at the drop-down gallery.

- Modify a style and all of the cells to which the style is applied automatically reflect the change. To modify a style, click the Cell Styles button in the Styles group on the HOME tab, right-click the desired style, and then click *Modify* at the shortcut menu.

- Styles are saved in the workbook in which they are created. Styles can be copied, however, to another workbook. Do this with options at the Merge Styles dialog box.

- With options at the Insert Hyperlink dialog box, you can create a hyperlink to a web page, another workbook, a location within a workbook, a new workbook, or an email. You can also create a hyperlink using a graphic.

- You can modify, edit, and remove hyperlinks.

- Excel provides preformatted templates for creating forms. Search for and download templates at the New backstage area.
- Templates contain unique areas where information is entered at the keyboard.

Commands Review

FEATURE	RIBBON TAB, GROUP/OPTION	BUTTON, OPTION	KEYBOARD SHORTCUT
cell styles	HOME, Styles		
Insert Hyperlink dialog box	INSERT, Links		
Merge Styles dialog box	HOME, Styles	, *Merge Styles*	
New backstage area	FILE, *New*		
new folder	FILE, *Open*	New folder	
Open backstage area	FILE, *Open*		Ctrl + O
Open dialog box			Ctrl + F12
Save As backstage area	FILE, *Save As*		Ctrl + S
Save As dialog box			F12
Style dialog box	HOME, Styles	, *New Cell Style*	

Concepts Check   Test Your Knowledge

Completion: In the space provided at the right, indicate the correct term, symbol, or command.

1. Perform file management tasks, such as copying, moving, and deleting workbooks, with options at the Open dialog box or this dialog box. _____

2. At the Open dialog box, a list of folders and files displays in this pane. _____

3. Rename a folder or file at the Open dialog box using a shortcut menu or this button. _____

4. At the Open dialog box, hold down this key while selecting nonadjacent workbooks. _____

5. Workbooks deleted from the hard drive are automatically sent to this location. _____

6. The most recently opened workbook names display in this list, which displays when the *Recent Workbooks* option is selected at the Open backstage area. _____

7. Do this to a workbook name you want to remain at the top of the Recent Workbooks list at the Open backstage area. _____

8. If you close a workbook without saving it, you can recover it with this option at the Open backstage area. _____

9. The Cell Styles button is located in this group on the HOME tab. _____

10. Click the *New Cell Style* option at the Cell Styles button drop-down gallery and this dialog box displays. _____

11. A style you create displays in this section of the Cell Styles button drop-down gallery. _____

12. Copy styles from one workbook to another with options at this dialog box. _____

13. To link a workbook to another workbook, click this button in the *Link to* section of the Insert Hyperlink dialog box. _____

14. Templates display at this backstage area. _____

Skills Check Assess Your Performance

Assessment

1 MANAGE WORKBOOKS

1. Display the Open dialog box with the EL1C6 folder the active folder.
2. Create a new folder named *O'Rourke* in the EL1C6 folder.
3. Copy **OEBudget.xlsx**, **OEPayroll.xlsx**, and **OEPlans.xlsx** to the O'Rourke folder.
4. Display the contents of the O'Rourke folder and then rename **OEBudget.xlsx** as **OEEquipBudget.xlsx**.
5. Rename **OEPlans.xlsx** as **OEPurchasePlans.xlsx** in the O'Rourke folder.
6. Change the active folder back to EL1C6.
7. Close the Open dialog box.

2 MOVE AND COPY WORKSHEETS BETWEEN SALES ANALYSIS WORKBOOKS

1. Open **DISales.xlsx** and then save the workbook with Save As and name it **EL1-C6-A2-DISales**.
2. Rename Sheet1 as *1st Qtr*.
3. Open **DIQtrs.xlsx**.
4. Rename Sheet1 as *2nd Qtr* and then copy it to **EL1-C6-A2-DISales.xlsx** following the 1st Qtr worksheet. (When copying the worksheet, make sure you insert a check mark in the *Create a copy* check box in the Move or Copy dialog box.)
5. Make **DIQtrs.xlsx** active, rename Sheet2 as *3rd Qtr*, and then copy it to **EL1-C6-A2-DISales.xlsx** following the 2nd Qtr tab. (Make sure you insert a check mark in the *Create a copy* check box.)
6. Make **DIQtrs.xlsx** active and then close it without saving the changes.
7. Open **DI4thQtr.xlsx**.
8. Rename Sheet1 as *4th Qtr* and then move it to **EL1-C6-A2-DISales.xlsx** following the 3rd Qtr worksheet.
9. With **EL1-C6-A2-DISales.xlsx** open, make the following changes to all four quarterly worksheets at the same time:
   a. Make 1st Qtr the active worksheet.
   b. Hold down the Shift key and then click the 4th Qtr tab. (This selects the four quarterly worksheet tabs.)
   c. Insert in cell E4 a formula to calculate the average of cells B4 through D4 and then copy the formula down to cells E5 through E9.
   d. Insert in cell B10 a formula to calculate the sum of cells B4 through B9 and then copy the formula across to cells C10 through E10.
   e. Make cell E4 active and apply accounting formatting with a dollar sign and no places after the decimal point.
10. Insert a footer on all worksheets that prints your name at the left, the page number in the middle, and the current date at the right.
11. Horizontally and vertically center all of the worksheets.
12. Save and then print all four worksheets.
13. Close **EL1-C6-A2-DISales.xlsx**.

3 DEFINE AND APPLY STYLES TO A PROJECTED EARNINGS WORKBOOK

1. At a blank worksheet, define a style named *C06Heading* that contains the following formatting:
   a. Font:14-point Cambria bold in dark blue
   b. Horizontal alignment: Center alignment
   c. Borders: Top and bottom in dark blue
   d. Fill: Light yellow (eighth column, second row)
2. Define a style named *C06Subheading* that contains the following formatting:
   a. Font: 12-point Cambria bold in dark blue
   b. Horizontal alignment: Center alignment
   c. Borders: Top and bottom in dark blue
   d. Fill: Light green (last column, second row)

3. Define a style named *C06Column* that contains the following formatting:
   a. Number: At the Style dialog box, click the *Number* check box to remove the check mark.
   b. Font: 12-point Cambria in dark blue
   c. Fill: Light green (last column, second row)
4. Save the workbook and name it **EL1-C6-A3-Styles**.
5. With **EL1-C6-A3-Styles.xlsx** open, open **ProjEarnings.xlsx**.
6. Save the workbook with Save As and name it **EL1-C6-A3-ProjEarnings**.
7. Make cell C6 active and then insert a formula that multiplies the content of cell B6 by the amount in cell B3. (When writing the formula, identify cell B3 as an absolute reference.) Copy the formula down to cells C7 through C17.
8. Make cell C6 active and then click the Accounting Number Format button.
9. Copy the styles from **EL1-C6-A3-Styles.xlsx** into **EL1-C6-A3-ProjEarnings.xlsx**. *Hint: Do this at the Merge Styles dialog box.*
10. Apply the following styles:
    a. Select cells A1 and A2 and then apply the C06Heading style.
    b. Select cells A5 through C5 and then apply the C06Subheading style.
    c. Select cells A6 through A17 and then apply the C06Column style.
11. Save the workbook again and then print **EL1-C6-A3-ProjEarnings.xlsx**.
12. With **EL1-C6-A3-ProjEarnings.xlsx** open, modify the following styles:
    a. Modify the C06Heading style so it changes the font color to dark green (last column, sixth row) instead of dark blue, changes the vertical alignment to center alignment, and inserts top and bottom borders in dark green (last column, sixth row) instead of dark blue.
    b. Modify the C06Subheading style so it changes the font color to dark green (last column, sixth row) instead of dark blue and inserts top and bottom borders in dark green (instead of dark blue).
    c. Modify the C06Column style so it changes the font color to dark green (last column, sixth row) instead of dark blue. Do not change any of the other formatting attributes.
13. Save and then print the workbook.
14. Close **EL1-C6-A3-ProjEarnings.xlsx** and then close **EL1-C6-A3-Styles.xlsx** without saving the changes.

Assessment

4   INSERT HYPERLINKS IN A BOOKSTORE WORKBOOK

1. Open **BGSpecials.xlsx** and then save the workbook with Save As and name it **EL1-C6-A4-BGSpecials.xlsx**.
2. Make cell E3 active and then create a hyperlink to www.microsoft.com.
3. Make cell E4 active and then create a hyperlink to www.symantec.com
4. Make cell E5 active and then create a hyperlink to www.nasa.gov.
5. Make cell E6 active and then create a hyperlink to www.cnn.com.
6. Make cell A8 active, type **Weekly specials!**, and then create a hyperlink to the workbook named **BGWklySpcls.xlsx**.
7. Click the hyperlink to the Microsoft website, explore the site, and then close the web browser.
8. Click the hyperlink to the NASA website, explore the site, and then close the web browser.
9. Click the <u>Weekly specials!</u> hyperlink, view the workbook, and then close the workbook.
10. Save, print, and then close **EL1-C6-A4-BGSpecials.xlsx**.

5

APPLY CONDITIONAL FORMATTING TO A SALES WORKBOOK

1. Use Excel Help files or experiment with the options at the Conditional Formatting button drop-down gallery to learn about conditional formatting.
2. Open **PSSales.xlsx** and then save the workbook with Save As and name it **EL1-C6-A5-PSSales**.
3. Select cells D5 through D19 and then use conditional formatting to display the amounts as data bars. (You choose the type of data bars.)
4. Insert a header that prints your name, a page number, and the current date.
5. Save, print, and then close **EL1-C6-A5-PSSales.xlsx**.

Visual Benchmark Demonstrate Your Proficiency

FILL IN AN EXPENSE REPORT FORM

1. Display the New backstage area, search for an expense report template, and then double-click the *Expense report* template shown in Figure 6.9.
2. With the expense report open, apply the Retrospect theme.
3. Select cells J1 through L1 and then apply the Note cell style.
4. Type the information in the cells as indicated in Figure 6.9.
5. Make cell L18 active and apply the Bad cell style.
6. Save the completed workbook and name it **EL1-C6-VB-OEExpRpt**.
7. Print and then close **EL1-C6-VB-OEExpRpt.xlsx**.

Figure 6.9 Visual Benchmark

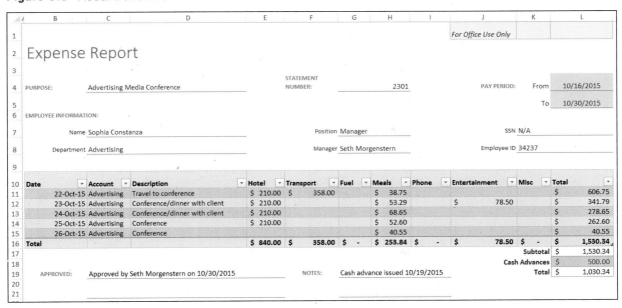

Case Study   Apply Your Skills

Part 1

You are the office manager for Leeward Marine and you decide to consolidate into one workbook several worksheets containing information on expenses. Open **LMEstExp.xlsx** and then save the workbook and name it **EL1-C6-CS-LMExpSummary**. Open **LMActExp.xlsx**, copy the worksheet into **EL1-C6-CS-LMExpSummary.xlsx**, make **LMActExp.xlsx** the active workbook, and then close it. Apply appropriate formatting to numbers and insert necessary formulas in each worksheet. (Use the Clear button in the HOME tab to clear the contents of cells N8, N9, N13, and N14 in both worksheets.) Include the company name, Leeward Marine, in both worksheets. Create styles and apply the styles to cells in both worksheets to maintain consistent formatting. Automatically adjust the widths of the columns to accommodate the longest entries. Save **EL1-C6-CS-LMExpSummary.xlsx**.

Part 2

You decide that you want to include another worksheet that displays the yearly estimated expenses, actual expenses, and variances (differences) between the two. With **EL1-C6-CS-LMExpSummary.xlsx** open, open **LMExpVar.xlsx**. Copy the worksheet into **EL1-C6-CS-LMExpSummary.xlsx**, make **LMExpVar.xlsx** the active workbook, and then close it. Rename the sheet tab containing the estimated expenses as *Estimated Exp*, rename the sheet tab containing the actual expenses as *Actual Exp*, and rename the sheet tab containing the variances as *Summary*. Recolor the three sheet tabs you just renamed.

Select the yearly estimated expense amounts (column N) in the Estimated Exp worksheet and then paste the amounts in the appropriate cells in the Summary worksheet. Click the Paste Options button and then click the Values & Number Formatting button in the *Paste Values* section of the drop-down list. (This pastes the value and the cell formatting, rather than the formula.) Select the yearly actual expense amounts (column N) in the Actual Exp worksheet and then paste the amounts in the appropriate cells in the Summary worksheet. Click the Paste Options button and then click the Values & Number Formatting button in the *Paste Values* section of the drop-down list. Apply appropriate formatting to the numbers and insert a formula to calculate the variances (differences) between estimated and actual expenses. Clear the contents of cells D8, D9, D13, and D14. Apply styles to the Summary worksheet so it is formatted similar to the Estimated Exp and Actual Exp worksheets.

Insert an appropriate header or footer in each worksheet. Scale the worksheets so each prints on one page. Save, print all of the worksheets, and then close **EL1-C6-CS-LMExpSummary.xlsx**.

Part 3

Based on the summary of the yearly expense variances, your supervisor has created projected expenses for next year and has asked you to format the worksheet. Open **LMProjectedExp.xlsx** and then save it and name it **EL1-C6-CS-LMProjectedExp**. Format the worksheet in a similar manner to the formatting you applied to **EL1-C6-CS-LMExpSummary.xlsx** (use the styles you created). Save and then close **EL1-C6-CS-LMProjectedExp.xlsx**. Open **EL1-C6-CS-LMExpSummary.xlsx**, make the Summary worksheet active and then insert a hyperlink to the **EL1-C6-CS-LMProjectedExp.xlsx** workbook. You determine the cell location and hyperlink text for the hyperlink. Save **EL1-C6-CS-LMExpSummary.xlsx** and then print only the Summary worksheet.

Part 4

You need to print a number of copies of the summary worksheet in the **EL1-C6-CS-LMExpSummary.xlsx** workbook and you want the company letterhead to print at the top of the page. You decide to use the letterhead in a Word document and copy the summary data from Excel into the Word letterhead document. To do this, open Word and then open the document named **LMLtrd.docx** (located in the EL1C6 folder on your storage medium). Press the Enter key two times. Make Excel the active program and with **EL1-C6-CS-LMExpSummary.xlsx** open, make the Summary worksheet active, select and then copy cells containing information on the yearly expense variances, and then paste them into the **LMLtrhd.docx** Word document as a picture object. (Click the Paste Options button and then click the Picture button.) Save the document with Save As and name it **EL1-C6-CS-LMExpSummary**. Print and then close **EL1-C6-CS-LMExpSummary.docx** and then close Word. In Excel, close **EL1-C6-CS-LMExpSummary.xlsx**.

MICROSOFT EXCEL

Creating Charts and Inserting Formulas

CHAPTER 7

PERFORMANCE OBJECTIVES

Upon successful completion of Chapter 7, you will be able to:

- Create a chart with data in an Excel worksheet
- Size, move, edit, format, and delete charts
- Print a selected chart and print a worksheet containing a chart
- Change a chart location
- Insert, move, size, and delete chart elements and shapes
- Write formulas with the PMT and FV financial functions
- Write formulas with the IF logical function

Tutorials

7.1	Creating Charts in Excel
7.2	Editing Chart Data
7.3	Formatting with Chart Buttons
7.4	Printing Charts
7.5	Changing Chart Design
7.6	Changing Chart Formatting
7.7	Inserting and Formatting a Shape
7.8	Moving, Sizing, and Deleting a Chart
7.9	Using Financial Functions
7.10	Using the Logical IF Function

In the previous Excel chapters, you learned to create data in worksheets. While a worksheet does an adequate job of representing data, some data are better represented visually with a chart. A *chart*, which is sometimes referred to as a *graph*, is a picture of numeric data. In this chapter, you will learn to create and customize charts in Excel. You will also learn how to write formulas using financial and logical functions. Model answers for this chapter's projects appear on the following pages.

Note: Before beginning the projects, copy to your storage medium the EL1C7 subfolder from the EL1 folder on the CD that accompanies this textbook and then make EL1C7 the active folder.

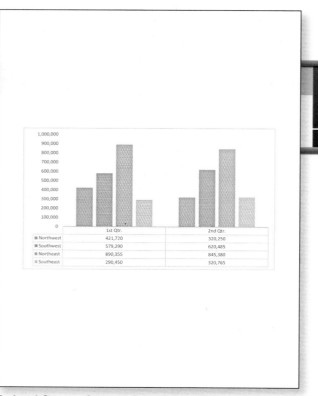

Project 1 Create a Quarterly Sales Column Chart

EL1-C7-P1-SalesChart.xlsx

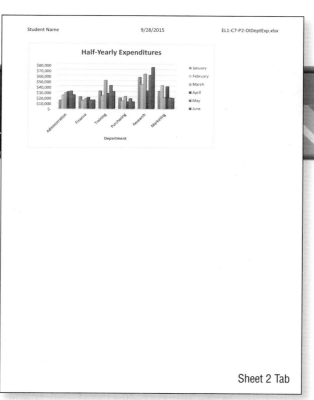

Sheet 2 Tab

Project 2 Create a Technology Purchases Bar Chart and Column Chart

EL1-C7-P2-DIDeptExp.xlsx

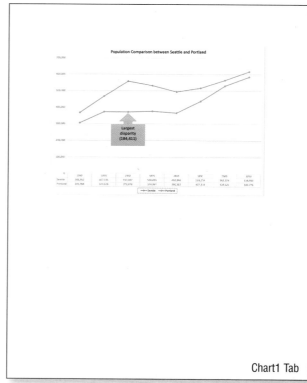

Chart1 Tab

Project 3 Create a Population Comparison Line Chart

EL1-C7-P3-PopComp.xlsx

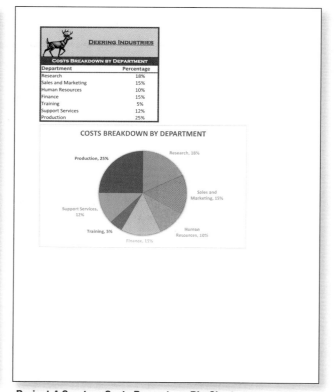

Project 4 Create a Costs Percentage Pie Chart

EL1-C7-P4-DIDeptCosts.xlsx

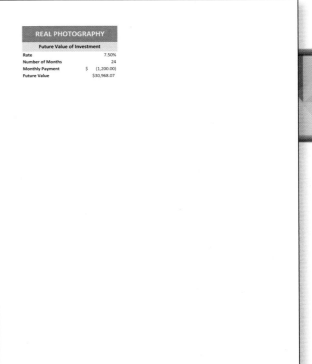

Project 5 Calculate Payments and the Future Value of an Investment

EL1-C7-P5-RPReports.xlsx

EL1-C7-P5-RPInvest.xlsx

Capstan Marine Products

Sales Department

Salesperson	Quota	Actual Sales	Bonus
Allejandro	$ 95,500.00	$ 103,295.00	$ 20,659.00
Crispin	137,000.00	129,890.00	-
Frankel	124,000.00	133,255.00	26,651.00
Hiesmann	85,500.00	94,350.00	18,870.00
Jarvis	159,000.00	167,410.00	33,482.00
Littleman	110,500.00	109,980.00	-

Sales Department

Product #	Price	Discount Price	Discount
C-2340	$ 1,250.00	$ 1,187.50	YES
C-3215	695.00	660.25	YES
C-4390	475.00	475.00	NO
E-2306	225.00	225.00	NO
E-3420	520.00	520.00	NO
G-2312	2,150.00	2,042.50	YES
G-4393	2,450.00	2,327.50	YES
J-1203	755.00	717.25	YES
J-3288	455.00	455.00	NO
J-4594	1,050.00	997.50	YES
M-2355	890.00	845.50	YES
M-3129	645.00	612.75	YES
M-4392	475.00	475.00	NO

New Employee Orientation

Name	Quiz 1	Quiz 2	Quiz 3	Average	Grade
Angelo	78	69	88	78	FAIL
Cunningham	90	95	86	90	PASS
Elliot	82	88	94	88	PASS
Kennedy	100	98	96	98	PASS
Lipscomb	64	76	62	67	FAIL

Project 6 Insert Formulas with the IF Logical Function

EL1-C7-P6-CMPReports.xlsx

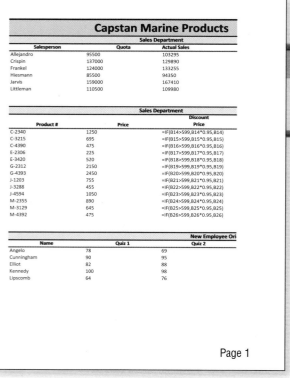

Page 1

Capstan Marine Products

Sales Department		
Salesperson	**Quota**	**Actual Sales**
Allejandro	95500	103295
Crispin	137000	129890
Frankel	124000	133255
Hiesmann	85500	94350
Jarvis	159000	167410
Littleman	110500	109980

Sales Department		
		Discount
Product #	**Price**	**Price**
C-2340	1250	=IF(B14>599,B14*0.95,B14)
C-3215	695	=IF(B15>599,B15*0.95,B15)
C-4390	475	=IF(B16>599,B16*0.95,B16)
E-2306	225	=IF(B17>599,B17*0.95,B17)
E-3420	520	=IF(B18>599,B18*0.95,B18)
G-2312	2150	=IF(B19>599,B19*0.95,B19)
G-4393	2450	=IF(B20>599,B20*0.95,B20)
J-1203	755	=IF(B21>599,B21*0.95,B21)
J-3288	455	=IF(B22>599,B22*0.95,B22)
J-4594	1050	=IF(B23>599,B23*0.95,B23)
M-2355	890	=IF(B24>599,B24*0.95,B24)
M-3129	645	=IF(B25>599,B25*0.95,B25)
M-4392	475	=IF(B26>599,B26*0.95,B26)

		New Employee Ori
Name	**Quiz 1**	**Quiz 2**
Angelo	78	69
Cunningham	90	95
Elliot	82	88
Kennedy	100	98
Lipscomb	64	76

Page 1

Page 2

Bonus
=IF(C4>B4,C4*0.2,0)
=IF(C5>B5,C5*0.2,0)
=IF(C6>B6,C6*0.2,0)
=IF(C7>B7,C7*0.2,0)
=IF(C8>B8,C8*0.2,0)
=IF(C9>B9,C9*0.2,0)

Discount
=IF(B14>599,"YES","NO")
=IF(B15>599,"YES","NO")
=IF(B16>599,"YES","NO")
=IF(B17>599,"YES","NO")
=IF(B18>599,"YES","NO")
=IF(B19>599,"YES","NO")
=IF(B20>599,"YES","NO")
=IF(B21>599,"YES","NO")
=IF(B22>599,"YES","NO")
=IF(B23>599,"YES","NO")
=IF(B24>599,"YES","NO")
=IF(B25>599,"YES","NO")
=IF(B26>599,"YES","NO")

entation		
Quiz 3	**Average**	**Grade**
88	=AVERAGE(B31:D31)	=IF(E31>79,"PASS","FAIL")
86	=AVERAGE(B32:D32)	=IF(E32>79,"PASS","FAIL")
94	=AVERAGE(B33:D33)	=IF(E33>79,"PASS","FAIL")
96	=AVERAGE(B34:D34)	=IF(E34>79,"PASS","FAIL")
62	=AVERAGE(B35:D35)	=IF(E35>79,"PASS","FAIL")

Page 2

EL1-C7-P6-CMReports(Formulas).xlsx

Project 1 — Create a Quarterly Sales Column Chart — 3 Parts

You will open a workbook containing quarterly sales data and then use the data to create a column chart. You will decrease the size of the chart, move it to a different location in the worksheet, and then make changes to sales numbers. You will also use buttons to customize and filter chart elements.

Creating a Chart

Quick Steps

Create a Chart
1. Select cells.
2. Click INSERT tab.
3. Click desired chart button.
4. Click desired chart style at drop-down gallery.

Recommended Charts

To provide a visual representation of your data, consider inserting data in a chart. With buttons in the Charts group on the INSERT tab, you can create a variety of charts, such as a column chart, line chart, pie chart, and much more. Excel provides ten basic chart types, as described in Table 7.1.

To create a chart, select the cells in the worksheet that you want to chart, click the INSERT tab, and then click the desired chart button in the Charts group. At the drop-down gallery that displays, click the desired chart style. If you are not sure what type of chart will best illustrate your data, consider letting Excel recommend a chart. To do this, select the data, click the INSERT tab, and then click the Recommended Charts button. This displays the data in a chart in the Insert Chart dialog box. Customize the recommended chart with options in the left panel of the dialog box. Click the OK button to insert the recommended chart in the worksheet. You can also insert a recommended chart in the worksheet with the keyboard shortcut Alt+ F1.

Table 7.1 Types of Charts

Chart	Description
area	Emphasizes the magnitude of change rather than time and the rate of change. Also shows the relationship of the parts to the whole by displaying the sum of the plotted values.
bar	Shows individual figures at a specific time or shows variations between components but not in relationship to the whole.
column	Compares separate (noncontinuous) items as they vary over time.
combo	Combines two or more chart types to make data easy to understand.
line	Shows trends and overall change across time at even intervals. Emphasizes the rate of change across time rather than the magnitude of change.
pie	Shows proportions and the relationship of the parts to the whole.
radar	Emphasizes differences and amounts of change over time and variations and trends. Each category has a value axis radiating from the center point. Lines connect all values in the same series.
stock	Shows four values for a stock: open, high, low, and close.
surface	Shows trends in values across two dimensions in a continuous curve.
xy (scatter)	Shows the relationships among numeric values in several data series or plots the interception points between x and y values. Shows uneven intervals of data and is commonly used in scientific data.

Sizing and Moving a Chart

When you create a chart, it is inserted in the same worksheet as the selected cells. Figure 7.1 displays the worksheet and chart you will create in Project 1a. The chart is inserted in a box, which you can size and/or move in the worksheet.

Change the size of the chart using the sizing handles (white squares) that display on the chart borders. Drag the top and bottom middle sizing handles to increase or decrease the height of the chart; use the left and right middle sizing handles to increase or decrease the width; and use the corner sizing handles to increase or decrease the height and width at the same time. To increase or decrease the size of the chart but maintain its proportions, hold down the Shift key while dragging one of the chart's corner borders.

To move the chart, make sure the chart is selected (border with sizing handles displays around the chart), position the mouse pointer on a border until the pointer displays with a four-headed arrow attached, hold down the left mouse button, and then drag to the desired position.

Editing Data and Adding a Data Series

The cells you select to create the chart are linked to it. If you need to change the data for a chart, edit the data in the desired cell and the corresponding section of the chart will be automatically updated. If you add data to cells within the range

▼ **Quick Steps**

Create a Recommended Chart
1. Select cells.
2. Click INSERT tab.
3. Click Recommended Charts button.
4. Click OK at Insert Chart dialog box.
OR
1. Select cells.
2. Press Alt + F1.

Hide rows or columns that you do not want to chart.

of cells used for the chart, called the source data, the new data will be included in the chart. If you add a data series in cells next to or below the source data, you will need to click in the chart to display the source data with sizing handles and then drag with a sizing handle to include the new data.

Figure 7.1 Project 1a Chart

Project 1a **Creating a Chart** Part 1 of 3

1. Open **SalesChart.xlsx** and then save the workbook with Save As and name it **EL1-C7-P1-SalesChart**.
2. Select cells A1 through E4.
3. Let Excel recommend a chart type by completing the following steps:
   a. Click the INSERT tab.
   b. Click the Recommended Charts button in the Charts group.

   c. At the Insert Chart dialog box, look at the options that display in the left panel and then click OK.

4. Slightly increase the size of the chart and maintain its proportions by completing the following steps:
   a. Position the mouse pointer on the sizing handle in the lower right corner of the chart border until the pointer turns into a two-headed arrow pointing diagonally.
   b. Hold down the Shift key and then hold down the left mouse button.
   c. Drag out approximately 0.5 inch. Release the mouse button and then release the Shift key.

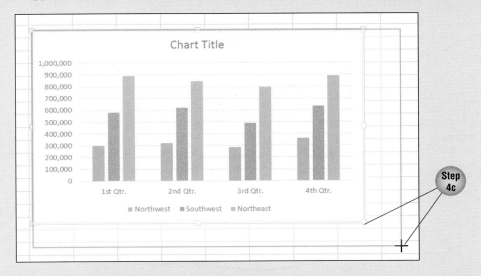

5. Move the chart below the cells containing data by completing the following steps:
   a. Make sure the chart is selected. (When the chart is selected, the border surrounding it displays with sizing handles.)
   b. Position the mouse pointer on the chart border until the pointer displays with a four-headed arrow attached.
   c. Hold down the left mouse button, drag the chart so it is positioned in row 6 below the cells containing data, and then release the mouse button.

6. Make the following changes to the specified cells:
   a. Make cell B2 active and then change *300,560* to *421,720*.
   b. Make cell D2 active and then change *287,460* to *397,460*.

	A	B	C	D	E	F
1	Region	1st Qtr.	2nd Qtr.	3rd Qtr.	4th Qtr.	
2	Northwest	300,560	320,250	287,460	360,745	
3	Southwest	579,290	620,485	490,125	635,340	
4	Northeast	890,355	845,380	795,460	890,425	
5						
6						
7				Chart Title		
8	1,000,000					

Step 5c

7. Add a new data series by typing data in the following cells:
   A5: Southeast
   B5: 290,450
   C5: 320,765
   D5: 270,450
   E5: 300,455

8. Add the new data series to the chart by completing the following steps:
   a. Click in the chart. (This selects the data source A1 through E4.)
   b. Position the mouse pointer on the sizing handle in the lower right corner of cell E4 until the pointer displays as a two-headed diagonally pointing arrow.
   c. Hold down the left mouse button, drag down to cell E5, and then release the mouse button. (This incorporates the data row E in the chart.)
9. Save **EL1-C7-P1-SalesChart.xlsx**.

Formatting with Chart Buttons

Chart Elements

When you insert a chart in a worksheet, three buttons display at the right side of the chart border. Click the top button, Chart Elements, and a side menu displays with chart elements, as shown in Figure 7.2. The check boxes containing check marks indicate the elements that are currently part of the chart. Add a new element to your chart by inserting a check mark in the check box for the desired element and remove an element by removing the check mark.

Chart Styles

Excel offers a variety of chart styles you can apply to your chart. Click the Chart Styles button that displays at the right side of the chart and a side menu gallery of styles displays, as shown in Figure 7.3 on the next page. Scroll down the gallery, hover your mouse over an option, and the style formatting is applied to your chart. In this way, you can scroll down the gallery and then choose the desired chart style.

In addition to applying a chart style, you can use the Chart Styles button side menu gallery to change the chart colors. Click the Chart Styles button and then click the COLOR tab that displays to the right of the STYLE tab. Click the desired color option at the color palette that displays. Hover your mouse over a color option to view how the color change affects the elements in your chart.

Chart Filters

Use the bottom button, Chart Filters, to isolate specific data in your chart. When you click the button, a side menu displays, as shown in Figure 7.4. Specify the series or categories you want to display in your chart. To do this, remove check marks from those elements that you do not want to appear in your chart. After removing the desired check marks, click the Apply button that displays toward the bottom of the side menu. Click the NAMES tab at the Chart Filters button side menu and options display for turning on/off the display of column and row names.

Figure 7.2 Chart Elements Button Side Menu Gallery

Click the Chart Elements button to display this side menu of chart elements. Add or remove chart elements by inserting or removing check marks from check boxes.

Figure 7.3 Chart Styles Button Side Menu Gallery

Figure 7.4 Chart Filters Button Side Menu

Click the Chart Styles button to display this side menu gallery of chart style options.

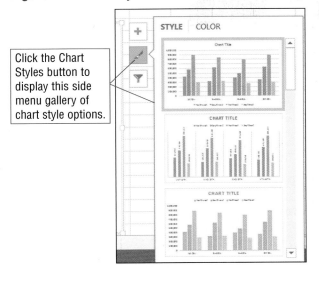

Click the Chart Fillers button to display this side menu. Isolate specific data in your chart by inserting check marks in check boxes for only those elements you want to appear in your chart.

Click this button to apply the selected options to the chart.

Project 1b **Formatting with Chart Buttons**   **Part 2 of 3**

1. With **EL1-C7-P1-SalesChart.xlsx** open, make the chart active by clicking inside the chart but outside any elements.
2. Insert and remove chart elements by completing the following steps:
    a. Click the Chart Elements button that displays outside the upper right side of the chart.
    b. At the side menu that displays, click the *Chart Title* check box to remove the check mark.
    c. Click the *Data Table* check box to insert a check mark.
    d. Hover your mouse over *Gridlines* in the Chart Elements button side menu and then click the right-pointing triangle that displays.
    e. At the side menu that displays, click the *Primary Major Vertical* check box to insert a check mark.
    f. Click the *Legend* check box to remove the check mark.

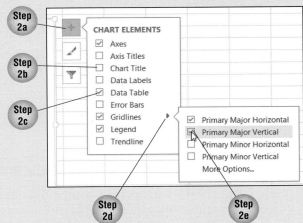

3. Apply a different chart style by completing the following steps:
   a. Click the Chart Styles button that displays outside the upper right side of the chart (below the Chart Elements button).
   b. At the side menu gallery, click the *Style 3* option (third option in the gallery).
4. Display only the first quarter and second quarter sales by completing the following steps:
   a. Click the Chart Filters button that displays outside the upper right corner of the chart (below the Chart Styles button).
   b. Click the *3rd Qtr.* check box in the *CATEGORIES* section to remove the check mark.
   c. Click the *4th Qtr.* check box in the *CATEGORIES* section to remove the check mark.
   d. Click the Apply button that displays toward the bottom of the side menu.
   e. Click the Chart Filters button to remove the side menu.

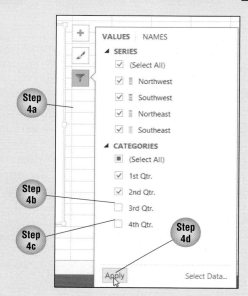

Step 3a

Step 3b

Step 4a

Step 4b

Step 4c

Step 4d

5. Save **EL1-C7-P1-SalesChart.xlsx**.

Printing a Chart ▪▪▪▪▪▪▪▪▪▪▪▪▪▪▪▪▪▪▪▪▪▪▪▪▪▪▪

In a worksheet containing data in cells as well as a chart, you have the option to print only the chart. To do this, select the chart, display the Print backstage area, and then click the Print button. With a chart selected, the first gallery in the *Settings* category is automatically changed to *Print Selected Chart*. A preview of the chart displays at the right side of the Print backstage area.

1. With **EL1-C7-P1-SalesChart.xlsx** open, make sure the chart is selected.
2. Click the FILE tab and then click the *Print* option.
3. At the Print backstage area, look at the preview of the chart that displays at the right side and notice that the first gallery in the *Settings* category is set to *Print Selected Chart*.
4. Click the Print button.
5. Save and then close **EL1-C7-P1-SalesChart.xlsx**.

Project **2** | **Create a Department Expenditures Bar Chart and Column Chart** | **2 Parts**

You will open a workbook containing expenditure data by department and then create a bar chart with the data. You will then change the chart type, layout, and style; add chart elements; and move the chart to a new worksheet.

Changing the Chart Design ■■■■■■■■■■■■■■■■■■■■■

Along with the buttons that display outside the upper right side of the chart, you can apply formatting to change the chart design with options on the CHART TOOLS DESIGN tab. This tab, shown in Figure 7.5, displays when you insert a chart in a worksheet. Use options on this tab to add chart elements, change the chart type, specify a different layout or style for the chart, and change the location of the chart so it displays in a separate worksheet.

Figure 7.5 CHART TOOLS DESIGN Tab

Changing the Chart Style

Quick Steps

Change the Chart Type and Style
1. Make chart active.
2. Click CHART TOOLS DESIGN tab.
3. Click Change Chart Type button.
4. Click desired chart type.
5. Click desired chart style.
6. Click OK.

Change Chart Type

The chart feature offers a variety of preformatted custom charts and varying styles for each chart type. You chose a chart style in Project 1b using the Chart Styles button that displays outside the right border of the chart. You can also choose a chart style with options in the Chart Styles group on the CHART TOOLS DESIGN tab. To do this, click the desired chart style thumbnail that displays in the Chart Styles group or click the More button that displays to the right of the thumbnails and then click the desired chart style thumbnail.

You can also choose a chart style with the Change Chart Type button in the Type group. Click this button and the Change Chart Type dialog box with the All Charts tab active displays, as shown in Figure 7.6. Click the desired chart type in the panel at the left side of the dialog box, click the desired chart style in the row of options at the top at the right, and then click a specific style that displays below the row of styles. Click the Recommended Chart tab to display chart styles recommended for the data by Excel.

Quick Steps

Switch Rows and Columns
1. Make chart active.
2. Click CHART TOOLS DESIGN tab.
3. Click Switch Row/Column button.

Switch Row/Column

Switching Rows and Columns

When creating a chart, Excel uses row headings for grouping data along the bottom of the chart (the horizontal axis) and uses column headings for the legend. You can change this order by clicking the Switch Row/Column button in the Data group on the CHART TOOLS DESIGN tab. When you click this button, Excel uses the column headings for grouping data along the horizontal axis and uses row headings for the legend.

Figure 7.6 Change Chart Type Dialog Box

1. Open **DIDeptExp.xlsx** and then save the workbook with Save As and name it **EL1-C7-P2-DIDeptExp**.
2. Create a bar chart by completing the following steps:
   a. Select cells A3 through G9.
   b. Click the INSERT tab.
   c. Click the Insert Bar Chart button in the Charts group.
   d. Click the *3-D Clustered Bar* option (first option in the *3-D Bar* section).
3. With the CHART TOOLS DESIGN tab active, change the chart type by completing the following steps:
   a. Click the Change Chart Type button located in the Type group.
   b. At the Change Chart Type dialog box, click the *Column* option in the left panel.
   c. Click the *3-D Clustered Column* option in the top row (fourth option from left).
   d. Click OK to close the Change Chart Type dialog box.
4. With the chart selected and the CHART TOOLS DESIGN tab active, click the Switch Row/Column button located in the Data group.

5. Save **EL1-C7-P2-DIDeptExp.xlsx**.

Changing Chart Layout and Colors

The CHART TOOLS DESIGN tab contains options for changing the chart layout and chart colors. Click the Quick Layout button in the Chart Layouts group and a drop-down gallery of layout options displays. Hover the mouse over a layout option at the drop-down gallery and the chart will reflect the layout. Change the colors used in the chart by clicking the Change Colors button in the Chart Styles group and then clicking the desired color at the drop-down gallery.

Quick Layout

Change Colors

Changing the Chart Location

Quick Steps

Change the Chart Location
1. Make chart active.
2. Click CHART TOOLS DESIGN tab.
3. Click Move Chart button.
4. Click *New Sheet* option.
5. Click OK.

Move Chart

Create a chart and the chart is inserted in the currently open worksheet as an embedded object. Change the location of a chart with the Move Chart button in the Location group on the CHART TOOLS DESIGN tab. Click this button and the Move Chart dialog box displays, as shown in Figure 7.7. To move the chart to a new sheet in the workbook, click the *New sheet* option; Excel automatically names the new sheet *Chart1*. Earlier in this chapter you learned that pressing Alt + F1 will insert a recommended chart in the currently open worksheet. If you want the recommended chart inserted into a separate worksheet, press F11.

If you move a chart to a separate sheet, you can move it back to the original sheet or move it to a different sheet within the workbook. To move a chart to a sheet, click the Move Chart button in the Location group. At the Move Chart dialog box, click the down-pointing arrow at the right side of the *Object in* option and then click the desired sheet at the drop-down list. Click OK and the chart is inserted in the specified sheet as an object that you can move, size, and format.

Adding, Moving, and Deleting Chart Elements

Add Chart Element

Quick Steps

Delete a Chart Element
1. Click chart element.
2. Press Delete key.
OR
1. Right-click chart element.
2. Click *Delete*.

As you learned earlier in this chapter, you can add chart elements to a chart with the Chart Elements button that displays at the right side of a selected chart. You can also add chart elements with the Add Chart Element button on the CHART TOOLS DESIGN tab. Click this button to display a drop-down list of elements, point to a category of elements, and then click the element you want to apply at the side menu that displays.

You can also move and/or size a chart element. To move a chart element, click the element to select it and then move the mouse pointer over the border line until the pointer turns into a four-headed arrow. Hold down the left mouse button, drag the element to the desired location, and then release the mouse button. To size a chart element, click to select the element and then use the sizing handles that display around it to increase or decrease the size. To delete a chart element, click the element to select it and then press the Delete key. You can also delete an element by right-clicking the element and then clicking *Delete* at the shortcut menu.

Figure 7.7 Move Chart Dialog Box

1. With **EL1-C7-P2-DIDeptExp.xlsx** open, make sure the CHART TOOLS DESIGN tab is active. (If it is not, make sure the chart is selected and then click the CHART TOOLS DESIGN tab.)

2. Change the chart style by clicking the *Style 5* thumbnail in the Chart Styles group (fifth option from the left).

3. Change the chart colors by clicking the Change Colors button in the Chart Styles group and then clicking the *Color 3* option (third row in the *Colorful* group).

4. Change the chart layout by clicking the Quick Layout button in the Chart Layouts group and then clicking the *Layout 1* option (first option in the drop-down gallery).

5. Add axis titles by completing the following steps:
   a. Click the Add Chart Element button in the Chart Layouts group on the CHART TOOLS DESIGN tab.
   b. Point to *Axis Titles* and then click *Primary Horizontal* at the side menu.
   c. Type **Department** and then press Enter. (The word *Department* will display in the Formula bar.)
   d. Click the Add Chart Element button, point to *Axis Titles*, and then click *Primary Vertical* at the side menu.
   e. Type **Expenditure Amounts** and then press Enter.

6. Click in the text *Chart Title* that displays toward the top of the chart, type **Half-Yearly Expenditures**, and then press Enter.

7. Delete the *Expenditure Amounts* axis title by clicking on any character in the axis title and then pressing the Delete key.

8. Move the legend by completing the following steps:
   a. Click on any character in the legend to select it.
   b. Move the mouse pointer over the border line until the pointer turns into a four-headed arrow.
   c. Hold down the left mouse button, drag up until the top border of the legend aligns with the top gridline in the chart, and then release the mouse button.

9. Move the chart to a new location by completing the following steps:

   a. Click the Move Chart button in the Location group.

   b. At the Move Chart dialog box, click the *New sheet* option and then click OK. (The chart is inserted in a worksheet named *Chart1*.)

10. Save **EL1-C7-P2-DIDeptExp.xlsx**.

11. Print the Chart1 worksheet.

12. Move the chart from Chart1 to Sheet2 by completing the following steps:

   a. Make sure Chart1 is the active worksheet and that the chart is selected (not just an element in the chart).

   b. Make sure the CHART TOOLS DESIGN tab is active.

   c. Click the Move Chart button in the Location group.

   d. At the Move Chart dialog box, click the down-pointing arrow at the right side of the *Object in* option box and then click *Sheet2* at the drop-down list.

   e. Click OK.

13. Change the amounts in Sheet1 by completing the following steps:

   a. Click Sheet1.

   b. Make cell B7 active and then change the amount from *10,540* to *19,750*.

   c. Make cell D8 active and then change the amount from *78,320* to *63,320*.

   d. Make cell G8 active and then change the amount from *60,570* to *75,570*.

   e. Make cell A2 active.

   f. Click the Sheet2 tab and notice that the chart displays the updated amounts.

14. Click outside the chart to deselect it.

15. Insert a header in the Sheet2 worksheet that prints your name at the left side, the current date in the middle, and the workbook file name at the right side.

16. Display the worksheet at the Print backstage area and make sure it will print on one page. If the chart does not fit on the page, return to the worksheet and then move and/or decrease the size of the chart until it fits on one page.

17. Print the active worksheet (Sheet2).

18. Save and then close **EL1-C7-P2-DIDeptExp.xlsx**.

Project 3 Create a Population Comparison Line Chart   2 Parts

You will open a workbook containing population comparison data for Seattle and Portland and then create a line chart with the data. You will move the chart to a new worksheet, format chart elements, and insert a shape in the chart.

Changing Chart Formatting ■■■■□■□□■□□■■□□■□□■■□■■

Customize the formatting of a chart and chart elements with options on the CHART TOOLS FORMAT tab, as shown in Figure 7.8. With buttons in the Current Selection group, you can identify specific elements in the chart and then apply formatting. Insert a shape in a chart with options in the Insert Shapes group and format shapes with options in the Shape Styles group. Apply WordArt formatting to data in a chart with options in the WordArt Styles group. Arrange, align, and size a chart with options in the Arrange and Size groups.

Formatting a Selection

Identify a specific element in a chart for formatting by clicking the Chart Elements button arrow in the Current Selection group on the CHART TOOLS FORMAT tab and then clicking the desired element at the drop-down list. This selects the specific element in the chart. Click the Reset to Match Style button to return the formatting of the element back to the original style. Use buttons in the Shapes Styles group to apply formatting to a selected object and use buttons in the WordArt Styles group to apply formatting to selected data.

Chart Elements

Figure 7.8 CHART TOOLS FORMAT Tab

Project 3a **Creating and Formatting a Line Chart**   Part 1 of 2

1. Open **PopComp.xlsx** and then save the workbook with Save As and name it **EL1-C7-P3-PopComp**.
2. Create a line chart and add a chart element by completing the following steps:
   a. Select cells A2 through I4.
   b. Click the INSERT tab.
   c. Click the Insert Line Chart button in the Charts group.
   d. Click the *Line with Markers* option at the drop-down list (first column, second row in the *2-D Line* section).
   e. Click the Chart Elements button that displays outside the upper right side of the chart.
   f. Hover your mouse over the *Data Table* option at the side menu, click the right-pointing triangle that displays, and then click *No Legend Keys* at the side menu that appears.
   g. Click the Chart Elements button to remove the side menu.
3. Move the chart to a new sheet by completing the following steps:
   a. Click the Move Chart button in the Location group on the CHART TOOLS DESIGN tab.
   b. At the Move Chart dialog box, click the *New sheet* option.
   c. Click OK.

4. Format the *Portland* line by completing the following steps:
   a. Click the CHART TOOLS FORMAT tab.
   b. Click the Chart Elements button arrow in the Current Selection group and then click *Series "Portland"* at the drop-down list.
   c. Click the Shape Fill button arrow in the Shape Styles group and then click the *Green* color at the drop-down color palette (sixth color in the *Standard Colors* section).

   d. Click the Shape Outline button arrow in the Shape Styles group and then click the *Green* color.
5. Type a title for the chart and format the title by completing the following steps:
   a. Click Chart Elements button arrow in the Current Selection group and then click *Chart Title* at the drop-down list.
   b. Type **Population Comparison between Seattle and Portland** and then press Enter.
   c. Click the *Fill - Black, Text 1, Shadow* WordArt style thumbnail in the WordArt Styles group (first WordArt style thumbnail).
6. Format the legend by completing the following steps:
   a. Click the Chart Elements button arrow in the Current Selection group and then click *Legend* at the drop-down list.
   b. Click the *Colored Outline - Blue, Accent 1* shape style thumbnail in the Shape Styles group (second shape style thumbnail).
7. Save **EL1-C7-P3-PopComp.xlsx**.

Inserting Shapes

▼ **Quick Steps**

Insert a Shape
1. Make chart active.
2. Click CHART TOOLS FORMAT tab.
3. Click More button at right side of shapes.
4. Click desired shape at drop-down list.
5. Click or drag to create shape in chart.

The Insert Shapes group on the CHART TOOLS FORMAT tab contains options for inserting shapes in a chart. Click a shape option and the mouse pointer turns into a thin, black plus symbol. Click in the chart or drag with the mouse to create the shape in the chart. The shape is inserted in the chart and the DRAWING TOOLS FORMAT tab is active. This tab contains many of the same options as the CHART TOOLS FORMAT tab. For example, you can insert a shape, apply a shape or WordArt style, and arrange and size the shape. Size a shape by clicking the up- or down-pointing arrows that display at the right side of the *Shape Height* or *Shape Width* measurement boxes in the Size group on the DRAWING TOOLS FORMAT tab. You can also select the current measurement and then type a specific measurement.

1. With **EL1-C7-P3-PopComp.xlsx** open, create a shape similar to the one shown in Figure 7.9 on the next page by completing the following steps:

    Step 1b

    a. Click the More button at the right side of the shapes in the Insert Shapes group on the CHART TOOLS FORMAT tab.
    b. Click the *Up Arrow Callout* shape in the *Block Arrows* section.
    c. Click in the chart to insert the shape.
    d. Click in the *Shape Height* measurement box in the Size group on the DRAWING TOOLS FORMAT tab, type **1.5**, and then press Enter.
    e. Click in the *Shape Width* measurement box, type **1.5**, and then press Enter.
    f. Apply a shape style by clicking the More button at the right side of the shape style thumbnails in the Shape Style group and then clicking the *Subtle Effect - Blue, Accent 1* option (second column, fourth row).

Step 1f

    g. Type **Largest disparity** in the shape, press Enter, and then type **(184,411)**.
    h. Select the text you just typed.
    i. Click the HOME tab.
    j. Click the Bold button in the Font group.
    k. Click the Font Size button arrow and then click *14*.
    l. Click the Center button in the Alignment group.
2. With the shape selected, drag the shape so it is positioned as shown in Figure 7.9.
3. Save **EL1-C7-P3-PopComp.xlsx**, print the Chart1 worksheet, and then close the workbook.

Figure 7.9 Project 3 Chart

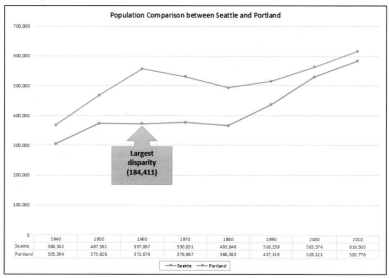

	1940	1950	1960	1970	1980	1990	2000	2010
Seattle	368,302	467,591	557,087	530,831	493,846	516,259	563,374	618,500
Portland	305,394	373,628	372,676	376,967	366,383	437,319	529,121	583,776

Population Comparison between Seattle and Portland

Largest disparity (184,411)

Project 4 Create a Costs Percentage Pie Chart   1 Part

You will create a pie chart, add data labels, apply a style, format chart elements, and then size and move the pie chart.

▼ **Quick Steps**

Display a Task Pane
1. Select chart or specific element.
2. Click CHART TOOLS FORMAT tab.
3. Click Format Selection button.

Format Selection

Applying Formatting at a Task Pane

To view and apply more formatting options for charts, display the formatting task pane by clicking the Format Selection button in the Current Selection group on the CHART TOOLS FORMAT tab. The task pane displays at the right side of the screen and the name of and contents in the task pane vary depending on what is selected. If the entire chart is selected, the Format Chart Area task pane displays, as shown in Figure 7.10. Format the chart by clicking the desired formatting options in the task pane. Display additional formatting options by clicking the icons that display toward the top of the task pane. For example, click the Effects icon in the Format Chart Area task pane and options for applying shadow, glow, soft edges, and 3-D formatting display.

Click a chart element and then click the Format Selection button and the task pane name and options change. You can also right-click a chart or chart element and then click the format option at the shortcut menu. The name of the format option varies depending on the selected element.

▼ **Quick Steps**

Change Chart Height and/or Width
1. Make chart active.
2. Click CHART TOOLS FORMAT tab.
3. Insert desired height and/or width with *Shape Height* and/or *Shape Width* measurement boxes.

Changing Chart Height and Width Measurements

As you learned earlier in this chapter, if you insert a chart into the current worksheet (not into a separate, new worksheet), you can size the chart by selecting it and then dragging a sizing handle. You can also size a chart to specific measurements. To do this, display the CHART TOOLS FORMAT tab and then click the up- or down-pointing arrow that displays at the right side of the *Shape*

Figure 7.10 Format Chart Area Task Pane

Display additional formatting options by clicking other icons in this section of the task pane.

This task pane displays if you click the Format Selection button with the chart selected. Apply formatting to the chart with options in the task pane.

Click an option to expand it and display additional options.

Height or *Shape Width* measurement box or select the current measurement and then type a specific measurement. In addition to using the *Shape Height* and *Shape Width* measurement boxes on the CHART TOOLS FORMAT tab, you can change the chart size with options at the Format Chart Area task pane.

Deleting a Chart

Delete a chart created in Excel by clicking once in the chart to select it and then pressing the Delete key. If you move a chart to a different worksheet in the workbook and then delete the chart, the chart will be deleted but the worksheet will not. To delete the worksheet as well as the chart, position the mouse pointer on the Chart1 tab, click the right mouse button, and then click *Delete* at the shortcut menu. At the message box telling you that selected sheets will be permanently deleted, click Delete.

▼ **Quick Steps**

Delete a Chart
1. Click once in chart.
2. Press Delete key.
OR
1. Right-click chart tab.
2. Click *Delete*.

Project 4   **Deleting a Chart and Creating and Formatting a Pie Chart**   Part 1 of 1

1. Open **DIDeptCosts.xlsx** and then save the workbook with Save As and name it **EL1-C7-P4-DIDeptCosts**.
2. Delete the column chart by completing the following steps:
   a. Click the column chart to select the chart. (Make sure the chart is selected and not a specific element in the chart.)
   b. Press the Delete key.
3. Create the pie chart shown in Figure 7.10 by completing the following steps:
   a. Select cells A3 through B10.
   b. Click the INSERT tab.

c. Click the Insert Pie or Doughnut Chart button.

d. Click the *Pie* option (first option in the *2-D Pie* section).

Step 3c

Step 3d

4. Insert data labels in the chart by completing the following steps:

a. Click the Chart Elements button that displays outside the upper right border of the chart.

b. Hover the mouse over the *Data Labels* option and click the right-pointing triangle that displays.

c. Click *Inside End* at the side menu.

d. Click the Chart Elements button to hide the side menu.

Step 4a

Step 4b   **Step 4c**

5. Click the *Style 6* thumbnail in the Chart Styles group.

6. Type a title and then apply a WordArt style to the title by completing the following steps:

a. Click the CHART TOOLS FORMAT tab.

b. Click the Chart Elements button arrow in the Current Selection group.

c. Click *Chart Title* at the drop-down list.

d. Type **C** and Excel's AutoComplete feature inserts the entire title *Costs Breakdown by Department* in the Formula bar. Accept this name by pressing the Enter key.

e. Click the More button at the right side of the WordArt style thumbnails in the WordArt Styles group.

f. Click the *Pattern Fill - Gray-50%, Accent 3, Narrow Horizontal, Inner Shadow* style thumbnail at the drop-down gallery (second column, fourth row).

7. Use the Format Legend task pane to apply formatting to the legend by completing the following steps:

a. Click the Chart Elements button arrow and then click *Legend* at the drop-down list.

b. Click the Format Selection button in the Current Selection group.

Step 7a

Step 7b

Step 7d

c. At the Format Legend task pane, click the *Left* option in the *LEGEND OPTIONS* section.

d. Click the Effects icon in the task pane. (This changes the options in the task pane.)

Step 7c

e. Click the *SHADOW* option. (This displays shadow options in the task pane.)

f. Click the Shadow button that displays to the right of *Presets* and then click the *Offset Diagonal Bottom Right* option (first option in the *Outer* section).

g. Click the Fill & Line icon in the task pane.

h. Click the *FILL* option.

i. Click the *Gradient fill* option.

j. Close the task pane by clicking the Close button located in the upper right corner of the task pane.

8. Use the Format Chart Area task pane to apply formatting to the chart by completing the following steps:

a. Click inside the chart but outside any chart elements.

b. Click the Format Selection button in the Current Selection group.

c. Make sure the Fill & Line icon in the Format Chart Area task pane is selected. (If not, click the icon.)

d. Make sure the *FILL* option is expanded. (If not, click the *FILL* option.)

e. Click the *Gradient fill* option.

f. Click the Size & Properties icon in the task pane.

g. Click the *SIZE* option to display size options.

h. Select the current measurement in the *Height* measurement box, type 4, and then press Enter.

i. Close the task pane.

9. Save **EL1-C7-P4-DIDeptCosts.xlsx** and then print only the chart.

10. Change the chart style by completing the following steps:

a. Click the CHART TOOLS DESIGN tab.

b. Click the More button at the right side of the chart style thumbnails.

c. Click the *Style 9* thumbnail at the drop-down gallery.

11. Change the size of the chart by completing the following steps:

a. Click the CHART TOOLS FORMAT tab.

b. Click in the *Shape Height* measurement box, type 3.5, and then press Enter.

c. Click in the *Shape Width* measurement box, type 5.5, and then press Enter.

12. Drag the chart so it is positioned below the cells containing data.

13. Click outside the chart to deselect it.

14. Display the Print backstage area, make sure the chart fits on the page with the data, and then click the Print button.

15. Save **EL1-C7-P4-DIDeptCosts.xlsx** and then close the workbook.

You will use the PMT financial function to calculate payments and the FV
financial function to find the future value of an investment.

Writing Formulas with Financial Functions ■■■■■■■■■

In Chapter 2, you learned how to insert formulas in a worksheet using
mathematical operators and functions. In this section, you will continue learning
about writing formulas with functions.

Excel provides a number of financial functions you can use in a formula.
With financial functions, you can determine different aspects of a financial loan
or investment, such as the payment amount, present value, future value, interest
rate, and number of payment periods. Each financial function requires some of the
variables listed below in order to return a result. Two such financial functions are
the PMT function and FV function. The **PMT function** calculates the payment for
a loan based on constant payments and a constant interest rate. The **FV function**
calculates the future value of an investment.

Financial functions use some of the following arguments:

- **Rate:** The rate is the interest rate for a payment period. The rate may need
  to be modified for the function to display the desired results. For example,
  most rate values are given as an APR (annual percentage rate), which is the
  percentage rate for one year, not a payment period. So a percentage rate may be
  given as 12% APR but if the payment period is a month, then the percentage
  rate for the function is 1%, not 12%. If your worksheet contains the annual
  percentage rate, you can enter the cell reference in the function argument and
  specify that you want it divided by 12 months. For example, if cell B6 contains
  the annual interest rate, enter *B6/12* as the Rate argument.

- **Nper:** The Nper is the number of payment periods in an investment. The Nper
  may also need to be modified depending on what information is provided. For
  example, if a loan duration is expressed in years but the payments are paid each
  month, the Nper value needs to be adjusted accordingly. A five-year loan has an
  Nper of 60 (five years times 12 months in each year).

- **Pmt:** The Pmt is the payment amount for each period. This variable describes
  the payment amount for a period and is commonly expressed as a negative
  value because it is an outflow of cash. However, the Pmt value can be entered
  as a positive value if the present value (Pv) or future value (Fv) is entered as a
  negative value. Whether the Pmt value is positive or negative depends on who
  created the workbook. For example, a home owner lists the variable as outflow,
  while the lending institution lists it as inflow.

- **Pv:** The Pv is the present value of an investment, expressed in a lump sum.
  The Pv variable is generally the initial loan amount. For example, if a person
  is purchasing a new home, the Pv is the amount of money the buyer borrowed
  to buy the home. Pv can be expressed as a negative value, which denotes it as
  an investment instead of a loan. For example, if a bank issues a loan to a home
  buyer, it enters the Pv value as a negative because it is an outflow of cash for
  the bank.

- **Fv:** The Fv is the future value of an investment, expressed in a lump sum amount. The Fv variable is generally the loan amount plus the amount of interest paid during the loan. In the example of a home buyer, the Fv is the sum of payments, which includes both the principle and interest paid on the loan. In the example of a bank, the Fv is the total amount received after a loan has been paid off. Fv can also be expressed as either a positive or negative value depending on which side of the transaction you review.

Finding the Periodic Payments for a Loan

The PMT function finds the payment for a loan based on constant payments and a constant interest rate. In Project 5a, you will use the PMT function to determine monthly payments for equipment and a used van as well as monthly income from selling equipment. The formulas you will create with the PMT function in Project 5a will include Rate, Nper, and Pv arguments. The Nper argument is the number of payments that will be made on the loan or investment, Pv is the current value of amounts to be received or paid in the future, and Fv is the value of the loan or investment at the end of all periods.

To write the PMT function, click the FORMULAS tab, click the Financial button in the Function Library group, and then click the PMT function at the drop-down list. This displays the Function Arguments palette with options for inserting cell designations for Rate, Nper, and Pv. (These are the arguments in bold. The palette also contains the Fv and Type functions, which are dimmed.)

Financial

| Project 5a | Calculating Payments | Part 1 of 2 |

1. Open **RPReports.xlsx** and then save the workbook with Save As and name it **EL1-C7-P5-RPReports**.
2. The owner of Real Photography is interested in purchasing a new developer and needs to determine monthly payments on three different models. Insert a formula that calculates monthly payments and then copy that formula by completing the following steps:
   a. Make cell E5 active.
   b. Click the FORMULAS tab.
   c. Click the Financial button in the Function Library group, scroll down the drop-down list, and then click *PMT*.

d. At the Function Arguments palette, type **C5/12** in the *Rate* text box. (This tells Excel to divide the interest rate by 12 months.)

e. Press the Tab key. (This moves the insertion point to the *Nper* text box).

f. Type **D5**. (This is the total number of months for the investment.)

g. Press the Tab key. (This moves the insertion point to the *Pv* text box.)

h. Type **B5**. (This is the purchase price of the developer.)

i. Click OK. (This closes the palette and inserts the monthly payment of *($316.98)* in cell E5. Excel displays the result of the PMT function as a negative number since the loan represents money going out of the company—a negative cash flow.)

j. Copy the formula in cell E5 down to cells E6 and E7.

3. The owner is interested in purchasing a used van for the company and wants an idea of what monthly payments would be at various terms and rates. Insert a formula that calculates monthly payments for a three-year loan at 5% interest by completing the following steps:

a. Make cell E12 active.

b. Make sure the FORMULAS tab is active

c. Click the Financial button in the Function Library group, scroll down the drop-down list, and then click *PMT*.

d. At the Function Arguments palette, type **C12/12** in the *Rate* text box. (This tells Excel to divide the interest rate by 12 months.)

e. Press the Tab key.

f. Type **D12** in the *Nper* text box. (This is the total number of months for the investment.)

g. Press the Tab key.

h. Type **B12** in the *Pv* text box.

i. Click OK. (This closes the palette and inserts the monthly payment of *($299.71)* in cell E12.)

j. Copy the formula in cell E12 down to cells E13 through E15.

Term in Months	Monthly Payments
36	($299.71)
36	($449.56)
36	($599.42)
36	($749.27)

Step 3j

4. The owner has discovered that the interest rate for a used van will be 6.25% instead of 5%. Change the percentages in cells C12 through C15 to 6.25%.

5. The owner is selling a camera and wants you to determine the monthly payments for a two-year loan at 4.5% interest. Determine monthly payments on the camera (income to Real Photography) by completing the following steps:

a. Make cell E20 active.

b. Make sure the FORMULAS tab is active.

c. Click the Financial button in the Function Library group, scroll down the drop-down list, and then click *PMT*.

d. At the Function Arguments palette, type **C20/12** in the *Rate* text box.

e. Press the Tab key.

f. Type **D20** in the *Nper* text box.

g. Press the Tab key.

h. Type **-B20**. In the *Pv* text box. (Excel displays the result of the PMT function as a negative number since the loan represents a negative cash flow. The sale of the camera represents a cash outflow because the business is selling the camera in order to receive payments—cash in flow).

i. Click OK. (This closes the palette and inserts the monthly income of *$185.92* in cell E20.)

6. Save, print, and then close **EL1-C7-P5-RPReports.xlsx**.

Finding the Future Value of a Series of Payments

The FV function calculates the future value of a series of equal payments or an annuity. Use this function to determine information such as how much money can be earned in an investment account with a specific interest rate and over a specific period of time.

Project 5b   **Finding the Future Value of an Investment**   Part 2 of 2

1. Open **RPInvest.xlsx** and then save the workbook with Save As and name it **EL1-C7-P5-RPInvest**.

2. The owner of Real Photography has decided to save money to purchase a new developer and wants to compute how much money can be earned by investing the money in an investment account that returns 7.5% annual interest. The owner determines that $1,200 per month can be invested in the account for three years. Complete the following steps to determine the future value of the investment account:

a. Make cell B6 active.

b. Make sure the FORMULAS tab is active.

c. Click the Financial button in the Function Library group.

d. At the drop-down list that displays, scroll down the list and then click *FV*.

e. At the Function Arguments palette, type **B3/12** in the *Rate* text box.

f. Press the Tab key.

g. Type **B4** in the *Nper* text box.

h. Press the Tab key.

i. Type **B5** in the *Pmt* text box.

j. Click OK. (This closes the palette and also inserts the future value of *$48,277.66* in cell B6.)

3. Save and then print **EL1-C7-P5-RPInvest.xlsx**.

4. The owner decides to determine the future return after two years. To do this, change the amount in cell B4 from *36* to *24* and then press Enter. (This recalculates the future investment amount in cell B6.)

5. Save, print, and then close **EL1-C7-P5-RPInvest.xlsx**.

Project 6 Insert Formulas with the IF Logical Function   3 Parts

You will use the IF logical function to calculate sales bonuses, determine pass/fail grades based on averages, and identify discounts and discount amounts.

Writing Formulas with the IF Logical Function ■■■■■■

A question that can be answered with true or false is considered a *logical test*. You can use the *IF function* to create a logical test that performs a particular action if the answer is true (condition met) and another action if the answer is false (condition not met).

For example, an IF function can be used to write a formula that calculates a salesperson's bonus as 10% if the salesperson sells more than $99,999 worth of product and 0% if he or she does not sell more than $99,999 worth of product. When writing a formula with an IF function, think about the words *if* and *then*. For example, the formula written out for the bonus example would look like this:

> *If* the salesperson sells more than $99,999 of product, *then* he or she receives a bonus of 10%.

> *If* the salesperson does not sell more than $99,999 of product, *then* he or she receives a bonus of 0%.

When writing a formula with an IF function, commas separate the condition and the action. The formula for the bonus example would look like this: *=IF(sales>99999,sales*0.1,0)*. The formula contains three parts:

- the condition or logical test: *IF(sales>99999*
- the action taken if the condition or logical test is true: *sales*0.1*
- the action taken if the condition or logical test is false: *0*

In Project 6a, you will write a formula with cell references rather than cell data. In the project, you will write a formula with an IF function that determines the following:

> *If* the sales amount is greater than the quota amount, *then* the sales-person will receive a 15% bonus.

> *If* the sales amount is not greater than the quota amount, *then* the sales-person will not receive a bonus.

Written with cell references in the project, the formula looks like this: *=IF(C4>B4,C4*0.15,0)*. In this formula the condition or logical test is whether or not the number in cell C4 is greater than the number in cell B4. If the condition is true and the number is greater, then the number in cell C4 is multiplied by 0.15 (providing a 15% bonus). If the condition is false and the number in cell C4 is less than the number in cell B4, then nothing happens (no bonus). Notice how commas are used to separate the logical test from the action.

1. Open **CMPReports.xlsx** and then save it with Save As and name it **EL1-C7-P6-CMPReports**.
2. Write a formula with the IF function that determines if a sales quota has been met and, if it has, inserts the bonus: 15% of actual sales. (If the quota has not been met, the formula will insert a 0.) Write the formula by completing the following steps:
   a. Make cell D4 active.
   b. Type =IF(C4>B4,C4*0.15,0) and then press Enter.

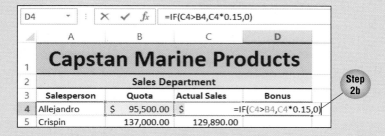

   c. Make cell D4 active and then use the fill handle to copy the formula to cells D5 through D9.
3. Print the worksheet.
4. Revise the formula so it inserts a 20% bonus if the quota has been met by completing the following steps:
   a. Make cell D4 active.
   b. Click in the Formula bar, edit the formula so it displays as =IF(C4>B4,C4*0.2,0), and then click the Enter button on the Formula bar.
   c. Copy the formula in cell D4 down to cells D5 through D9.
   d. Apply accounting formatting with a dollar sign and two places beyond the decimal point.
5. Save **EL1-C7-P6-CMPReports.xlsx**.

Writing Formulas with an IF Function Using the Function Arguments Palette

You can type a formula containing an IF function directly into a cell or you can use the Function Arguments palette to help you write the formula. To use the Function Arguments palette to write a formula with the IF function, click the FORMULAS tab, click the Logical button in the Function Library group, and then click *IF* at the drop-down list. This displays the Function Arguments palette, shown in Figure 7.11. The Function Arguments palette displays the information you will type in the three argument text boxes for Project 6b.

Logical

At the Function Arguments palette, click in the *Logical_test* text box and information about the Logical_test argument displays in the palette. In this text box, type the cell designation followed by what is evaluated. In the figure, the *Logical_test* text box contains *B14>599*, indicating that what is being evaluated is whether or not the amount in cell B14 is greater than $599. The *Value_if_true* text box contains *B14*0.95*, indicating that if the logical test is true, then multiply the amount in cell B14 by 0.95. (The discount for any product price greater than $599

Figure 7.11 Function Arguments Palette

Insert in this text box the logical test (what is being evaluated).

Insert in this text box the action that will occur if the logical test is true.

Insert in this text box the action that will occur if the logical test is false.

is 5% and multiplying the product price by 0.95 determines the price after the 5% discount is applied.) The *Value_if_false* text box contains *B14*, indicating that if the logical test is false (the product price is not greater than $599), then simply insert the amount from cell B14.

Project 6b

Writing a Formula with an IF Function Using the Function Arguments Palette

Part 2 of 3

1. With **EL1-C7-P6-CMPReports.xlsx** open, insert a formula with an IF function using the Function Arguments palette by completing the following steps:
   a. Make cell C14 active.
   b. Click the FORMULAS tab.
   c. Click the Logical button in the Function Library group.
   d. Click *IF* at the drop-down list.
   e. At the Function Arguments palette, type **B14>599** in the *Logical_test* text box.
   f. Press the Tab key and then type **B14*0.95** in the *Value_if_true* text box.
   g. Press the Tab key and then type **B14** in the *Value_if_false* text box.
   h. Click OK to close the Function Arguments palette.

Step 1e

Step 1f

Step 1g

2. Copy the formula in cell C14 down to cells C15 through C26.
3. Apply accounting formatting with a dollar sign and two places after the decimal point to cell C14.
4. Save **EL1-C7-P6-CMPReports.xlsx**.

Writing IF Formulas Containing Text

If you write a formula with an IF function and want text inserted in a cell rather than a value, you must insert quotation marks around the text. For example, in Step 2 of Project 6c, you will write a formula with an IF function that, when written out, looks like this:

> *If* the employee averages more than 79 on the quizzes, **then** he or she passes.

> *If* the employee does not average more than 79 on the quizzes, **then** he or she fails.

When writing the formula in the project, the word *PASS* is inserted in a cell if the average of the new employee quizzes is greater than 79 and inserts the word *FAIL* if the condition is not met. To write this formula in Project 6c, you will type **=IF(E31>79, "PASS", "FAIL")**. The quotation marks before and after *PASS* and *FAIL* identify the data as text rather than a value.

You can use the Function Arguments palette to write a formula with an IF function that contains text. For example, in Step 3 of Project 6c, you will write a formula with an IF function using the Function Arguments palette that, when written out, looks like this:

> *If* the product price is greater than $599, **then** insert *YES*.

> *If* the product price is not greater than $599, **then** insert *NO*.

To create the formula in Step 3 in the Function Arguments palette, display the palette and then type **B14>599** in the *Logical_test* text box, **YES** in the *Value_if_true* text box, and **NO** in the *Value_if_false* text box. When you press Enter after typing YES in the *Value_if_true* text box, Excel automatically inserts quotations marks around the text. Excel will do the same thing for NO in the *Value_if_false* text box.

Project 6c | **Writing IF Statements Containing Text** | Part 3 of 3

1. With **EL1-C7-P6-CMPReports.xlsx** open, insert quiz averages by completing the following steps:
   a. Make cell E31 active and then insert a formula that calculates the average of the test scores in cells B31 through D31.
   b. Copy the formula in cell E31 down to cells E32 through E35.
2. Write a formula with an IF function that inserts the word *PASS* if the quiz average is greater than 79 and inserts the word *FAIL* if the quiz average is not greater than 79. Write the formula by completing the following steps:
   a. Make cell F31 active.
   b. Type **=IF(E31>79,"PASS","FAIL")** and then press Enter.

   c. Copy the formula in cell F31 down to cells F32 through F35.

3. Write a formula with an IF function using the Function Arguments palette that inserts the word *YES* in the cell if the product price is greater than $599 and inserts the word *NO* if the price is not greater than $599. Write the formula by completing the following steps:
  a. Make cell D14 active.
  b. Click the FORMULAS tab.
  c. Click the Logical button in the Function Library group.
  d. Click *IF* at the drop-down list.
  e. Type B14>599 in the *Logical_test* text box.
  f. Press the Tab key and then type YES in the *Value_if_true* text box.
  g. Press the Tab key and then type NO in the *Value_if_false* text box.
  h. Click OK to close the Function Arguments palette.
  i. Copy the formula in cell D14 down to cells D15 through D26.

4. Save and then print **EL1-C7-P6-CMPReports.xlsx**.
5. Press Ctrl + ` to turn on the display of formulas.
6. Print the worksheet again. (The worksheet will print on two pages.)
7. Press Ctrl + ` to turn off the display of formulas.
8. Save and then close **EL1-C7-P6-CMPReports.xlsx**.

Step 3e   Step 3f   Step 3g

Function Arguments

IF

Logical_test	B14>599	= TRUE
Value_if_true	"YES"	= "YES"
Value_if_false	NO	=

Chapter Summary

- A chart is a visual presentation of data. Excel provides 11 basic chart types: area, bar, bubble, column, doughnut, line, pyramid, radar, stock, surface, and xy (scatter).

- To create a chart, select the cells containing data you want to chart, click the INSERT tab, and then click the desired chart button in the Charts group. Click the Recommended Charts button in the Charts group and Excel will recommend a type of chart for the data.

- A chart you create is inserted in the same worksheet as the selected cells.

- Change the size of a chart using the mouse by dragging one of the sizing handles that display around the border of the chart. When changing the chart size, maintain the proportion of the chart by holding down the Shift key while dragging a sizing handle.

- Move a chart by positioning the mouse pointer on the chart border until the pointer displays with a four-headed arrow attached and then dragging with the mouse.

- The data in cells used to create the chart are linked to the chart. If you change the data in cells, the chart reflects the changes.

- Three buttons appear outside the right border of a selected chart. Use the Chart Elements button to insert or remove chart elements, use the Chart Styles button to apply a chart style, and use the Chart Filters button to isolate specific data in the chart.

- Print a chart by selecting the chart, displaying the Print backstage area, and then clicking the Print button.

- When you insert a chart in a worksheet, the CHART TOOLS DESIGN tab is active. Use options on this tab to add chart elements, change the chart type, specify a different layout or style, and change the location of the chart.

- Choose a chart style with options in the Chart Styles group on the CHART TOOLS DESIGN tab or at the Change Chart Type dialog box.

- Click the Switch Row/Column button in the Data group to change what Excel uses to determine the grouping of data along the horizontal axis and legend.

- Use the Quick Layout button in the Chart Layouts group to change the chart layout.

- Use the Change Colors button to apply different colors to a chart.

- By default, a chart is inserted in the active worksheet. You can move the chart to a new worksheet within the workbook with the *New sheet* option at the Move Chart dialog box.

- Add chart elements with the Add Chart Element button arrow in the Chart Layouts group on the CHART TOOLS DESIGN tab.

- Move a chart element by selecting the element and then dragging it with the mouse. Use the sizing handles that display around a chart element to change the size of the element. Delete a chart element by selecting it and then pressing the Delete key or right-clicking the selected element and then clicking Delete at the shortcut menu.

- Customize the formatting of a chart and chart elements with options on the CHART TOOLS FORMAT tab. With options on the tab, you can identify specific elements in the chart for formatting, insert a shape, apply formatting to a shape, apply WordArt formatting to data in a chart, and arrange, align, and size a chart.

- Insert a shape by clicking the desired shape in the Insert Shapes group on the CHART TOOLS FORMAT tab and then clicking or dragging in the chart.

- Excel provides additional formatting options at a formatting task pane. A formatting task pane displays at the right side of the screen and the name and the contents in the task pane vary depending on whether the entire chart or an element in the chart is selected. Display a task pane by clicking the chart or element in the chart and then clicking the Format Selection button in the Current Selection group on the CHART TOOLS FORMAT tab.

- Change the size of a chart with shape height and width measurement boxes on the CHART TOOLS FORMAT tab or at the Format Chart Area task pane.

- To delete a chart in a worksheet, click the chart to select it and then press the Delete key. To delete a chart created in a separate sheet, position the mouse pointer on the chart tab, click the right mouse button, and then click *Delete*.

- Write a formula with the PMT function to calculate the payment for a loan based on constant payments and a constant interest rate. Write a formula with the FV function to calculate the future value of an investment based on periodic, constant payments and a constant interest rate.

- A logical test is a question that can be answered with true or false. Use the IF function to create a logical test that performs a particular action if the answer is true (condition met) or another action if the answer is false (condition not met).

Commands Review

FEATURE	RIBBON TAB, GROUP	BUTTON, OPTION	KEYBOARD SHORTCUT
Change Chart Type dialog box	CHART TOOLS DESIGN, Type	📊	
chart in separate sheet			F11
chart or chart element task pane	CHART TOOLS FORMAT, Current Selection	🖌	
financial functions	FORMULAS, Function Library	🖹	
logical functions	FORMULAS, Function Library	🖹	
Move Chart dialog box	CHART TOOLS DESIGN, Location	🖼	
recommended chart	INSERT, Charts	📊	Alt + F1

Concepts Check   Test Your Knowledge

Completion: In the space provided at the right, indicate the correct term, symbol, or command.

1. Let Excel determine a chart type for selected data in a worksheet by clicking this button in the Charts group on the INSERT tab. _____

2. This type of chart shows proportions and relationships of the parts to the whole. _____

3. When you create a chart, the chart is inserted in this location by default. _____

4. Size a chart by dragging one of these on the selected chart border. _____

5. When a chart is selected, three buttons display at the right side of the chart border: the Chart Elements button, the Chart Styles button, and this button. _____

6. Select a chart in a worksheet, display the Print backstage area, and the first gallery in the *Settings* category is automatically changed to this option. _____

7. The Switch Row/Column button is located in this group on the CHART TOOLS DESIGN tab.

_____

8. Click this option at the Move Chart dialog box to move the chart to a separate sheet.

_____

9. Insert a shape in a chart and this tab is active.

_____

10. Select a chart (not a chart element), click the Format Selection button in the Current Selection group on the CHART TOOLS FORMAT tab, and this task pane displays at the right side of the screen.

_____

11. This function finds the payment for a loan based on constant payments and a constant interest rate.

_____

12. Suppose cell B2 contains the total sales amount. Write a formula that inserts the word *BONUS* in cell C2 if the sales amount is greater than $49,999 and inserts the words *NO BONUS* if the sales amount is not greater than $49,999.

_____

Skills Check   Assess Your Performance

Assessment

1   CREATE A NET PROFIT CHART

 Grade It

1. Open **NetProfit.xlsx** and then save the workbook with Save As and name it **EL1-C7-A1-NetProfit**.
2. Select cells A2 through E7 and then create a chart using the Recommended Charts button. (Accept the chart recommended by Excel.)
3. Use the Chart Elements button that displays outside the right border of the chart to insert a data table and remove the legend.
4. Use the Chart Styles button that displays outside the right border of the chart to apply the Style 7 chart style.
5. Use the Chart Filters button that displays outside the right border of the chart to display only New York and Philadelphia net profits in the chart. (Make sure you click the Apply button.)
6. Click the text *Chart Title*, type **Net Profit by Office**, and then press Enter.
7. Move the chart below the cells containing data, deselect the chart, make sure the data and chart fit on one page, and then print the worksheet (data and chart).
8. Save and then close **EL1-C7-A1-NetProfit.xlsx**.

Assessment

2   CREATE A COMPANY SALES COLUMN CHART

1. Open **CMSales.xlsx** and then save the workbook with Save As and name it **EL1-C7-A2-CMSales**.
2. Select cells A3 through C15 and then create a column chart with the following specifications:
   a. Click the *3-D Clustered Column* option at the Insert Column Chart button drop-down list.
   b. At the CHART TOOLS DESIGN tab, click the Quick Layout button and then click the *Layout 3* option at the drop-down gallery.
   c. Apply the Style 11 chart style.
   d. Click the text *Chart Title*, type 2015 Company Sales, and then press Enter.
   e. Move the location of the chart to a new sheet.
3. Print only the worksheet containing the chart.
4. Save and then close **EL1-C7-A2-CMSales.xlsx**.

Assessment

3   CREATE QUARTERLY DOMESTIC AND FOREIGN SALES BAR CHART

1. Open **CMPQtrlySales.xlsx** and then save the workbook with Save As and name it **EL1-C7-A3-CMPQtrlySales**.
2. Select cells A3 through E5 and then create a bar chart with the following specifications:
   a. Click the *3-D Clustered Bar* option at the Insert Bar Chart button drop-down list.
   b. Apply the Layout 2 quick layout. (Use the Quick Layout button.)
   c. Apply the Style 6 chart style.
   d. Type **Quarterly Sales** as the chart title. (Excel will convert the text to uppercase letters.)
   e. Click in the chart but outside any chart element.
   f. Click the CHART TOOLS FORMAT tab and then apply the Subtle Effect - Gold, Accent 4 shape style (fifth column, fourth row).
   g. Click the Chart Elements button arrow, click *Series "Foreign"* at the drop-down list, and then apply Dark Red shape fill. (Use the Shape Fill button arrow in the Shape Styles group and choose Dark Red in the *Standard Colors* section.)
   h. Select the chart title and then apply the Fill - Black, Text 1, Shadow WordArt style (first column, first row).
   i. Increase the height of the chart to 4 inches and the width to 6 inches.
3. Move the chart below the cells containing data, deselect the chart, make sure the data and chart fit on one page, and then print the worksheet (data and chart).
4. Save and then close **EL1-C7-A3-CMPQtrlySales.xlsx**.

Assessment

4 CREATE A FUND ALLOCATIONS PIE CHART

1. Open **SMFFunds.xlsx** and then save the workbook with Save As and name it **EL1-C7-A4-SMFFunds**.
2. Select cells A3 through B7 and then create a pie chart with the following specifications:
   a. Click the *3-D Pie* option at the Insert Pie or Doughnut Chart button drop-down gallery.
   b. Apply the Layout 1 quick layout.
   c. Apply the Style 2 chart style.
   d. Change the color to Color 3.
   e Move the pie chart to a new worksheet.
   f. Change the title to *Fund Allocations*.
   g. Click the CHART TOOLS FORMAT tab, make sure the chart is selected and not a chart element, and then click the Format Selection button.
   h. At the Format Chart Area task pane, make sure the Fill & Line icon is active, click the *FILL* option to display additional options, click the *Gradient fill* option, and then close the task pane.
   i. Use the Chart Elements button arrow to select *Series "Allocation" Data Labels*.
   j. With the data labels selected, click the Text Fill button arrow (located in the WordArt Styles group) and then click the *Orange, Accent 2, Darker 50%* option (sixth column, bottom row in the *Theme Colors* section).
   k. With the data labels still selected, click the HOME tab and then change the font size to 18 points.
3. Print only the worksheet containing the chart.
4. Save and then close **EL1-C7-A4-SMFFunds.xlsx**.

Assessment

5 WRITE A FORMULA WITH THE PMT FUNCTION

1. Open **CMRefiPlan.xlsx** and then save the workbook with Save As and name it **EL1-C7-A5-CMRefiPlan**.
2. The manager of Clearline Manufacturing is interested in refinancing a loan for either $125,000 or $300,000 and wants to determine the monthly payments. Make cell E4 active and then insert a formula using the PMT function. (For assistance, refer to Project 5a. The monthly payment amounts will display as negative numbers representing outflows of cash.)
3. Copy the formula in cell E4 down to cells E5 through E7.
4. Save, print, and then close **EL1-C7-A5-CMRefiPlan.xlsx**.

Assessment

6 WRITE A FORMULA WITH THE FV FUNCTION

1. Open **CMInvest.xlsx** and then save the workbook with Save As and name it **EL1-C7-A6-CMInvest**.
2. Make cell B6 active and then use the FV function to insert a formula that calculates the future value of the investment.
3. Save and then print the worksheet.

4. Make the following changes to the worksheet:
   a. Change the percentage in cell B3 from *6.5%* to *8.0%*.
   b. Change the number in cell B4 from *48* to *60*.
   c. Change the amount in cell B5 from *(-1000)* to *-500*.
5. Save, print, and then close **EL1-C7-A6-CMInvest.xlsx**.

7 WRITE A FORMULA WITH THE IF FUNCTION

1. Open **DISalesBonuses.xlsx** and then save the workbook with Save As and name it **EL1-C7-A7-DISalesBonuses**.
2. Insert a formula in cell C4 that inserts the word *YES* if the amount in B4 is greater than 99999 and inserts *NO* if the amount is not greater than 99999. Copy the formula in cell C4 down to cells C5 through C14.
3. Make cell D4 active and then insert the formula =IF(C4="YES",B4*0.05,0). If sales are over $99,999, this formula will multiply the sales amount by 5% and then insert the product (result) of the formula in the cell. Copy the formula in cell D4 down to cells D5 through D14.
4. Apply accounting formatting with a dollar sign and no places past the decimal point to cell D4.
5. Save and then print **EL1-C7-A7-DISalesBonuses.xlsx**.
6. Display the formulas in the worksheet and then print the worksheet.
7. Turn off the display of formulas.
8. Save and then close **EL1-C7-A7-DISalesBonuses.xlsx**

8 CREATE A STACKED COLUMN CHART

1. Use Excel's Help feature to learn more about chart types and specifically about 3-D stacked column charts.
2. Open **CMPerSales.xlsx** and then save the workbook with Save As and name it **EL1-C7-A8-CMPerSales**.
3. With the data in the worksheet, create a 3-D 100% stacked column chart in a separate sheet. Create an appropriate title for the chart and apply any other formatting to enhance the appearance of the chart.
4. Print only the worksheet containing the chart.
5. Close **EL1-C7-A8-CMPerSales.xlsx**.

9   LEARN ABOUT EXCEL OPTIONS

1. Learn about specific options in the Excel Options dialog box by completing the following steps:
   a. At a blank workbook, display the Excel Options dialog box by clicking the FILE tab and then clicking *Options*.
   b. At the Excel Options dialog box, click the *Advanced* option in the left panel.
   c. Scroll down the dialog box and look for the section *Display options for this workbook* and then read the information in the section. Also read the information in the *Display options for this worksheet* section.
   d. Write down the check box options available in the *Display options for this workbook* section and the *Display options for this worksheet* section and identify whether or not the check box contains a check mark. (Record only check box options and ignore buttons and options preceded by circles.)

2. With the information you wrote down about the options, create an Excel worksheet with the following information:
   a. In column C, type each option you wrote down. (Include an appropriate heading.)
   b. In column B, insert an X in the cell that precedes any option that contains a check mark in the check box. (Include an appropriate heading.)
   c. In column A, write a formula with the IF function that inserts the word *ON* in the cell if the cell in column B contains an X and inserts the word *OFF* if it does not (the cell is blank). (Include an appropriate heading.)
   d. Apply formatting to improve the appearance of the worksheet.

3. Save the workbook and name it **EL1-C7-A9-DisplayOptions**.
4. Turn on the display of formulas.
5. Print the worksheet.
6. Turn off the display of formulas.
7. Save, print, and then close **EL1-C7-A9-DisplayOptions.xlsx**.

Visual Benchmark Demonstrate Your Proficiency

CREATE AND FORMAT A PIE CHART

1. At a blank workbook, enter data and then create a pie chart in a separate sheet, as shown in Figure 7.12. Use the information shown in the pie chart to create the data. Format the pie chart so it appears similar to what you see in Figure 7.12. (Apply the Layout 4 quick style and the Style 8 chart style. Create and format the title as shown in the figure and change the size of the data labels to 12 points.)
2. Save the completed workbook and name it **EL1-C7-VB-CMFebExp**.
3. Print both worksheets in the workbook.
4. Close **EL1-C7-VB-CMFebExp.xlsx**.

Figure 7.12 Visual Benchmark

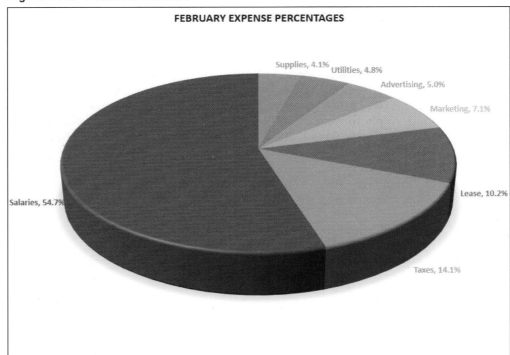

FEBRUARY EXPENSE PERCENTAGES

Supplies, 4.1% Utilities, 4.8%
Advertising, 5.0%
Marketing, 7.1%
Lease, 10.2%
Taxes, 14.1%
Salaries, 54.7%

Case Study   Apply Your Skills

You are an administrator for Dollar Wise Financial Services and need to prepare charts indicating home loan and commercial loan amounts for the past year. Use the information below to prepare a chart in Excel. You determine the type and style of the chart and the layout and formatting of the chart. Insert a shape in the Commercial Loans chart that contains the text *All-time High* and points to the second quarter amount (*$6,785,250*).

Home Loans
1st Qtr.	=	$2,675,025
2nd Qtr.	=	$3,125,750
3rd Qtr.	=	$1,975,425
4th Qtr.	=	$875,650

Commercial Loans
1st Qtr.	=	$5,750,980
2nd Qtr.	=	$6,785,250
3rd Qtr.	=	$4,890,625
4th Qtr.	=	$2,975,900

Save the workbook and name it **EL1-C7-CS-DWQtrSales**. Print only the chart and then close **EL1-C7-CS-DWQtrSales.xlsx**.

You need to present information on the budget for the company. You have the dollar amounts and need to convert each amount to a percentage of the entire budget. Use the information below to calculate the percentage of the budget for each item and then create a pie chart with the information. You determine the chart style, layout, and formatting.

Total Budget: $6,000,000
Building Costs	=	$720,000
Salaries	=	$2,340,000
Benefits	=	$480,000
Advertising	=	$840,000
Marketing	=	$600,000
Client Expenses	=	$480,000
Equipment	=	$420,000
Supplies	=	$120,000

Save the workbook containing the pie chart and name it **EL1-C7-CS-DWBudget**. Print only the chart and then close **EL1-C7-CS-DWBudget.xlsx**.

Part

3

The loan officer for Dollar Wise Financial Services has asked you to prepare a sample home mortgage worksheet to show prospective clients. This mortgage worksheet will show the monthly payments on variously priced homes with varying interest rates. Open the **DWMortgageWksht.xlsx** worksheet and then complete the home mortgage worksheet by inserting the following formulas:

- Since many homes in your area sell for at least $400,000, you decide to use that amount in the worksheet with down payments of 5%, 10%, 15%, and 20%. (Insert the amount $400,000 in cells A11 through A14.)
- In column C, insert a formula that determines the down payment amount.
- In column D, insert a formula that determines the loan amount.
- In column G, insert a formula using the PMT function. (The monthly payment will display as a negative number.)

Save the worksheet and name it **EL1-C7-CS-DWMortgageWksht**.

Part

4

If home buyers put down less than 20% of the home's purchase price, mortgage insurance is required. With **EL1-C7-CS-DWMortgageWksht.xlsx** open, insert an IF statement in the cells in column H that inserts the word *NO* if the percentage in column B is equal to or greater than 20% and inserts the word *YES* if the percentage in column B is less than 20%. Save and then print **EL1-C7-CS-DWMortgageWksht.xlsx**.

Part

5

You need to prepare information on mortgage interest rates for a community presentation. You decide to provide the information on mortgage rates in a chart for easy viewing. Use the Internet to search for historical data on the national average for mortgage interest rates. Determine the average mortgage rate for a 30-year FRM (fixed-rate mortgage) for each January and July beginning with the year 2011 and continuing to the current year. Also include the current average interest rate. Use this information to create the chart. Save the workbook and name it **EL1-C7-CS-DWRates**. Print only the chart and then close **EL1-C7-CS-DWRates.xlsx**.

EXCEL
MICROSOFT®

Adding Visual Interest to Workbooks

PERFORMANCE OBJECTIVES

Upon successful completion of Chapter 8, you will be able to:

- Insert symbols and special characters
- Insert, size, move, and format images
- Insert a screenshot
- Draw, format, and copy shapes
- Insert, format, and type text in a text box
- Insert a picture image as a watermark
- Insert and format SmartArt graphics
- Insert and format WordArt

Tutorials

8.1 Inserting Symbols and Special Characters

8.2 Inserting and Modifying Images from the Insert Picture dialog box

8.3 Inserting and Modifying Images from Office.com

8.4 Creating and Inserting Screenshots

8.5 Inserting and Formatting a Shape

8.6 Drawing and Formatting Text Boxes

8.7 Inserting a Picture as a Watermark

8.8 Inserting and Formatting a SmartArt Graphic

8.9 Creating WordArt

Microsoft Excel includes a variety of features that you can use to enhance the appearance of a workbook. Some methods for adding visual appeal that you will learn in this chapter include inserting and modifying pictures and clip art images, screenshots, shapes, text boxes, SmartArt, and WordArt. Model answers for this chapter's projects appear on the following pages.

EL1C8

Note: Before beginning the projects, copy to your storage medium the EL1C8 subfolder from the EL1 folder on the CD that accompanies this textbook and make EL1C8 the active folder.

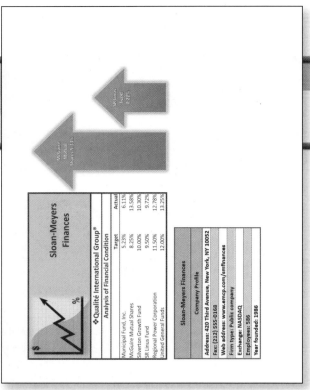

Project 1 Insert a Clip Art Image and Shapes in a Financial Analysis Workbook EL1-C8-P1-SMFFinCon.xlsx

Project 2 Insert a Picture and Text Box in a Division Sales Workbook EL1-C8-P2-SPDivSales.xlsx

Division	1st Half	2nd Half	Total
Northeast	$ 934,210	$ 1,002,390	$ 1,936,600
Southeast	745,231	88,732	833,963
Northwest	884,423	745,932	1,630,355
Southwest	342,091	441,293	783,384
European	554,205	441,230	995,435
Asian	779,040	523,490	1,302,530

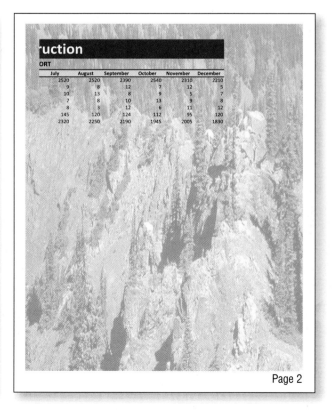

Project 3 Insert a Watermark in an Equipment Usage Workbook
EL1-C8-P3-HCEqpRpt.xlsx

Total Sales tab

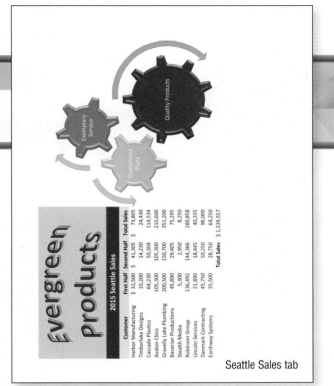

Seattle Sales tab

Project 4 Insert and Format SmartArt Graphics in a Company Sales Workbook　　　EL1-C8-P4-EPSales.xlsx

---

Project ▣ 1　Insert a Clip Art Image and Shapes in a Financial Analysis Workbook　　5 Parts

You will open a financial analysis workbook and then insert symbols and move, size, and format an image in the workbook. You will also insert an arrow shape, type and format text in the shape, and then copy the shape.

Inserting Symbols and Special Characters ■ ■ ■ ■ ■ ■ ■ ■ ■ ■

Use the Symbol button on the INSERT tab to insert special symbols in a worksheet. Click the Symbol button in the Symbols group on the INSERT tab and the Symbol dialog box displays, as shown in Figure 8.1. At the Symbol dialog box, double-click the desired symbol and then click Close or click the desired symbol, click the Insert button, and then click Close. At the Symbol dialog box with the Symbols tab selected, you can change the font at the *Font* option box. When you change the font, different symbols display in the dialog box. Click the Special Characters tab at the Symbol dialog box and a list of special characters displays. Click the desired character, click the Insert button, and then click the Close button.

▼ Quick Steps
Insert a Symbol
1. Click in desired cell.
2. Click INSERT tab.
3. Click Symbol button.
4. Double-click desired symbol.
5. Click Close.

Symbol

Insert a Special Character
1. Click in desired cell.
2. Click INSERT tab.
3. Click Symbol button.
4. Click Special Characters tab.
5. Double-click desired special character.
6. Click Close.

H I N T

You can increase or decrease the size of the Symbol dialog box by positioning the mouse pointer on the lower right corner until the pointer displays as a two-headed arrow and then dragging with the mouse.

Figure 8.1 Symbol Dialog Box with Symbols Tab Selected

Click this tab to display a list of special characters.

Use the *Font* option box to select the desired set of characters.

This section of the dialog box displays the most recently used symbols.

Project 1a   **Inserting Symbols and Special Characters**   Part 1 of 5

1. Open **SMFFinCon.xlsx** and then save the workbook with Save As and name it **EL1-C8-P1-SMFFinCon**.
2. Insert a symbol by completing the following steps:
   a. Double-click in cell A2.
   b. Delete the *e* that displays at the end of *Qualite*.
   c. With the insertion point positioned immediately right of the *t* in *Qualit*, click the INSERT tab.
   d. Click the Symbol button in the Symbols group.
   e. At the Symbol dialog box, scroll down the list box and then click the *é* symbol (located in approximately the ninth through eleventh row).
   f. Click the Insert button and then click the Close button.

Step 2e

Step 2f

3. Insert a special character by completing the following steps:
   a. With cell A2 selected and in EDIT mode, move the insertion point so it is positioned immediately right of *Group*.
   b. Click the Symbol button in the Symbols group.
   c. At the Symbol dialog box, click the Special Characters tab.
   d. Double-click the ® symbol (tenth option from the top).
   e. Click the Close button.
4. Insert a symbol by completing the following steps:
   a. With cell A2 selected and in EDIT mode, move the insertion point so it is positioned immediately left of the *Q* in *Qualité*.
   b. Click the Symbol button in the Symbols group.
   c. At the Symbol dialog box, click the down-pointing arrow at the right side of the *Font* option box and then click *Wingdings* at the drop-down list. (You will need to scroll down the list to display this option.)
   d. Click the ❖ symbol (located in approximately the fifth or sixth row).
   e. Click the Insert button and then click the Close button.
5. Click in cell A3.
6. Save **EL1-C8-P1-SMFFinCon.xlsx**.

Inserting Images ■■■■■■■■■■■■■■■■■■■■■■■■■■■■■■

Insert an image, such as a picture or clip art, in an Excel workbook with buttons in the Illustrations group on the INSERT tab. Click the Pictures button to display the Insert Picture dialog box, where you can specify the desired picture file, or click the Online Pictures button and search for images online. When you insert an image in a worksheet, the PICTURE TOOLS FORMAT tab displays, as shown in Figure 8.2.

▼ **Quick Steps**

Insert a Picture
1. Click INSERT tab.
2. Click Pictures button.
3. Navigate to desired folder.
4. Double-click desired picture.

Pictures

Figure 8.2 PICTURE TOOLS FORMAT Tab

Customizing and Formatting an Image

Use buttons in the Adjust group on the PICTURE TOOLS FORMAT tab to remove unwanted portions of an image, correct the brightness and contrast, change the image color, apply artistic effects, change to a different image, and reset the image back to the original formatting. Use the Compress Pictures button in the Adjust group to compress the size of an image file and reduce the amount of space the image requires on your storage medium. Use buttons in the Picture Styles group to apply a predesigned style to the image, change the image border, or apply other effects to the image. With options in the Arrange group, you can position the image on the page, specify how text will wrap around it, align the image with other elements in the worksheet, and rotate the image. Use the Crop button in the Size group to remove any unnecessary parts of the image and use the *Shape Height* and *Shape Width* measurement boxes to specify the image size.

Compress
Pictures

Crop

In addition to the PICTURE TOOLS FORMAT tab, you can customize and format an image with options at the shortcut menu. Display this menu by right-clicking the image. With options at the shortcut menu, you can change the image, insert a caption, choose text wrapping, size and position the image, and display the Format Picture task pane.

Sizing and Moving an Image

Change the size of an image with the *Shape Height* and *Shape Width* measurement boxes in the Size group on the PICTURE TOOLS FORMAT tab or with the sizing handles that display around the selected image. To change size with a sizing handle, position the mouse pointer on a sizing handle until the pointer turns into a double-headed arrow and then drag in or out to decrease or increase the size of the image. Use the middle sizing handles at the left and right sides of the image to make the image wider or thinner. Use the middle sizing handles at the top and bottom of the image to make the image taller or shorter. Use the sizing handles at the corners of the image to change both the width and height at the same time. Hold down the Shift key while dragging a sizing handle to maintain the proportions of the image.

HINT

You can use arrow keys on the keyboard to move a selected image. To move the image in small increments, hold down the Ctrl key while pressing one of the arrow keys.

Move an image by positioning the mouse pointer on the image border until the pointer displays with a four-headed arrow attached and then dragging the image to the desired location. Rotate the image by positioning the mouse pointer on the white, round rotation handle until the pointer displays as a circular arrow. Hold down the left mouse button, drag in the desired direction, and then release the mouse button.

Project 1b **Formatting an Image** Part 2 of 5

1. With **EL1-C8-P1-SMFFinCon.xlsx** open, insert a picture by completing the following steps:
   a. Click the INSERT tab and then click the Pictures button in the Illustrations group.
   b. At the Insert Picture dialog box, navigate to the EL1C8 folder on your storage medium and then double-click *WallStreet.jpg*.
2. Change the size of the image by clicking in the *Shape Height* measurement box in the Size group on the PICTURE TOOLS FORMAT tab, typing 2, and then pressing Enter.
3. Remove the yellow background from the image by completing the following steps:
   a. Click the Remove Background button in the Adjust group.
   b. Position the mouse pointer on the middle sizing handle at the top of the image until the pointer displays as an up-and-down-pointing arrow.

c. Hold down the left mouse button, drag the border up to the top of the image, and then release the mouse.

d. Position the mouse pointer on the middle sizing handle at the bottom of the image until the pointer displays as an up-and-down-pointing arrow.

e. Hold down the left mouse button, drag the border up approximately 0.25 inch, and then release the mouse button.

f. Click the Keep Changes button in the Close group on the BACKGROUND REMOVAL tab.

4. Change the color by clicking the Color button in the Adjust group and then clicking the *Blue, Accent color 1 Light* option (second column, third row in the *Recolor* section).

5. Apply a correction by clicking the Corrections button and then clicking the *Brightness: +20% Contrast: +20%* option (fourth column, fourth row in the *Brightness and Contrast* section).

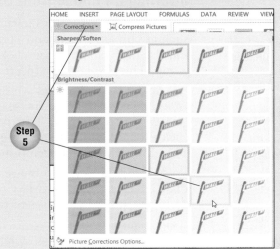

6. Apply an artistic effect by clicking the Artistic Effects button and then clicking the *Glow Edges* option (last option in the drop-down gallery).

7. Move the image by completing the following steps:

a. Position the mouse pointer on the image (displays with a four-headed arrow attached).

b. Hold down the left mouse button, drag the image to the upper left corner of the worksheet, and then release the mouse button.

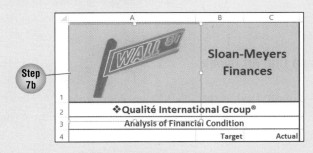

8. Save and then print **EL1-C8-P1-SMFFinCon.xlsx**.

Formatting an Image at the Format Picture Task Pane

In addition to the PICTURES TOOLS FORMAT tab, the Format Picture task pane is available for formatting an image. Click the Picture Styles group task pane launcher or the Size group task pane launcher and the Format Picture task pane displays at the right side of the screen. If you click the Picture Styles group task pane launcher, the task pane displays with the Effects icon selected, and if you click the Size group task pane launcher, the Size & Properties icon is selected. Two other icons are also available in this task pane: the Fill & Line icon and the Picture icon. You may need to display (expand) the formatting options within the icons. For example, click SIZE with the Size & Properties icon selected and options for changing the size of the image display. Close the task pane by clicking the Close button located in the upper right corner of the task pane.

Inserting an Image from Office.com

▼ **Quick Steps**

Insert an Image from Office.com
1. Click INSERT tab.
2. Click Online Pictures button.
3. Type search word or topic.
4. Press Enter.
5. Double-click desired image.
6. Click desired image.

Online Pictures

Microsoft Office includes a gallery of media images you can insert in a worksheet, such as clip art images and photographs. To insert an image in a worksheet, click the INSERT tab and then click the Online Pictures button in the Illustrations group. This displays the Insert Pictures window, as shown in Figure 8.3.

At the Insert Pictures window, click in the search text box to the right of *Office.com Clip Art*; type the search word(s), term, or topic; and then press Enter. Images that match your search text display in the window. To insert an image, click the desired image and then click the Insert button or double-click the image. This downloads the image from the Office.com website to your worksheet.

When you insert an image in the worksheet, the image is selected and the PICTURE TOOLS FORMAT tab is active. Use buttons on this tab to customize an image, just as you learned to customize a picture.

Figure 8.3 Insert Pictures Window

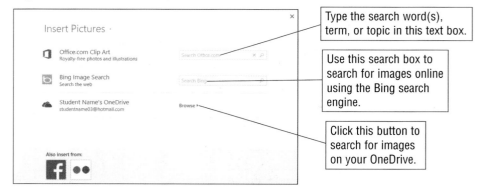

Type the search word(s), term, or topic in this text box.

Use this search box to search for images online using the Bing search engine.

Click this button to search for images on your OneDrive.

Project 1c | **Inserting and Formatting a Clip Art Image** | **Part 3 of 5**

1. With **EL1-C8-P1-SMFFinCon.xlsx** open, delete the Wall Street sign image by clicking the image and then pressing the Delete key.
2. Insert a clip art image by completing the following steps:
   a. Make cell A1 active.
   b. Click the INSERT tab and then click the Online Pictures button in the Illustrations group.

c. At the Insert Pictures window, type **charts, graphs, stock market** in the search box and then press Enter.

d. Double-click the image shown below and to the right.

Step 2c

3. Apply a border to the image by clicking the Picture Border button arrow, pointing to *Weight* at the drop-down list, and then clicking *1 pt* at the side menu.

4. Change the image border to a picture style by clicking the *Soft Edge Rectangle* thumbnail in the Picture Styles group (sixth thumbnail).

Step 4

Step 2d

5. Display the Format Picture task pane with the Size & Properties icon selected by clicking the Size group task pane launcher on the PICTURE TOOLS FORMAT tab.

6. If necessary, click *SIZE* in the task pane to display the sizing options.

7. Change the height of the image by selecting the current measurement in the *Height* measurement box, typing 1.7, and then pressing Enter. (The width automatically changes to maintain the proportions of the image.)

8. Change the properties of the image by clicking PROPERTIES to expand the options and then clicking the *Move and size with cells* option. (With this option selected, if you change the size of the row, the size of the image will also change.)

9. Apply a correction to the image by completing the following steps:

a. Click the Picture icon located toward the top of the task pane.

b. Click PICTURE CORRECTIONS to expand the options.

c. Select the current percentage in the *Brightness* text box and then type **-23**.

d. Select the current percentage in the *Contract* text box, type **45**, and then press Enter.

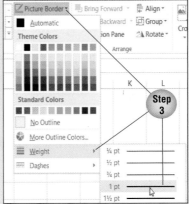

Step 3

10. Close the Format Picture task pane by clicking the Close button in the upper right corner of the task pane.

11. Click outside the clip art image to deselect it.

12. Increase the height of row 1 to 126.00 pixels and notice that the image size increases with the row height.

13. Save **EL1-C8-P1-SMFFinCon.xlsx**.

Step 6

Step 7

Step 10

Step 9a

Step 9b

Step 9c

Step 9d

Creating and Inserting Screenshots ■■■■■■■■■■■■■■■

▼ Quick Steps

Insert a Screenshot
1. Open workbook.
2. Open another file.
3. Display desired information.
4. Make workbook active.
5. Click INSERT tab.
6. Click Screenshot button.
7. Click desired window at drop-down list.
OR
6. Click Screenshot button and then Screen Clipping.
7. Drag to specify capture area.

Screenshot

The Illustrations group on the INSERT tab contains a Screenshot button you can use to capture all or part of the contents of a screen as an image. This is useful for capturing information from a web page or a file in another program. If you want to capture the entire screen, display the desired web page or open the desired file from a program, make Excel active, and then open a workbook or blank workbook. Click the INSERT tab, click the Screenshot button, and then click the desired screen thumbnail at the drop-down list. The currently active worksheet does not display as a thumbnail at the drop-down list—only any other file or program you have open. If you do not have another file or program open, the Windows desktop displays. When you click the desired thumbnail, the screenshot is inserted as an image in the open workbook, the image is selected, and the PICTURE TOOLS FORMAT tab is active. Use buttons on this tab to customize the screenshot image.

In addition to making a screenshot of an entire screen, you can make a screenshot of a specific portion of the screen by clicking the *Screen Clipping* option at the Screenshot button drop-down list. When you click this option, the open web page, file, or Windows desktop displays in a dimmed manner and the mouse pointer displays as crosshairs (a plus sign). Using the mouse, draw a border around the specific area of the screen you want to capture. The specific area you identify is inserted in the workbook as an image, the image is selected, and the PICTURE TOOLS FORMAT tab is active. If you have only one workbook or file open when you click the Screenshot button, clicking the *Screen Clipping* option will cause the Windows desktop to display.

Project 1d Inserting and Formatting a Screenshot   Part 4 of 5

1. With **EL1-C8-P1-SMFFinCon.xlsx** open, make sure that no other programs are open.
2. Open Word and then open the document named **SMFCoProfile.docx** from the EL1C8 folder on your storage medium.
3. Click the Excel button on the Taskbar.
4. Insert a screenshot of the table in the Word document by completing the following steps:
   a. Click the INSERT tab.
   b. Click the Screenshot button in the Illustrations group and then click *Screen Clipping* at the drop-down list.
   c. When the **SMFCoProfile.docx** document displays in a dimmed manner, position the mouse crosshairs in the upper left corner of the table, hold down the left mouse button, drag down to the lower right corner of the table, and then release the mouse button. (This creates a screenshot of the entire table.)

5. With the screenshot image inserted in the **EL1-C8-P1-SMFFinCon.xlsx** workbook, make the following changes:
   a. Click in the *Shape Width* measurement box in the Size group on the PICTURE TOOLS FORMAT tab, type **3.7**, and then press Enter.

b. Click the Corrections button and then click the *Sharpen: 25%* option (fourth option in the *Sharpen/Soften* section).

c. Click the Corrections button and then click the *Brightness: 0% (Normal) Contrast: -40%* (third column, first row in the *Brightness/Contrast* section).

d. Using the mouse, drag the screenshot image one row below the data in row 10.

6. Make cell A4 active.

7. Save **EL1-C8-P1-SMFFinCon.xlsx**.

8. Click the Word button on the Taskbar, close **SMFCoProfile.docx**, and then close Word.

Inserting and Copying Shapes ■■■■■■■■■■■■■■■■■

In Chapter 7, you learned how to insert shapes in a chart. With the Shapes button in the Illustrations group on the INSERT tab, you can also insert shapes in a worksheet. Use the Shapes button to draw shapes in a worksheet, including lines, basic shapes, block arrows, flow chart shapes, callouts, stars, and banners. Click a shape and the mouse pointer displays as crosshairs. Click in the worksheet or position the crosshairs where you want the shape to begin, hold down the left mouse button, drag to create the shape, and then release the mouse button. If you click or drag in the worksheet, the shape is inserted in the worksheet and the DRAWING TOOLS FORMAT tab, shown in Figure 8.4, becomes active. Use the buttons on this tab to change the shape, apply a style to the shape, arrange the shape, and change the size of the shape.

If you choose a shape in the *Lines* section of the Shapes button drop-down list, the shape you draw is considered a line drawing. If you choose an option in the other sections of the drop-down list, the shape you draw is considered an enclosed object. When drawing an enclosed object, you can maintain the proportions of the shape by holding down the Shift key while dragging with the mouse to create the shape. You can type text in an enclosed object and then use buttons in the WordArt Styles group (or options on the HOME tab) to format the text.

Copy a shape in a worksheet by selecting the shape and then clicking the Copy button in the Clipboard group on the HOME tab. Make active the cell where you want to copy the shape and then click the Paste button. You can also copy a selected shape by holding down the Ctrl key while dragging the shape to the desired location.

▼ Quick Steps

Insert a Shape
1. Click INSERT tab.
2. Click Shapes button.
3. Click desired shape at drop-down list.
4. Click or drag in worksheet.

Copy a Shape
1. Select shape.
2. Click Copy button.
3. Position insertion point in desired location.
4. Click Paste button.
OR
1. Select shape.
2. Hold down Ctrl key.
3. Drag shape to desired location.

Shapes

Figure 8.4 DRAWING TOOLS FORMAT Tab

1. With **EL1-C8-P1-SMFFinCon.xlsx** open, create the larger arrow shown in Figure 8.5 on page 284 by completing the following steps:
   a. Click the INSERT tab.
   b. Click the Shapes button in the Illustrations group and then click the *Up Arrow* shape (third column, top row in the *Block Arrows* section).
   c. Position the mouse pointer (displays as crosshairs) near the upper left corner of cell D1 and then click the left mouse button. (This inserts the arrow shape in the worksheet.)

   d. Click in the *Shape Height* measurement box and then type 3.7.
   e. Click in the *Shape Width* measurement box, type 2.1, and then press Enter.
   f. If necessary, drag the arrow so it is positioned as shown in Figure 8.5 on page 284. (To drag the arrow, position the mouse pointer on the border of the selected arrow until the pointer displays with a four-headed arrow attached, hold down the left mouse button, drag the arrow to the desired position, and then release the mouse button.)
   g. Click the More button at the right side of the thumbnails in the Shape Styles group on the DRAWING TOOLS FORMAT tab and then click the *Intense Effect - Blue, Accent 1* option (second column, bottom row).

h. Click the Shape Effects button in the Shape Styles group, point to *Glow*, and then click the *Orange, 11 pt glow, Accent color 2* option (second column, third row in the *Glow Variations* section).

2. Insert text in the arrow shape by completing the following steps:
   a. With the arrow shape selected, type **McGuire Mutual Shares 5.33%**.
   b. Select the text you just typed (*McGuire Mutual Shares 5.33%*).
   c. Click the More button at the right side of the thumbnails in the WordArt Styles group and then click the *Fill - White, Outline - Accent 2, Hard Shadow - Accent 2* option (fourth column, third row).
   d. Press Ctrl + E to center the text.

3. With the arrow selected, copy the arrow by completing the following steps:
   a. Hold down the Ctrl key.
   b. Position the mouse pointer on the arrow border until the pointer displays with a square box and plus symbol attached.
   c. Hold down the left mouse button and drag to the right so the outline of the arrow is positioned at the right side of the existing arrow.
   d. Release the mouse button and then release the Ctrl key.

4. Format the second arrow by completing the following steps:
   a. With the second arrow selected, click in the *Shape Height* measurement box on the DRAWING TOOLS FORMAT tab and then type 2.
   b. Click in the *Shape Width* measurement box, type 1.6, and then press Enter
   c. Select the text *McGuire Mutual Shares 5.33%* and then type **SR Linus Fund 0.22%**.
   d. Drag the arrow so it is positioned as shown in Figure 8.5.

5. Change the orientation to landscape. (Make sure the cells containing data, the screenshot image, and the arrows will print on the same page.)

6. Save, print, and then close **EL1-C8-P1-SMFFinCon.xlsx**.

Figure 8.5 Project 1e

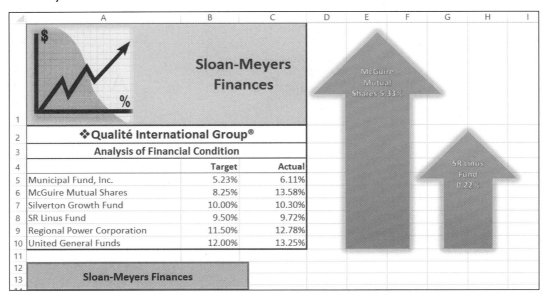

Project 2   Insert a Picture and Text Box in a Division Sales Workbook   1 Part

You will open a division sales workbook and then insert, move, and size a picture. You will also insert a text box and then format the text.

Drawing and Formatting Text Boxes ■■■■■■■■■■■■■■■■

Use the Text Box button on the INSERT tab to draw a text box in a worksheet. To draw a text box, click the INSERT tab and then click the Text Box button in the Text group. This causes the mouse pointer to display as a long, thin, crosslike pointer. Position the pointer in the worksheet and then drag to create the text box. When a text box is selected, the DRAWING TOOLS FORMAT tab displays with options for customizing the text box.

Click a text box to select it and a dashed border and sizing handles display around the text box. If you want to delete the text box, click the text box border again to change the dashed border lines to solid border lines and then press the Delete key.

Project 2   Inserting and Customizing a Picture and Text Box   Part 1 of 1

1. Open **SPDivSales.xlsx** and then save the workbook with Save As and name it **EL1-C8-P2-SPDivSales**.
2. Make the following changes to the bird clip art image:
   a. Click the bird clip art image to select it.
   b. Click the PICTURE TOOLS FORMAT tab.

c. Click the Rotate button in the Arrange group and then click *Flip Horizontal* at the drop-down list.

Step 2c

3. Insert and format a picture by completing the following steps:
   a. Click in cell A1 outside the bird image.
   b. Click the INSERT tab.
   c. Click the Pictures button in the Illustrations group.
   d. At the Insert Picture dialog box, navigate to the EL1C8 folder on your storage medium and then double-click *Ocean.jpg*.
   e. With the picture selected, click the Send Backward button in the Arrange group on the PICTURE TOOLS FORMAT tab.

Step 3e

   f. Use the sizing handles that display around the picture image to move and size it so it fills cell A1, as shown in Figure 8.6.
   g. If necessary, click the bird clip art image and then drag the image so it is positioned as shown in Figure 8.6 on the next page.

4. Save **EL1-C8-P2-SPDivSales.xlsx**.

5. Draw a text box by completing the following steps:
   a. Click the INSERT tab.
   b. Click the Text Box button in the Text group.
   c. Drag in cell A1 to draw a text box the approximate size and shape shown at the right.

Step 5c

6. Format the text box by completing the following steps:
   a. Click the DRAWING TOOLS FORMAT tab.
   b. Click the Shape Fill button arrow in the Shape Styles group and then click *No Fill* at the drop-down gallery.
   c. Click the Shape Outline button arrow in the Shape Styles group and then click *No Outline* at the drop-down gallery.

Step 6b

7. Insert text in the text box by completing the following steps:
   a. With the text box selected, click the HOME tab.
   b. Click the Font button arrow and then click *Lucida Calligraphy* at the drop-down gallery. (You will need to scroll down the gallery to display this font.)
   c. Click the Font Size button arrow and then click *32* at the drop-down gallery.
   d. Click the Font Color button arrow and then click *White, Background 1* (first column, first row in the *Theme Colors* section).
   e. Type **Seabird Productions**.

8. Move the text box so the text is positioned in cell A1 as shown in Figure 8.6.

9. Save, print, and then close **EL1-C8-P2-SPDivSales.xlsx**.

Figure 8.6 Project 2

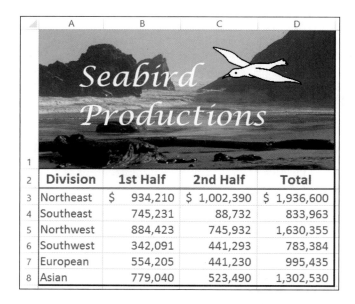

Project 3 Insert a Watermark in an Equipment Usage Workbook   1 Part

You will open an equipment usage report workbook and then insert a picture as a watermark that prints on both pages of the worksheet.

Inserting a Picture as a Watermark ■■■■■■■■■■■■■■■

▼ **Quick Steps**

Insert a Picture as a Watermark
1. Click INSERT tab.
2. Click Header & Footer button.
3. Click Picture button.
4. Click Browse button.
5. Navigate to desired folder.
6. Double-click desired picture.
7. Click Format Picture button.
8. Change size, brightness, and contrast of image.
9. Click OK.

A *watermark* is a lightened image that displays behind data in a file. You can create a watermark in a Word document but the watermark functionality is not available in Excel. You can, however, insert a picture in a header or footer and then resize and format the picture to display behind each page of the worksheet.

To create a picture watermark in a worksheet, click the INSERT tab and then click the Header & Footer button in the Text group. With the worksheet in Print Layout view, click the Picture button in the Header & Footer Elements group on the HEADER & FOOTER TOOLS DESIGN tab. At the Insert Pictures window, click the Browse button to the right of the *From a file* option. At the Insert Picture dialog box, navigate to the desired folder and then double-click the desired picture. This inserts &[Picture] in the header. Resize and format the picture by clicking the Format Picture button in the Header & Footer Elements group. Use options at the Format Picture dialog box with the Size tab selected to specify the size of the picture and use options in the dialog box with the Picture tab selected to specify brightness and contrast.

Format Picture

1. Open **HCEqpRpt.xlsx** and then save it and name it **EL1-C8-P3-HCEqpRpt**.
2. Insert a picture as a watermark by completing the following steps:
   a. Click the INSERT tab.
   b. Click the Header & Footer button in the Text group.
   c. Click the Picture button in the Header & Footer Elements group on the HEADER & FOOTER TOOLS DESIGN tab.
   d. At the Insert Pictures window, click the Browse button that displays to the right of the *From a file* option.
   e. At the Insert Picture dialog box, navigate to the EL1C8 folder on your storage medium and then double-click *Olympics.jpg*.
   f. Click the Format Picture button in the Header & Footer Elements group.
   g. At the Format Picture dialog box with the Size tab selected, click the *Lock aspect ratio* check box in the *Scale* section to remove the check mark.
   h. Select the current measurement in the *Height* measurement box in the *Size and rotate* section and then type **10**.
   i. Select the current measurement in the *Width* measurement box in the *Size and rotate* section and then type **7.5**.
   j. Click the Picture tab.
   k. Select the current percentage in the *Brightness* measurement box in the *Image control* section and then type **75**.
   l. Select the current percentage in the *Contrast* measurement box and then type **25**.
   m. Click OK to close the Format Picture dialog box.
3. Click in the worksheet.
4. Display the worksheet in the Print backstage area to view how the image will print on page 1 and page 2 and then print the worksheet.
5. Save and then close **EL1-C8-P3-HCEqpRpt.xlsx**.

Project ④ Insert and Format SmartArt Graphics in a Company Sales Workbook   4 Parts

You will open a workbook that contains two company sales worksheets. You will insert and format a SmartArt cycle graphic in one worksheet and insert and format a SmartArt relationship graphic in the other. You will also create and format WordArt text.

Inserting SmartArt Graphics ■■■■■■■■■■■■■■■■■■

▼ Quick Steps

Insert a SmartArt Graphic
1. Click INSERT tab.
2. Click SmartArt button.
3. Double-click desired graphic.

SmartArt

Generally, you would use a SmartArt graphic to represent text and a chart to represent numbers.

Text Pane

Use the SmartArt feature included in Excel to insert graphics, such as diagrams and organizational charts, in a worksheet. SmartArt offers a variety of predesigned graphics that are available at the Choose a SmartArt Graphic dialog box, shown in Figure 8.7. Display this dialog box by clicking the INSERT tab and then clicking the SmartArt button in the Illustrations group. At the dialog box, *All* is selected in the left panel and all available predesigned graphics display in the middle panel. Use the scroll bar at the right side of the middle panel to scroll down the list of graphic choices. Click a graphic in the middle panel and the name of the graphic displays in the right panel along with a description of the graphic type. SmartArt includes graphics for presenting a list of data; showing data processes, cycles, and relationships; and presenting data in a matrix or pyramid. Double-click a graphic in the middle panel of the dialog box and the graphic is inserted in the worksheet.

Entering Data in a SmartArt Graphic

Some SmartArt graphics are designed to include text. Type text in a graphic by selecting a shape in the graphic and then typing text in the shape or you can display a text pane and then type text in the pane. Display the text pane by clicking the Text Pane button in the Create Graphic group on the SMARTART TOOLS DESIGN tab. Turn off the display of the pane by clicking the Text Pane button or clicking the Close button that displays in the upper right corner of the text pane.

Figure 8.7 Choose a SmartArt Graphic Dialog Box

Choose the SmartArt graphic category from options in this panel.

Double-click the desired SmartArt graphic in this panel to insert the graphic in the worksheet.

Use the scroll bar to view the entire list of choices.

Click a SmartArt graphic in the middle panel and then read a description of the graphic here.

Sizing, Moving, and Deleting a SmartArt Graphic

Increase or decrease the size of a SmartArt graphic by dragging one of the sizing handles that display around the selected graphic. Use the corner sizing handles to increase or decrease the height and width at the same time. Use the middle sizing handles to increase or decrease the height or width of the SmartArt graphic.

To move a SmartArt graphic, select the graphic and then position the mouse pointer on the graphic border until the pointer displays with a four-headed arrow attached. Hold down the left mouse button, drag the graphic to the desired position, and then release the mouse button. Delete a graphic by selecting the graphic and then pressing the Delete key.

Project 4a **Inserting, Moving, and Sizing a SmartArt Graphic in a Worksheet**   Part 1 of 4

1. Open **EPSales.xlsx** and then save the workbook with Save As and name it **EL1-C8-P4-EPSales**.
2. Create the SmartArt graphic shown in Figure 8.8 on page 291. To begin, click the INSERT tab.
3. Click the SmartArt button in the Illustrations group.
4. At the Choose a SmartArt Graphic dialog box, click *Cycle* in the left panel.
5. Double-click *Radial Cycle* in the middle panel.
6. If the text pane is not open, click the Text Pane button in the Create Graphic group. (The text pane will display at the left side of the SmartArt graphic.)
7. With the insertion point positioned after the top bullet in the text pane, type **Evergreen Products**.
8. Click the *[Text]* placeholder below *Evergreen Products* and then type **Seattle**.
9. Click the next *[Text]* placeholder and then type **Olympia**.
10. Click the next *[Text]* placeholder and then type **Portland**.
11. Click the next *[Text]* placeholder and then type **Spokane**.
12. Click the Text Pane button to turn off the display of the text pane.
13. Drag the SmartArt graphic so it is positioned as shown in Figure 8.8. To drag the graphic, position the mouse pointer on the graphic border until the pointer displays with a four-headed arrow attached. Hold down the left mouse button, drag the graphic to the desired position, and then release the mouse button.
14. Use the sizing handles that display around the SmartArt graphic to increase or decrease the size of the graphic so it displays as shown in Figure 8.8.
15. Save **EL1-C8-P4-EPSales.xlsx**.

Changing the SmartArt Graphic Design

To restore the SmartArt default layout and color, click the Reset Graphic button in the Reset group on the SMARTART TOOLS DESIGN tab.

When you double-click a SmartArt graphic at the Choose a SmartArt Graphic dialog box, the graphic is inserted in the worksheet and the SMARTART TOOLS DESIGN tab is active. Use options and buttons on this tab to add objects, change the graphic layout, apply a style to the graphic, and reset the graphic back to the original formatting.

Project 4b **Changing the SmartArt Graphic Design** Part 2 of 4

1. With **EL1-C8-P4-EPSales.xlsx** open, make sure the SMARTART TOOLS DESIGN tab is active and then click the *Spokane* circle shape in the graphic to select it.
2. Click the Right to Left button in the Create Graphic group. (This switches *Olympia* and *Spokane*.)
3. Click the More button located at the right side of the SmartArt Styles group and then click the *Polished* option at the drop-down list (first column, first row in the *3-D* section).

4. Click the Change Colors button in the SmartArt Styles group, scroll down the drop-down gallery, and then click the *Gradient Range - Accent 6* option (third option in the *Accent 6* section).
5. Click outside the SmartArt graphic to deselect it.
6. Change the orientation to landscape. (Make sure the graphic fits on the first page.)
7. Save **EL1-C8-P4-EPSales.xlsx** and then print the Total Sales worksheet.

Figure 8.8 Projects 4a and 4b

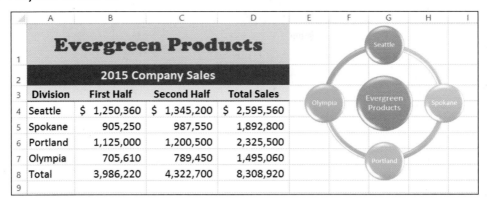

Changing the SmartArt Graphic Formatting

Click the SMARTART TOOLS FORMAT tab and options display for formatting a SmartArt graphic. Use buttons on this tab to insert and customize shapes; apply a shape style; apply WordArt styles; and specify the position, alignment, rotation, wrapping style, height, and width of the graphic.

Project 4c   **Changing the SmartArt Graphic Formatting**   Part 3 of 4

1. With **EL1-C8-P4-EPSales.xlsx** open, click the Seattle Sales worksheet tab.
2. Create the SmartArt graphic shown in Figure 8.9 on the next page. To begin, click the INSERT tab and then click the SmartArt button in the Illustrations group.
3. At the Choose a SmartArt Graphic dialog box, click *Relationship* in the left panel and then double-click *Gear* in the middle panel.
4. Click *[Text]* in the bottom gear and then type **Quality Products**.
5. Click *[Text]* in the left gear and then type **Customized Plans**.
6. Click *[Text]* in the top gear and then type **Exemplary Service**.
7. Click inside the SmartArt graphic border but outside any graphic element.
8. Click the More button that displays at the right side of the SmartArt Styles group and then click the *Inset* option (second column, first row in the *3-D* section).

9. Click the Change Colors button in the SmartArt Styles group and then click the *Gradient Loop - Accent 6* option (fourth option in the *Accent 6* section).
10. Click the SMARTART TOOLS FORMAT tab.
11. Click in the *Shape Height* measurement box in the Size group and then type 4.
12. Click in the *Shape Width* measurement box, type 4.5, and then press Enter.

13. Click the bottom gear to select it.
14. Click the Shape Fill button arrow in the Shape Styles group and then click the *Green, Accent 6, Darker 50%* option (last column, last row in the *Theme Colors* section).
15. Click the top gear to select it.
16. Click the Shape Fill button arrow and then click the *Green, Accent 6, Darker 25%* option (last column, fifth row in the *Theme Colors* section).
17. Change the orientation to landscape.
18. Move the SmartArt graphic so it fits on the first page and displays as shown in Figure 8.9.
19. Click outside the chart to deselect it.
20. Save **EL1-C8-P4-EPSales.xlsx** and then print the Seattle Sales worksheet.

Figure 8.9 Project 4c

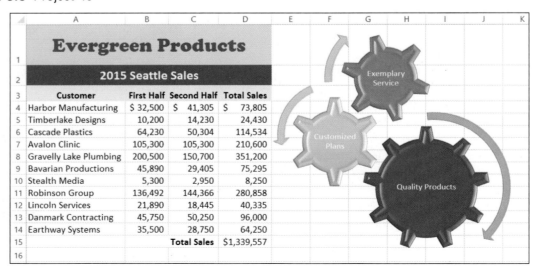

Creating, Sizing, and Moving WordArt ■■■■■■■■■■■■■

With the WordArt feature, you can distort or modify text to conform to a variety of shapes. This is useful for creating company logos and headings. With WordArt, you can change the font, style, and alignment of text. You can also use different fill patterns and colors, customize border lines, and add shadow and three-dimensional effects.

To insert WordArt in an Excel worksheet, click the INSERT tab, click the Insert WordArt button in the Text group, and then click the desired option at the drop-down list. This inserts the text *Your text here* in the worksheet, formatted in the WordArt option you selected at the drop-down list. Type the desired text and then use the buttons on the DRAWING TOOLS FORMAT tab to format the WordArt.

WordArt text inserted in a worksheet is surrounded by white sizing handles. Use these sizing handles to change the height and width of the WordArt text. To move WordArt text, position the arrow pointer on the border of the WordArt text box until the pointer displays with a four-headed arrow attached and then drag the outline of the WordArt text box to the desired location.

Conform WordArt text to a variety of shapes using the *Transform* option from Text Effects button drop-down list. When you apply a transform shape, the WordArt border displays with a small, purple, square shape. Use this shape to change the slant of the WordArt text.

Project 4d — Inserting and Formatting WordArt

Part 4 of 4

1. With **EL1-C8-P4-EPSales.xlsx** open, click the Total Sales worksheet tab.
2. Make cell A1 active and then press the Delete key. (This removes the text from the cell.)
3. Increase the height of row 1 to 137 points.
4. Click the INSERT tab.
5. Click the Insert WordArt button in the Text group and then click the *Fill - Black, Text 1, Outline - Background 1, Hard Shadow - Background 1* option (first column, third row).
6. Type **Evergreen**, press the Enter key, and then type **Products**.
7. Click the WordArt border to change the border to a solid line (not a dashed line).
8. Click the Text Fill button arrow in the WordArt Styles group and then click the *Green, Accent 6, Darker 50%* option (last column, last row in the *Theme Colors* section).

Step 5

Step 8

9. Click the Text Effects button in the WordArt Styles group, point to *Transform*, and then click the *Can Up* option (third column, fourth row in the *Warp* section).

10. Position the mouse pointer (turns into a white arrow) on the small, purple square that displays right below the *d* in *Products*, hold down the left mouse button, drag up approximately 0.25 inch, and then release the mouse button. (This changes the slant of the text.)

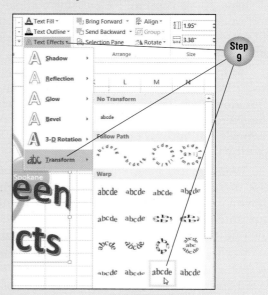

11. Drag the WordArt text so it is positioned in cell A1.

12. If necessary, resize the SmartArt graphic and position it so it prints on one page with the data.

13. Click the Seattle Sales worksheet tab and then complete steps similar to those in Steps 2 through 11 to insert *Evergreen Products* as WordArt in cell A1.

14. Make sure the SmartArt graphic fits on the page with the data. If necessary, decrease the size of the graphic.

15. Save **EL1-C8-P4-EPSales.xlsx** and then print both worksheets.

16. Close **EL1-C8-P4-EPSales.xlsx**.

Chapter Summary

- Insert symbols with options at the Symbol dialog box with the Symbols tab or the Special Characters tab selected.

- With buttons in the Illustrations group on the INSERT tab, you can insert a picture, clip art image, screenshot, shape, or SmartArt graphic.

- Insert a picture by clicking the INSERT tab, clicking the Pictures button in the Illustrations group, and then double-clicking the desired picture at the Insert Picture dialog box.

- When you insert an image, such as a picture or clip art image, in a worksheet, the PICTURE TOOLS FORMAT tab is active and includes options for adjusting the image, applying preformatted styles, and arranging and sizing the image.

- Change the size of an image with the *Shape Height* and *Shape Width* measurement boxes in the Size group on the PICTURE TOOLS FORMAT tab or with the sizing handles that display around the selected image.

- Move an image by positioning the mouse pointer on the image border until the pointer displays with a four-headed arrow attached and then drag the image to the desired location.

- Insert an image from Office.com with options at the Insert Pictures window. Display this window by clicking the INSERT tab and then clicking the Online Pictures button in the Illustrations group.

- Use the Screenshot button in the Illustrations group on the INSERT tab to capture all or part of the contents of a screen.
- To draw shapes in a workbook, click the INSERT tab, click the Shapes button in the Illustrations group, and then click the desired shape at the drop-down list. Click or drag in the worksheet to insert the shape. To maintain the proportions of the shape, hold down the Shift key while dragging in the worksheet.
- Copy a shape with the Copy and Paste buttons in the Clipboard group on the HOME tab or by holding down the Ctrl key while dragging the shape.
- Draw a text box in a worksheet by clicking the INSERT tab, clicking the Text Box button in the Text group, and then clicking or dragging in the worksheet. Use options on the DRAWING TOOLS FORMAT tab to format and customize the text box.
- A watermark is a lightened image that displays behind data in a file. Create a picture watermark in a worksheet by inserting a picture in a header or footer and then changing the size and formatting of the picture.
- Insert a SmartArt graphic in a worksheet by clicking the INSERT tab, clicking the SmartArt button in the Illustrations group, and then double-clicking the desired graphic at the Choose a SmartArt Graphic dialog box. Customize a SmartArt graphic with options on the SMARTART TOOLS DESIGN tab and the SMARTART TOOLS FORMAT tab.
- Use WordArt to create, distort, modify, and/or conform text to a variety of shapes. Insert WordArt in a worksheet with the WordArt button in the Text group on the INSERT tab. Customize WordArt text with options on the DRAWING TOOLS FORMAT tab.

Commands Review

FEATURE	RIBBON TAB, GROUP	BUTTON
Choose a SmartArt Graphic dialog box	INSERT, Illustrations	
Insert Picture dialog box	INSERT, Illustrations	
Insert Pictures window	INSERT, Illustrations	
Insert WordArt button drop-down list	INSERT, Text	
screenshot	INSERT, Illustrations	
Shapes button drop-down list	INSERT, Illustrations	
Symbol dialog box	INSERT, Symbols	
text box	INSERT, Text	

Concepts Check   Test Your Knowledge

Completion: In the space provided at the right, indicate the correct term, symbol, or command.

1. The Symbol button is located on this tab.

2. The *Font* option is available at the Symbol dialog box with this tab selected.

3. Insert a picture, clip art image, screenshot, shape, or SmartArt graphic with buttons in this group on the INSERT tab.

4. Display the Insert Pictures window by clicking this button on the INSERT tab.

5. When you insert an image, such as a picture or clip art, in a worksheet, this tab is active.

6. Maintain the proportions of an image by holding down this key while dragging a sizing handle.

7. To move an image, position the mouse pointer on the image border until the mouse pointer displays with this attached and then drag the image to the desired location.

8. To capture a portion of a screen, click the Screenshot button and then click this option at the drop-down list.

9. To copy a shape, hold down this key while dragging the shape.

10. When you draw a text box in a worksheet and then release the mouse button, this tab is active.

11. This term refers to a lightened image that displays behind data in a file.

12. Click the SmartArt button in the Illustrations group on the INSERT tab and this dialog box displays.

Skills Check   Assess Your Performance

Assessment

1   INSERT A CLIP ART IMAGE AND WORDART IN AN EQUIPMENT SALES WORKBOOK

1. Open **MSSalesPlans.xlsx** and then save the workbook with Save As and name it **EL1-C8-A1-MSSalesPlans**.
2. Insert a formula in cell E4 using the PMT function that calculates monthly payments. (Type a minus sign before the cell designation in the *Pv* text box at the Function Arguments palette.) ***Hint: For assistance, refer to Chapter 7, Project 5a.***

3. Copy the formula in cell E4 down to cells E5 and E6.
4. Insert a formula in cell F4 that calculates the total amount of the payments.
5. Copy the formula in cell F4 down to cells F5 and F6.
6. Insert a formula in cell G4 that calculates the total amount of interest paid.
7. Copy the formula in cell G4 down to cells G5 and G6.
8. Insert the clip art image shown in Figure 8.10 with the following specifications:
   a. Click the INSERT tab and then click the Online Pictures button. At the Insert Pictures window, search for images related to maple leaves. (The colors of the original clip art image are green and white.)
   b. Apply the Orange, Accent color 2 Dark clip art image color (third column, second row).
   c. Apply the Brightness: -20% Contrast: +20% correction (second column, fourth row).
   d. Apply the Drop Shadow Rectangle picture style (fourth thumbnail).
   e. Size and move the image so it is positioned as shown in Figure 8.10.
9. Insert the company name *Maplewood Suppliers* in cell A1 as WordArt with the following specifications:
   a. Click the WordArt button on the INSERT tab and then click the *Fill - White, Outline - Accent 2, Hard Shadow - Accent 2* option (fourth column, third row).
   b. Apply the Orange, Accent 2, Darker 50% text fill (sixth column, bottom row in the *Theme Colors* section).
   c. Apply the Orange, Accent 2, Lighter 60% text outline (sixth column, third row in the *Theme Colors* section).
   d. Using the Text Effects button, apply the Square transform text effect.
   e. Change the width of the WordArt to 5 inches.
   f. Move the WordArt so it is positioned in cell A1 as shown in Figure 8.10.
10. Change the worksheet orientation to landscape.
11. Save, print, and then close **EL1-C8-A1-MSSalesPlans.xlsx**.

Figure 8.10 Assessment 1

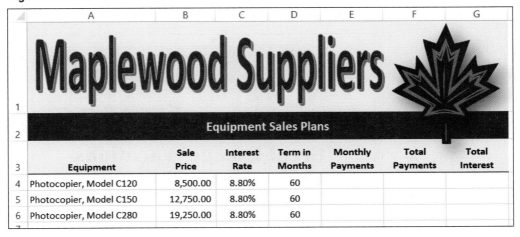

Assessment

2 INSERT FORMULAS AND FORMAT A TRAVEL COMPANY WORKBOOK   Grade It

1. Open **TSGEVacs.xlsx** and then save the workbook with Save As and name it **EL1-C8-A2-TSGEVacs**.
2. Insert appropriate formulas to calculate the prices based on 10% and 20% discounts and apply the appropriate number formatting. *Hint: For the 10% discount column, multiply the price per person by 0.90 (which determines 90% of the price) and for the 20% discount column, multiply the price per person by 0.80 (which determines 80% of the price).*
3. Format the image of the airplane and position it as shown in Figure 8.11 with the following specifications:
   a. Use the Remove Background button in the Adjust group on the PICTURE TOOLS FORMAT tab to remove a portion of the yellow background so the image displays similar to what you see in the figure.
   b. Rotate the image to flip it horizontally.
   c. Apply the Brightness: +20% Contrast: +20% correction.
   d. Change the height of the image to 1.4 inches and then position the image as shown in the figure.
4. Open Word and then open the document named **TSAirfare.docx** located in the EL1C8 folder on your storage medium. Click the Excel button on the Taskbar and then use the Screenshot button (with the *Screen Clipping* option) to select and then insert the airfare information in **EL1-C8-A2-TSGEVacs.xlsx**. Position the information at the right side of the data in the worksheet.
5. Change the orientation to landscape.
6. Make sure the data and the airfare information display on one page and then print the worksheet.
7. Save and then close **EL1-C8-A2-TSGEVacs.xslx**.
8. Click the Word button on the Taskbar, close **TSAirfare.docx**, and then close Word.

Figure 8.11 Assessment 2

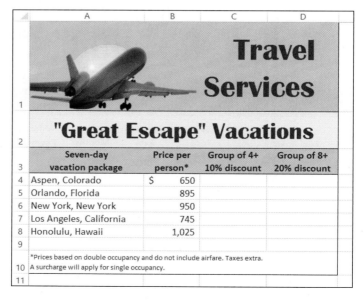

3   INSERT AND FORMAT SHAPES IN A COMPANY SALES WORKBOOK

1. Open **MGSales.xlsx** and then save the workbook with Save As and name it **EL1-C8-A3-MGSales**.
2. Use the Isosceles Triangle shape located in the *Basic Shapes* section of the Shapes drop-down palette to draw a triangle as shown in Figure 8.12.
3. Apply Green, Accent 6, Darker 50% shape outline color (last column, last row in the *Theme Colors* section) to the triangle.
4. Apply Green, Accent 6, Darker 25% shape fill (last column, fifth row in the *Theme Colors* section) to the triangle.
5. Copy the triangle three times.
6. Position the triangles as shown in Figure 8.12.
7. Select the second and fourth triangles and then apply the Green, Accent 6, Lighter 80% shape fill (last column, second row in the *Theme Colors* section).
8. Insert the total amounts in cells B10 through D10. (If you use the fill handle to copy the formula from B10 to cells C10 and D10, use the Auto Fill options button to fill without formatting.)
9. Insert an arrow pointing to *$97,549* with the following specifications:
   a. Use the Left Arrow shape to draw the arrow.
   b. Change the height of the arrow to 0.6 inch and the width to 1.2 inches.
   c. Apply Green, Accent 6, Darker 25% shape fill (last column, fifth row in the *Theme Colors* section) to the arrow.
   d. Type the text **Largest Order** in the arrow and then select the text and change the font to 10-point Calibri bold.
   e. Position the arrow as shown in Figure 8.12.
10. Save, print, and then close **EL1-C8-A3-MGSales.xlsx**.

Figure 8.12 Assessment 3

	A	B	C	D	E	F
1	**Mountain Group**					
2	FIRST QUARTER SALES - 2015					
3	Customer	January	February	March		
4	Lakeside Trucking	$ 84,231	$ 73,455	$ 97,549	← Largest Order	
5	Gresham Machines	33,199	40,390	50,112		
6	Real Photography	30,891	35,489	36,400		
7	Genesis Productions	72,190	75,390	83,219		
8	Landower Company	22,188	14,228	38,766		
9	Jewell Enterprises	19,764	50,801	32,188		
10	**Total**					
11						

4 INSERT AND FORMAT A SMARTART GRAPHIC IN A SALES WORKBOOK

1. Open **PS2ndQtrSales.xlsx** and then save the workbook with Save As and name it **EL1-C8-A4-PS2ndQtrSales**.
2. Change the orientation to landscape.
3. Insert the Pyramid List SmartArt graphic at the right side of the worksheet data with the following specifications:
   a. Apply the Gradient Loop - Accent 2 color (fourth option in the *Accent 2* section).
   b. Apply the Cartoon SmartArt style (third column, first row in the *3-D* section).
   c. In the bottom text box, type **Red Level**, press Enter, and then type **$25,000 to $49,999**.
   d. In the middle text box, type **Blue Level**, press Enter, and then type **$50,000 to $99,999**.
   e. In the top text box, type **Gold Level**, press Enter, and then type $100,000+.
   f. Apply fill color to each text box to match the level color. (Use the Orange fill color for the Gold Level text box.)
4. Size and/or move the SmartArt graphic so it displays attractively at the right side of the worksheet data. (Make sure the entire graphic will print on the same page as the worksheet data.)
5. Save, print, and then close **EL1-C8-A4-PS2ndQtrSales.xlsx**.

5 CREATE AND INSERT A SCREENSHOT

1. Open **RPRefiPlan.xlsx**, save it with Save As and name it **EL1-C8-A5-RPRefiPlan**, and then display the formulas by pressing Ctrl + `.
2. Insert the arrow shape shown in Figure 8.13 on the next page. Add fill to the shape, remove the shape outline, bold the text in the shape, and then determine how to rotate the shape using the rotation handle (white circle). Rotate, size, and position the arrow as shown in the figure.
3. Open Word.
4. At a blank document, press Ctrl + E to center the insertion point, press Ctrl + B to turn on bold, type **Excel Worksheet with PMT Formula**, and then press the Enter key twice.
5. Click the INSERT tab, click the Screenshot button, and then click the thumbnail of the Excel worksheet.
6. Save the Word document and name it **EL1-C8-A5-PMTFormula**.
7. Print and then close the document and then close Word.
8. In Excel, save and then close **EL1-C8-A5-RPRefiPlan.xlsx**.

Figure 8.13 Assessment 5

	A	B	C	D	E	F
1			**REAL PHOTOGRAPHY**			
2			**Refinance Plan**			
3						
4	**Lender**	**Amount**	**Interest Rate**	**Term in Months**	**Monthly Payments**	**Total Payments**
5	Castle Credit Union	400000	0.065	300	=PMT(C5/12,D5,-B5)	=E5*D5
6	Castle Credit Union	500000	0.062	300	=PMT(C6/12,D6,-B6)	=E6*D6
7	Millstone Bank	400000	0.064	240	=PMT(C7/12,D7,-B7)	=E7*D7
8	Millstone Bank	500000	0.061	240	=PMT(C8/12,D8,-B8)	=E8*D8
9						
10						
11						

PMT Formula

Visual Benchmark   Demonstrate Your Proficiency

INSERT FORMULAS, WORDART, AND CLIP ART IN A WORKSHEET

1. Open **TSYrlySales.xlsx** and then save the workbook with Save As and name it **EL1-C8-VB-TSYrlySales**.

2. Insert formulas that will calculate the results shown in the worksheet in Figure 8.14 on the next page. (**Do not** type the data in the cells. Instead, insert the following formulas. The results of your formulas should match the results you see in the figure.)

   - Cells C4 through C14: Insert a formula with an IF function that inserts *5%* if the amount in the cell in column B is greater than $249,999 and inserts *2%* if the amount is not greater than $249,999.

   - Cells D4 through D14: Insert a formula that multiplies the amount in column B with the amount in column C.

   - Apply accounting formatting with a dollar sign and no places past the decimal point to cell D4.

3. Insert the company name *Target Supplies* as WordArt with the following specifications:

   - Choose the *Fill - Black, Text 1, Outline - Background 1, Hard Shadow - Accent 1* option (second column, third row).

   - To type the WordArt text, press Ctrl + L (which changes to left text alignment), type **Target**, press Enter, and then type **Supplies**.

   - Apply Orange, Accent 2, Darker 50% text fill color (sixth column, bottom row in the *Theme Colors* section).

   - Apply the Orange, Accent 2, Lighter 40% text outline color (sixth column, fourth row in the *Theme Colors* section).

   - Move the WordArt so it is positioned as shown in Figure 8.14.

4. Insert the target clip art image (use the Insert Pictures window and search with the words *archery, arrows, target* to find this clip art image) with the following specifications:

   - Apply the Orange, Accent color 2 light color (third column, third row).

   - Apply the Brightness: -20% Contrast: -20% correction (second column, second row).

   - Size and position the clip art image as shown in the figure.

5. Draw the shape that displays below the data with the following specifications:
   - Use the Bevel shape (located in the *Basic Shapes* section).
   - Type the text in the shape, apply bold formatting, and change to center and middle alignment.
   - Apply the Orange, Accent 2, Darker 50% shape fill color (sixth column, bottom row in the *Theme Colors* section).
   - Apply the Orange, Accent 2 shape outline color (sixth column, top row in the *Theme Colors* section).
6. Save and then print the worksheet.
7. Press Ctrl + ` to turn on the display of formulas and then print the worksheet again.
8. Turn off the display of formulas and then close the workbook.

Figure 8.14 Visual Benchmark

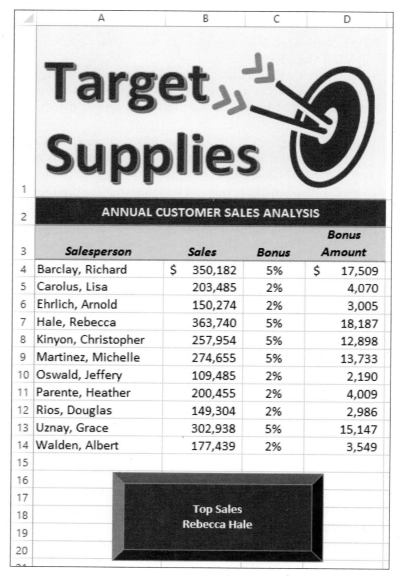

	A	B	C	D
2	ANNUAL CUSTOMER SALES ANALYSIS			
3	Salesperson	Sales	Bonus	Bonus Amount
4	Barclay, Richard	$ 350,182	5%	$ 17,509
5	Carolus, Lisa	203,485	2%	4,070
6	Ehrlich, Arnold	150,274	2%	3,005
7	Hale, Rebecca	363,740	5%	18,187
8	Kinyon, Christopher	257,954	5%	12,898
9	Martinez, Michelle	274,655	5%	13,733
10	Oswald, Jeffery	109,485	2%	2,190
11	Parente, Heather	200,455	2%	4,009
12	Rios, Douglas	149,304	2%	2,986
13	Uznay, Grace	302,938	5%	15,147
14	Walden, Albert	177,439	2%	3,549
15				
16				
17		Top Sales		
18		Rebecca Hale		
19				
20				

Case Study

Apply Your Skills

Part 1

You are the office manager for Ocean Truck Sales and are responsible for maintaining a spreadsheet of the truck and SUV inventory. Open **OTSales.xlsx** and then save the workbook and name it **EL1-C8-CS-OTSales**. Apply formatting to improve the appearance of the worksheet and insert at least one clip art image (related to a truck or ocean). Save **EL1-C8-CS-OTSales.xlsx** and then print the worksheet.

Part 2

With **EL1-C8-CS-OTSales.xlsx** open, save the workbook with Save As and name it **EL1-C8-CS-OTSalesF&C**. You make the inventory workbook available to each salesperson at the beginning of the week. For easier viewing, you decide to divide the workbook into two worksheets, with one worksheet containing all Ford vehicles and the other worksheet containing all Chevrolet vehicles. Rename the worksheet tabs to reflect the contents. Sort the data in each worksheet by price from most expensive to least expensive.

The owner offers incentives each week to help motivate the sales force. Insert in the first worksheet a SmartArt graphic of your choosing that contains the following information:

> Small-sized truck: $200
>
> 2WD regular cab: $150
>
> SUV 4x4: $100

Copy the SmartArt graphic in the first worksheet and then paste it into the second worksheet. Change the orientation to landscape and then save, print, and close both worksheets in **EL1-C8-CS-OTSalesF&C.xlsx**.

Part 3

You have been asked to save the inventory worksheet as a web page for viewing online. Open **EL1-C8-CS-OTSales.xlsx**, display the Save As dialog box, click the *Save as type* option, and then determine how to save the workbook as a single-file web page (*.mht, *.mhtml). Save the workbook as a single-file web page with the name **EL1-C8-CS-OTSales-WebPage**. Open your Internet browser and then open the web page. Look at the information in the file and then close the Internet browser.

Part 4

As part of your weekly duties, you post the incentive SmartArt graphic in various locations throughout the company. You decide to insert the graphic in PowerPoint for easy printing. Open **EL1-C8-CS-OTSalesF&C.xlsx** and then open PowerPoint. Change the slide layout in PowerPoint to Blank. Copy the SmartArt graphic in the first worksheet and paste it into the PowerPoint blank slide. Increase and/or move the graphic so it better fills the slide. Print the slide and then close PowerPoint without saving the presentation. Close **EL1-C8-CS-OTSalesF&C.xlsx**.

MICROSOFT® EXCEL® Performance Assessment

Excel
EL1U2

Note: Before beginning unit assessments, copy to your storage medium the EL1U2 subfolder from the EL1 folder on the CD that accompanies this textbook and then make EL1U2 the active folder.

Assessing Proficiency ■■■■■■■■■■■■■■

In this unit, you have learned how to work with multiple windows; move, copy, link, and paste data within and between workbooks and applications; create and customize charts with data in a worksheet; write formulas with PMT, FV, and IF functions; save a workbook as a web page; insert hyperlinks; and insert and customize images, shapes, SmartArt graphics, and WordArt.

Assessment 1 Copy and Paste Data and Insert WordArt in a Training Scores Workbook

1. Open **RLTraining.xlsx** and then save the workbook with Save As and name it **EL1-U2-A01-RLTraining**.
2. Delete row 15 (the row for *Kwieciak, Kathleen*).
3. Insert a formula in cell D4 that averages the percentages in cells B4 and C4.
4. Copy the formula in cell D4 down to cells D5 through D20.
5. Make cell A22 active, turn on bold formatting, and then type **Highest Averages**.
6. Display the Clipboard task pane and make sure it is empty.
7. Select and then copy each of the following rows (individually): 7, 10, 14, 16, and 18.
8. Make cell A23 active and then paste row 14 (the row for *Jewett, Troy*).
9. Make cell A24 active and then paste row 7 (the row for *Cumpston, Kurt*).
10. Make cell A25 active and then paste row 10 (the row for *Fisher-Edwards, Theresa*).
11. Make cell A26 active and then paste row 16 (the row for *Mathias, Caleb*).
12. Make cell A27 active and then paste row 18 (the row for *Nyegaard, Curtis*).
13. Click the Clear All button in the Clipboard task pane and then close the task pane.
14. Insert in cell A1 the text *Roseland* as WordArt. Format the WordArt text to add visual appeal to the worksheet.
15. Save, print, and then close **EL1-U2-A01-RLTraining.xlsx**.

Assessment 2 Manage Multiple Worksheets in a Projected Earnings Workbook

1. Open **RLProjEarnings.xlsx** and then save the workbook with Save As and name it **EL1-U2-A02-RLProjEarnings**.
2. Delete *Roseland* in cell A1. Open **EL1-U2-A01-RLTraining.xlsx**, copy the *Roseland* WordArt text, and then paste it into cell A1 in **EL1-U2-A02-RLProjEarnings.xlsx**. If necessary, increase the height of row 1 to accommodate the WordArt text.
3. Close **EL1-U2-A01-RLTraining.xlsx**.
4. Insert a new worksheet in the **EL1-U2-A02-RLProjEarnings.xlsx** workbook.
5. Select cells A1 through C11 in Sheet1 and then copy and paste the cells to Sheet2, keeping the source column widths.
6. With Sheet2 displayed, make the following changes:
   a. Increase the height of row 1 to accommodate the WordArt text.
   b. Delete the contents of cell B2.
   c. Change the contents of the following cells:
   - A6: Change *January* to *July*
   - A7: Change *February* to *August*
   - A8: Change *March* to *September*
   - A9: Change *April* to *October*
   - A10: Change *May* to *November*
   - A11: Change *June* to *December*
   - B6: Change *8.30%* to *8.10%*
   - B8: Change *9.30%* to *8.70%*
7. Make Sheet1 active, copy cell B2, and then paste link it to cell B2 in Sheet2.
8. Rename Sheet1 *First Half* and rename Sheet2 *Second Half*.
9. Make the First Half worksheet active and then determine the effect on projected monthly earnings if the projected yearly income is increased by 10% by changing the number in cell B2 to *$1,480,380*.
10. Horizontally and vertically center both worksheets in the workbook and insert a custom header that prints your name at the left, the current date in the center, and the sheet name (click the Sheet Name button in the Header & Footer Elements group on the Header & Footer Tools Design tab) at the right.
11. Print both worksheets.
12. Determine the effect on projected monthly earnings if the projected yearly income is increased by 20% by changing the number in cell B2 to *$1,614,960*.
13. Save the workbook again and then print both worksheets.
14. Close **EL1-U2-A02-RLProjEarnings.xlsx**.

Assessment 3 Create Charts in Worksheets in a Sales Totals Workbook

1. Open **EPYrlySales.xlsx** and then save the workbook with Save As and name it **EL1-U2-A03-EPYrlySales**.
2. Rename Sheet1 as *2013 Sales*, rename Sheet2 as *2014 Sales*, and rename Sheet3 as *2015 Sales*.
3. Select all three sheet tabs, make cell A12 active, turn on bold formatting, and then type **Total**. Make cell B12 active and then insert a formula to total the amounts in cells B4 through B11. Make cell C12 active and then insert a formula to total the amounts in cells C4 through C11.
4. Make the 2013 Sales worksheet active, select cells A3 through C11 (being careful not to select the totals in row 12), and then create a column chart. Click the Switch Row/Column button on the Chart Tools Design tab. Apply formatting to increase the visual appearance of the chart. Drag the chart below the worksheet data. (Make sure the chart fits on one page.)
5. Make the 2014 Sales worksheet active and then create the same type of chart you created in Step 4.
6. Make the 2015 Sales worksheet active and then create the same type of chart you created in Step 4. Filter the records in this chart so that only the following companies display: *Harbor Manufacturing*, *Avalon Clinic*, and *Stealth Media*.
7. Save the workbook and then print the entire workbook.
8. Close **EL1-U2-A03-EPYrlySales.xlsx**.

Assessment 4 Create and Format a Line Chart

1. Open **ProfitCompare.xlsx** and then save the workbook with Save As and name it **EL1-U2-A04-ProfitCompare**.
2. Use the data in the workbook to create a line chart with the following specifications:
   a. Apply the Style 11 chart style.
   b. Include the chart title *NET PROFIT COMPARISON*.
   c. Apply the Green shape fill and shape outline color of the Asia series (in the *Standard Colors* section).
   d. Move the chart to a new worksheet.
3. Save the workbook and then print only the worksheet containing the chart.
4. Close **EL1-U2-A04-ProfitCompare.xlsx**.

Assessment 5 Create and Format a Pie Chart

1. Open **EPProdDept.xlsx** and then save the workbook with Save As and name it **EL1-U2-A05-EPProdDept**.
2. Create a pie chart as a separate worksheet with the data in cells A3 through B10. You determine the type of pie chart. Include an appropriate title for the chart, as well as percentage labels.
3. Print only the worksheet containing the chart.
4. Save and then close **EL1-U2-A05-EPProdDept.xlsx**.

Assessment 6 Use the PMT Function and Apply Formatting to a Workbook

1. Open **HERSalesInfo.xlsx** and then save the workbook with Save As and name it **EL1-U2-A06-HERSalesInfo**.
2. The owner of Hilltop Equipment Rental is interested in selling three tractors owned by the business and needs to determine the possible monthly income from the sales. Using the PMT function, insert a formula in cell E4 that calculates monthly payments. (Type a minus sign before the cell designation in the *Pv* text box at the Function Arguments palette.)
3. Copy the formula in cell E4 down to cells E5 and E6.
4. Insert a formula in cell F4 that multiplies the amount in cell E4 by the amount in cell D4.
5. Copy the formula in cell F4 down to cells F5 and F6.
6. Insert a formula in cell G4 that subtracts the amount in cell B4 from the amount in cell F4. *Hint: The formula should return a positive number.*
7. Copy the formula in cell G4 down to cells G5 and G6.
8. Save, print, and then close **EL1-U2-A06-HERSalesInfo.xlsx**.

Assessment 7 Use the IF Function and Apply Formatting to a Workbook

1. Open **PSQtrlySales.xlsx** and then save the workbook with Save As and name it **EL1-U2-A07-PSQtrlySales**.
2. Insert an IF statement in cell F4 that inserts *Yes* if cell E4 contains a number greater than 74999 and inserts *No* if the number in cell E4 is not greater than 74999. Copy the formula in cell F4 down to cells F5 through F18. Center align the text in cells F4 through F18.
3. Insert a footer that prints your name at the left, the current date in the middle, and the current time at the right.
4. Turn on the display of formulas, print the worksheet in landscape orientation, and then turn off the display of formulas. (The worksheet will print on two pages.)
5. Save and then close **EL1-U2-A07-PSQtrlySales.xlsx**.

Assessment 8 Insert a Text Box and Hyperlinks in a Travel Workbook

1. Open **TravDest.xlsx** and then save the workbook with Save As and name it **EL1-U2-A08-TravDest**.
2. Insert a text box in the workbook with the following specifications:
   a. Draw the text box at the right side of the clip art image.
   b. Type **Call 1-888-555-1288 for last-minute vacation specials!**
   c. Select the text and then change the font to 24-point Forte and apply the Blue color in the *Standard Colors* section.
   d. Size and position the text box so it appears visually balanced with the travel clip art image.
3. Make sure you are connected to the Internet and then, for each city in the worksheet, search for sites that might be of interest to tourists. Write down the web address of the best web page you find for each city.
4. Create a hyperlink with each city name to the web address you wrote down in Step 3. (Select the hyperlink text in each cell and change the font size to 18 points.)
5. Test each hyperlink to make sure you entered the web address correctly. Click the hyperlink and then close the web browser after the page has loaded.
6. Save, print, and then close **EL1-U2-A08-TravDest.xlsx**.

Assessment 9 Insert an Image and a SmartArt Graphic in a Workbook

1. Open **SalesQuotas.xlsx** and then save the workbook with Save As and name it **EL1-U2-A09-SalesQuotas**.
2. Insert a formula in cell C3 using an absolute reference to determine the projected quotas at a 10% increase of the current quotas.
3. Copy the formula in cell C3 down to cells C4 through C12. Apply the Accounting format with two places past the decimal point and a dollar sign to cell C3.
4. In row 1, insert a clip art image related to money. You determine the size and position of the clip art image. If necessary, increase the height of the row.
5. Insert a SmartArt graphic at the right side of the data that contains three shapes. Insert the following quota ranges in the shapes and apply the specified fill colors:
    $50,000 to $99,999 (apply a green color)
    $100,000 to $149,999 (apply a blue color)
    $150,000 to $200,000 (apply a red color)
6. Apply formatting to the SmartArt graphic to improve the visual appearance.
7. Insert a custom header that prints your name at the left, the current date in the middle, and the file name at the right.
8. Change the orientation to landscape and make sure the graphic fits on the page.
9. Save, print, and then close **EL1-U2-A09-SalesQuotas.xlsx**.

Assessment 10 Insert a Symbol, WordArt, and Screenshot in a Sales Workbook

1. Open **CISales.xlsx** and then save the workbook with Save As and name it **EL1-U2-A10-CISales**.
2. Delete the text *Landower Company* in cell A7 and then type **Económico** in the cell. (Use the Symbol dialog box to insert *ó*.)
3. Insert a new row at the beginning of the worksheet.
4. Select and then merge cells A1 through D1.
5. Increase the height of row 1 to approximately 141.00 points.
6. Insert the text *Custom Interiors* as WordArt in cell A1. You determine the formatting of the WordArt. Move and size the WordArt so it fits in cell A1.
7. Open Word and then open **CICustomers.docx** located in the EL1U2 folder on your storage medium. Click the Excel button and with **EL1-U2-A10-CISales.xlsx** open, make a screenshot (using the *Screen Clipping* option) of the customer information in the Word document. Position the screenshot image below the data in the cells.
8. Insert a custom footer that prints your name at the left and the file name at the right.
9. Make sure the data in the cells and the screenshot display on the same page and then print the worksheet.
10. Save and then close **EL1-U2-A10-CISales.xlsx**.
11. Make Word the active program, close **CICustomers.docx**, and then close Word.

Assessment 11 Insert and Format a Shape in a Budget Workbook

1. Open **SEExpenses.xlsx** and then save the workbook with Save As and name it **EL1-U2-A11-SEExpenses**.
2. Make the following changes to the worksheet so it displays as shown in Figure U2.1:
   a. Select and then merge cells A1 through D1.
   b. Add fill to the cells as shown in Figure U2.1. (Use the Green, Accent 6, Lighter 40% fill color.)
   c. Increase the height of row 1 to the approximate size shown in Figure U2.1.
   d. Make cell A1 active, type **SOLAR**, press Alt + Enter, and then type **ENTERPRISES**. Set the text you just typed in 20-point Calibri bold, center and middle aligned, and change the font color to *Green, Accent 6, Darker 25%*.
   e. Insert the sun shape (located in the *Basic Shapes* section of the Shapes button drop-down list). Apply orange shape fill (using the Orange option in the *Standard Colors* section) and change the shape outline to *Green, Accent 6, Darker 25%*. Copy the shape in the cell and then size and position the shapes as shown in the figure.
3. Save, print, and then close **EL1-U2-A11-SEExpenses.xlsx**.

Figure U2.1 Assessment 11

	A	B	C	D
1				
2	*Expense*	*Actual*	*Budget*	*% of Actual*
3	Salaries	$ 126,000.00	$ 124,000.00	98%
4	Benefits	25,345.00	28,000.00	110%
5	Commissions	58,000.00	54,500.00	94%
6	Media space	8,250.00	10,100.00	122%
7	Travel expenses	6,350.00	6,000.00	94%
8	Dealer display	4,140.00	4,500.00	109%
9	Payroll taxes	2,430.00	2,200.00	91%
10	Telephone	1,450.00	1,500.00	103%
11				

Writing Activities ▪■▪■▪▪▪▪▪■▪▪■▪■▪▪▪

The following activities give you the opportunity to practice your writing skills along with demonstrating an understanding of some of the important Excel features you have mastered in this unit. Use correct grammar, appropriate word choices, and clear sentence constructions.

Activity 1 Prepare a Projected Budget

You are the accounting assistant in the financial department of McCormack Funds and you have been asked to prepare a proposed annual department budget. The total amount available to the department is $1,450,000. You are given these percentages for the proposed budget items: salaries, 45%; benefits, 12%; training, 14%; administrative costs, 10%; equipment, 11%; and supplies, 8%. Create a worksheet with this information that shows the projected yearly budget, the budget items in the department, the percentage for each item, and the amount for each item. After the worksheet is completed, save the workbook and name it **EL1-U2-Act1-MFBudget**. Print and then close the workbook.

Optional: Using Word 2013, write a memo to members of the McCormack Funds Finance Department explaining that the proposed annual department budget is attached for their review. Comments and suggestions are to be sent to you within one week. Save the file and name it **EL1-U2-Act1-MFMemo**. Print and then close the file.

Activity 2 Create a Travel Tours Bar Chart

Prepare a worksheet in Excel for Carefree Travels that includes the following information:

Scandinavian Tours

Country	Tours Booked
Norway	52
Sweden	62
Finland	29
Denmark	38

Use the information in the worksheet to create and format a bar chart as a separate sheet. Save the workbook and name it **EL1-U2-Act2-CTTours**. Print only the sheet containing the chart and then close **EL1-U2-Act2-CTTours.xlsx**.

Activity 3 Prepare a Ski Vacation Worksheet

Prepare a worksheet for Carefree Travels that advertises a snow skiing trip. Include the following information in the announcement:

- At the beginning of the worksheet, create a company logo that includes the company name *Carefree Travels* and a clip art image related to travel.
- Include the heading *Whistler Ski Vacation Package* in the worksheet.
- Include the following details below the heading:
  - Round-trip air transportation: $395
  - Seven nights' hotel accommodations: $1,550
  - Four all-day ski passes: $425
  - Compact rental car with unlimited mileage: $250
  - Total price of the ski package: (calculate the total price)

- Include the following information somewhere in the worksheet:
  - ◦ Book your vacation today at special discount prices.
  - ◦ Two-for-one discount at many of the local ski resorts.

Save the workbook and name it **EL1-U2-Act3-CTSkiTrips**. Print and then close **EL1-U2-Act3-CTSkiTrips.xlsx**.

Internet Research ▪▪▪▪▪▪▪▪▪▪▪▪▪▪▪▪▪▪▪▪

Find Information on Excel Books and Present the Data in a Worksheet

Locate two companies on the Internet that sell new books. At the first new book company site, locate three books on Microsoft Excel. Record the title, author, and price for each book. At the second new book company site, locate the same three books and record the prices. Create an Excel worksheet that includes the following information:

- Name of each new book company
- Title and author of each book
- Prices for each book from the two book company sites

Create a hyperlink to the website of each book company. Then save the completed workbook and name it **EL1-U2-IR-Books**. Print and then close the workbook.

Job Study ▪▪▪▪▪▪▪▪▪▪▪▪▪▪▪▪▪▪▪▪▪▪▪▪▪▪

Create a Customized Time Card for a Landscaping Company

You are the manager of Landmark Landscaping Company and are responsible for employee time cards. At the New backstage area, search for and download a time card using the words *weekly time sheet portrait* to narrow the search. Use the template to create a customized time card workbook for your company. With the workbook based on the template open, insert additional blank rows to increase the spacing above the Employee row. Insert a clip art image related to landscaping or gardening and position and size it attractively in the form. Include a text box with the text *Lawn and Landscaping Specialists* inside the box. Format, size, and position the text attractively in the form. Fill in the form for the current week with the following employee information:

Employee: Jonathan Holder
Manager: (Your name)
Employee phone: (225) 555-3092
Employee email: None
Regular hours: 8 hours for Monday, Tuesday, Wednesday, and Thursday
Overtime: 2 hours on Wednesday
Sick hours: None
Vacation: 8 hours on Friday
Rate per hour: $20.00
Overtime pay: $30.00

Save the completed form and name it **EL1-U2-JS-TimeCard**. Print and then close **EL1-U2-JS-TimeCard.xlsx**.

Index

313

Excel 2013 Quick Reference

Excel 2013 Feature	Ribbon Tab, Group/Option	Button	Keyboard Shortcut
Accounting format	HOME, Number		
align text left, center, or right	HOME, Alignment		
align text top, middle, or bottom	HOME, Alignment		
bold text	HOME, Font		Ctrl + B
borders	HOME, Font		
cell styles	HOME, Styles		
change file type	FILE, Export		
close Excel			Alt + F4
close workbook	FILE, *Close*		Ctrl + F4
Comma format	HOME, Number		
comments	REVIEW, Comments		
conditional formatting	HOME, Styles		
Consolidate	DATA, Data Tools		
convert text to columns	DATA, Data Tools		
copy selected cells	HOME, Clipboard		Ctrl + C
cut selected cells	HOME, Clipboard		Ctrl + X
data table	DATA, Data Tools		
data validation	DATA, Data Tools		
decrease decimal places	HOME, Number		
decrease indent	HOME, Alignment		Ctrl + Alt + Shift + Tab
delete cells, rows, or columns	HOME, Cells		
display formulas	FORMULAS, Formula Auditing		Ctrl + `

Excel 2013 Feature	Ribbon Tab, Group/Option	Button	Keyboard Shortcut
fill color	HOME, Editing		
financial functions	FORMULAS, Function Library		
Find & Select	HOME, Editing		Ctrl + E
Flash Fill	DATA, Data Tools		
font color	HOME, Font		
Format Cells dialog box	HOME, Number		
Format Painter	HOME, Clipboard		
Goal Seek	DATA, Data Tools		
group and ungroup	DATA, Outline		Shift + Alt + Right Arrow key, Shift + Alt + Left Arrow key
header and footer	INSERT, Text		
Help			F1
hyperlink	INSERT, Links		Ctrl + K
import from Access, web page, or text file	DATA, Get External Data		
increase decimal places	HOME, Number		
increase indent	HOME, Alignment		Ctrl + Alt + Tab
inspect workbook	FILE, Info		
insert cells, rows, or columns	HOME, Cells		
Insert Chart dialog box	INSERT, Charts		
Insert Function dialog box	FORMULAS, Function Library		Shift + F3
italicize text	HOME, Font		Ctrl + I
logical functions	FORMULAS, Function Library		

Excel 2013 Feature

Excel 2013 Feature	Ribbon Tab, Group/Option	Button	Keyboard Shortcut
lookup and reference functions	FORMULAS, Function Library		
macros	VIEW, Macros		Alt + F8
mark workbook as final	FILE, Info		
math and trigonometry functions	FORMULAS, Function Library		
merge and center cells	HOME, Alignment		
Name Manager dialog box	FORMULAS, Defined Names		Ctrl + F3
New backstage area	FILE, New		
number format	HOME, Number	General	
online pictures	INSERT, Illustrations		
Open backstage area	FILE, Open		Ctrl + O
Orientation	HOME, Alignment		
page orientation	PAGE LAYOUT, Page Setup		
paste selected cells	HOME, Clipboard		Ctrl + V
Percent format	HOME, Number		Ctrl + Shift + %
PivotTable or PivotChart	INSERT, Tables, INSERT Charts, or PIVOTTABLE TOOLS ANALYZE, Tools		
Print backstage area	FILE, Print		Ctrl + P
protect worksheet	REVIEW, Changes		
recommended chart	INSERT, Charts		Alt + F1
remove duplicates	DATA, Data Tools or TABLE TOOLS DESIGN, Tools		
Save As backstage area	FILE, Save As		Ctrl + S, F12
save as PDF/XPS	FILE, Export		
Scenario Manager	DATA, Data Tools		
screenshot	INSERT, Illustrations		

Excel 2013 Feature	Ribbon Tab, Group/Option	Button	Keyboard Shortcut
share workbook	REVIEW, Changes		
Slicer	INSERT, Filters or TABLE TOOLS DESIGN, Tools or PIVOTTABLE TOOLS ANALYZE, Filter		
SmartArt graphic	INSERT, Illustrations		
sort and filter data	HOME, Editing		
Sparklines: Line, Column, Win/Loss	INSERT, Sparklines		
spelling checker	REVIEW, Proofing		F7
statistical functions	FORMULAS, Function Library		
subtotals	DATA, Outline		
SUM function	HOME, Editing OR FORMULAS, Function Library		Alt + =
Symbol dialog box	INSERT, Symbols		
table	INSERT, Table		
text box	INSERT, Text		
text functions	FORMULAS, Function Library		
themes	PAGE LAYOUT, Themes		
Timeline	INSERT, Filters or PIVOTTABLE TOOLS ANALYZE, Filter		
trace dependents or trace precedents	FORMULAS, Auditing		
Track Changes	REVIEW, Changes		
underline text	HOME, Font		Ctrl + U
unlock cells	HOME, Cells		
update formulas	FORMULAS, Calculation		F9
wrap text	HOME, Alignment		